INDEPENDENT INTELLECTUALS
IN THE UNITED STATES, 1910–1945

The American Social Experience Series
GENERAL EDITOR: JAMES KIRBY MARTIN
EDITORS: PAULA S. FASS, STEVEN H. MINTZ,
CARL PRINCE, JAMES W. REED & PETER N. STEARNS

24. *The Dutch-American Farm*
DAVID STEVEN COHEN

25. *Independent Intellectuals in the United States, 1910–1945*
STEVEN BIEL

INDEPENDENT INTELLECTUALS IN THE UNITED STATES, 1910–1945

STEVEN BIEL

NEW YORK UNIVERSITY PRESS

NEW YORK AND LONDON

NEW YORK UNIVERSITY PRESS
New York and London

Library of Congress Cataloging-in-Publication Data
Biel, Steven, 1960-
Independent intellectuals in the United States, 1910–1945 / Steven
Biel.
p.   cm. — (The American social experience series ; 25)
Includes bibliographical references and index.
ISBN 0-8147-1188-X (cloth : alk. paper)
1. United States—Intellectual life—20th century.
2. Intellectuals—United States—History—20th century.   I. Title.
II. Series.
E169.12.B53   1992
973.9—dc20   92-14935
CIP

New York University Press books are printed on acid-free paper
and their binding materials are chosen for strength and durability.

Manufactured in the United States of America

c 10 9 8 7 6 5 4 3 2 1

For Jean

I have a profound belief in criticism and in the great work criticism, and criticism alone, can do for America in the immediate future. I believe there is a large and growing class of young men whose minds are set on the problem of making American life richer, more personal, more expressive, more disinterested. —VAN WYCK BROOKS

Contents

Acknowledgments

There are some parallels, which I would not want to exaggerate, between the life of a historian starting out in the 1980s and the lives of independent intellectuals in the first half of the century: financial anxieties, concerns about autonomy and purpose, yearnings to escape the university. In my case, as in theirs, the effort was sustained and redeemed by a sense of intellectual community. The basement of Robinson Hall in the corner of Harvard Yard provided camaraderie, criticism, humor, and solidarity throughout the completion of this project. I would especially like to thank Mark Peterson, Bruce Venarde, Vince Tompkins, and Eric Hinderaker; theirs has been the "spark" of "other minds to rub up against" that Randolph Bourne defined as the essence of friendship. I would also like to thank Marc Forster, Karla Goldman, Fran MacDonnell, Tom Siegel, Maureen Miller, Michael Prokopow, and Gerry Prokopowicz, all of whom give hope for the future of professional history as a humanity.

I began to write this book immediately after a conference in honor of Donald Fleming. The tributes of so many outstanding historians confirmed for me my good fortune in studying with a teacher of extraordinary intellectual generosity. One of the organizers of the conference, John L. Thomas, gave the first college history lecture I heard, introduced me to intellectual history, read this manuscript, and continues to be an invaluable source of ideas and suggestions. My debts to these two mentors are enormous. Brian Balogh, with his remarkable grasp of twentieth-century American history, helped illuminate the connections between my subject and the historiography of the professions and expertise. In addition, I am grateful to Alan Brinkley, Terry Cooney, Paula Fass, Joanne

Meyerowitz, Zane Miller, Hilda Smith, and Dan Terris for comments and advice at various stages of my work.

The librarians and staffs at several archives deserve mention for facilitating my research: the Rare Book and Manuscript Library, Columbia University; the Houghton Library, Harvard University; the Lilly Library, Indiana University; the Manuscript Division of the Library of Congress; the Rare Books and Manuscripts Division of the New York Public Library; and the Sterling and Beinecke Libraries at Yale University. Nancy Shawcross and Daniel Traister of the Van Pelt-Dietrich Library Center at the University of Pennsylvania were particularly accommodating. Colin Jones and Despina Gimbel of New York University Press guided the book through to publication with great care and efficiency.

My parents' idea that there is something precarious and not entirely conventional about an academic career suggests how much has changed since the period of this study. Claire and Morton Biel share some of the blame for my decision to become a historian, and I thank them for their unwavering interest and encouragement. Dana Rosenfeld, Eric Biel, David Saltzman, Scott Gutterman, and Jamie Kay graciously put me up, put up with me, and filled in the hours after the libraries had closed during my visits to Washington and New York.

No matter how much I have brooded over this book, Jean Kolling, to whom it is dedicated, has been the real center of my life for the last seven years.

If there is such a person as the non-professional reader (and the characters who populate my discussion acted on the belief that there is), he or she will find some of the names that appear in the text more familiar than others. Academic readers will know most if not all of them. I make no pretenses of having unearthed forgotten figures from our cultural past. Nor do I claim that I am offering the last word on them. My goal is a more modest one: to treat them in a way that they have not been fully treated before. There are certainly other contexts in which they can be situated, alternative approaches to their writings, aspects of their identities that I ignore. It should be clear from what follows that I believe they merit further study, and I hope this book suggests some points of departure.

I also want to thank the following for giving me permission to quote from their sources:

Excerpts from the American Fund for Public Service Records are quoted by permission of the Rare Books and Manuscripts Division, The New York Public Library, Astor, Lenox and Tilden Foundations.

Excerpts from the Randolph Bourne Papers are quoted by permission of the Rare Book and Manuscript Library, Columbia University.

Excerpts from the Van Wyck Brooks Collection are quoted by permission of Special Collections, Van Pelt-Dietrich Library Center, University of Pennsylvania, and Peter Stimson Brooks.

A letter written by Malcolm Cowley is quoted by permission of Robert Cowley.

Four letters written by John Dos Passos are quoted by permission of Elizabeth H. Dos Passos.

Excerpts from the Max Eastman, Eliena Krylenko Eastman, and Claude McKay Papers are quoted by permission of The Lilly Library, Indiana University, and Yvette Eastman.

Excerpts from the Waldo Frank Collection are quoted by permission of Special Collections, Van Pelt-Dietrich Library Center, University of Pennsylvania and Jonathan W. Frank.

Excerpts from the Benjamin W. Huebsch Papers are quoted by permission of the Manuscript Division, The Library of Congress.

Excerpts from the Walter Lippmann Papers are quoted by permission of Manuscripts and Archives, Yale University Library.

Excerpts from the Lewis Mumford Collection are quoted by permission of Special Collections, Van Pelt-Dietrich Library Center, University of Pennsylvania, and the Gina Maccoby Literary Agency.

Excerpts from the John Reed Papers are quoted by permission of The Houghton Library, Harvard University.

Excerpts from the Paul Rosenfeld Papers are quoted by permission of the Yale Collection of American Literature, Beinecke Rare Book and Manuscript Library, Yale University.

Excerpts from the Margaret Sanger Papers are quoted by permission of the Manuscript Division, The Library of Congress.

Excerpts from the Edmund Wilson Papers are quoted by permission of the Yale Collection of American Literature, Beinecke Rare Book and Manuscript Library, Yale University.

Introduction

H. L. Mencken, already well known for his caustic dismissals of "mountebanks advocating birth control, free verse, free love, and other such juvenile propaganda," surprised Max Eastman in the early 1920s by praising the *Liberator*. "You produce the best magazine in America," Mencken told him, "—not now and then, but steadily every month. It is informing, it is good tempered, it is often brilliant." Coming from a critic whose tolerance for the "whole red-ink bunch" was limited at best, these words carried special meaning. They suggested to Eastman that he had succeeded, despite his strong support for Bolshevism, in creating an intellectual voice that transcended politics. Mencken reassured Eastman that they shared a common ground as critics and intellectuals that could withstand even the most pronounced ideological differences. "Here at least is one customer among the opposition that you will have as long as you go on," Mencken wrote. In his reflections on the exchange after Mencken's death in 1956, Eastman recalled his "surprised admiration" for Mencken's "imagination as a critic" and "the flexibility of his judgment."[1]

The temptation when writing about groups of intellectuals is to arrange them according to their political views or ideological conflicts. Such an approach carries the advantage of allowing historians to play groups and ideas off one another by accentuating important distinctions and disagreements. But it also runs the risk of ignoring a larger story toward which the Mencken-Eastman exchange points. Intellectuals, committed as they are to critical interchange, thrive on argument. The seriousness with which they approach and hold ideas often translates into verbal warfare. Yet the commitment to argument and the attachment to ideas can themselves serve as the bases for an underlying sense of community.

As Thomas Bender has observed, "[t]he solidarity that characterizes communities does not mean . . . that all is unity and harmony within." Bender offers what he calls "a historically grounded concept of community" which recognizes that modes of "human interaction" change over time and that communal forms evolve to meet new situations.[2] Historians and sociologists no longer speak in terms of a simple distinction between gemeinschaft and gesellschaft, nor do they assume modernity's obliteration of community. Communities, often of a voluntaristic character, have continued to develop within urban industrial societies, even where individualism is the dominant ethos. Intellectual and professional communities, for example, consciously attempt to mediate between the claims of the group and the autonomy of its individual members, sometimes by actively encouraging disagreement and debate.

It is my contention that in the 1910s and 1920s, a new community came together in the United States outside the established centers of intellectual life—the universities and the professions. The new intellectual community cohered around a unique set of "shared understandings," to use another of Bender's terms, and developed its own "sense of obligation."[3] This book explores the assumptions upon which the independent intellectual community was formed, presents a picture of the personal, vocational, generational, institutional (and anti-institutional) ties that bound it together, and analyzes some of the problems and tensions that it encountered over time.

By "independent intellectuals" I mean in part the social type that Russell Jacoby and others have designated "public intellectuals" or "men and women of letters"—"writers and thinkers who address a general and educated audience."[4] Like Jacoby, I am concerned with critics rather than fiction writers, poets, or dramatists, although many of the characters who appear here can be labeled critics only as a convenient shorthand; their hostility to boundaries and specialties compelled them toward a self-conscious generalism. Their criticism itself was diverse, ranging in subject matter from literature and the fine arts to politics, economics, sociology, education, history, urban planning, and national character. If Walter Lippmann was primarily a political commentator, he was also a writer on social psychology, class structure, morals, and culture in its broadest sense. Van Wyck Brooks frustrates any attempt to categorize him as a literary critic since so little of his work seems to deal with actual texts and all of it addresses larger issues of American culture and society. Max Eastman was variously a Marxist critic, aesthetic theorist, popularizer of Freud, psychologist of humor, political editorialist, traveling lecturer, poet, novelist, and radio game show host.

Unlike Jacoby, I am concerned with the emergence rather than the disappearance of twentieth-century American public intellectuals. In certain ways, this makes the story I tell more positive than Jacoby's bleak tale of "a vacancy in culture, the absence of younger voices, perhaps the absence of a generation" of public intellectuals at the end of the twentieth century.[5] There are certainly young voices and a generational presence in the pages that follow. But one of the purposes of this book is to call into question the nostalgic vision of a Golden Age of public intellectuals. Never in this century have circumstances been especially conducive to a general critical discourse. The era of the university was already well under way by 1900. Specialized knowledge, professional authority, and the cult of expertise have been with us since the progressive period. The educated middle-class public may have been at its most homogeneous in the 1910s and 1920s, but its size and arguably its receptivity to new ideas increased after the Second World War.[6] It is too easy to exaggerate the opportunities for a public intellectual life before 1945. I want to convey how difficult an undertaking this was even early in the century.

There is a tendency among historians to conflate "public intellectuals" with "The New York Intellectuals." I will confess my own guilt in this matter in advance, since the intellectual community I describe was centered in New York and because I ignore many thriving regional intellectual communities, located in various universities, the most famous being the Nashville Agrarians and Howard Odum's group at Chapel Hill. "The New York Intellectuals," however, has become more than geographically specific. The label refers to a group of critics who started out in the thirties, to borrow Alfred Kazin's phrase, came to maturity in the forties, and congregated around such publications as the *Partisan Review*, *Commentary*, and *Dissent*. They themselves expropriated the New York Intellectual label, so that perhaps historians are not to blame for using it with exclusive reference to this group. I would simply point out that there were New York intellectuals long before The New York Intellectuals, and that their pioneering work in carving out and defining a public intellectual life opened the way for successive generations.

Although several historians have recognized antecedents, too often The New York Intellectuals' own claims to uniqueness have gone unchallenged. The recent contention that there was something new and dramatic in their ultimate "allegiance to intellectualism rather than political leftism"[7] fails to recognize that the priority of establishing a strong intellectual culture animated a previous generation and that these earlier critics also gave the intellectual life precedence over politics in any limited sense of the term.[8] If, however, politics is defined more broadly than factional contests for power and quarrels over specific matters of policy, the work of building a critical community was unquestionably a political act. Opposition, dissent, the revitalization of public discourse, and the imagination of alternative cultures can seem apolitical only when politics is conceived as a narrow range of positions along a conventional left-to-right spectrum.

In the title and elsewhere, I use the adjective "independent" rather than "public" because it more accurately describes the intellectuals who are the subject of this book.[9] There have been and still are (despite Jacoby's jeremiad) public intellectuals who hold university positions, while the individuals I discuss were not only non-academic but anti-academic. Independence, moreover, was the cornerstone of their communal identity. As I will show, they expended tremendous effort to define and secure intellectual independence, which they believed was the essential condition for a viable public intellectual life in the United States.

Intellectual historians have come to see the early twentieth century as an age of specialization and professionalization. Formal mechanisms were instituted to determine competence and control membership as the professions matured. Professional communication became increasingly internal with the proliferation of specialized journals and conferences.[10] Recognizing these trends, however, is not to concede John Higham's claim that the only serious criticism of specialization was "a lament, a protest, and a rear-guard action" by "the beleaguered defenders of gentility."[11] Beginning in about 1910, younger critics mounted a determined challenge to both the genteel tradition and the growing division of intellectual labor. The community with which I am concerned emerged in

direct opposition to the developments that Higham and others have described; it was an adversarial, even *anti*-professional community which
refused to surrender the future entirely to the academic disciplines and
their esoteric specialties.

To the extent that independent intellectuals shunned institutional commitments, the task of treating them collectively becomes somewhat more
difficult than identifying and studying communities with solid organizational bases, clearly established leaders, and standard recruiting and cer-
tification procedures. In aspiring to be public intellectuals, they resisted
the movement toward concentrated expertise and private modes of communication. Yet even as they avoided the insularities of the academic
disciplines and the communities of experts, their work was extremely
self-referential. Although they addressed public issues and reached for a
non-specialized audience, they simultaneously and constantly spoke to
the problem of how to be independent intellectuals in the modern United
States. It is therefore possible to see them as engaged in a collective effort
to create an alternative kind of intellectual life. To examine this effort in
some of its diversity is the central purpose of this book.

What I have attempted here is a cultural history of intellectuals rather
than a formal history of ideas. My concern, as I have suggested, is with
what Christopher Lasch called "the intellectual as a social type" rather
than with the systematic treatment of individual thinkers and their work.
While I have no interest in minimizing differences and conflicts, I do
think that a broader picture has been obscured by attempts to classify
intellectuals according to political or ideological persuasions.[12] The project of reconstructing American intellectual life that began in the 1910s
allowed for a range of personalities and critical positions, yet was communal in its guiding purpose of making a place in American society for
independent and socially engaged intellectuals. David A. Hollinger has
observed that the essential feature of an intellectual community is a
shared set of questions rather than complete agreement on the answers.
Questions, he writes, "are the dynamics whereby membership in a community of discourse is established, renewed, and sometimes termi-
nated."[13] Among the non-academic intellectuals, there was no consensus
on how to achieve critical independence, how to secure public influence,
or how to reconcile two such difficult and disparate goals. But these
concerns, expressed most succinctly in the title of Van Wyck Brooks'
1918 book *Letters and Leadership*, formed the discursive core of an intellec-

tual community. Around them revolved an array of specific arguments which only rarely went so far as to destroy the sense of common identity and struggle.

My approach, to borrow Peter Novick's terminology, is both internalist and externalist.[14] It would seem artificial to concentrate exclusively on either internal dynamics or external influences when discussing a community which was committed at once to autonomy and social engagement. On the externalist side, I describe the development of this community as an ongoing response to a variety of perceived cultural conditions: the failure of a technologically proficient and materially abundant society to wrestle with larger questions of value and purpose; America's devaluation of art and criticism; the insularity of the universities and the timidity of the professoriate. Moreover, the independent intellectuals' belief that human beings can function consciously as historical agents and act constructively for change grew out of an intellectual and cultural context of pragmatism and progressivism.

At the same time, internal factors determined the issues they discussed and shaped the way they discussed them. They conversed with one another, directly and indirectly, as members of a critical community; that they simultaneously spoke to a larger book-buying and magazine-reading public meant that their ideas developed both esoterically and exoterically. As I suggest in a number of examples, their responses to public issues and events were phrased in terms that reflected their personal concerns as independent intellectuals. Yet it is not my intention to debunk their claims to disinterestedness by pointing out that they were very much involved with problems of their own vocation. Disinterestedness—the freedom from all compromising ties that would foster a truly independent criticism—always remained an ideal rather than a reality, normative rather than descriptive. Balanced against the concern for engagement, their commitment to this ideal was never absolute. Pure disinterestedness, as Michael Walzer has said, implies complete detachment, abstraction, and impersonality—none of which they sought.[15] On the whole, the reflective dimension of their writing was animating; it was probably inevitable as well.

With the goal of illuminating a larger intellectual culture, I have chosen to structure the discussion thematically and chronologically rather than biographically. A biographical arrangement, it seemed to me, would undermine the collective emphasis.[16] The generational framework is intentionally loose, because American intellectuals (unlike their European contemporaries) did not think systematically in generational terms.[17] Even Randolph Bourne spoke inclusively of "youth" as a radical and experimental attitude toward life which could be chosen and cultivated regardless of actual age or experience. If, for a time, younger critics such as Kenneth Burke, Malcolm Cowley, and Matthew Josephson thought of themselves as members of a different generation from that of Bourne, Van Wyck Brooks, and Waldo Frank, this generational consciousness faded after the mid-1920s and collapsed completely in the 1930s. Edmund Wilson and Lewis Mumford, who were closer in age to Burke, Cowley, and Josephson, identified from the beginning of their careers with the older critics. While there was an important element of generational self-awareness among independent intellectuals, it would defy their own flexibility to adopt an excessively rigid scheme. The generation to which I will refer was bracketed on one side by its college professors and on the other by critics who came of age during the Depression. Nearly all the intellectuals who populate these pages were born between 1881 and 1899.

The generational dimension is most evident in the first chapter, which frames the discussion that follows by addressing the issue of dissatisfaction with the universities. Without denying the importance of a revolt against gentility, I am concerned to locate a more specific context for the emergence of an independent intellectual community.[18] Chapter 1 thus traces the rise in status of the university and the professoriate around the turn of the century and the almost simultaneous emergence of critical and subversive voices from within the academy. I argue that these critics, especially William James, John Dewey, and Thorstein Veblen, struck a chord with some of their later students and younger readers, who absorbed their critique, expanded it, and translated it into the decision to seek out a different basis for the intellectual life. The independent intellectuals' position outside the academy remained a vital component of identity throughout their careers.

The following three chapters begin to address the question of how they created an alternative to the university. Chapter 2 examines the problem of securing creative autonomy without the financial support of a teaching position and considers the possibilities and difficulties of intellectual journalism. If the ideal was the independent life of letters, the reality was often a routine editorial position or free-lance hackwork. Chapter 3 discusses some of the attempts to combine this precarious independence with public influence. Here I bring out the tensions and dilemmas of direct involvement in politics and social movements, with the First World War serving as a particularly wrenching experience. Most of the critics, I argue, came to embrace a form of what Bourne called "the impossibilist élan"—a faith in the ultimate inspiriting power of criticism that rejected binding political or institutional affiliations and thus seemed conducive to intellectual independence. Chapter 4 treats the issue of geographical location in relation to the problems of autonomy and engagement. Specifically, it discusses the critics' ambivalence about New York, their settlement in semi-rural enclaves sufficiently removed from the city to foster critical distance but close enough to furnish a sense of involvement, and the implications of expatriation.

Women's involvement in the critical community receives separate attention in chapter 5. While many women were members of a larger community of writers, artists, and activists, relatively few chose to pursue free-lance criticism as a career. I contend that women's choices played a role in this development; a consciousness of exclusion led many of them into forms of social and political activity that the male critics largely shunned. But I also argue that the male critics' quest to de-marginalize the intellectual life led them to conceive of the critical community as a primarily masculine domain.

As I summarize what is included in my discussion, I must also point out a subject that is absent: the work of African-American intellectuals during the period of this study. If women were partially excluded from the critical community I describe, blacks were almost completely shut out. The racial attitudes of the members of this community ranged from the stereotypical to the relatively progressive, but issues of race did not figure prominently in their criticism, nor were interracial associations common among them. The notable exceptions were Max Eastman's long friendship with Claude McKay and Waldo Frank's shorter but more complex relationship with Jean Toomer, neither of which was exempt from paternalism and condescension. H. L. Mencken's comments about racial inferiority are now well known, yet he knew and published more African-American writers than any other white critic of his time. The literary historian William E. Cain recently observed that two of the twentieth century's most important men of letters, W. E. B. Du Bois and Edmund Wilson, never even "referred to one another."[19] I make no apologies for my choice of subject, but I share Cain's belief that intellectual segregation—the failure to build bridges to black critics and the general neglect of issues of race by white critics—significantly impoverished their work and their community.

Chapters 6 through 8 draw out connections between the critics' personal concerns about the terms of the intellectual life and their ideas about education, morality, and history. A belief in the general compatibility of self-fulfillment and the communal good surfaced not only in their ideal of the free and socially involved intellectual but in their reflections on pedagogy and moral codes as well. My discussion of the "usable past" concentrates on the effort to discover an American tradition of intellectual freedom and influence which would bolster the independent intellectuals' own project.

Finally, in chapter 9, I consider the attraction of many critics to Marxism as part of the continuing attempt to reconcile independence and engagement. While in some cases this led to a tipping of the scale in favor of an uncritical sense of social involvement, in most it took the form of an intellectual search for a non-ideological Marxism that established the critical mind at the center of the task of social reconstruction. The epilogue carries the story into the Second World War, when disillusionment with Marxism and the threat of fascism combined to produce spirited calls to preserve the integrity of critical values against challenges to intellectual freedom. By the early 1940s, the impossibilist alternative seemed the only hope for influence that did not endanger independence. Meanwhile, a new generation was emerging with its own ideas, its own agenda, and a dismissive attitude toward its old-fashioned predecessors.

CHAPTER I

The Repudiation of the University

America in the progressive period offered unprecedented opportunities to scholars. By the turn of the century, social and economic interdependence had gone far toward undermining older faiths in common sense and an omnicompetent citizenry and toward producing a demand for expert knowledge. As the ability to identify the causes of social problems, economic changes, physical, political, and historical events receded further and further into the distance, those who possessed the tools for discovering esoteric truths won new prestige and respect. To meet the demand for expertise, to foster authoritative thinking, scholars forged institutions that defined disciplines, established methodologies, set professional standards, and allowed for intradisciplinary communication. Beginning with the American Historical Association in 1884 and the American Economics Association in 1885, professional organizations proliferated around the turn of the century and gradually screened out quacks and charlatans in the quest to establish mastery over a specific field of knowledge. The difficulty in tracing causation in the modern world necessitated an intellectual division of labor, not only between disciplines but within them. Professionalization had as its goal what Charles Sanders Peirce called a "community of the competent" and what Thomas Haskell has renamed a "community of inquiry" in which truth became the product of cooperative effort rather than common sense or individual investigation. Working under standards and expectations established by professional peers, individual scholars sacrificed a degree of personal autonomy, while the profession as a whole gained significant group autonomy by casting itself as the authoritative voice on those matters that came within its investigative domain. Membership in professional communities conferred upon scholars the exclusive right to interpret a particular sphere of life, subject in theory only to the control of their colleagues and free from the interference of laymen.[1]

The assertion of professional authority coincided with changes in the complexion of American higher education. While professional organizations admitted amateur scholars to bolster their membership and absorb potential adversaries, they were dominated from the start by academic men. Academic professionals looked to the universities for additional legitimization, which came in the form of new departments. Universities strengthened their commitment to specialized research by creating the basic structures necessary for sustained investigation: sabbaticals, teaching assistantships, and other means of reducing teaching loads; new facilities, additional books and equipment; research institutes and funds specifically earmarked for research projects. Though the "Golden Age" of the American research university did not come until the 1920s, the emphasis on productive scholarship became more and more pronounced after 1890, and scholars could look with growing confidence to the universities as the home of intellectual inquiry and authority. Claims of authority, meanwhile, helped scholars inclined toward public service find a place for themselves in progressive governments. Drafting regulations and legislation, and serving on investigative commissions, professors assumed what Richard Hofstadter recognized as the new role of "the serviceable expert."[2] Whether or not they chose to translate their knowledge into public policy, scholars in this age of professionalization and specialization had good reason to believe that they and their abilities were valued now as never before. The reputation of the professor had reached an all-time peak.

Yet the preferred path toward intellectual authority—the path of organization, division of labor, esoteric knowledge, and intradisciplinary communication—did not go unchallenged. For some thoughtful irreconcilables within the universities, and for the intellectual offspring who followed their teachers' critique to its logical conclusion, the costs of this path to authority were prohibitive. The innovations that most scholars saw as inevitable and welcomed optimistically, these irreconcilables received critically and with a sense of foreboding. What seemed to the majority the only way to adapt the scholarly life to modern circumstances and to elevate thinkers to their deserved status in American society struck critical minds as an adaptation that could easily lead to extinction; in pursuing this course, scholars were altering the life of the mind to the point where it was no longer recognizable as such. As they developed and articulated their criticism, those who did not share the pervasive sense of promise and satisfaction held to a different image of the intellectual life in America. It was out of this criticism and out of this alternative vision that an independent intellectual community was born.

I.

In the greatest autobiographical account of an American intellectual's search for place, Henry Adams described the experience of marginalization. Adams' expectation that his mind and his lineage guaranteed a position of social and political leadership foundered upon the reality of an academic career. When he recalled his years from 1871 to 1877 as a Harvard professor, Adams judged himself a "failure." Not only did he doubt his abilities as a teacher, he also questioned the legitimacy of the university as a nurturer of intellect. The routine of teaching interfered with the more important work of thinking, as he "exhausted all his strength in trying to keep one day ahead of his duties." Nor could Harvard satisfy his longings for influence in the world of affairs. The university, he wrote in the *Education*, "produced at great waste of time and money results not worth reaching."[3]

Adams' disillusionment came at a time when many scholars were looking to the universities as the great hope for the life of the mind in America, when reform and expansion promised to raise the higher learning to a new position of importance and respect. Charles William Eliot became Harvard's president and began the task of reclaiming the university only two years before Adams joined the faculty. "The college had pleaded guilty" to uselessness, according to Adams, "and tried to reform." Shortly before Adams quit his teaching career, Johns Hopkins opened its doors and under Daniel Coit Gilman commenced to revolutionize the American university system. Adams sensed that in his misery at Harvard, as in most things, he was out of touch with his times. He confessed that he "never knew whether his colleagues shared his doubts about their own utility."[4] The enthusiasm with which his contemporaries greeted the new and improved universities suggests that Adams was isolated, even if prophetic, in his despair. For many, the development of the modern university represented a realization of the centrality of independent thought in confronting the problems and opportunities of the Gilded Age.

While university reformers did not share Henry Adams' sense of futility, they did recognize a crisis in American intellectual life. Scholars committed to freedom of thought and concerned with constructing a meaningful social role for themselves found the colleges moribund in the period following the Civil War. "The college," one historian has written, "became a seat of useless theory, cut off from the world of practice; the college quietly contemplated ideas, while other men busied themselves in the arena of action in politics or in business." In a culture which celebrated material progress and the active life, defending the college as a spiritual retreat was increasingly difficult and pointless. A younger generation of scholars chafed at the "images of uselessness, impracticality and scholasticism" associated with academic careers.[5] No less disconcerting than this removal from the hard realities of American life was the colleges' dogmatic approach to knowledge. Moral philosophy and religious doctrine, the curricular barriers to contact with the material world, obstructed the disinterested pursuit of truth essential to an age of science and progress. Rescuing the intellect from narrowness and marginality demanded the recasting of academic institutions and a redefinition of the scholarly life.

The new university presidents, often in competition with one another over appointments and at odds over specific policies, agreed that the reformed universities must forge a social role for themselves and their faculties. In an address marking the ninth anniversary of Johns Hopkins in 1885, Gilman enumerated the academic disciplines—new and old— and insisted upon their practical value as an "influence upon civilization." The universities, he said, possess "innumerable . . . opportunities of conveying their benefits to the outside world." Woodrow Wilson, then a professor of jurisprudence and political economy and soon to be president of Princeton, reflected in an 1896 *Forum* article that Princeton's separation from society in the post-Civil War period had been an anomaly. "It has never been natural," Wilson argued, "it has seldom been possible, in this country for learning to seek a place apart and hold aloof from affairs." In place of "spirit," the new presidents substituted the word "service." The "true university," proclaimed William Rainey Harper of the University of Chicago, "the university of the future, is one the motto of which will be: service for mankind wherever mankind is, whether within scholastic walls or without those walls and in the world at large."[6]

This rhetoric of service fulfilled several purposes. In quest of philanthropic support, presidents such as Harper and Gilman needed to justify their institutions to capitalist benefactors who ranked culture second to practical affairs. To counter charges of elitism, university publicists emphasized the democratic character of scholarship and its potential benefits for society at large. Gilman stressed this public role when he spoke at the Columbian Exposition in Chicago in 1893: "The results of scholarly thought and acquisition are not to be treasured as secrets of a craft; they are not esoteric mysteries known only to the initiated; they are not to be recorded in cryptograms or perpetuated in private notebooks. They are to be given to the world."[7] External pressures from a society with little tolerance for cloistered elites and idle contemplation doubtless came to bear on spokesmen for American higher education. The frequency with which these spokesmen insisted upon what Charles W. Eliot called "the modern democratic spirit of serviceableness" and David Starr Jordan of Stanford described as a movement "toward reality and practicality" suggests a genuine concern about public opinion.[8]

There were also internal pressures for the universities to search out a place of greater involvement in outside affairs. Scholars themselves demanded a role at the center rather than at the periphery of American life. John Dewey, as a young philosopher at the University of Michigan, rejected all scholarship lacking a social orientation as "scraps and fragments" without "a unity in the human, in the social." Dewey defended "the democratic idea in education . . . the idea that higher education, as well as the three R's, is of and for the people, and not for some cultivated classes" against the bankrupt concept of "university education as a sort of sacred scholarship to be preserved, at all hazards, from the contaminating touch of the masses." Not content to dwell in "barren isolation," Dewey and his contemporaries vowed to thrust the intellect into "[r]elationship to man, to his interests and purposes," to "throw its fund out again into the stress of life," and to redeem the scholarly pursuits from the margins of American civilization.[9] Ideally, the university would bridge the worlds of affairs and contemplation, protecting independent thought while fostering the application of knowledge to social, economic, and political problems. As Woodrow Wilson envisioned it, the university would be

the home of sagacious men, hard-headed and with a will to know, debaters of the world's questions every day and used to the rough ways of democracy; and yet a place removed—calm Science seated there, recluse, ascetic, like a nun, not knowing that the world passes, not caring, if the truth but come in answer to her prayer; and Literature, walking within her open doors, in quiet chambers, with men of olden time, storied walls about her, and calm voices infinitely sweet; her "magic casements, opening on the foam of perilous seas, in fairy lands forlorn," to which you may withdraw and use your youth for pleasure; there windows open straight upon the street, where many stand and talk, intent upon the world of men and business.[10]

Dewey's pursuit of a socialized intellect would have implications for his philosophical development as early as the 1880s. His embrace of Hegelianism under the guidance of George S. Morris was a rejection of Kantian dualism and its separation of the mind from the external world. Hegel's idealism made the mind and reality one; in the Hegelian scheme, subject and object were reconciled, and ideas became motive forces in history. "Here," as J. O. C. Phillips has stated it, "was an ideology which was able to provide Dewey with the comforting reassurance that in following his own desire to become a philosopher, he was also serving his society and his God."

By the time he left Michigan for the University of Chicago in 1894, however, Dewey had discovered inadequacies in philosophical idealism. Hegel's concept of individual thought as a passive, incomplete component of a universal consciousness left the human mind with little or no creative influence. Idealism implied that individual ideas were always imitative of the Absolute, and once again Dewey found the intellect too far removed from reality. At Chicago, he began to develop a new philosophy that would rescue the mind from isolation and impotence. William James' and George Herbert Mead's biological analogies allowed Dewey to recast the mind in evolutionary terms as existing for purposes of adaptation, competition, survival, and action. Ideas "became plans of action, working hypotheses. Ideas were a function of a particular mind in a particular dynamic situation."[11] Dewey's instrumentalism, with James' pragmatism, provided new philosophical justifications for the intellectual life. In Dewey's system, thoughts could not have an independent existence; intellect was naturally poised for action. He had succeeded in crafting a philosophy that would reassure scholars of their social value.

Yet philosophical reassurances were not sufficient even for Dewey. Scholars needed more visible means of linking their academic labors to the movement of events outside the universities, and in the process of university modernization in the last quarter of the nineteenth century, administrators and faculties attempted to forge direct connections between their institutions and a larger American public. The urge to communicate, to reach beyond the classrooms and laboratories, accounts for the tremendous enthusiasm with which scholars greeted such innovations as university extensions, university presses, and scholarly journals.

Harper's plans for the University of Chicago included an extension program which would serve, he declared, to bring the university "into direct contact with human life and activity." Similarly, "publication" would be the "indispensable extension" of knowledge to an audience outside the university proper. For Harper, "the extension and the press" were "phases of a single work" through which "the University comes in contact with the outside world." Gilman, in his celebration of higher education's public functions at the Columbian Exposition, also touted university extension and learned publications. The older conception of knowledge as private and obscure, Gilman indicated, was yielding to a new belief in dissemination. The new scholar knew that he "must not merely print; he must publish." Dewey, too, wrote of the tendency "towards the distribution of . . . ideas" and hailed university extension as evidence of such a tendency. From 1889 to 1892, Dewey unsuccessfully conspired with the New York City journalist Franklin Ford to create a magazine called *Thought News* to help popularize current developments in American philosophy. Gilman also exhorted scholars to contribute to the popular press, confident that the university's image could only be enhanced as a result. In the exhilaration of university reform, nobody anticipated that rising expectations and the invitation to write for a larger public would give professors the impetus to attack the same institutions that had urged them to reach out in the first place.[12]

2.

The shared sense of possibility among scholars and university reformers, never universal (as the dissent of Henry Adams suggests), eroded in the first years of the twentieth century. By 1900, critical voices within the universities were growing stronger, aware that the promise of a general audience for scholarship had not materialized. The assumptions behind the innovations of the 1870s, 1880s, and 1890s began to appear naive. University extension programs, presses, and journals failed to meet expectations almost immediately and, from the critics' perspective, produced results far different from what their advocates had anticipated.

Almost immediately, extension lecturers discovered that their audiences were smaller and less receptive than extension advocates had anticipated. Jane Addams, still calling for "socialized education" and still convinced of the merits of the Hull House Shakespeare Club in 1910, had long since recognized the problem of attracting working-class listeners to lectures on "the spectrum analyses of star dust, or the latest theory concerning the milky way." Scholars immersed in the "habit of research" and driven by "the desire to say the latest word upon any subject" failed to arouse "the sympathetic understanding" of their audiences; too often the extension lecturer fell "into the dull terminology of the classroom." With the knowledge "that the educational efforts of a Settlement should not be directed primarily to reproduce the college type of culture," Addams and her associates moved toward replacing lectures with instruction in manual skills. Frederick Jackson Turner, an active supporter of the extension program at the University of Wisconsin, quickly perceived problems in the "character of the audiences" and suggested "specially adapted courses" to draw working people.[13]

Critics increasingly challenged the assumption that the content of university courses and the products of scholarly research would naturally appeal to a larger public. The idea that uninhibited thought could easily translate into popular knowledge—that the disinterested intellect required only the proper forum for expression to acquire a social function —could not bear the weight of experience. After the mid-1890s, as the incompatibility of university teaching methods and public demands became evident, enthusiasm for extension programs declined rapidly. When the movement was revived in the 1910s, vocational training dominated the curricula, and there was no serious attempt to renew the effort to disseminate scholarship through popular lectures. The progressives' emphasis on expertise, epitomized by Charles R. Van Hise's "Wisconsin Idea," implied a shift away from the earlier belief that the American public could grasp the ideas of university minds.[14]

Different difficulties tempered the initial enthusiasm for university publications. Launched in the hope of ending intellectual isolation, the university presses and scholarly journals instead reinforced the ivory tower image and helped create the new problem of overspecialization. Even while boasting of the possibilities of the university extension, Dewey perceived a "tendency towards specialization, towards minute personal research" which could only be offset by the dissemination of the "resulting ideas." But the publishing boom which accompanied the development of graduate seminars, research laboratories, and academic organizations did not obliterate Gilman's distinction between publishing and printing. As early as 1891, Dewey warned against a new scholasticism—scholarship's increasing "abstraction from life"—characterized by narrow-minded academics who, like the medieval scholastics, pored over an increasingly obscure body of knowledge. In Dewey's analogy, "monographs, journals without end" now occupied "the void left by the commentators upon Aristotle."[15] The problem of communicating esoteric ideas to a larger American public was complicated by competition between institutions and disciplines. Academic rivalries made any concerted effort to bridge the widening gap between the universities and the public impossible, and the proliferation of journals only exacerbated the problem. If the advancement of knowledge required competition and specialization, Hugh Hawkins has written, "the price had to be paid in pages that were sterile, involuted, supercilious, and narrow."[16] To critics within the universities, the mechanisms for establishing direct, meaningful contact with "real life" which had held so much promise in the 1870s and 1880s became by 1900 signs of the failure of the university, of its overspecialization and marginality.

The idea that the universities fostered freedom of thought also came under critical scrutiny at the turn of the century. For many scholars, teaching itself was an obstacle to the genuine work of the intellect. William James complained in 1896 that his energy was "more than consumed by [the] duties of teaching" and that almost none was "left over for writing." In 1903, he wrote to his brother Henry that he yearned to live the remainder of his life in "a different manner, contemplatively namely, and with leisure and simplification for the one remaining thing, which is to report in one book, at least, such impression as my own intellect has received from the universe." James' diary for the last months of 1905 expressed an ongoing internal struggle over whether to resign his position at Harvard, which he resolved in favor of staying on only after changing his mind at least four times.[17] His colleague George Santayana recalled the strain of teaching on James, Josiah Royce, and himself, noting that "they were obliged to divide their energies externally, giving to their daily tasks as professors and pedagogues what duty demanded, and only the remainder to scholarship, reflection, and literary work." The routine of lecturing compartmentalized the intellectual process, forcing ideas to "come when the bell rings and stop approximately when the bell rings a second time." Santayana questioned whether the university was the proper place for thinking at all and urged philosophers, only half-facetiously, to make their living polishing lenses like Spinoza or selling catalogues and taking umbrellas at museums. Quitting the universities, as Santayana did in 1911, would free thinkers from the burdens of teaching and place them closer to reality. Some more "innocent" way of supporting themselves "would not prejudice their meditations and would keep their eyes fixed, without undue affection, on a characteristic bit of the real world which it is their business to understand."[18] Thorstein Veblen, a far more outspoken critic of the university than James and Santayana, saw the independent intellect "going to seed in routine work" and included higher education in his broader attack on conspicuous waste.[19]

Veblen's discussion of the universities in *The Theory of the Leisure Class* (1899) and its elaboration in *The Higher Learning in America* (1918) stressed the "ritual and paraphernalia" of academic life which impeded the intellect while serving as emblems of leisure-class status. With its emphasis on display in the form of ceremonies, degrees, and dress, the university continued to demonstrate "an habitual aversion to what is merely useful, as contrasted with what is merely honorific in learning." The cap and gown, for example, fit "into the leisure-class scheme of life as involving a notable element of conspicuous waste."[20] William James, excoriating what he called the "Ph.D octopus," also noted this distinction between learning and display. America, he wrote in 1903, is "rapidly drifting towards a state of things in which no man of science or letters will be accounted respectable unless some kind of badge or diploma is stamped upon him," and the university risked becoming "some title-giving machine" instead of a nurturer of "truth and disinterested labor." James' hostility toward academic ritual extended as far as course requirements which interfered with a student's "more immediate intellectual aims." Gertrude Stein told the story of how she chose to enjoy a spring day in Cambridge rather than take the final examination in James' course. Stein left a note explaining this decision to James on her exam paper, and he responded by giving her the highest grade in the course. Veblen was known to give every student the same grade on an exam and explained his randomness by saying, "My grades are like lightning. They are liable to strike anywhere."[21]

Similarly contemptuous of the standard emblems of achievement, Santayana wrote of students "stamped" with degrees, while David Starr Jordan bemoaned the "doctors of philosophy turned out in such numbers from the great hot-houses of university culture." Irving Babbitt, the outspoken Harvard literature professor, based his critique of the doctorate on a distinction between the "philologist" and the "humanist." The philologist—the Ph.D.—made a fetish out of "endless accumulations of facts" and failed "to disengage from these accumulated stores their permanent human values." The "present superstition of the doctor's degree" with its "barbed-wire entanglements" excluded the "humanistically inclined" student from higher education. Babbitt felt "a sort of intellectual nausea" at the displacement of wide learning and meaningful ideas by the "dry rot" of specialization.[22]

These assaults on the trappings of the modern university were responses to the bureaucratization of academic life which had accompanied modernization. Dissident scholars spoke of the universities as factories or machines, churning out diplomas and standardizing the educational process to the point where authentic intellectual endeavor seemed threatened with extinction. William James warned President Eliot of "the extraordinary scrupulousness and conscientiousness with which our [academic] machine is being organized now" and "the risk of overwhelming the lives of men whose interest is more in learning than in administration." Eliot himself feared that his successes would be measured in terms of "lands, buildings, collections, money and thousands of students" and that future generations would view him as a "Philistine." Santayana likened the faculty to "a registry office" finding jobs for its "nurslings."

It was Veblen, however, who made the most systematic effort to portray the modern university as "a bureaucratic organization" run by businessmen with no concern for the intellectual life. With the basic arguments in place by 1899, Veblen in 1918 expanded his critique into a full-scale attack on business's "bootless meddling with academic matters." Corporate interests sitting on university governing boards had transformed the institutions of higher learning into the equivalents of modern corporations, where the "love of knowledge" was sacrificed to the efficient

production of diplomas for "genteel students" who required college degrees as symbols of status. Veblen's recurring difficulties in securing
academic positions, combined with the celebrated academic freedom cases
involving Richard T. Ely at Wisconsin in 1894, Edward T. Bemis at
Chicago in 1895, and Edward A. Ross at Stanford in 1900, had made him
dubious about the possibilities for intellectual independence in the universities long before the big clampdown on academic freedom during World
War I. Businessmen's "coercive control" and the "standardization of tasks,"
Veblen argued, had "given the schools something of the character of a
penal settlement." In this repressive atmosphere, disinterested scholarship was "thrown into the background," and so vanished the hope of
scholars redressing the ills of American society through the unimpeded
pursuit of truth.[23]

To its critics, the university had failed to provide an adequate place
for the life of the mind in the United States. The mundanities of teaching
and the machinations of anti-intellectual governing bodies had prevented
scholars from giving themselves freely to the development of their ideas.
Without this freedom, and with the trends toward overspecialization,
overqualification, and esoteric knowledge, the university could not serve
as the legitimate conduit of ideas into society at large. Already by 1899,
Veblen was contending that the most important intellectual work in
America was being done outside the academy.

3.

Most academics, of course, did not share the beliefs of these malcontents,
but the critical voices were heard by a younger generation of students and
readers. For those who became America's first self-styled intellectuals,
the direct and indirect presence of a few professorial sages, along with
their own negative experiences in higher education and the influence of
important figures from outside the academy, helped set the terms of the
intellectual life in the 1910s and 1920s. James, Dewey, Santayana, Veblen,
and several other key mentors did not abandon the ideal of the independent but worldly intellectual, but they did make clear to their students
that the next generation of American thinkers would be better off creating
a place for itself outside the universities. The words and examples of
these subversive scholars, however limited their effect on established
institutions, guided some younger intellects to seek out alternative ar-

rangements for the life of the mind in the twentieth-century United States.

William James' resonance among his later students and their contemporaries had less to do with the nuances of his philosophy and psychology than with the general thrust of his thought and character. John Reed remembered James as one of Harvard's "révoltes," "great men," and "independent thinkers"—a model of the unspecialized scholar who stood in lonely opposition to the clubbish, business-dominated Harvard of the early 1900s. Reed drew inspiration from James' essay "The True Harvard," which celebrated the university's "more truth-seeking and independent and often very solitary sons" and rued the "day when Harvard shall stamp a single hard and fast type of character upon her children." This vision of the intellectual as disinterested, unfettered, and expansive provided encouragement to those, like Reed, who were taking their first tentative steps outside the conventional career channels. James also offered the reassurance that independent thought guaranteed its own influence. "[W]hen God lets loose a thinker on the world," he wrote, "all things then have to rearrange themselves." In "The Social Value of the College-Bred," he repeated the claim that ideas inevitably spilled over into action: "The ceaseless whisper of the more permanent ideals, the steady tug of truth and justice, give them but time, *must* warp the world in their direction." [24] Reed's Harvard classmate Walter Lippmann looked to James as a model of intellectual breadth and tolerance. Eulogizing James in 1910, Lippmann remarked, "I think he would have listened with an open mind to the devil's account of heaven, and I'm sure he would have heard him out on hell." For Lippmann, in Ronald Steel's phrase, James was a "culture hero" who resisted narrowness and dogma and asserted a social function for the disinterested thinker. He "listened for truth from anybody, and from anywhere, and in any form," Lippmann insisted, and never lost his "sense of the pace of things," his "glad, sweaty sense of life itself." [25]

Randolph Bourne, a student of Dewey at Columbia, derived similar sustenance from James' defense of the free intellect and its inherent social role. "I should like to know your reaction to James," he wrote to a friend in 1913. "[H]e has settled so many of my own worries that I preach him as a prophet." [26] Until he broke with Dewey over American involvement in World War I, Bourne also found in his mentor the right blend of detachment and involvement. Dewey's "simplicity of manner, his dread of show or self-advertisement," his disregard for the "whole business of impressing yourself on other people," spoke to his intellectual integrity; he stood fast against the temptation to conform and expressed "horror" at "having his ideas petrified into a system." Despite his self-effacing character and his "innate contempt for propaganda," Dewey assumed the role of society's teacher. "A prophet dressed in the clothes of a professor of logic," Bourne wrote adoringly, "his influence goes on increasing to an extent of which he is almost innocently unconscious."[27] Max Eastman, another Dewey student, admired his teacher's "moral force" and "rigorous self-discipline." As Lippmann had done with James, Eastman compared Dewey with Walt Whitman in homage to open-mindedness and free expression. Dewey's "social attitude," Eastman recalled, embodied "the very essence of democracy."[28]

The pragmatic conception of the mind as flexible, wide-ranging, adaptive, and always poised on the brink of action had an emboldening effect on the intellectual generation that came of age between 1910 and 1920. James and Dewey taught that the life of the mind need not mean obscurity and ineffectuality—that ideas, as John Macy proclaimed in celebration of William James, could be "redeemed" from "rigid and jejeune abstraction" and made "alive for living people."[29] The professorial sages proved that a meaningful intellectual life, freed from the blight of specialization and involved with the real business of the world, was possible in the United States. Edmund Wilson described his Princeton teacher Christian Gauss as "the least didactic of sages" who "gave the impression of keeping in touch . . . with everything that was going on everywhere, as well as everything that had ever gone on." Gauss' "extreme flexibility and enormous range" were worthy of emulation. Thorstein Veblen and Patrick Geddes impressed Lewis Mumford with their expansiveness and helped forge for him an image of the twentieth-century intellectual as boundless and relentless in his social criticism: "Both men refused to recognize the no-trespass signs that smaller minds erected around their chosen fields of specialization." The young Lippmann praised Santayana's "ability to see the world steady and whole."[30] For aspiring minds fresh out of college, these models of intellectual courage were of enormous importance; they instilled a sense that compromise and intellectual atrophy could be resisted.

Yet the professorial sages stood out as exceptions within the universities. They themselves were critical of the stifling atmosphere of higher education and seemed to thrive despite the hostile environment. Bourne noted the contrast between Dewey and the academic types who expressed "their views on every question of the day in the old caked and frozen language, thinking along the old lazy channels." Gauss, according to Wilson, "seemed to meet the academic world with a slightly constrained self-consciousness at not having much in common with it." "[H]ow few the Gausses and Kemp Smiths are," he remarked in 1919, "and how sterile most university teaching is." In his semi-autobiographical novel *I Thought of Daisy*, Wilson distinguished Professor Grosbeake, a character based on Alfred North Whitehead, "from the essential triviality of mind which academic arrogance or complacency so often tries to disguise." Matthew Josephson found only a few "vital personalities" on the Columbia faculty, and even the presence of Charles Beard, James Harvey Robinson, Franz Boas, and Dewey could not fully salvage his undergraduate education. Columbia, he remembered, "contributed only a modest increment to my store of learning; the real profits were intangible and extracurricular."[31]

The rule of the universities, as the sages knew and reported, was something other than the expansive intellect, and however heroic they had been in their efforts to transcend the limits of the universities, their influence had suffered for their cloistered existence. "I feel a savage indignation that Professor Dewey should not be out in the arena of the concrete, himself interpreting current life," Bourne wrote. He blamed Columbia for Dewey's failure to assume a position of immediate involvement in American affairs. Lippmann chastised Santayana for his aloofness from "the common hopes of ordinary men" but was less sanguine than Bourne about the possibilities of reconciling dispassionate observation and meaningful participation. Still, Lippmann complained, "There is something of the pathetic loneliness of the spectator about him. You wish he would jump on the stage and take part in the show."[32] Bourne, Lippmann, and their contemporaries were not entirely content with assurances that good ideas inevitably produced practical results. In addition to inspiring lessons about intellectual integrity and versatility, they learned from their mentors that academic careers erected barriers against the real world. The spread of ideas from the universities was too gradual and accidental; the professor who wrote for and reached a larger public was a rare exception.

4.

It was not only the words and examples of important teachers that created hostility to the academy among the younger intellectuals. Their own experiences with higher education also contributed to the belief that the university failed to foster the independent and influential intellect. Those concerned about knowledge and ideas saw themselves as an embattled minority; isolation is the dominant motif in their letters and recollections about college life. Van Wyck Brooks concluded that the mediocrity of his professors and the stupidity of his classmates summed up "Undergraduate Culture" at Harvard. "Nothing in college surprises me so much as the ignorance of them in high places," Brooks confessed as a freshman. "The so-called literary bigbugs by having any claim to preeminence but illustrate the deplorable darkness of the multitude of ignoramuses that make up the other five thousand."[33] Randolph Bourne managed to find "many who thought as I did" and formed "an interesting social group" but knew himself to be on the fringes of undergraduate life nonetheless. Most Columbia students "have about as many modern ideas and as broad an outlook on life as a child of two," Bourne observed. "I am assuming that all my friends are highly endowed, interesting, and charming and that outside my circle, such creatures don't exist."[34] Outside the small bands of thinkers, the colleges were populated by narrow-minded careerists— "easy materialists and hedonists," Harold Stearns called them, "specialists who saw in terms of bread and butter the future value of their present work." In an article entitled "The Confessions of a Harvard Man," Stearns complained "that men interested in intellectual things are often unwarrantably lonely." Harvard, where "the greater number of the student body were depressingly matter-of-fact, intellectually shallow, utilitarian, interested, the same as crass Philistines outside of college, only in money-making, women and amusement," had been a most inhospitable place for intellectual development.[35] Stearns claimed to be able to count on one hand the authentic intellectuals he had met as an undergraduate.

Critics' revulsion at the university's Philistinism did not, however, lead them to compensate by embracing the university's abstract thought. Abstraction was another of higher education's pathologies. Given Brooks' attitudes toward his own college experience, it is not surprising that he chose the university as the primary target of his famous assault on highbrow culture. In Brooks' scheme, Philistinism thrived because the professors had failed to challenge it, opting instead to dwell in the realm of vagueness and intangibility. The "typical university man," believing that theory had nothing to do with reality, could pass through college without encountering any challenge to his faith in "a world of dollars." Brooks described the American university as a place "where ideals are cherished precisely because they are ineffectual, because they are ineptly and mournfully beautiful."[36] Opposed to both abstraction and narrow utilitarianism, he rejected the university itself as being simultaneously out of touch with the hard realities of American life and uncritically accepting of America's grasping materialism.

Mumford rooted his own early critique of genteel culture in an attack on academic aloofness. His 1914 short story "Fruit" described the travails of a Latin professor named Jarvis—a defender of the bankrupt idea of culture as a sphere removed from everyday experience—who comes to realize that what he teaches is useless. Overcome by doubts, Jarvis stumbles out into his garden and begins to dig, discarding abstractions and renewing his contact with reality. Malcolm Cowley similarly located the false view of culture in the universities, which he characterized in terms derived from Veblen and Brooks. "Essentially we were taught to regard culture as a veneer, a badge of class distinction—," he wrote of Harvard, "as something to be assumed like an Oxford accent or a suit of English clothes"; to Cowley, the colleges were little more than "mansions of air." John Reed railed at professors who went through "a dull round of dates, acts, half-truths and rules for style, without questioning, without interpreting and without seeing how ridiculously unlike the world their teachings are." "In the universities," Lippmann observed in 1920, "men should be able to think patiently and generously for the good of society. If they do not, surely one of the reasons is that thought terminates in doctor's theses and brown quarterlies."[37]

To escape such insularity, these critics concluded, to establish a more direct relationship between ideas and action, required that American intellectual life be removed from the universities and placed somewhere closer to the lowbrow realities. Max Eastman stated it succinctly in 1908: "If the meaning of an idea is its result in action, then the meaning of Pragmatism is to resign your chair in philosophy." Eastman made clear his sentiments about the incompatability of an academic career and a meaningful intellectual life by fulfilling all the requirements for a Ph.D. and then expressing his "scorn of scholastic trinkets by not taking the degree." Earlier he had declined a teaching job at Williams in the belief that "the highest good is the right union of the active and the contemplative life."[38]

In some cases, additional experiences and outside advice helped shape the decision to avoid the academy. Brooks had the example of the painter John Butler Yeats, the poet's father, who dispensed wisdom from his seat at Petitpas' restaurant in lower Manhattan. To the recent graduate, Yeats suggested the possibilities of intellectual freedom in a way that Brooks' professors had not. He "was so much more my teacher than Harvard was," Brooks later said of this "true sage." "He taught me to cherish the concrete, eschewing the abstract and the speculative wherever one could" and thus to strive for something other than the university's highbrow conception of culture.[39] From 1911 to 1913, Brooks taught English at Stanford and learned first-hand that teaching was a distraction from the more important work of writing books. After applying for a position at Columbia in 1915, he never again ventured toward an academic career. By 1922, he was able to advise his own protégé Newton Arvin "to get what the universities can give you without belonging to a university"— to try to "be a genuine scholar and a free man at the same time."[40] Bourne sought the counsel of Ellery Sedgwick, editor of the *Atlantic*, who at first suggested that Bourne follow the advice of a Columbia dean, become a professor, and "rejoice in belonging to a profession" which offered "so large a liberty" to continue writing. But one of Bourne's friends warned him that he had as much chance of securing a teaching post "as Voltaire would have had of obtaining a bishopric," and Sedgwick soon changed his mind and told Bourne that he "would find a professor's chair too narrow to sit in" and "would be about as unhappy in college as . . . in the priesthood."[41] The prospect of finding an alternative to an academic position was daunting, but Bourne's unwillingness to accept a role he found confining kept him out of the university.

Lippmann and Reed drew from the advice and experience of Lincoln Steffens, whose muckraking adventures had allied him with Reed's father in Oregon and brought him to Harvard in search of talented recruits. Steffens himself had undergone a vocational crisis after college; he had studied philosophy in Europe before concluding that "self-culture" was inadequate and determining to find a place for himself in "practical life." When Reed was nearing graduation, Steffens readily offered his assessment of the university: "There is not enough intellectual curiosity in your college; there is little in any American college." In 1911, the recently widowed Steffens moved into a Greenwich Village apartment with Reed and three of Reed's college friends and established himself as mentor to "a clever group of young Harvard men," helping them with "love-scrapes, jobs, and money troubles." The lesson of Steffens' life was evident to Reed: free expression and legitimate influence might be reconcilable, but only away from the university. Reed dedicated his 1913 poem "The Day in Bohemia" to his mentor-roommate, proclaiming him "One of Us; The Only Man Who Understands My Arguments," symbol of "light-hearted Liberty."[42]

The idea that the university obstructed liberty and denied an immediate relationship with the world of affairs formed the basis for a more general animosity toward institutions. Attempts at relocating the intellectual life after 1910 would enlarge the problem of the university into a problem of affiliations of any kind. When Veblen, Dewey, Charles A. Beard, James Harvey Robinson, and several other professors established the New School for Social Research in 1919, they envisioned an anti-institutional institution which would circumvent the constraints and remoteness of the established schools and instead "seek an unbiased understanding of the existing order, its genesis, growth, and present working, as well as of those exigent circumstances which are making for its revision."[43] But the rejection of an academic career was the first act of resistance to regimentation and routine by those who, like Lippmann, sought ways to avoid the "ossification of mind" they had perceived in higher education. Mumford never regretted his decision to avoid the academy; it had released him from any obligation "to court official approval or academic good will" and left him "free to explore neglected areas or unorthodox approaches without current academic sanction." Long before he established himself as a writer, Mumford boasted that he never expected to receive a college degree and that he had learned more from New York's museums and libraries than from his courses at Columbia, Washington Square College, and CCNY. These non-academic institutions allowed him to work according to his "own needs" rather than the demands "of a system" and helped him "to recover from the disastrous results of a thorough education."[44]

While there would be other obstacles to intellectual independence, the repudiation of the university was a crucial step in the redefinition of American intellectual life.[45] By itself, this repudiation did not secure for younger intellectuals the freedom to think and write as they pleased; it did not bring them into closer contact with everyday experience and reality. Randolph Bourne, yearning "to do something direct and useful in the world," dismissed further study as "too much of an invitation to dawdle"—"an ineffective waste of time in a world where there are as many things to be done and done at once." Bourne knew that "to do them" required more than the choice against an academic career. "If only I had some confidence in my ability to persuade by writing," he agonized. "Now this is no attitude for a would-be man-of-letters, a would-be man with a message, who wants to be a preacher, and even a prophet."[46] Bourne and his contemporaries had no clear idea of how they were to go about being thinkers without traditional institutional supports, and self-doubt would persist. But the movement to find a home for the intellect outside the university renewed the promise of independence and involvement, gave aspiring intellectuals like Bourne a sense of purpose, and meant for them that they were opening a new and better phase in the life of the mind in the United States.

CHAPTER 2

Making a Living

Van Wyck Brooks summed up what he called the "ordeal" of Mark Twain as a conflict between the "creative instinct" and the "acquisitive instinct." Brooks believed that Twain had failed as an artist by succumbing to the "unconscious conspiracy" which "activated all America against the creative spirit"; he "had abdicated that spiritual independence without which the creative life is impossible." Twain's sin, according to Brooks, was to compromise with conventional expectations about career and success. Jane Clemens had raised her son to resist "every sort of personal deviation from the accepted types" and had exacted a promise from young Samuel upon her husband's death "to be a faithful and industrious man, and upright, like his father." This "solemn oath," in Brooks' clumsy Freudian scheme, doomed Twain to a life of conflict between individuality and conformity, between expression and acquisition. "To become such a conventional citizen as his father would have approved of, to make money and restore the fallen fortunes of his family—that old pledge was fixed in the back of his mind" as he made his way as a writer.[1] The sad conclusion was that Twain confused art with a trade and became a humorist to satisfy his perverse need for material success. Even his choice of a pseudonym indicated compromise with convention; Mark Twain had opted for safe water.

Malcolm Cowley described *The Ordeal of Mark Twain* as one of Brooks' "cautionary tales" to his contemporaries, replete with "lessons of courage in self-expression."[2] The book is more compelling in what it reveals about the concerns of Van Wyck Brooks than in its critical assessment of Twain

and his work. Foremost among these concerns was the problem of maintaining independence in a commercial society which constantly threatened to co-opt artists and intellectuals. Independence was impossible if
the lure of money became too strong, as for Twain. But independence
was equally impossible if writers had no reliable source of income, and
the removal from the universities had cut off the most stable means of
financial support for the intellectual life. While Brooks castigated Twain
for becoming "the mouthpiece" of "worldly interests," he could not will
away the mundane problem of making a living.[3] Like it or not, the need
for money determined where and how intellectuals lived and worked.
Brooks' discussion of Twain suggests his own deep apprehensions about
financial matters, apprehensions shared by many of those who were
trying to construct an independent intellectual life in the United States.

1.

Ideally, intellectuals would remain free of any vocation resembling a
career, which connoted enslavement to routine, specialization, and capitulation to what Harold Stearns disdainfully termed the "cash nexus."
Stearns imagined the young intellectual standing in opposition to "the
smooth, round, tasteless monotony" of living in a business civilization,
forging some "other kind of life than the monotonous majority-ruled,
unimaginative existence of the great average." An early experience with
factory work had acted upon Stearns to make him "hate the monotony
and stupidity of piece work on machines with an intensity that more or
less altered the emotional direction of my whole life."[4] Randolph Bourne
counseled "aloofness from drudgery" and the rejection of "painful obligation" in favor of "excellent spontaneity" and "self-expression." Bourne,
too, had worked at several unpleasant jobs before enrolling in college,
including an underpaid position making piano rolls in New Jersey. In a
prescriptive essay titled "The Dodging of Pressures," he noted "the incredible stupidity of our civilization where so much of the work is unin-
teresting and monotonous." For the young Edmund Wilson, the " 'valuable experience' " that fathers urged their children to obtain was merely
"an American euphemism for the drudgery of money-getting."[5]

Formal employment intruded on creativity by structuring lives and
diverting them toward non-productive ends. Hutchins Hapgood, a fre-

quenter of Mabel Dodge's salon with such younger lights as Walter Lippmann, John Reed, and Max Eastman, expressed his fear of "crystallization." "Held to one or the other form of work . . . , either through economic necessity lasting for the better part of one's life or the passion for position and power, the familiar elements of one's personality become so definite that eventually there is little room for new elements which again point to a completer personality and keep the individual esthetically alive." Brooks, whose father had deteriorated under the burdens of an unsuccessful business career, contrasted "getting a living" with "living" itself. Intellectuals, he wrote in 1915, were properly engaged not in the rituals of "economic self-assertion" but in the quest for "self-fulfillment." "A man is either living, or earning his living," according to Max Eastman. "He is never doing these two things, purely, at once." Lewis Mumford drew a similar distinction between "senseless external activity" and expression; in 1934 he still revolted against a "maniacal concentration upon work" at the expense of life—art, education, play, sex. The ideal creative life would not include the "joyless enforced labor," the sacrifice of time "divinely precious, in the treadmill of making a living" that John Dos Passos and Sherwood Anderson repudiated in early critical essays.[6]

Proclaiming their liberation from ordered, purposeless work, independent intellectuals constructed a myth of autonomy central to their self-definition. The conscious decision to resist traditional paths toward success and distinction amounted to a generational break. Some, like Brooks and Bourne, agonized over the decision. "A boy is born," Brooks wrote of conventional expectations. "The first thought is, what will he be? And this question not from the standpoint, how much good can he do, or can he be great, but how much salary will he be able to draw." While touring England after college, Brooks struggled with these expectations: "Meanwhile, how am I making my living, preparing for my responsibilities?" Bourne suffered under "that awful glowering family eye of rich guarding relatives" when he chose to forsake a career in business. "I felt like a criminal," he confessed, "because it meant my withdrawing from the possibility of earning money for my family." The temptation to "justify my existence by getting a job" was difficult to resist.[7] David Bauer, the hero of Paul Rosenfeld's autobiographical novel *The Boy in the Sun*, senses the discomfiting gaze of his grandmother and projects for himself a life of intolerable labor: " 'Your grandfather and uncles were business men: it's

good enough for you! Earn your living!' and David saw himself in faint
subaqueous light an office-boy or Western Union messenger in a uniform."[8]

The galvanizing effects of this break, however, compensated for the
doubts. By renouncing binding affiliations and declaring instead their
intent to operate outside common career channels, aspiring intellectuals
fostered a belief in their own uniqueness. Rhetorically, at least, they
distanced themselves from the dehumanizing forces of twentieth-century
America—greed, standardization, mechanization, regimentation—and
imagined themselves capable of producing genuinely disinterested social
criticism. "I have the firm conviction that some day our will will begin to
operate freely and creatively, when we get oriented in the world and get
a certain poise and surety," Bourne wrote, "and our activity is now bent
to getting that poise and understanding the chaotic world about us."[9]
Such understanding seemed possible to free-lance intellectuals, those
without ties to universities, without stultifying jobs, beyond the corrupt-
ing influences of business civilization. In their minds, they were attempting something new; the first free thinkers in America, they were fashioning an alternative to a way of life based on accumulation and meaningless
toil.

2.

To sustain a sense of autonomy, it was necessary to insist that financial
matters were inconsequential and could not interfere with independent
expression. Floyd Dell juxtaposed the artist-intellectual with the American mass, "the passing crowds" who all "did the same, essentially the
same, sort of thing for a living." In *Moon-Calf*, Dell's alter ego Felix Fay
witnesses his brother's sacrifice of a painter's life and resists a similar fate
for himself: "Why should he ask something better—something like the
fancied life of the butterfly? Yet he did . . ." Dell later recalled his father's
failure as a businessman and his own rejection "of the obligation of being
a good ordinary citizen who got a job and did his duty by his family."[10]
Dramatic renunciations of ties to the business civilization were accompanied by the celebration of a scaled-down life conspicuously free of all
acquisition beyond bare necessity. Brooks admired the poet Edwin Ar-
lington Robinson for his adherence to "a cult of poverty that appealed to
me as a real and vital element of the literary life"—real and vital because

it signified independence and disinterestedness. When Edmund Wilson was about to return from army service in Europe and contemplated his future, he too settled on the cult of poverty. "I have been worrying for some time now as to how I am going to earn an honest living when I get back," he wrote in 1919, "and have about decided that I won't do so at all but, instead, will spend a life of simplicity, more or less poverty, and relentless application in the service of Apollo." [11] Beneath the mock seriousness of Wilson's declaration lay an apprehension of the conflict between career and culture, acquisitiveness and truth. In an imaginary conversation between Brooks and F. Scott Fitzgerald, Wilson made clear his belief in the incompatibility of expression and acquisition. Speaking through Brooks, Wilson castigates his friend Fitzgerald for his admission that he "can't live down at Great Neck on anything under thirty-six thousand a year." "In allowing your art to become a business," Wilson's Brooks tells Fitzgerald, "you have made intellectual unity impossible and given yourself up to the competitive anarchy of American commercial enterprise." [12] Intellectual integrity required a conscious determination to avoid conventional measures of success and enslavement to excessive material desires.

The dodging of pressures and the cult of poverty are dominant motifs in the literature of intellectual self-definition. Marks of failure in mainstream America became badges of a different kind of success in this alternative culture. Sherwood Anderson urged his comrades to get "training in what is called poverty," not simply because poverty was their fate but because it was an essential part of the creative life. Speaking of herself and Hutchins Hapgood, Mabel Dodge boasted that "[w]e both felt like failures from the angle of worldly success, and we were proud of it." Even at 87, Mumford was proud that he had "often disregarded financial rewards and been impervious to financial pressures." [13]

Poverty, Eastman suggested, not only demonstrated freedom from the acquisitive instinct; it also brought the creative mind—"always in danger of removing itself from real life"—into contact with common experience and thus helped bridge the gap between the intellect and reality. The "dominant feature of real life is the pressure of necessity," Eastman pointed out, "and the artist, the writer, ought to taste that, and taste it strong." It may have been Eastman's lingering resistance to financial success that prompted H. L. Mencken's ironic remark concerning the former's *Enjoyment of Laughter* in 1936: "I hope the book becomes a best seller, and makes you rich." During the Depression, Mumford reminded Waldo Frank of the benefits of material deprivation for social critics:

It is part of our experience of humanity to know, through our life-curve, those harassing restrictions, those daily deficits and defeats, which all our fellow work-ers know as part of their routine: it is indeed only by such suffering as we have encountered that we can experience imaginatively the daily lot of mankind in our era, a lot beside which our material constrictions count as wealth and affluence.[14]

In contrast to what Wilson called "all the sterilizing and demoraliz-ing forces—industrialism, physical depletion, dissipation, careerism and cynicism," intellectuals posited a self-fulfilling life of letters which would operate on its own time with its own values. "[W]hat I wanted to escape was the business man's harness," wrote the future stage designer Lee Simonson in 1913. "What I felt . . . most keenly was not a certain sort of work, but a certain type of life. An aristocratic life—a pleasant life—where all day one did only what it was a pleasure to do, never *had* to do anything, had plenty of leisure, was generally a privileged person."[15] Floyd Dell and Max Eastman tried to separate the creative process from financial necessity by compartmentalizing their lives. "Writing was a part of an ideal world—," according to Dell, and "it had nothing to do with making a living." Eastman determined that "economic security" would not taint his life of "ideas and opinions" and told his sister Crystal in 1906 that "writing" had to be kept separate from "making my living." "By earning a small living at noncreative work, with time free for writing," he wrote to Oswald Garrison Villard in declining a job at the New York *Evening Post*, "I shall foster my real purposes."[16]

Simonson's ideal of leisure, with its emphasis on privilege as something other than economic aggrandizement, suggests that the model for the intellectual life resided in an imagined precommercial past. Generally hostile to American history, American intellectuals in the 1910s and 1920s located this past imprecisely, in a vague time before industry intruded upon craftsmanship and made money rather than beauty and self-fulfillment the standards of value. When Vernon Parrington referred to "poets and essayists and novelists and dramatists, the eager young intellectuals of a drab generation" as America's "men of letters," he placed these "free souls" and "free thinkers" in opposition to "the professional custodians of official views."[17] These young intellectuals, according to Parrington, were amateurs who did their thinking for the sake of self (in the sense of fulfillment rather than selfishness) and society; "men of letters" recalled a time before specialization and professionalization. Sherwood Anderson called for "a quieter, more leisurely and altogether more charming way of life [that] we might begin to live, here in America" and went so far in decrying professionalism as to argue that the idea that "one should get money by writing, painting, making music is in some way false." [18]

Anderson conceived of the artist-intellectual as a craftsman, one who thought "more of quality than of quantity and more of living than accumulating." Alfred Stieglitz, for example, had "the craftsman's love of his tools and his materials" and created something "sound and sweet." Gertrude Stein, "who cares for the handmade goodies and who scorns the factory-made foods," was "making something with her materials, something sweet to the tongue and fragrant to the nostrils." In Anderson's scheme, the artists and the intellectuals were the only contemporary Americans not alienated from their labor. "The arts are after all but the old crafts intensified," he reasoned, "followed with religious fervor and determination by men who love them[,] and deep down within him perhaps every man wants more than anything else to be a good craftsman." The life of letters was a path away from the cheapened, standardized life of modern America, a way "to reach down through all the broken surface distractions of modern life to that old love of craft out of which culture springs." Parrington proclaimed Anderson one of America's most important artists and summarized his message to the aspiring writer: "He must pull himself free from a deadening and devastating routine of an industrial society with its empty ambitions. And having found his craft he finds a recompense in life." [19]

Few were as insistent as Anderson in celebrating the writer as craftsman, but many shared his belief that the life of letters was the only remaining sphere in which quality superseded quantity and individual happiness mattered more than money. Anderson acknowledged an intellectual debt to Brooks and the circle around the *Seven Arts*, where some of the first Winesburg stories were published, and it was Brooks who supplied the language for understanding artists and critics as the preservers of "the quality, the spiritual value of life." Brooks lashed out at the division of labor for removing all joy from work and for ignoring "the element of the unexplainable in hand-made work, that curious product of human ambition and pride called quality." For Brooks, too, the artist-intellectual was one of the last true producers in a speculative, alienating, consumption-oriented civilization. The independent farmer, a vanishing type, was the only other holdout: "By his labour he is actually bringing something into the world, not merely transferring something already produced. And the artist also creates."[20] As the farmer and the craftsman passed into oblivion, the critic and the artist stood alone as the saving remnants of a productive society. The writer, said Anderson, worked only with "the materials of his craft"—"a sheet of white paper," a "true and vital economy of ink," and ideas. In this uncorrupted state, nothing intruded between creator and creation; the writer was fully independent, driven exclusively by what Lewis Mumford called "delight in production" and Randolph Bourne termed "an instinct for workmanship." Mark Twain, in Brooks' portrayal, had tasted independence as a riverboat pilot; Brooks quoted Twain's description of the pilot as "the only unfettered and entirely independent human being that lived in the earth." But Twain failed to transfer "the ideal of craftsmanship" he had absorbed from this experience to his writing—he failed to cherish being "morally free" in the pursuit of his craft—and succumbed to "a world given over to exploitation." Speaking as Brooks, Wilson described "serious men of letters" as those who "followed their art with a high sense of its dignity," meaning those who resisted the lure of commercial success. The independent, unspecialized life of letters, Mumford declared, was "a life lived for its own values, instead of a life on the make," an example of the possibility in twentieth-century America of an alternative to numbing work and empty materialism.[21] Familiar with the handicraft utopianism of Ruskin and Morris, Brooks and Mumford added a strange twist. Rather than endorsing the English antimodernist solution of a return to hand work, they recast the independent life of letters as a kind of productive labor akin to the old crafts: free, skilled, creative, fulfilling, and socially beneficial.

3.

The turn away from the university closed off an outlet for publication as well as a source of income, leaving journalism as the most inviting alternative on both counts.[22] With the exception of Max Eastman, who soon violated his pledge anyway, few aspiring intellectuals attempted to separate writing from earning a living. For a time, Eastman supported himself by lecturing on women's suffrage, but by 1914 he had committed himself to paid full-time editorial work. Journalism offered the chance to write for money, to sharpen critical skills, develop a reputation, reach an audience, and still avoid less pleasant and more routine employment. Lincoln Steffens had also tried to live a dual life—by day "a merchant and an active citizen in political life," by night a man engaged in "study and writing." Steffens, however, found that he could reconcile the "practical life" with the literary life through journalism; after a struggle to gain a foothold, he was able to boast to his father that he had succeeded and was now earning from sixteen to twenty dollars a week by writing.[23] Steffens, in turn, helped dissuade Walter Lippmann from becoming a lawyer and set up Lippmann and John Reed as professional journalists. When Lippmann joined Steffens at *Everybody's* in 1910, his friend Alfred Booth Kuttner contrasted his own choice of medical school, which he believed was transforming him into "a materialistic machine," to Lippmann's "swift" and "progressive move." Kuttner confessed, "I envy you your tutelage under Steffens."[24]

Even Steffens' generation, however, recognized that there were problems with steady newspaper or magazine work. At best, commercial journalism was an imperfect approximation of the independent life of letters, constrained by "business managers" and the obligation to complete assignments, follow routines, and conform to rules about style and content. As early as 1895, Steffens complained that he was "sinking more and more deeply" into his "profession" and felt "helpless humiliation" at his "descent." He saw himself succumbing to the tendency "more and more to become absorbed in the newspaper work to the exclusion of scientific and literary work" and agreed with his colleagues that journalism was a distraction from the real stuff of writing: "I find that the other reporters are ambitious of literary careers and feel that reportorial work is beneath them and temporary. I think the same . . ." In his *Autobiography*, Steffens recalled his "dread of becoming a professional newspaper man," his fear that "the conditions of journalism would make of me what I saw it make of old reporters and editorial writers, a Greek slave in Rome, a writer of the master's opinions."[25]

Other members of the muckraking generation who influenced the development of younger writers shared these concerns about journalism. Albert Jay Nock, later the editor of Brooks, Mumford, and Geroid Robinson at the *Freeman*, joined the *American* magazine when Steffens bought it in 1906 but quit in 1915 (long after Steffens' departure) because of the magazine's "mad passion for size and popularity." Hutchins Hapgood wrote for the New York *Commercial Advertiser* under Steffens' editorship and remembered how its "individuality of writing" made it "a delightful form of self-expression" in contrast to the competition: "We all had a freer hand in our work than men on the other papers." Steffens, too, played up the exceptionality of the paper, announcing that he wanted it staffed not by newspaper men but by writers who would get the news "as material for poetry, plays, or fiction" and "for practice."[26] Steffens and Hapgood were the elder statesmen of the Dodge salon and brought their ideas about journalism to the younger generation.

4.

Wary of any impediments to full freedom of expression, this generation approached journalism suspiciously, with the understanding that newspaper and magazine writing was merely an expedient. Most adopted the attitude that no job was permanent, that even a regular staff position would not last long enough to become routine, that the proper way to avoid stagnation was to become a free-lancer. Free-lancing changed journalism into a kind of anti-career for intellectuals, characterized by frequent movement, a sense of autonomy and integrity, resistance to specialization and professionalization, and an unwillingness to conform to commercial demands.

The experience of commercial journalism contributed to the conception of free-lancing as an alternative vocation and to a search for other modes of publication. When Floyd Dell reflected on his days as a cub reporter in Davenport, Iowa, he focused on the destruction of self-expression among the old-timers. "Reporting was so devastating a job," he wrote, "it reduced anyone to such a poor, unrepresentative wraith of his individual self, that in order to recover the sense of being a particular person with thoughts and feelings of his own, some reporters [*sic*] had apparently to get drunk every so often." An awareness of the traps of journalism, Dell believed, allowed intellectuals to subvert this loss of self. At the Chicago *Evening Post*, Dell served as assistant on the literary supplement to Francis Hackett, later a *New Republic* editor. There, according to Dell, it "was the object of the intellectuals on the staff to make the best possible use of the means which the proprietor provided to spread ideas of the kind that he was known to deplore."[27] But the possibilities for internal subversion were limited, and aspiring intellectuals caught in the routine of regular journalism knew that they were wasting time. In *Moon-Calf*, Dell's Felix Fay quickly loses his initial enthusiasm for reporting and finds his writing, "as pabulum offered by a daily newspaper to its readers, unpalatable." John Reed derided his employers in a show he wrote for the Dutch Treat Club in 1913 and titled *Everymagazine, An Immorality Play;* his theme was the timidity and tepidness of the popular magazines. Four years later, Reed complained about having to write a "pot-boiler" for a "silly Aeroplane magazine" and lamented of his work at the New York *Evening Mail*, "I don't like the desperate grind of this job." Waldo Frank's father lined him up with a job at Oswald Garrison Villard's New York *Evening Post* and even paid his son's salary to establish him in the newspaper business, but Frank found the work inadequate and depressing. Joining the *New York Times* in 1912, he discovered a gap between the "glamor" and the "inward reality" of commercial journalism and failed to find compensation in the good pay he received as a reporter.[28] Paul Rosenfeld's idea that a year at the Columbia School of Journalism would "be a great training" and his initial enthusiasm for a job at the New York *Press* gave way after five months to a different feeling altogether. "I am exaspirated [*sic*] with the Press," he told a friend. "I have been having a rotten time of it lately, and am beginning to hate it." When he quit, he explained that "while I was on the 'Press,' the beauty of making something fine, useful, and sincere came over me, and now's my chance."[29] Writing was not a craft at the mass-circulation newspapers and magazines; it was factory work.

Dell, Frank, Rosenfeld, and their contemporaries looked for redemption in a free-lance life which treated commercial journalism as an expedient for paying the bills while leaving enough time for more meaningful work. Their critical attitude toward the established press gave impetus to an alternative journalism which, in its conception, offered an outlet for free expression and a chance to compensate themselves and the public for the unpleasantness of writing for money. Dell described his involvement with the socialist press as "a spiritual relief to me" after the unhappy experience of newspaper work.[30] In *Journalism versus Art* (1916), Eastman presented a full-scale critique of commercial journalism, arguing that most newspapers and magazines were "presided over by the monotonous desire to do business." The effect of "the commercial preoccupation" was "to please everybody a little and displease none," and the cost was intellectual freedom. This preoccupation with "profits in competition" was like a disease which began with the owners, then passed "along the editor's nerves and outward to the brains of his contributors." Eastman concluded that journalism must "be free of the tyranny of this demand that everybody be pleased with it—free to make enemies as well as friends." As an example of free journalism, he cited the *Masses*, the magazine he edited with the assistance of Dell and Reed. "The fact that nobody is trying to make dividends out of *The Masses*," Eastman boasted, "has given it a unique character, has given the freedom for a perfectly wilful play of the creative faculties, such as would inevitably produce unique works of art." For added emphasis, he made public his "inflexible rule . . . never to try to earn money by writing," though perhaps without trying, he was earning $150 a month at the *Masses* in 1916.[31]

Similar dreams of independence and involvement informed the founding of the *New Republic*. In his proposal for the magazine, Herbert Croly predicted that it would be "self-sustaining" rather than "profitable." The staff "should be willing . . . to accept no more than a living wage for their work," not only because this was a "business necessity" but also because it was a "moral necessity," signifying the magazine's freedom from external influences. A self-conscious repudiation of financial motives would demonstrate "an ardent and disinterested belief in the value of the enterprise and the value of the ideal" of progressive criticism. Croly envisioned the *New Republic* as a living example of cooperative rather than competitive effort, from which the primary reward would be the joy of "laboring in cooperation with right-minded associates for the benefit of an ultimate human ideal." Freed from the snares of profit and pandering, it would also remain unattached to "any fixed or narrow creed" which might compromise the "disinterested motive" and critical independence of its founders and contributors. The magazine would not be political in the confining sense of advocating a particular party or agenda. Instead, Croly insisted, it would stand "for a higher quality of human expression in American life—for moral freedom, intellectual integrity, social sympathy, and improved technical methods in all the practical and fine arts." For its writers, it would be a functional alternative to commercial journalism, a forum for independent criticism untainted by meddlesome owners trying to appeal to the lowest common denominator. Slowly, inevitably, it would gain an audience, "accelerate and guide" the "American national consciousness," and become "a power in the formation of American public opinion."[32]

Lippmann agreed with Croly's assessment of the *New Republic*'s possibilities. Writing to Van Wyck Brooks in 1914, he claimed for the magazine "the opportunity of focussing the young men in America" through disinterested criticism and asked Brooks to think of himself "as one of our group." Though Brooks had not yet completed *America's Coming-of-Age*, he had articulated its organizing theme in a letter to Lippmann, who now conceived of the *New Republic* as a way of reconciling the highbrow and lowbrow. "We may be able to do what you ask for in your letter—to define the issues on the 'robust middle plane,' " Lippmann wrote. The free play of ideas in touch with social reality would give the magazine "a real sense of the relation between the abstract and the concrete, between the noble dream and the actual limitations of life." The fact that it had "a paid up capital—God save us—of $200,000" would keep the publication free from the cash nexus, and without any "party axe or propaganda axe to grind," it would allow for full freedom of expression.[33] Randolph Bourne approached the new weekly with equal enthusiasm. Completing a fellowship in Europe at the beginning of 1914, he wished for "some forum, when I get back to America, from which I could preach some disagreeable truths to my countrymen." With the help of Charles Beard and Ellery Sedgwick, Bourne managed to secure a slot as a regular contributor to the *New Republic*. "It seems like just the opportunity that I have wanted to get myself expressed," he wrote shortly before the magazine's debut, "and I am only hoping to be able to be really big enough for the opportunity."[34]

From the 1910s through the boom time of the little magazines in the 1920s, this promise of intellectual freedom was constantly renewed. In the first issue of the *Seven Arts*, published in November 1916, the editors explicitly distanced themselves from commercial journalism. Waldo Frank, speaking for his associates Brooks and James Oppenheim, announced, "What we ask of the writer is simply self-expression without regard to current magazine standards." John Reed, still frustrated with the necessity of earning money by writing for the popular press, took "real delight" in the *Seven Arts*' acceptance of one of his articles.[35] Albert Jay Nock's *Freeman* presented itself in 1920 as "a paper which desires disinterestedly to serve its age," dedicated to "the promotion of free popular discussion."

Extreme tolerance became the defining feature of the intellectual magazines. Free from the control of advertisers and outwardly unconcerned with their own financial stability, they conceived of themselves as the primary vehicles for independent thought in modern America.

Most agreed with the early observations of Croly, Lippmann, and the *New Republic* that institutional partisanship and dogma precluded disinterested criticism. Intellectual adversity was a positive presence, a kind of security against stagnation. And if disagreement proved inadequate to avoid what Gorham Munson of *Secession* called the danger of "moribundity," then the instability of the little magazines would be a sufficient guarantee of free expression. Munson, in fact, followed through on his pledge to scrap the magazine after two years if routine appeared to be setting in: "Beyond a two year span, observation shows, the vitality of most reviews is lowered and their contribution, accomplished, becomes repetitive and unnecessary."[36] In the search for a place for independent thought, intellectuals achieved brief successes through these alternative media. While the output of the intellectual magazines was inconsistent, the enthusiasm with which critics and artists created new publications translated into substantial work, some of it important in its own right and much of which served as the basis for subsequent books.

5.

Vigilance against stagnation, however, did not forestall the conclusion that even an alternative journalism might be an obstacle to genuine intellectual endeavor. An independent press had its own routines and requirements, standards and hierarchies, and in many cases deadlines and editorial responsibilities seemed to intrude into time better spent writing books. Eastman thought of his work at the *Masses* as "secondary" and "supplemental." He told his brother in 1913, "I never intended to be an editor at all. I've not written a word on my book." The job "simply doesn't leave enough strength (or rather enough vigorous idleness) for real creative thought or imagination."[37] Bourne, who had craved "some tight little niche to work around in for a while" without selling out to a conventional career and had welcomed the chance to write for the *New Republic* in 1914, soon came to view this work as a distraction. By the summer of 1916 he was complaining that the *New Republic* "continues to sidetrack me" and that the editors had become more rigid about the articles they were willing to assign and accept. Even Lippmann soon admitted that his *New Republic* work "wouldn't do as a permanent job." In a memorandum to his fellow editors, he warned against the "danger" that the magazine was exhausting its "original impulse" and its "original stock of ideas" and might begin to "run on tradition and routine" instead of "a genuine freshness of mind."[38]

At the *Freeman*, Brooks' passage from enthusiasm to disillusionment was equally rapid. Promised full "freedom to express himself" by publisher B. W. Huebsch, Brooks initially thought it "fine to be driven to do just so much every week." Within a year and a half, however, he confessed to Alfred Stieglitz that the routine of the magazine was detracting from his writing. "I am not proud of this work which I do under pressure," he wrote. "A weekly article is not to my taste and I always express myself inadequately." Huebsch had also promised that the job "need not necessarily be a full-time one" and that Brooks would have three or four days a week "for creative work" beyond the "creative thinking" he would be doing at the *Freeman*. But Brooks found the work all-consuming—a tremendous "nuisance" as he described it to Sherwood Anderson in 1923. "The business of keeping up a job" which involved "writing an article and fifty letters a week, reading mss. for B.W.H., etc., etc." did not even allow him time for "keeping up the few big personal relations that I will keep up or bust." With such an intrusion into his personal and intellectual lives, Brooks could only conclude that he had been "marking time" with the *Freeman*. His experiences in journalism impelled him to advise Newton Arvin to avoid even "the best *jobs* in the world," for his was, he admitted, "the best, the freest, etc. It simply hasn't permitted me to write a book." By the early 1920s, Brooks was no longer willing to accept any institutional mediation between the critic and his work. "To throw yourself into journalism on terms dictated entirely to you by outer circumstances would not be a good thing," he warned Arvin. After the *Freeman* folded in 1924, Brooks never again held a regular job in journalism. In 1947, he responded to a request for an article by saying that he had "resolved years ago to do no miscellaneous writing and in fact never write a line that was not prompted by my own thoughts."[39]

Not all of Brooks' contemporaries were so adamant about staying away from magazine and newspaper jobs. Lippmann and H. L. Mencken, for example, made the adjustment to careers in journalism and remained with the commercial press throughout their lives. But both men had doubts about this kind of work, even after their reputations as America's foremost intellectual journalists were well established. Lippmann periodically informed his friends that his positions at the *New Republic* and the New York *World* obstructed more important writing. "Journalism," he told Bernard Berenson in 1919, "takes much time, and interrupts too much." Explaining his decision in the summer of 1921 to join the *World*, Lippmann gave only a lukewarm assessment of his prospects: "I'm not passionate about journalism, but variety improves it." The advice he received from some of his friends could not have lessened his ambivalence. Robert Hallowell, a *New Republic* colleague, said he shuddered to think of Lippmann "caged" into a daily newspaper job. "If you can keep out of the damn cage—that's all. So few of them do." The playwright and critic Laurence Stallings was even more direct: "Will you please get on with your books and let journalism go to hell?" Henry Seidel Canby sent Lippmann a copy of a letter he received from Carl Becker in 1928 asking, "Can't something be done to induce Walter Lippmann to stop writing editorials and devote his extraordinary talents to the writing of books—of literary criticism, or whatever?" After more than eight years at the *World*, Lippmann confessed to Berenson that he had "never taken newspaper work very seriously" and "wanted to cut loose entirely from journalism" for awhile in order "to get along with a book" he had started.[40]

Mencken revelled in 1918 at his liberation from "regular journalism," his new status at the Baltimore *Sun* which left him "under no obligation to produce any definite amount of copy." At long last, he boasted to Ellery Sedgwick, he had a "chance to enrich and embellish the beautiful letters of this grand and glorious république." Though this freedom was short-lived, he thanked his "escape from daily journalism" for allowing him to write five books. Returning to the grind in 1920, Mencken condemned the "hard hack work" and "newspaper slavery" to which he and his friends George Jean Nathan and Burton Rascoe found themselves consigned out of economic necessity. The editorship of the *American Mercury* afforded him almost complete freedom to exercise his opinions, but by 1933, after ten years, he was ready to rid himself of this "editorial routine" as well. "My true business, after all, is writing books, not editing magazines," he argued, "and I concluded after long prayer and soul-searching that I had better get to it before it was too late."[41]

Yet Mencken also recognized the relationship between intellectual freedom and a secure income. "Economic independence," he noted, "is the foundation of the only sort of freedom worth a damn." Mencken himself dismissed the cult of poverty as "nonsense" and suggested moderation instead. "Do I advocate, then, the ceaseless, senseless hogging of money?" he asked. "I do not. All I advocate—and praise as virtuous—is the hogging of enough to provide security and ease." Finding the right balance between disinterestedness and financial security proved difficult for many of Mencken's contemporaries. If too much money implied a compromise with business civilization, too little meant a constant struggle which diverted energies from serious work. Efforts to distance themselves from Philistine values, to rid themselves of the acquisitive impulse, to know, in Bourne's phrase, "the glories of spiritual free-lancing," often undermined the quest for autonomy by making intellectuals almost wholly dependent on the hazards of the marketplace. Stuart Chase, who worked as a "journeyman" C.P.A. to support his writing, noted that the "greater one's economic insecurity, the greater the tendency to sacrifice spiritual independence and to chant in dreary unison the simple credo of the yes man."[42] Free-lancing often meant a hand-to-mouth existence and assignments from editors whose first concern was not for the writer's own intellectual interests, even at the non-commercial publications. Editorial positions, which supplied a steady income, were time-consuming and dominated by routine, whether at the factories of commercial journalism or at the craft shops of the alternative press.

Whatever balance an individual struck between free-lancing and full-time staff work and between commercial and non-commercial writing, journalism had a pronounced effect on intellectual production and lifestyle. To make even a subsistence living, intellectual journalists were compelled to write constantly—to dash off reviews, to cover unfamiliar subjects, to spin off minor variations on single themes. Essays often appeared in two or more forms, first as magazine pieces, then in collections, and finally perhaps in book-length versions. Brooks, for example, published "Highbrow and Lowbrow" in the *Forum*, expanded it into *America's Coming-of-Age* in 1915, collected his *Seven Arts* essays as *Letters and Leadership* in 1918, contributed "The Literary Life" to Stearns' *Civilization in the United States* in 1922, and reissued everything together as *Three Essays on America* in 1934. Edmund Wilson's imaginary dialogues initially appeared in the *New Republic*, then as *Discordant Encounters* (1926), and again in *The Shores of Light* (1952). For *Virgin Spain* (1926), Waldo Frank assembled essays he had published over a five-year period in the

Commonweal, the *Dial*, the *Menorah Journal*, the *Nation*, the *New Republic*, the *North American Review*, the *Saturday Review*, the *Virginia Quarterly*, and a Madrid magazine. At its best, this work of churning out articles, rehashing, revising, expanding, and reissuing helped writers perfect their prose and keep their minds active. At its worst, it made for repetition, hurried writing, superficial thinking, and books that seemed more like patchwork than integrated wholes. Malcolm Cowley captured the dilemma when he praised Wilson as "the only writer I know who has been successfully leading a double life—that is, who has been earning a living out of literature and at the same time writing good books." As of 1929, Cowley's opinion of his own literary life was that he had "rather failed in both sides of it."[43]

6.

Beneath the sustaining myth of the cult of poverty, those who dismissed the idea of a career faced real problems in trying to create a stable economic basis for an independent intellectual life. Bourne's public swaggering about his generation's freedom from material preoccupations concealed tremendous personal anxiety about earning a living. "Poverty is a hideous thing," he wrote in 1916. "Not to have enough to command the resources of mere getting around, of having what you need, is appalling. And still worse to have the slender minimum resources that you have, so uncertain." Two years with the *New Republic* failed to ease Bourne's fears that he was doomed to the "life of a hermit philosopher living on a bare pittance." He despaired at the "New Republic starvation wages" and the "mounting" cost of living and took only meager comfort in the fact that most of his friends were "in a like unlucky state." The "calm stability of comfort, place and mood" necessary for disinterested criticism seemed to elude him: "I must always expect to be poor and unloved and obscure."[44]

Bourne's income was, in fact, precarious. Between 1910 and 1914, when he was a student and a regular contributor to the *Atlantic*, his total earnings were only $4075. In 1915, with steady work at the *New Republic*, he made $1666; his peak salary at the magazine was one hundred dollars a month in 1916. Under these pressures, Bourne had trouble living in New York and occasionally faced the unpleasant prospect "of living again in the dull old house and town" in New Jersey where he had "so many thwartings to remember." The problem with the independent magazines, as Bourne's struggles suggest, was that they could not pay particularly well (if at all) for the privilege of free expression; they could not always remove the necessity of hack writing. In Bourne's case, a tenuous security came only at the end of his life when he was fired from the editorial board of the *Dial* but continued to draw his salary, leaving him "much freer" than ever before. He left $827 in the bank at his death in 1918.[45] The martyrology created about Bourne in the 1920s was distorted in its claims that he died in poverty as a result of his views on the war. But he did live most of his life as a writer on the edge of subsistence, never able to achieve the comfort and stability requisite to a free man of letters.

Bourne's mother apparently did not look with favor upon her son's hazardous existence, because Bourne justified himself by explaining to her in 1918 that he was the envy of Van Wyck Brooks, who was burdened with a regular job at the moment. Brooks, he told her, "has been tied to a desk in the Century Co., and he looks on me as one who leads the ideal, free, dignified, leisurely life of a true man of letters, making my living by my pen with no sordid job to hold down." This "ideal" life eluded Brooks as it eluded Bourne. Brooks took the publishing job after the collapse of the *Seven Arts* and continued to suffer from financial worries—the "problem" of winning "an independent footing" he described to Waldo Frank in 1919—until he joined the *Freeman*. Then for a time he could boast that "I'm making enough money for us all to live on! This has never happened before," though even in his brief time of prosperity, Brooks had to beware "not to be fat," not to become too enamored of material success. When the *Freeman* closed down, he again found himself with "a good deal of time but not quite enough money" and worried that he would have to find a job to supplement his part-time work at Harcourt, Brace. By the end of 1925, Brooks had to "interrupt" work on his Ralph Waldo Emerson book to do some translating, as he found himself "in the worse [sic] financial hole yet."[46] It was not until he achieved commercial success with *The Flowering of New England* in 1936— at the age of fifty—that Brooks finally became fully self-supporting. No longer needing help from his wife's family, he wrote her cousin Henry Stimson thanking him for the "endless kindness" that had "made this work possible." Brooks found in the "happy circumstance" of a best-seller relief from the "anxiety" of scrambling for a living. At last he could say that "my work can well provide for our family needs."[47]

Cycles of hardship and short-lived security could make the independent intellectual life unstable to the point where claims of autonomy seemed merely wishful. Unable to support himself by writing for the *Masses*, Reed explained that he was "pretty strapped" and had to "keep on at this terrible newspaper work" to remain afloat. "I'm so in debt," he mourned to Louise Bryant in 1917, "and there doesn't seem to be more or other work." When he was hospitalized in Baltimore with kidney problems, Reed could barely afford to send for Bryant and nearly had to endure the ordeal of surgery and recovery alone. Income from hack work came as a relief; "two new checks" convinced him that "we have plenty of money," and he told Bryant that she "mustn't feel cramped anymore." After the lean times of 1917—in which he had been forced to pawn his father's gold watch and sell his mortgaged Cape Cod house to Margaret Sanger—Reed was finally "in the process of making some money for us to take it easy on, thank God." Under these circumstances, the ideal life that Reed had imagined in *Insurgent Mexico* continued to escape him: a life based on a "barefooted mestizo's conception of *Liberty* . . . the only correct definition of *Liberty—to do what I want to!*"[48]

Mumford, Edmund Wilson, and Francis Hackett also knew the determining influence of personal finances on intellectual production. Brooks supported Mumford's application for a Guggenheim Fellowship in the early thirties with the explanation that "he has all the qualifications & no means of earning money except at the expense of what he wants to do." Wilson returned to the *New Republic* in 1924 because he was "completely broke and under a great necessity of making money." He recognized, too, that his friends Gilbert Seldes, Burton Rascoe, and John Peale Bishop faced similar problems. They "have to spend so much thought and energy on earning a living," Wilson wrote, "that their minds are rarely free for anything else." Compelled to write an introduction to a Hans Christian Andersen collection and in debt to his publisher, Hackett spoke longingly of being "free to do *real* work." The *New Republic*, he feared, was "*destroying*" him, and he dreaded the possibility of falling into "that great class of literary hacks who give up creativeness to be eunuchs in the palace." Hackett's concerns also took the form of advice to others. "I hope you stay on the outside," he urged Mumford. "The editorial inside-job is dangerous for a writer, and you are a writer with a darned good start."[49]

When his royalties dried up and he had problems publishing articles because of his outspoken opposition to Stalin, Eastman had to rely on his wife's help and a variety of money-making expedients. He went back to lecturing in the early 1930s, traveling the circuit repeatedly while Eliena taught Russian classes and did translations for publishers. In 1938, he hosted a game show called "Word Game" on CBS radio. Only in 1942, when he joined the *Reader's Digest* as a "roving editor," did Eastman find assurance that he "would never have to worry about money again." And then he had to cope with the guilt of writing for a lowbrow commercial magazine—offset just slightly by his association with the unprofitable, highbrow *New Leader*.[50]

Common as financial insecurity was among intellectuals, not all encountered these obstructions to the life of letters. Paul Rosenfeld was helped by a $5000 annual income from an inheritance.[51] Family wealth also provided a safety net for Matthew Josephson, who turned to his banker father as a last resort while living abroad. Josephson's early association of "the world of business" with the "condition of 'slavery' " did not prevent him from experimenting in 1921 with "the treadmill of a commercial publishing office in New York" and, after his return from Europe, going to work as a stockbroker on Wall Street. A degree of security came through an inheritance in 1927, investments (which were severely diminished by the Crash but not wiped out), the successes of *Zola and His Time* (1928) and *The Robber Barons* (1934), and regular contributions to the *New Yorker* and *New Republic* after 1931. In Josephson's view, however, it was a life of "plain living if not enough high thinking" that allowed him and his contemporaries to weather the Depression; "they were able to subsist on little and were not immediately affected by the Great Slump."[52]

The only time Lippmann seems to have been strapped was just after he completed his World War I service, when he tried to collect on a four-year-old loan to Harold Stearns. Stearns was a notorious borrower, especially after he went off to Europe in the 1920s and became the model for the indigent pest Harvey Stone in Hemingway's *The Sun Also Rises*. In 1919, however, Lippmann entertained hopes of recovering his hundred dollars, explaining to Stearns that "you have had an opportunity to earn normal pay, whereas I have not." Otherwise, Lippmann enjoyed a comfortable income from journalism, book royalties, and investments. From $5000 in 1916, his annual income rose to $15,000 in 1921, $21,000 in 1924, $31,000 in 1926, and $45,000 by the time the Depression set in.[53]

Ironically, it was Lippmann, the defector to commercial journalism, who had the most stable economic basis for the free life of letters. Wilson privately criticized Lippmann in 1921 for his bourgeois existence, his "stodginess," and his "extreme conventionality and respectability." A year later, however, he wanted to share the benefits of a steady income and wrote Lippmann, "I don't suppose there is any place on *The World* now for a literary and dramatic critic? I have about come to the end of my free-lancing and should be [in need] of a job."[54] Wilson's vacillating earnings contrasted dramatically with Lippmann's stability. As a *New Republic* editor in the late twenties, Wilson had a comfortable salary of $7500. In 1935, however, he had to rely on a modest Guggenheim Fellowship, and as late as the period from 1947 to 1951 his annual income averaged only $2000.[55] If Lippmann felt constrained by the routine of a regular job, Wilson experienced the tensions between the free-lance life and real financial independence. Both were trying to find the best conditions for free expression, and both had to adjust to the realities of the marketplace and the imperfections of American intellectual life.

The problem of making a living also had positive outcomes. Awareness of the difficulties confronting writers fostered a common identity and a sense of shared purposes, strengthening ties across ideological boundaries, at least until the lines hardened in the late 1930s. When Paul Rosenfeld fell on hard times during the Depression, Mumford tried to get him regular work at the *New Yorker*, and Wilson loaned him money and gave him books to review for the *New Republic*. Wilson had temporarily resumed his old position as literary editor and used the opportunity to help his friend. In thanking him, Rosenfeld repeated the refrain about extended editorial responsibilities. "I'm glad you are out of it," he remarked after Wilson's period as Malcolm Cowley's replacement had ended, even though Rosenfeld's finances would suffer as a result. He was pleased that Wilson would now be returning to his "own good work."[56]

Individual fortunes, as Rosenfeld's case suggests, did not follow the same trajectories, but a cooperative ethos helped during bad spells. From his stable position, Lippmann functioned as a kind of clearinghouse for intellectuals, many of whom approached him in search of temporary jobs or publishers. Robert Edmond Jones, the stage designer, requested that Lippmann pledge $20 a month for six months to give their friend David Carb "one last chance" to "keep going" as a writer. Reed later asked Lippmann to help Jones, who was "about at the end of his rope," find a job and a cheap place to live. Among others who enlisted Lippmann's help were Waldo Frank, Floyd Dell, Eastman, Stuart Chase, Mumford,

Stearns, Gilbert Seldes, George Soule, Leo Stein, Mabel Dodge, Hendrik Van Loon, Louis Untermeyer, Stark Young, and Frank Tannenbaum. The painter and critic Marsden Hartley, protesting that he could not "sacrifice" himself "in any way commercially," hoped that Lippmann might be able to alert him to some of the "opportunities for patronage among the rich" and "find a way to make something happen without too much effort on your part."[57]

Lippmann was one of the better-connected members of an intellectual community which cohered around the struggle for disinterested expression. Amid fluctuating fortunes and frequent changes in jobs, those who were momentarily in positions to get work published or find sources of support did so with the assurance that they were furthering the cause of the intellect in America. Randolph Bourne's imploring question, "What then is a literary man to do if he has to make his living by his pen?" reflected the frustrations of a critic looking to voice his opinions without financial concerns and without institutional interference. In the search for this ideal life of letters, Bourne had the compensation of companionship and the knowledge that there were outlets, however imperfect, for the ideas of American intellectuals. Brooks took note of Bourne's ability to keep himself "afloat in a society where his convictions prevented him from following any of the ordinary avenues of preferment and recognition" and celebrated, through Bourne, the "daily miracles of audacity and courage" in the lives of intellectuals with incomes and affiliations only "of the most precarious kind."[58]

CHAPTER 3

From Expression to Influence

The struggle for disinterestedness represented only one side of a vocational crisis complicated by the desire of American intellectuals to make
themselves influential. Even as they sought to set themselves apart from
mass society—defining themselves against a mercenary civilization—
they also looked for ways to join and rechannel the mainstream of American life. Few believed that the creation of a comfortable niche for arts
and letters was sufficient; to accept a safe place at the periphery would
have been to concede the irrevocable triumph of Philistinism and the
marginality of culture. Legitimizing the life of self-expression in a society
that valued action over thought required the unification of action and
thought. The repudiation of the universities, implying a return of thinkers to the "real" world, was the beginning of a long search for this unity.
When Brooks hit upon the highbrow/lowbrow distinction, he supplied a
powerful set of terms to describe the central preoccupation of American
intellectuals in the first forty years of the twentieth century: the task of
making ideas matter, of socializing the intellect.

If one of the universal features of mass society is the eradication of the
individual's sense of an autonomous self, then intellectuals developed
unique responses to this loss of autonomy. Beginning in the 1910s, the
first generation of non-academic intellectuals devised strategies for asserting the effectiveness of individual effort—strategies which centered around
an insistence on the transforming power of ideas. No matter how difficult

it might have been to achieve independence, intellectual freedom alone was not sufficient to define and justify the critic's life. Removed from conventional positions of power and decision, intellectuals tried to create alternative modes of influence while preserving, as far as was possible, their integrity and disinterestedness.

1.

Before he took over the *Masses* late in 1912, Max Eastman sought to reconcile expression and involvement by dividing his life into two distinct spheres. The craving for action was channeled into his work for the Men's League for Woman Suffrage, founded in 1909 by Eastman, Oswald Garrison Villard, and Rabbi Stephen Wise. Public speaking on the suffrage issue promised direct contact with a receptive audience and coincided with the "immediate influence" of his sister Crystal and the "general mood of America" toward reform activity rather than mere contemplation and writing. Meanwhile, Eastman reserved his time away from the agitator's sphere to cultivate "the poet in me." But the inadequacies of this segmented life soon became clear. Separating thought from action, even while engaging in both, did not solve the problem of integration. Instead, it merely reinforced Eastman's sense that his "true function of thinking-studying-writing" was a leisure-time diversion with no connection to other lives and actual events.[1]

Given these concerns, it is not surprising that Eastman's first book explored the relation between poetry and reality. Warning poets to be on guard against writing that was "private and incommunicable," Eastman ventured in *Enjoyment of Poetry* (1913) to place poets—and by implication all writers—in a new social role. Rather than standing aloof and detached, he argued, the poet possessed a natural "zest for experience." The very "essence of the poetic temper" was "a wish to experience life and the world," and the heightened sensibility of poets made them particularly capable of apprehending truth in all its complexity. Their "agility and fervor of realization" allowed them to know life more fully than most people. According to Eastman, the social function of writing was inherent; the writer used words to communicate reality, to distill "the present" and make it vivid. Poetry was "simply the giving to any object, or thought, or event, or feeling, the name that makes its nature shine forth to you." In this remarkable inversion, it was the non-writer who stood further from reality and needed the writer to convey the "qualities" of "things" and "a sense of the actual existence of those things."[2] Experience was only made conscious through words.

After rescuing poetry from "the library" and the "serious madness of abstraction," Eastman constructed a claim for writing beyond realization and communication. Writers, he asserted, accomplished more than description; not only did they "show us the world," but in their efforts to "intensify experience," they could also "rouse us" to alter the world. The writer was a "restorer" who "nourishes the waking spirit, nourishes the gift of vision." The process of writing itself was a suspension of action, but the moment of reflection tended inexorably toward renewed action because it resulted in an art capable of inspiring others. This was the true social importance of thinking and writing—translating experience into vision. "We cannot but conclude that poetry is of high practical value," Eastman declared; "it is of value to purposive conduct and adjustment for the future."[3] *Enjoyment of Poetry* cleverly mended the split in Eastman's life. But it glossed over the problem of a specific subject matter for art and criticism and left ambiguous whether all experience was valid, whether every poem served a social purpose, whether writing invariably inspired action (some poetry, after all, was too "private"), and whether it inspired the right kind of action. Eastman's reconciliation was tenuous and provisional in 1913.

Others who joined Eastman in proclaiming the inspirational capacity of art and criticism were more attentive to the relationship between content and effectiveness and to the fragility of the connection between individual intellectual effort and larger social influence. Randolph Bourne bemoaned the "perverse fate" that had "imposed" on him a "desperately unpractical" philosophy "of scorn for institutions, combined with a belief in their reform" and "a fanatical belief in mass-movements and mass ideals, combined with a sensitiveness to unique and distinctive personality." For Bourne, the reconciliation of these dualisms lay in his conviction that the young intellectual must plunge into American life in pursuit of objective experience before translating experience into vision. "We are seldom conscious enough of the ground we are rooted in and the air we breathe," he confessed. "We can know ourselves best by knowing others." Unlike Eastman, Bourne drew a clear distinction between personal and social experience, insisting that "the task of this intellectual generation" was "to conquer the paradoxes by admitting the validity of both the matter-of-fact view and the mystic." The new breed of thinkers could guarantee the resonance of their ideas by grounding them in common realities and so invalidate "the antithesis between mystic and scientific."[4]

Once Bourne's intellectual had gained social knowledge, he could count on the public's docility and imitativeness to allow him "to rouse and teach it": "[H]e launches boldly his personality into society, confident of its effect in polarizing the ideas and attitudes of the wistful."[5] In the minds of Bourne and his contemporaries, the removal from the academic ivory tower did not destroy the educational function of thinkers and writers. On the contrary, the descent into rough-and-tumble reality broadened the potential for persuasive influence, as the entire literate public became an inchoate student body susceptible to the ideas of free-lance intellectuals.

It was Brooks, however, who most clearly articulated the problematic relationship between subject matter and the power of ideas. Six years before he found the terms to make vivid the gap between abstract thought and mundane affairs, Brooks issued his first warning to critics and artists that they must immerse themselves in the American context if they hoped to awaken and transform it. Those who would be "great constructors, great positive forces," who would "bind together the estranged fragments of society," had to be "trained to one deep, local, indigenous attitude toward life." Brooks understood the critic's role—his own role—to be that of an exhorter, urging nascent artists to use native materials to reach and redeem a pliant American public, and much of Brooks' writing through the 1920s had a markedly hortatory flavor. Yet he also recognized early on the non-intellectual basis for artistic expression and human response. The artist, he admitted, "can produce great and lasting work only out of the materials which exist in him by instinct." Whether ideas could persuade, whether intellectuals could teach through the reasoned discourse of literary and social criticism remained unclear. "We must put aside anything that tends to make us self-conscious in this matter of American tradition and simply *be* American," Brooks concluded, "teach our pulses to beat with American ideas and ideals, absorb American life."[6] But how could creative minds "teach" themselves to "*be* American" without being "self-conscious" about it? How could critics exhort artists to draw on "instinct?" Such insoluble contradictions led Brooks, like

Bourne, Eastman, and others, to a reliance on some vague ability to inspire, half-intellectual and half-emotional, as the basis for intellectual efficacy.

However elusive the idea that critics encouraged artists who in turn transformed society, it served as the ideological foundation for both the *New Republic* and the *Seven Arts*. Under the early influence of Brooks, Lippmann delineated in 1913 the cultural basis for social and political change:

Culture is the name for what people are interested in, their thoughts, their models, the books they read and the speeches they hear, their table talk, gossip, controversies, historical sense and scientific training, the values they appreciate, the quality of life they admire. All communities have a culture. It is the climate of their civilization. Without a favorable culture political schemes are a mere imposition. They will not work without a people to work them.

Lippmann's definition of culture offered a more expansive version of the caste of creative spirits than did Brooks, who was concerned almost exclusively with critics, poets, and fiction writers. Lippmann allowed enlightened scientists, engineers, and even politicians to qualify as cultural redeemers, as members of an intellectual leadership class "capable of moving mountains . . . when mountains stand in their way."[7] Herbert Croly's plan for the *New Republic* appealed directly to Lippmann's belief in the untapped power of an American intelligentsia. Not only did Croly speak of the pursuit of an unspecified "ultimate human ideal," he also revealed "a realistic practical method of making it prevail." The method was simply to construct "a serious publication" which, through the sheer force of its ideas, would be "sufficiently large and influential" to "improve conditions of life among our fellow countrymen." Education was the key to effectiveness; the magazine would alter the cultural fabric of the United States by functioning as "a power in the formation of American public opinion." Croly concluded the proposal with an appeal to the self-consciousness of an independent intellectual community in its own process of formation. Educating and inspiring the American people through cogent criticism and the example of a cooperative enterprise such as the *New Republic* were vital components of the task of cultural transformation, and, according to Croly, "not many" were "capable of doing it right."[8]

The *Seven Arts* stated even more directly its redemptive purpose. Waldo Frank introduced the magazine in November 1916 by defining it as an organ for the socialization of art. "In short," he wrote, "the *Seven*

Arts is not a magazine for artists, but an expression of artists for the community." Frank's translation of an article of support by the French novelist Romain Rolland complemented this explicit rejection of insularity. Rolland urged the new magazine to take up the mantle of intellectual leadership and invoked the recurrent image of the public as a malleable mass eagerly awaiting the wisdom and the will of the articulate few. "They—the people—whose indifference to art oppresses you, are the Dumb," counseled Rolland. "And since they cannot express themselves, they cannot know themselves. You must be their Voice." How the creative mind was to overcome this indifference, how an indifferent public would be disposed to accept the leadership of artists and intellectuals, he did not spell out. This was left to Paul Rosenfeld, who had already discovered in Alfred Stieglitz his model for the artist as a social force. Stieglitz, in Rosenfeld's view, was using photography to merge the real and the ideal, to transform the mundane into the beautiful, to reach an audience through familiar material and then infuse it with the artist's vision of a better life based on creation and expression in place of accumulation and consumption. Rosenfeld paid homage to Stieglitz's "lofty conception of art, not as a divertissement, a refuge from the world, but as a bridge to consciousness of self, to life, and through that, to new life and new creation again." Alfred Booth Kuttner, one of the first American translators of Freud, recognized this creative fusion of reality and vision in terms of modern psychology. The artist, according to Kuttner, was "the great mediator between phantasy and reality" who "hurts us by reminding us of the pain of living" but also seduces us by "showing us the joy of what life might be in the ideal." Here again creative individuals —and these included critics as well as literary and plastic artists and musicians—were recast as the types most capable of apprehending real life, provided they remained aware of what Brooks called "the necessary correspondence between expression and experience."[9]

2.

The promise of influence at some distant hazy place of education or inspiration did not fully satisfy the urge toward decisive action which nagged some intellectuals into the pursuit of more direct kinds of involvement. John Reed was the motive force behind a more daring adventure in fusing harsh reality and visionary art than Brooks, Bourne, Lippmann, and even Eastman were willing to attempt. Reed and Eastman both took up the cause of the striking mill workers of Paterson, New Jersey, in 1913; both experienced the brief surge of addressing a rally of strikers, of seeing words inspire a crowd. But Reed also managed to get himself arrested and jailed, returning to New York to transform the strike into a massive work of socialized art. Mabel Dodge remembered having conceived the idea of the Paterson Pageant, and she joined her soon-to-be lover Reed, along with Big Bill Haywood, Margaret and William Sanger, Alexander Berkman, Hutchins Hapgood, and other frequenters of her salon on the planning committee. Reed commuted back and forth between Paterson and New York to rehearse the musical drama he was constructing out of the materials of a brutal labor war. Under his supervision, mill workers became actors in a hyper-realistic work of inspired imagination that would strengthen the will of the strikers, convey the ugliness of greed and oppression, and infuse a larger audience with visions of an alternative America based on free expression and fulfilling work. "Imagine suddenly teaching 2,000 people of various nationalities how to present their case in a huge, graphic, orderly art form!" Dodge wrote in an attempt to recapture the spirit of the moment. "Imagine planning an event to fill Madison Square Garden, a whole city block, where we were used to going to see Barnum and Bailey's Circus, with three rings and two bands going at once, and having it audible, visible, and composed enough to be convincing!"[10] The Pageant was an exhilarating experience of leadership and participation, contact with the world of events and the creative representation of those events. Yet Reed's bold quest for immediacy ultimately depended on the same potential to rouse and teach that other defenders of art and criticism invoked to justify their chosen work. The strike, after all, began without intellectual or artistic guidance; the Pageant's most tangible contribution was its unknowable effect on public opinion.

For Reed, however, Paterson had a more lasting significance. It was in his strike article for the *Masses* that he found the journalistic style that characterized his most memorable writing and brought him closest to the decisive presence in events he craved. Shaped by his apprenticeship in muckraking with Steffens, Reed's reporting blurred the distinction between observation and participation to the point where the writer was intimately involved in the drama he was recreating. "War in Paterson" began as a witness's description of the picket lines but quickly evolved into a first-person account of Reed's own arrest, trial, imprisonment, and release. In the series of articles for the *Metropolitan* magazine later assembled as *Insurgent Mexico*, Reed perfected this amalgamation of subject and object. Now he rode with soldiers, advised Pancho Villa, and unabashedly took sides in the Mexican Revolution. Meanwhile his friend and mentor was busy counseling Carranza and, by Steffens' own account, single-handedly convincing Woodrow Wilson not to go to war with Mexico.[11]

Still Reed's sense of participation and influence was fleeting and inadequate. His frontline reporting on the Great War did not fulfill him as the Mexican experience had done, largely because there were no sides to take in a conflict between imperialist powers and therefore no real feeling of being caught up in the events he described. By the spring of 1917, he found himself "drifting with the wind," yearning to plunge "joyously into a new role," yet dangerously close to foreswearing further involvement in the sphere of action. "I love beauty and chance and change," he wrote, "but less now in the external world and more in my mind. I suppose I'll always be a Romanticist." In this time of directionlessness, Reed confessed to Louise Bryant that instead of "getting a hero" she "only got a vicious little person who is fast losing any spark he may have had."[12]

The October Revolution ended Reed's drifting by anchoring him again at the center of momentous events and satisfying a paradoxical impulse to be swept up in history and to shape it. As Eastman shrewdly observed, Reed "could only be satisfied to be in the heart of the most tremendous events of history—and to be on the right side." In *Ten Days That Shook the World*, Reed took a view of the revolution that downplayed the role of individual leadership (the "incoherent multiple will" became "one will") while celebrating Lenin as a "strange popular leader—a leader purely by virtue of intellect." The book itself was intended to rally American support behind the Bolshevik cause much as the Paterson show was supposed to move the public behind the strikers, and Reed even described the revolution as "the pageant of the Rising of the Russian Masses."[13] He spent the last period of his life as a Communist Labor party and Comintern official, still not certain whether he could be most influential as a political organizer or as a journalist-intellectual-poet trying to reach the hearts and minds of the masses through the art of writing, or whether he could have any genuine influence at all.

3.

American participation in the First World War threw into relief the dilemmas of intellectual involvement and prompted more careful considerations of the proper relationship between the life of the mind and the world of affairs. Croly's memorandum notwithstanding, the *New Republic* had wavered from its inception between a simple commitment to the articulation of ideas and the establishment of tangible connections to the sources of political decision making. As Charles Forcey has admirably detailed, Croly, Lippmann, and Walter Weyl "sought a more direct influence than their published words could bring." In their lopsided relationships with Theodore Roosevelt, Woodrow Wilson, and other political figures, the *New Republic* editors "hovered like moths on the flaming edges of power."[14] In 1914, Lippmann revised his ideas about a wholesale cultural transformation produced by the superior intuitive powers of artists and critics and came out for a pragmatic adjustment of American life. "We have to deal with it deliberately," he wrote in *Drift and Mastery*, "devise its social organization, alter its tools, formulate its method, educate and control it." Lippmann was beginning to conceive of intellectuals less as inspirational figures seeking to touch the collective imagination and more as scientific advisers guiding the actions of progressive statesmen. His "increasing interest in administrative problems and constructive solutions" encouraged and justified his movement "nearer to the Progressives," and in his diary, he rationalized this shift by claiming that informed criticism required personal ties to powerful individuals: "A writer on public affairs can't pretend to despise reputation, for reputation is not only flattering to his vanity, it is the only way of meeting the people you've got to know in order to understand the world."[15] The war brought Lippmann into formal contact with those he had met as an intellectual journalist and tested his belief that intellectuals could develop and apply their ideas most effectively from within the established power structure.

Amid all the discussions of diplomacy, strategy, the nature and purpose of American involvement, intellectuals approached the war as a debate over their own social role. Their analyses of the war's moral and political implications were consistently self-referential, emphasizing the delicate balance between integrity and sway. When Lippmann joined the War Department, he staked his decision on the "great abilities," "the mind and heart" of Secretary of War Newton Baker, confident that his association with Baker would encourage disinterested thought and its translation into important policy. An administrative position seemed to offer an answer to his agonizing question "What does theorizing amount to after all?" Doubtless Lippmann was encouraged by Graham Wallas' admiration for his "pluck in chucking journalism and taking to responsible administration just at the right moment for your country (and humanity) and for your own intellectual life."[16]

More aloof from the "flaming edges of power" than the *New Republic* editors, the staff of the *Seven Arts* grappled publicly with the intellectual implications of the war to the complete exclusion of any discussion of its policy implications. In March 1917, James Oppenheim suggested that American entry would represent a welcome departure from what the "younger generation" perceived as "the soft ideal of universal comfort and the ennui of a colorless social life, a purposeless round of petty sensations." Claiming that the martial spirit arose in response to the drift and emptiness of modern life, Oppenheim argued that "a race that has gone out time and again to suffer and die for ideas and symbols, for abstract conceptions like 'freedom' and 'democracy,' cannot be content alone with factory-work, or business, or the flat metallic taste of money." American involvement in the war would be one way, perhaps the inevitable way, of resisting the malaise of business civilization. But Oppenheim, echoing William James, preferred a moral equivalent, an alternative life of self-expression ushered in and epitomized by artists and intellectuals. Creative minds would offer the public a heightened sense of value and a new national identity based on shared "intuitions," "longings," and "aspirations."[17]

With the declaration of war in April, the *Seven Arts* reevaluated the meaning of American participation, belatedly calling for "preparedness" and scoffing at the "good-natured dreams of pacifists who think they can handle life by evading it." Guiding the war through ideas and art, creative thinkers would awaken the nation from its materialist stupor, furnish purpose beyond mere acquisition, and prepare the way for America's cultural independence from Europe. "Let there be a preparation of our spirit and our forces," the editors declared in this moment of rapture. "Out of our momentary plight there may be born the much-heralded, the long-dreamed-of America." Leaving the task of preparing the forces to the government, the *Seven Arts* assigned critics and artists the work of preparing the spirit. It was in this frame of mind that the magazine published John Dewey's assessment of American involvement. Dewey suggested that the nation had hesitated to fight because it had required time to discover its own goals and purposes. Even now there was hesitation, and it would persist "until the almost impossible happens, . . . until the Allies are fighting on our terms for our democracy and civilization." America could only realize and convey its will by testing it in action. In any event, an inspired nation would enter the war with its own spirit and its own agenda, shaped by strong minds.[18]

By May, however, Oppenheim was beginning to have doubts about the war as a step toward a transformed America. He confessed that he was "full of confusion" and no longer knew whether the war could be directed by intellectuals, whether it was "a social workers' affair," "an experience we need," or an entanglement "in the skein of European dynastic politics" that would mean the end of America's "growing independence." The lessons of the Civil War and its barren aftermath were troubling. That war had created and glorified America's captains of industry, who were "already at work while the rest of the nation fought and bled." Oppenheim wondered whether every generation had to experience war to learn that for all but a few it brings only grief.[19] Randolph Bourne's arrival at the *Seven Arts* in June ended Oppenheim's confusion.

To Bourne, the *New Republic*'s support for the war and Lippmann's direct participation in its conduct were acts of intellectual self-annihilation. Publicly and privately Bourne accused pro-war intellectuals of caving in to business and the state, the natural enemies of the free intellect and the interests against which disinterested criticism defined itself. Those who claimed to maintain their integrity and autonomy while supporting American involvement were deluding themselves. Within the first two months of participation, Bourne observed, the "results of war on the intellectual class" were "already apparent." Pro-war thought had become "little more than a description and justification of what [was] going on." The war was rapidly demonstrating the fragility of intellectual independence; critics surrendered their distinctiveness when they allied themselves with the forces of thoughtlessness and embraced the ethos of a mechanical civilization preoccupied with means and blind to "the quality of living." The most flagrant exercise in self-deception was to claim that intellectuals could jump into the fray and still maintain the critical perspective necessary to direct events toward a desired outcome. In Bourne's view, any compromise with the enemies of the intellect was "inexorable." Participating in the "loosing of a war-technique" without foreseeing "how quickly aims and purposes would be forgotten" indicated a kind of intellectual death wish. Former heroes like Dewey and Lippmann now crumbled under the pressures against intellectual autonomy. In a penetrating piece of social psychology, Bourne described the "gregarious impulse" which drove intellectuals into this submergence of identity. The yearning for immediate influence and the "feeling of being with and supported by the collective herd" were components of the intellectual's "will to power, the nourishment of which the organism so constantly demands." What began as a quest for autonomy ended in conformity and self-destruction: "You feel powerful by conforming, and you feel forlorn and helpless if you are out of the crowd. While even if you do not get any access of power by thinking and feeling just as everybody else in your group does, you get at least the warm feeling of obedience, the soothing irresponsibility of protection." [20]

While Bourne was passionate in his criticism of Dewey—the fallen hero of "Twilight of Idols"—the defection of Lippmann was equally if not more upsetting. An admiring Bourne had confessed in 1915 that *Drift and Mastery* was "a book one would have given one's soul to have written." Now, however, Lippmann's " 'mastery' becomes 'drift,' tangled in the fatal drive toward victory as its own end." [21] Lippmann's crimes against the intellect were greater than Dewey's. He had done more than merely articulate a pro-war position; he had given himself body and soul to the machinery of war-making. In August 1917, Bourne directly challenged Lippmann to justify his position on Newton Baker's staff by agreeing to intervene on behalf of Bourne's friend, "Edward Murray, musician," who had been drafted and wanted "to conscientiously object to military service."

If you have any influence as the "confidential adviser of the Secretary of War," can you not see that some democratic and liberal arrangements are speedily made that will keep my friend and others of his type from being made martyrs and victims? If you could, I should be more convinced of the sincerity of the Government in conducting a democratic war, and in your assumption of the power of liberal forces to control it. You once said to me, when I complained about something at the [New Republic], — "We are very busy men." I fancy you reacting in the same way to my letter. Yet it is exactly efforts like this which I am bringing to your attention which would justify your presence in Washington, indeed, almost be the essence of that justification.

Lippmann made no promises in his reply but told Bourne, "You are quite wrong in your guess as to how I react to your letter. I don't believe a day has passed since I have been in Washington in which I hav'nt [sic] had this thing on my mind."[22] The exchange itself suggests that a sense of intellectual common ground survived even wartime conflict, but Bourne was clearly pained by Lippmann's actions. For however disillusioning Dewey's acquiescence had been, Dewey was of an older generation and a member of the professoriate. Lippmann was a contemporary, part of the movement of young intellectuals to carve out a meaningful place for themselves outside the institutions that corrupted or isolated creative minds, and in this sense, Lippmann's sellout was more disturbing than Dewey's.

What is most remarkable about Bourne's anti-war essays, however, is not the mood of disillusionment but the ultimate spirit of affirmation. "The War and the Intellectuals" ended with a call for "a heightened energy and enthusiasm for the education, the art, the interpretation that make for life in the midst of the world of death." "A War Diary" closed with the "hope that in the recoil from war we may find the treasures we are looking for." "Twilight of Idols" concluded with the observation that a "more skeptical, malicious, desperate, ironical mood may actually be the sign of more vivid and more stirring life fermenting in American today."[23] Even more revealing than these exhortations and prophecies is Bourne's judgment of the intellectuals' role in the coming of the war. In condemning the pro-war intellectuals, Bourne never denied them a determining influence on the course of events. Though he was speaking derisively when he wrote, "A war made deliberately by the intellectuals!," he was not being cynical. The intellectuals may have been duped by "the least democratic forces in American life" into justifying American participation, but it was the intellectuals who had finally been responsible for "jockeying the nation into war," for leading "an apathetic nation into an irresponsible war."[24] For Bourne, the blunder of intellectual involvement in the Great War confirmed that intellectual engagement and leadership had to take the form of critical discussion with a potential public rather than administrative service. The negative example of intellectuals manipulating public opinion left open the possibility of positive intellectual influence, free of ties to the war-making state, in the future.

Did Bourne genuinely believe that creative minds could rise and lead in postwar America? When he wrote Brooks in the spring of 1918 to praise him for *Letters and Leadership*, Bourne pointed out "a certain youthful arrogance in your implication that it is we and our friends who are to be the masters." Such arrogance was welcome—perhaps essential—if the intellectual life was to survive the war. Bourne proceeded to classify Brooks' idea of intellectual leadership as a "vital myth," a faith needed to sustain critics and artists in their work even if it bore no immediate relation to reality. Without this vital myth, he suggested, they would have to admit their own superfluousness and the impossibility of creating an inhabitable America. Whether or not their impact was tangible—and Bourne warned against "pointing complacently to tangible results"—intellectuals had to believe in its existence. Bourne testified to his own faith by prophesying to Brooks that future " 'leaders' will be simply those articulate souls who can express most convincingly [the] desired values."[25]

4.

The war and the perceived debacle of the peace encouraged fuller discussions of the place and purpose of intellectuals in the 1920s. Some used the memory and martyrdom of Bourne to restate ideas about the prophetic function of thinkers and artists. Harold Stearns celebrated Bourne's "splendid isolation," by which he meant not aloofness but a willingness to brook unpopularity for the sake of truth and ultimate effectiveness. According to Stearns, the war had exposed the dangerous attraction of "the gospel of accomplishment," the readiness with which intellectuals would compromise themselves to appear "pragmatic." Bourne, in contrast, had demonstrated that opposition and independence, while precluding instant accomplishment, guaranteed greater influence in the long run. "The true and permanent influence of the intellectual," Stearns wrote in 1920, "is never so much the result of what he specifically advocates as of the example he sets, and of the ideas that he clarifies and sets in motion."[26] Inspiring, not policy-making, was the intellectuals' bridge to society. Paul Rosenfeld felt certain that Bourne's message of "self-reliant humanity" would be heard and heeded in postwar America and that his supreme sacrifice for "the life of ideas and of spiritual distinction" would touch and transform the national soul. "It is certain," Rosenfeld predicted, "that his figure will stretch as the years go by, and become even more generally visible. His fame and future are with the

cycles of life." Brooks, accepting Bourne's idea of the vital myth, proclaimed in 1920 that Bourne's involvement in "the common struggle" of
"the creative spirit" and his "sense of a new socialized world groping its
way upward" had "made him, not the critic merely, but the leader."
Critics and artists seeking to redeem America would have to adopt nothing less than what Lewis Mumford recognized as Bourne's "impossibilist
élan."[27]

In books such as Rosenfeld's *Port of New York*, Waldo Frank's *Our
America*, Mumford's *The Golden Day*, Wilson's *Discordant Encounters*, and
the Stearns symposium *Civilization in the United States*, the dual themes of
opposition and experience received elaborate attention. Wilson privately
acknowledged that intellectual acts of destruction would have to precede
the task of renovation—that intellectual and artistic leadership began in
opposition to the common and conventional. Writers like Mencken, Sinclair Lewis, and the Brooks of *The Ordeal of Mark Twain* were engaged in
a "devastating criticism of America" that was "a prelude to its being made
what the above authors want to see it be." Stearns' ambitious effort to
create a united intellectual front against the "emotional and aesthetic
starvation" of American life cohered around a common belief in the
necessity of debunking—what Mumford later called "a bit of preliminary
housecleaning and rubbish-removing." Criticism, Stearns announced in
the preface to the *Civilization* collection, was the first step toward the
national "self-understanding" essential for social renewal. This collabora-
tive immersion in the ugly realities of American life would expose the
rottenness that needed to be cut out and begin to clear the way for
change: "We wished to speak the truth about American civilization as we
saw it, in order to do our share in making a real civilization possible."
Stearns undertook the symposium in a conscious attempt to make intellectuals into a distinct social group, separate from both the corrupt interests
and the deluded mass. Allying themselves against society yet near enough
to understand it, critics could attain the perspective from which influence
eventually would come. Relentless criticism would awaken the mass to a
sense of its own degradation and thus alert it to the possibility of something different. Speaking for Rosenfeld in one of his imaginary dialogues,
Wilson lauded those writers who had "dared to oppose" American civilization and had ventured "to blurt out one desperate word, against vulgar-
ity and routine, for the honor of the human spirit!"[28] The war had
confirmed that intellectuals and artists must remain a class apart at least

until they succeeded in producing a popular change of heart. In the meantime, they would be determined, uncompromising, even muscular in their struggle to comprehend and remake America. Already in 1919 Waldo Frank could see "groups of well-equipped and intellectual athletes, schooled and travelled, take the lead in the stern and ugly business of social warfare."[29]

The next phase in this story of destruction followed by renewal was the creation of new values, and it was artists and intellectuals who, by the act of creative expression itself, provided the example of an alternative life. Frank described the Chicago poets as writers who "create values out of chaos." Carl Sandburg was a "true poet—and living a true life" who showed the possibilities of true life to others. Sherwood Anderson had found "health and sanity—as must all his people—in the elemental let of self-expression." Alfred Stieglitz, Frank's "true Apostle of self-liberation," was Rosenfeld's model artist also. In touch with the materials and realities of American life, Stieglitz was showing "the face of expressivity to a trading society living by middle-class conventions." According to Rosenfeld, Stieglitz proved the falseness of the old dualism of subject and object by giving artistic expression to the external world. The photographer immersed himself in the common life and elevated it by transforming it into works of vision and spirit; he had succeeded in "realizing all the possibilities for life shut inside one, and simultaneously finding oneself one with the people."[30] Joseph Freeman, a young poet and critic involved with Eastman's *Liberator* and later the *New Masses*, neatly summarized the continuing mission of American intellectuals in the 1920s: "to resolve, if only by a tour de force of the mind, the dualism which hampered us."[31]

5.

The persistent faith in the ultimate power of truthful writing did not preclude new ideas about a more direct kind of efficacy. Lippmann spent the first half of the twenties exploring ways for intellectuals to circumvent the destructive force of public opinion and to translate their own better informed opinions into active policy. Chastened by the frustrating effort to formulate the terms of a just peace settlement, he now recognized the limits of direct involvement in the political sphere and sought a formal advisory role for an American intelligentsia. In 1922, Lippmann called for "an independent, expert organization for making the unseen facts

intelligible to those who have to make the decisions." Such an organization would bring intellectuals into close and influential contact with
powerful individuals without compromising their integrity. The "disinterested expert" who "finds and formulates the facts for the man of
action" could maintain intellectual independence while exerting "real
control" over events and outcomes. Even though "the staff which investi-
gates" was to be kept separate from "the staff which executes," the
investigative minds would be able to see their ideas produce results. But
Lippmann went farther than most of his contemporaries in accepting a
specialized function for intellectuals. Always an advocate of expertise,
Lippmann shifted after the war from a vision of an unspecialized, free-
floating intellectual elite to a demand for specific competence. Still smart-
ing from the intellectual battles of 1917, he noted in 1925 how "excellent
automobile manufacturers, literary critics and scientists often talk such
nonsense about politics" and argued that their "congenital excellence, if it
exists, reveals itself only in their own activity." Lippmann, however,
never allowed expertise and specialization to confine his own work; he
remained a generalist despite his calls for compartmentalized knowledge
and ventured in the late twenties into the realm of morals and ethics. His
claims for administrative control should be weighed against his continued
role as a public intellectual, which at least tacitly recognized the possibility of widespread critical discussion. Like Dewey's earlier *Thought News*,
Lippmann's intelligence agency did not materialize, and he still shared
with his old friends and adversaries the problem of reaching "a squirming
mass of humanity at which one throws one's contributions and gets no
response." Meanwhile, he continued to gravitate toward men of power as
an informal adviser.[32]

This tension between expertise and a revitalized public discourse was
even more pronounced in the work of Stuart Chase and George Soule,
both of whom spoke as generalists on behalf of radical planning by
managerial elites. Their intended audience, Soule pointed out, was "the
non-professional reader," and their aim was to "convey a sense that
economic research and economic experiment are capable of enhancing the
values of human life." Chase, too, viewed intelligent planning as the
means toward "a maximum of living and a minimum of existing"—
toward universal economic security, more fulfilling work and leisure, the
renewal of cities, a beautified landscape, an organic culture. Both became
increasingly disenchanted with capitalism for subverting the social good

in favor of private profit. Under a system of "socialized planning," they predicted, the predations and waste of finance capital would be eliminated, and a "functional society" would replace the "acquisitive society."[33]

To achieve these decidedly radical ends, Soule and Chase looked to "enlightened and professional management" in the persons of "the new executive," "the instrumental and experimental economist," "the man of science—the social scientist, the engineer." Neither was willing to offer specific names, and when Chase called for rule by "philosophical engineers," he confessed that he was projecting an ideal rather than a present type; the engineer of the future, he insisted, must no longer be "at the bidding" of the "bungling profiteers." Although they left the specifics to the managers, Soule and Chase urged the creation of a national planning board or industrial general staff "composed, not of bargaining representatives of various interests, but of qualified experts representing the nation as a whole." Whether this general staff would be selected through a process of "industrial self-government," national elections, executive appointment, or a coup d'état was also left open. Chase's conception of the planning board as "a fact gatherer and in turn adviser to Congress, President, industry, trade union, banker, state government" competed with a vision of a "wise" and "practical dictatorship." By 1934, he would tolerate political democracy only insofar as it did not directly interfere with the general staff's "dictatorial powers" over the economy; the public could vote for its managers but could not participate in "technical" decisions. "Work will be carefully allocated," he wrote in an uncharacteristically harsh tone, "and what the general staff requires, citizens will have to perform."[34]

The idealization of scientific management did not, however, relegate the non-expert intellectual to a passive and deferential role. Because "expertness" currently served the interests of "some one trying to make a profit," it was the responsibility of independent intellectuals to issue the summons to the philosopher engineers. "Where are the riders with their whirling ropes," asked Chase in his search for heroic managers; "where [are] the light-hearted youths to mount, be thrown, and rise to mount again?" Planning would "require a pooling of the best brains we possess to work out the needed blueprints," and Chase's function was "to call for those brains."[35] In addition, the public needed to be prepared to accept (or perhaps demand) the planned society. Soule and Chase both contended that even before the Depression, underlying conditions made planning imperative. Yet old habits and beliefs conspired to preserve the current "economy of a madhouse" until it collapsed completely. To combat this "cultural lag," to create "the mental apparatus which is necessary as a tool to bring a new society out of the old," was the function of the intellectuals. Soule suggested that a "revolution in ideas" had to precede any "shifts in power" and that this "idea struggle" would, "at least in the immediate future, probably have more importance than the class struggle." Chase had the same revolutionary goal in mind when he referred to himself as "a sort of a statistical Don Quixote." The irony of fostering a "mobilized and conscious" public which would then defer to an industrial general staff seems to have escaped both writers. So did the irony of supporting a system which, in James Gilbert's words, would "make the critics themselves irrelevant."[36]

6.

Generalist advocates of expertise located their potential influence somewhere between established centers of power and an educated public. For most independent intellectuals, however, the problem of influence had nothing at all to do with advising present or future elites. Their paramount concern was with the revival or creation of a public, and they accordingly directed their attention to matters and modes of communication. In February 1921, Michael Gold (still in his final months as Irwin Granich) uttered his first demand for something called "proletarian art," which he initially meant as any form that captured "the primitive monotony of Life" and its "deep truths and instincts." At this stage he was largely echoing the ideas of Eastman, Brooks, and Rosenfeld who had also lashed out at artists concerned exclusively "with some transient personal mood." Gold, however, condemned those critics who believed that exhortation could produce resonant creative work, branding them "a few phrase-intoxicated intellectuals." He suggested instead that effective expression had to be a product of intuition, had to come "freely and without forethought." The notion that the proper material was to be found in "the soil of life" was nothing new, but Gold was looking at more than content; in invoking the new term "proletarian art" and in declaring the ineffectiveness of hortatory writing, he implied that the mode of presentation was equally important.[37]

Gold was not alone in discovering that writing had to be less "intellectual" if it was to have social force. Rosenfeld criticized his former *Seven Arts* colleague James Oppenheim for writing poetry too "deliberately." In 1924, Rosenfeld used the occasion of the appearance of a collection of Oppenheim's work to reflect on the *Seven Arts* group, which he now criticized for overrationalizing the process of artistic creation. Prewar criticism, he observed, "was couched too frequently in the shape of moral exhortations and appeals to the conscious will."[38] To inspire resonant art, criticism itself had to assume new forms; it had to work on the emotions as much as the intellect if it hoped to drive artists toward the kinds of expression that would touch a popular nerve.

Paradoxically, this increased attention to the means by which art communicates produced a much more self-conscious and rationalized criticism than in the *Seven Arts*, *New Republic*, or *Masses* before the war. Gorham Munson analyzed the work of Waldo Frank in 1923 and stated plainly that the choice of subject—the discovery of the common life—was not enough to guarantee effective writing. "It is not contact with reality," Munson wrote, "but the solved presentation of such a contact that is rare." Frank, he argued, had found the proper form—an "esthetic of mobility" which was capable of penetrating the hearts of modern Americans because it was rooted in "the larger collective forces smelted by a civilization of populous centers, rapid communications, and wholesale standardizations." Only by finding such an esthetic had Frank realized the possibility of communicating "experience" so effectively as "to modify profoundly human lives." Munson upheld the redemptive potential of expression while explaining in the most intellectual terms how Frank's esthetic produced an emotional response in his readers. How criticism of this sort could foster the "transforming religious spirit" which Munson detected in Frank's writing he did not specify.[39]

As a rule, younger critics like Munson and Kenneth Burke possessed a deeper interest in problems of form and showed a much greater sympathy for literary experimentation and modernism than did Eastman, Dell, or Brooks, who frequently complained about unintelligibility. Burke would probably be excluded from a stricter generational study, in large part because of his abiding concern with form and his technical approach to criticism. In 1921, he asserted his generational distinctiveness by referring to Paul Rosenfeld, who had tried to enlist him in a magazine venture, as "a greasy Jew" and "next to Waldo Frank the sloppiest critic in America." But two years later, he expressed his "great respect and admiration" for Frank's "devotion to ideas" and announced his convergence with Frank, Brooks, and their "religion" of "humanism." Burke consistently viewed his study of form as a kind of social inquiry, especially into the effects of literature on its audiences. He consciously rejected the narrower concern with form as a purely aesthetic problem and tried to bridge the gap between rigorous literary analysis and a more general social philosophy. "How, for instance, can I reconcile my extreme technical interest in letters with my extreme detest [sic] for the modern trait of specialization?" he asked Malcolm Cowley after meeting Brooks. "Specialization is technique, and technique is the opposite of humanism. The basis of humanism is not form, but subject matter, as Brooks very rightly pointed out." By the fall of 1922, Burke was warning Frank against allowing art too much freedom from external reality: "I feel that art should be rescued from all these individualist leaks, that we should fight to preserve the main broad current, that art—to possess its full dignity—must be given a cultural content, a formative power, a humanistic deepening. I *know* that you feel the same."[40]

Burke was especially concerned with the relation between writer and audience and recognized that communication—which was the purpose of "all competent art"—was a considerably more complex matter than simply enlisting an inert public through clear representations or distillations of experience. In Burke's view, the process of communication was complicated by the presence of what Veblen called "trained incapacity" and Dewey termed "occupational psychosis"—orientations that made it difficult for artists and critics "to gain favor" with potential audiences. The task of reorientation required an imaginative appropriation and manipulation of symbols ("the evocation of emotion by mechanism") and involved negotiation rather than a pure tour de force on the writer's part. "He will accept it that the pieties of others are no less real or deep though being different from his," Burke urged in *Permanence and Change* (1935), "and he will seek to recommend his position by considering such orders of recalcitrance and revising his statements accordingly." If writers ignored the "authority" of their audience, they would find themselves producing "otherworldly art" and abandoning their public role completely.[41]

Criticism's unique function was to provide "perspective by incongruity"—to point out the limits and contradictions of a given orientation and to suggest a "wider frame of reference" to replace it. Burke saw critics and their opponents, those who would maintain the status quo, locked in a struggle he described as "the stealing back and forth of symbols." The success of criticism depended upon its adoption of a broad, undogmatic, uncynical "comic frame" that would "enable people *to be observers of themselves, while acting.*" Only by stepping back and developing an understanding of "the nature of linguistic, or symbolic, or literary action" could critics gain "command" over "a resource" by which they could "shift the rules of the game." Only by explaining to the public how language and motives were connected, how a given situation inevitably produced linguistic strategies, could critics contribute to a necessary change in attitudes. In other words, they had to convey that literary problems were not merely academic; all action sprang from frames of reference which were essentially literary in that they gave meaning to experience through symbols.[42]

While Burke and Munson looked for the precise ways in which literature could serve public ends, Gilbert Seldes accused his fellow critics of ignoring expressive forms which by definition attracted mass audiences. In *The Seven Lively Arts* (1924), Seldes announced his discovery of "our actual form of expression"—the popular arts—and disparaged his intellectual friends for dwelling in the rarified air of the so-called "great arts." That "exceptionally sluggish beast—the New York intellectual" had failed to encourage "genuine, honest native" productions such as the films of Charlie Chaplin and the "Krazy Kat" cartoons of George Herriman. For a number of intellectuals, Chaplin was a cultural hero—an unflappable artist who maintained his integrity while penetrating and transforming the popular consciousness. Waldo Frank, who befriended Chaplin in the twenties, referred to him in 1919 as "our most significant and most authentic dramatic figure." Eastman and Chaplin struck up a friendship in 1919, and for a short time both were romantically involved with the actress Florence Deshon. Edmund Wilson wrote a ballet expressly for Chaplin, who gracefully declined to participate.[43] Seldes, ignoring the fact that others joined him in seeing Chaplin as an artist who effectively erased the highbrow/lowbrow distinction, called him "the one man who has destroyed the world and created it in his own image!"

In the revelry of his discovery, Seldes blasted American critics and artists for their excessive self-consciousness; worrying about great art made the creative process all the more unnatural and difficult. When the

best comic strips were measured against American fiction, Seldes concluded, the comics clearly came out ahead in their ability to communicate
common experience: "I am convinced that none of our realists in fiction
come so close to the facts of the average man, none of our satirists are so
gentle and so effective. Of course they are all more serious and more
conscious of their mission; but—well, exactly who cares?" Matthew
Josephson, who had moved in Dada circles in Paris and Berlin from 1921
to 1923, was similarly concerned with "exploring the arts naturally prop-
agated" in machine-age America and admired *The Seven Lively Arts* accordingly. Seldes, however, went beyond insisting that intellectuals were
merely out of touch; in a curious way, he gave them enormous power
over popular taste. According to Seldes, the popular arts were now being
corrupted by what he called the "faux bon." Instead of remaining true to
themselves, they were incorporating false notions of what constituted
good art, and the result was an "irretrievably bogus" hybrid. A good part
of the blame resided with critics whose highbrow conceptions had shamed
and confused the producers of popular forms. The "pretentious intellectual," Seldes wrote, "is as much responsible as any one for what is
actually absurd and vulgar in the lively arts."[44]

In drawing this conclusion, Seldes undermined what might have been
a highly original argument about the failure of American critics to appreciate the active role of the public in the processes of cultural production.
Instead, he left it to Burke to take on the issue that had produced so much
ambiguity in the work of independent intellectuals: whether the public
was a docile mass subject to limitless manipulation or a diverse citizenry
capable of participating in a cultural conversation.[45] The problem with
Seldes' analysis was that it posited a strong critical sensibility among
popular audiences only to make them the easy victims of highbrow
intellectuals. *The Seven Lively Arts* initially suggested the possibility of a
more fruitful engagement of critics with popular culture but concluded
that there was no need for criticism at all. Though Seldes continued to
insist on a role for the "creative intelligence," his book represents the
crowning achievement of intellectual anti-intellectualism in the 1920s.
Critics were left with nothing to do but affirm the presence and goodness
of American popular culture, since any other position could only foster
pretentiousness. The paradox of *The Seven Lively Arts* was that it condemned intellectuals and celebrated popular expression in the language of
a Harvard-educated intellectual. In his search for a kind of criticism that

would reach the public, Seldes could not escape the persistent dilemma of how to jump into the mainstream without committing intellectual suicide.

7.

Nobody in the 1920s wrestled with the problem of form and influence with greater concern and insight than Edmund Wilson. Wilson spent the second half of the decade examining the dualism in literature between subject and object and, after a nervous collapse in 1929, concluded the inquiry with the publication of the brilliant *Axel's Castle* in 1931. As early as 1926, he noted the vast separation of literature from life, its inherent artificiality and subjectivity. "All of literature gives a false view of life," Wilson observed, "because it is the obverse of the reality—the artist fills in the holes in his character or experience by the fabrication of imaginary spiritual material." Any author's attempt to find common ground with the literate public was complicated by the inevitable tendency of the work, "no matter how intelligent, elaborate (Proust) or rich and vigorous in imagination," to "constitute some particular set of values." Wilson raised this problem again in his 1929 novel *I Thought of Daisy*, where the narrator recognizes the anti-social basis of his art. Wilson may have been making a confession of his own when he had his narrator admit that "the instinct to produce a work of art was merely a self-protective reflex like another."[46] By the time of his breakdown, Wilson was on the verge of despair over whether a writer could ever transcend self-justification and individual psychic needs. As with Brooks, then in the midst of his own longer and more serious breakdown, mental illness corresponded with severe doubts about the possibility of any writer closing the gap between the highbrow and the lowbrow.

As he proceeded with the work on *Axel's Castle*, however, Wilson began to entertain hopes for a new literature that would break free from the bounds of excessive subjectivity. In May 1929, he conveyed these vague hopes to Allen Tate: "I begin to wonder whether the time hasn't arrived for the intellectuals, etc., to identify themselves a little more with the general life of the country." In November, he announced his own intention to search out a less reflective form of expression. "As for a confession d'un enfant du siècle," he wrote Christian Gauss, "I fear that I shall never write one. That kind of thing is really repugnant to me, and I expect to become more and more objective instead of more and more personal."[47]

Axel's Castle, Wilson's study of the literary movement he labeled "Symbolism," displayed an understanding of modern literature far beyond the capacities of Brooks and other contemporaries; the discussions of Proust, Joyce, and Eliot were particularly sympathetic. But the general tone of the book was condemnatory. The Symbolist authors and their characters, Wilson observed, "would rather drop out of the common life than have to struggle to make themselves a place in it—they forego their mistresses, preferring dreams." They "found themselves out of touch with their fellows and thrown in upon their own private imaginations." Wilson used his examination of the movement to declare it dead—an important chapter in the history of world literature now fortunately concluded. The Symbolists' "world of the private imagination in isolation from the life of society," he determined, "seems to have been exploited and explored as far as for the present is possible."[48] Similarly for Wilson the publication of *Axel's Castle* marked the culmination of a long struggle to comprehend the writer's relationship with the world. Seeking a form that would break down the barriers between literature and the public and bring him closer to reality, he ventured in the first half of the 1930s into experiments in reportage. For *The American Jitters* (1932) and *Travels in Two Democracies* (1936), Wilson placed himself physically and spiritually in direct contact with the realities of Depression-era America and the Soviet Union. After his confrontation with the problems of rhetoric and the inherently mediating quality of language, he reaffirmed his faith in communicability and common understanding—a faith that would remain central to the critical project as a whole. As an observer and recorder, Wilson temporarily solved the problem of the socialized intellect which had absorbed his creative energies for a decade.[49]

Reportage represented an embrace of empiricism—an attempt to infuse literature with the authority of science and to reclaim for it some capacity to grasp and convey truth. More directly than Wilson, Eastman addressed the jurisdictional conflict between science and "the literary mind" and revised in the process his earlier assumptions about the writer's ability to communicate experience and precipitate regenerative action. The essays in *The Literary Mind*, published in the same year as Wilson's *Axel's Castle*, explained current literary movements as reactions against the encroachments of the scientist into areas of understanding once reserved exclusively for literature. Taking on what he called "the Cult of Unintelligibility," Eastman argued that Wilson's Symbolist writers were producing "private literature" and "intra-cerebral art" because they had been displaced by scientists in the effort to comprehend and alter life. James Joyce, for example, was "doing an intellectual and imaginative labor gigantic in its proportions, obdurate in its persistence, with no practical end in view whatever, not even that of communicating his experience, but solely to perfect himself in the art of playing by himself in public." The explanation for this literary masturbation, for this turning inward, was that modern poets and novelists had come to the realization that "they don't know anything about life." Science and literature "had parted company," and science now assumed complete responsibility for adjusting or remaking the world. Irving Babbitt's and Paul Elmer More's New Humanism and T. S. Eliot's neoclassicism were the reactionary responses of "the demoted men-of-letters"—"last ditch" attempts to defend "the territorial preserves of their trade against the advance of technical and specialized understanding." Seeking to recover for literature its lost authority, they were really defending "their right to make important choices on the basis of amateur, accidently inherited, unchecked, and unverified information."[50]

Though at one point Eastman insisted that there was "nothing to do . . . but smile patiently and turn to the books of science and wait for better days," he too was unwilling to abandon the claims of the literary mind to a determinative social function. Literature, by repudiating unintelligibility, could resume the communication of experience and the sharing of "vivid consciousness." But the best hope for an effective literature in the modern age lay in the acceptance and assimilation of science by the literary mind. The writer who wanted to be "once more as of old a prophet and a truth-speaker" had to acquire "some genuine and verified, and as we say 'systematic,' knowledge of his own"; writers had "to read some science deeply and become at home in the temple of science." Eastman believed that he was meeting this demand by making himself into an authority on Marxism and the science of revolution, which, along with his study of psychology, furnished the necessary knowledge for understanding humanity and charting its course. Critics, he proclaimed, had "no other choice" but to become psychologists. In science resided "the sole possibility of again combining in one great intellectual leader the critic of literature as poetry and the critic of the knowledge that reaches us through books," the only hope of transforming American intellectuals into influential social critics. The unpleasant alternative was for criticism to "dwindle and die away until it is generally regarded as a harmless parlor entertainment or a rudimentary survival like alchemy and the quack forms of therapeutics."[51]

Whatever form a writer chose and no matter how much a work of literature disguised the author's subjective voice, any hope of social impact still hinged upon the ability to persuade, inspire, or realize. Wilson's reportage, no less than his criticism and fiction and no less than Eastman's science of revolution, Reed's revolutionary journalism, Lippmann's editorials, Seldes' musings on popular culture, or Brooks' cautionary tales, required the same faith that Bourne had summed up as the "vital myth" of American intellectual life. Writing of Herman Melville in 1929, Lewis Mumford distinguished between "raw experience," which was essentially meaningless, and the "realization" of that experience through the construction of forms. "It is the artist, the knower, the sayer," Mumford summarized, "who realizes human experience, who takes the raw lump of ore we find in nature, smelts it, refines it, assays it, and stamps it into coins that can pass from hand to hand and make every man who touches them the richer." If at times there was utopianism or naiveté in the search for influence, more often the vital myth involved "the tragic sense of life" —a faith in human effort tempered by a realistic awareness of limitations. This was an outlook that was neither defeatist nor utopian, that recognized "the spirit of man" as "small and feeble" yet "purposive," and that insisted on the constant pitting of "purpose against the blank senselessness of power."[52] When Mumford moved in the thirties from small thematic and period studies to the massive, sweeping history of *Technics and Civilization* (1934) and *The Culture of Cities* (1938), he did not alter what had long been his ultimate means toward social regeneration. Arguing the historical necessity of regional planning, Mumford cast himself as a prophet whose works of visionary history would help usher in a saner, more humane world. In many ways he had left Bourne and his ideas behind. But Mumford clung to the "impossibilist élan" he had found in Bourne, because nobody had discovered a more powerful credo for sustaining intellectual commitment and the hope for influence. "Impossible?" he asked about the regionalist future. "No: for however modern science and technics have fallen short of their inherent possibilities, they have taught mankind at least one lesson: Nothing is impossible."[53]

A Note on H. L. Mencken

Mencken's reputation as the premier debunker raises questions about his place in a community trying to make itself heard as a constructive voice for social change. He consistently ridiculed moralists, reformers, up-lifters, and "forward-lookers," particularly those responsible for Prohibition, Comstockery, and anti-vice crusading. Increasingly after 1920, he also derided advocates of "constructive criticism" for similarly falling victim to "our national disease" of "messianic delusion." Critics who looked for sweeping transformations in American life were only less malignant versions of the standard American type: the Puritan. "Of all the sentimental errors which reign and rage in this incomparable repub-lic," Mencken wrote, "the worst, I often suspect, is that which confuses the function of criticism, whether aesthetic, political or social, with the function of reform." In defense of debunking—exposing myths, errors, and stupidities rather than urging new truths—he insisted on the futility and misguidedness of most alternative schemes.[54]

At times, Mencken's response to demands that he supply a construc-tive alternative was to deny criticism any public function. Too many of his contemporaries, he observed, falsely equated criticism with pedagogy and therefore differed little from the professors who concentrated exclu-sively on the moral content of literature. "The true aim of the critic" was "certainly not to make converts." In his most cynical moments, Mencken veered toward a kind of criticism-for-criticism's-sake of which the pur-poses and satisfactions were almost entirely private. "I am wholly devoid of public spirit," he proclaimed in 1922. The sole motive and aim of the critic was "to express himself" and "to achieve thereby for his own inner ego the grateful feeling of a function performed, a tension relieved, a *katharsis* attained." Moreover, critics were free to indulge their "preju-dices, biles, naivetés, humors," since they were not responsible for dis-covering truths.[55]

It is tempting, based on such essays in self-analysis, to write off Mencken as an exception, as a political conservative with an anti-social conception of the intellectual life. Yet his insistence on the value of self-expression unquestionably resonated with other critics and suggests that he shared at least one of the vital concerns of the larger intellectual community. If his denunciations of democracy were more strident and direct than those of most of his contemporaries, he was hardly alone in characterizing the American public as Puritan, Philistine, and an obstruction to a healthy culture. His call for critics and artists to be "autonomous, curious, venturesome, courageous" in the face of "the national fear of ideas" could quite as easily have come from Brooks or Bourne. His hostility to "all movements" was a particularly strident version of the anti-institutionalism and anti-dogmatism that guided so many of his contemporaries. "I am against Puritanism to the last gasp," he explained to Theodore Dreiser in one of his most forceful statements of intellectual independence; "but when anti-Puritanism comes to a program and a theory I find myself against it almost as strongly. This is a temperamental lack that I can't help. I'd spoil even a good enterprise if I had anything to do with it." And Mencken's characterization of the professoriate as "the antithesis of all free inquiry, of all honest hospitality to ideas, of all intellectual independence and integrity" captured in a single phrase the core of his generation's self-definition.[56]

Few of Mencken's fellow critics publicly expressed aristocratic leanings; most, of course, saw in the notion of aristocracy either the genteel culture's isolation from reality or the triumph of industrial and financial elites, both of which they deplored. But Mencken distinguished between the "bugaboo aristocracy" of "wealthy industrials in the interior-decorator and country-club stage of culture" and what he called a "genuine aristocracy" dedicated to "freedom in thought" and "the liberty to try and err." This latter class, he pointed out, did not exist in the United States. In calling for its creation, he was really urging the development of an intellectual community, "secure in its position, animated by an intelligent curiosity, skeptical of all facile generalizations, superior to the sentimentality of the mob, and delighting in the battle of ideas for its own sake." Everywhere else there was such a class of "men[,] differing enormously among themselves, but still united in common cause against the lethargy and credulity of the mass."[57] Mencken may have been too skeptical to speak in terms of disinterestedness, but he did invoke the ideal of intellectual autonomy and the free exchange of ideas (or intelligent "prejudices") as a counterweight to the dogmatism, narrowness, and superficiality of the plutocracy and the mob. The prejudices of the independent critic, tempered by unfettered discussion, were of a different order from "the illogical and often quite unintelligible prejudices, instincts and mental vices" of the American public.[58]

Even in his most limited conception of criticism's functions, Mencken ultimately qualified his claim that nothing mattered but the personal delight in articulating a point of view. In the same passage in which he declared ego-gratification to be the critic's essential goal, he explicitly connected this personal satisfaction to the public resonance of his writing: "He is trying to arrest and challenge a sufficient body of readers, to make them pay attention to him, to impress them with the charm and novelty of his ideas, to provoke them into an agreeable (or shocked) awareness of him." Unlike many of his colleagues, who spoke more broadly of social renewal and a transvaluation of values, Mencken always saw the critic as appealing to and enlarging a civilized minority—a permanent opposition to the vulgar majority. The existence of a thriving intellectual community, operating in "an atmosphere of hearty strife," was the best guarantee that criticism would engage the attention of a growing audience. Intellectual conflict, he argued, "melodramatizes the business of the critic, and so convinces thousands of bystanders, otherwise quite inert, that criticism is an amusing and instructive art, and that the problems it deals with are important. What men will fight for seems to be worth looking into."[59]

While it is customary to label Mencken an iconoclast and to distinguish him from the cultural radicals—Bourne, Brooks, Frank, and Mumford, for example—such a division seems arbitrary when Mencken is observed in his more expansive moments. He was equally committed to the work of cultural awakening and similarly involved in the critic's task of encouraging artists to free themselves from the country's anti-intellectual, anti-aesthetic forces. Though he could present the critic's aim modestly—"to find out what an author is trying to do, and to beat a drum for him when it is worth doing and he does it well"—he also wrote of the critic's role in creating the necessary conditions for a vital culture. "He makes the work of art live for the spectator; he makes the spectator live for the work of art," Mencken proclaimed. "Out of the process comes understanding, appreciation, intelligent enjoyment—and that is precisely what the artist tried to produce." In 1924, he confessed his "faint shadow of a hope" that "leadership in the arts, and especially in all the art of letters" might "eventually" pass from Europe to the United States.[60] If this was not quite the rapturous prophecy of the *Seven Arts*, neither was it the unmitigated cynicism of a pure iconoclast. A healthy native culture might not subvert the vapidity and Puritanism of the masses, but at least it would serve as an alternative—an intelligent and stable minority voice.[61]

There were even occasions when Mencken ventured beyond the idea of a permanent opposition toward the very notion of social change that at other times he mocked. Perhaps art and criticism were not meant to instruct; they might still, as he said of Dreiser, seek "to stir, to awaken, to move." In a critique of J. E. Spingarn's New Criticism, Mencken contended that literature had "its social, its political, even its moral implications," and that it was especially valuable when it questioned the conventional. While he scoffed at "Men of Vision, all pining for Service," he conceived of his intelligentsia or aristocracy as "the custodian of the qualities that make for change and experiment," "the class that organizes danger to the service of the race," and that boldly stands "in the forefront of the fray." Here was a hint that the critical intelligence might reach deeper into society, might actually possess a public spirit. "The brewery cellar, in these days, is as impossible as the ivory tower," he confessed to Edmund Wilson in 1921. "For a while the show is simply farce, but inevitably every man feels an irresistable [sic] impulse to rush out and crack a head—in other words, to do something positive for common decency." On the sixtieth anniversary of the *Nation*, Mencken praised the magazine's "independence and honesty" and then offered a prediction of the larger effects of an intellectual minority. The *Nation* had recognized "the capital fact" that members of the intelligentsia "alone count—that the ideas sneaked into them to-day will begin to sweat out of the herd day after to-morrow."[62]

It would be wrong to make too great a claim for Mencken as a cultural radical. His remarks on the role of criticism and culture were inconsistent and often contradictory. Sometimes he stopped with the goal of an intellectual community concerned only with its own ideas and its own liberties; other times he seemed to embrace an alternative kind of service and to perceive culture as a genuine antidote to the disease of a Puritan-Philistine civilization. Regardless of his vacillations, however, Mencken was clearly involved in the discussions of autonomy and community, independence and efficacy that occupied and motivated his fellow intellectuals. Not least because he steadily encouraged such discussions was he a central presence in the critical community.

CHAPTER 4

The Geography of
the Intellectual Life

Professional communities maintain their identity and coherence through a variety of institutions: permanent associations, periodic conferences, specialized publications, a common discourse, jargon. They do not depend upon the geographical proximity of their members; they exist as communities without the traditional ties of locality. In its maturity, the community of independent intellectuals achieved its own level of decentralization, but it never ceased to look to New York as its physical and spiritual center. New York—and Greenwich Village in particular—stood in place of the professional communities as a source of common identity and shared purpose, becoming in the 1910s and 1920s something much greater than a vaguely attractive location for aspiring writers who had opted against the academy and the professions.[1]

The larger meanings of New York, explicit statements of the necessary connection between the city and the new intellectual life, emerged only after these young writers had settled there for rather mundane reasons. For all their later disquisitions on the city's marvels and menaces, they left little or no record of the choice to locate in New York, and it appears as if these decisions were almost automatic. Those who grew up in Manhattan, including Lippmann, Mumford, Waldo Frank, and Paul Rosenfeld, simply returned home after college or a trip abroad. Bourne, Brooks, and Wilson, who spent their youth in the Wall Street suburbs of New Jersey, gave equally little thought to the matter; New York was the place where people went to work.

One of the city's obvious attractions to novice writers was its publishing business. By 1910, New York had no rivals for the title of America's publishing capital; Boston and Philadelphia had slipped as early as the 1880s. The turn of the century marked the maturation of older houses such as Scribner's, Doubleday, Henry Holt, and E. P. Dutton and the arrival of some important newcomers to the expanding New York industry. For a generation of thinkers already committed to reaching a non-academic audience, close contact with the book business and the general circulation magazines was essential. Consolidation, however, had not proceeded so far as to choke off opportunities for unknowns; the relative openness of the industry made this a golden time at which to enter the writer's trade. Although "the criterion of salability was paramount," one historian of American publishing has observed, the heads of the houses also "considered their calling a public service." The break-even point for book sales remained low in these years, rising only from one thousand to fifteen-hundred copies from 1880 to 1914. Because it still required very little capital to enter the business, individuals such as Mitchell Kennerley, B. W. Huebsch, Horace Liveright, Albert and Charles Boni, Alfred A. Knopf, Alfred Harcourt, and Donald Brace were able to launch their companies between 1900 and 1920. Kennerley started out with an investment of about $3000 and picked up the rights to British titles "on deferred payment." Mumford acknowledged this "liberated state of publishing" as a spur to himself and his contemporaries, who had the good fortune to find in New York a centralized national industry not yet at the level of corporate giantism and not yet driven to an overly cautious consideration of the bottom line.[2]

Subsequent generations would also flock to the city hoping to get their books and stories and essays published, but none would be drawn by quite the same sense of opportunity. Kennerley, a transplanted Englishman, bought the unbound sheets of Brooks' *The Wine of the Puritans* from an English press for forty dollars in 1909 and issued it in the United States despite his reader's opinion that Brooks' "style, if not the matter, would militate against popularity" and that "it would probably be best not to buy the book." By exempting first printings from royalties and not offering advances, Kennerley could afford to take the risk of publishing first-time authors. Lippmann's *A Preface to Politics* also bore the Kennerley imprint, and some of Mumford's earliest published work appeared in the *Forum*, the magazine Kennerley owned from 1910 to 1916. Mumford

signed on as a reader for the house in 1916 but quit after a month because
Kennerley failed to give him regular work or pay him. Brooks and
Lippmann finally found themselves demanding royalty payments that
never came. No matter how shabbily they were treated, however, Brooks
and Mumford could look back on Kennerley with affection and gratitude,
not as a charlatan but as a symbol of an inviting New York and a
remarkable period in the history of publishing. "What did it matter that
he sometimes played a double game?" Brooks asked. "He made little or
nothing out of his exasperated authors, and who else would have printed
them, who else would have looked at their first little books, which Kennerley delightedly acclaimed and so charmingly published?"[3]

1.

Beyond its importance as a place to establish credentials with publishers,
New York drew Brooks' generation in its role as America's business
center. Concerns about marginalization fed a desire to establish a physical
as well as intellectual presence in the thick of activity, and no place was
more active and decisive in the nation's life than New York. The city was
a test of mettle—a sign of the willingness of young intellectuals to
struggle to make contact with reality. In Eastman's recollection, throwing
himself into the maelstrom of New York after the serenity of Elmira and
Williamstown was "the stiffest purgatory I could put myself through."
The decision to follow his sister Crystal there was a difficult one, and for
a time he countered her arguments "about living in the city and meeting
humanity" with a lingering Thoreauvian "desire to live in the country
and meet the universe." Crystal's plea for engagement, and perhaps the
assurance of her protection, soon won him over. When he joined her as a
suffrage speaker in the city's crowded squares, Eastman felt his first
closeness to the public life of a metropolitan civilization.[4] Mumford went
through no such trauma in making contact with the city. With his grandfather, he had begun to explore New York at an early age, gradually
expanding his urban experience beyond Manhattan into the other bor-
oughs. This process of self-education combined a full-scale immersion in
the realities of twentieth-century city life with analysis and writing. In
1916, he plunged into the world of the sweatshops as an investigator of
the garment industry for an arbitration board, deepening his relations
with the social life of the city. For Mumford, living in New York rooted

the budding intellect in reality and prevented it from drifting off into abstraction. Here he could satisfy his strong "appetite for the concrete and the contemporary."[5] Nobody else approached the city as systematically and thoroughly as Mumford, but many attached similar meanings to it. With its masses, its money and power, New York served as a symbol of engagement for the intellectual generation that located there in the 1910s.

This image of the city as the center of modern America contributed to the relocation of the intellectual core of the Chicago Renaissance by 1915. Francis Hackett, editor of the important *Friday Literary Review* of the Chicago *Evening Post*, departed in 1911 and arrived in New York in 1913 to help plan the *New Republic*. Hackett left his associate Floyd Dell in charge, and Dell hired his friend George Cram Cook to help run the supplement. But Cook left for New York in 1912, and Dell himself followed a year later. On Dell's part, the decision to move had as much to do with the breakup of his marriage as anything else. Yet he and Cook, like Susan Glaspell and Edna Kenton earlier, could not help thinking that remaining in Chicago would consign them to the margins of the nation's cultural life. In a letter to Kenton, written after her move and before his own, Dell referred to "the Chicago myth" of cultural pre-eminence. En route to New York, he wrote of his desire "to commence all over again the adventure of life" and swore off idealism in favor of a deeper relationship with humanity. Dell now conceived of his migration from Iowa to Chicago to New York as a progression toward reality.[6]

Beneath all this, New York's grasp on the publishing trade contributed to the sense that Chicago's intellectual and artistic impact would always be secondary. The Irish critic Mary Colum, who visited Chicago in 1915, later remarked on the city's losses. "It always seemed to me a great pity that so many Chicago intellectuals moved to New York," she wrote, "for Chicago was then heading for its own place in the sun and was developing its own brand of middle-western culture." But "what it lacked was a couple of first-rate book-publishing houses, for it is publishing houses that mysteriously cause a city to be regarded as an intellectual center." The problem in Chicago was not getting into print; the problem was publishing in the sense of reaching out past the city and the region. No doubt Dell felt Chicago's limitations when he had to send writings that he hoped would find a national audience to magazines like *McClure's* and

Harper's. New York, it seemed, was the place of greatest influence. New York directed the affairs of the nation and spoke to the largest public.[7]

In the lore of Greenwich Village, Dell serves as the symbol of the young man from the provinces come in search of liberation. True to the extent that he became the Village's leading apostle (and perhaps its leading practitioner) of free love, the myth of Bohemia minimizes the seriousness of his quest. The Village was most significant to those with a genuine commitment to critical writing as a haven for free inquiry on the edge of greater New York. Dell indicated something of this symbolic landscape in a retrospective comment. "The Bohemian world of Murger did not please me," he recalled. "[I]t was too pathetic—people were always dying in those garrets, and dying without an idea in their silly heads. The Bohemia I approved of was the one seen for a moment in every history of Parisian revolutionary uprisings, in which Bohemian students fought and died behind barricades in each crisis of liberty."[8] Dell's Village—and that of his friends—was an intellectual colony situated on the brink of action, readying its ideas through open discussion to carry forth into the city and nation beyond. The arrival of the Eastmans, Reed, Lippmann, Dodge, Brooks, Bourne, Dell, Stearns, and their contemporaries signaled the transformation of Greenwich Village from a place of mild aestheticism to the home of the new intellectual life. "Pretenders" remained and would come in greater numbers after 1920, but by 1912–13, a nascent critical community resided within the larger Bohemia, headquartered at the Liberal Club and the Dodge salon. Brooks, looking back on this period as the final chapter in his cultural history of America, captured the meaning of the Village to his generation—its freedom and openness, its commitment to national regeneration: "As Boston had fermented in 1840, New York was fermenting in 1912 on a scale that was no longer provincial but continental, and Greenwich Village swarmed with the movers and shakers who were expressing the new insurgent spirit." Dell conveyed a similar impression from the vantage point of 1926, identifying the Village as an "exciting young world, full of high purpose and serious endeavor." Here, between Wall Street and uptown, was a "little republic" of letters in which "free self-expression and the passion of propaganda" were "for one moment happily mated."[9] There is more to these memories than nostalgia; they contain clues to the convergence of these writers in New York and to the evolution of a shared mission. The Village gave physical substance to the vision of locating an independent intellectual community at the center of American civilization.

Coming together downtown also meant a liberation from confining backgrounds. Whether from Brooks' Plainfield, Reed's Portland, or Rosenfeld's Upper West Side, the migration to the Village (most often via college) represented an effort to transcend narrowness. The Village and the Lower East Side provided the basis for Bourne's announcement of a "new cosmopolitan outlook"—what David A. Hollinger has defined as "the desire to transcend the limitations of any and all particularisms in order to achieve a more complete human experience and a more complete understanding of that experience."[10] The Greenwich Village friendships of Anglo-Saxons and Jews, such as those between Brooks, Bourne, Frank, Rosenfeld, and Oppenheim at the *Seven Arts*, came to signify the intellectuals' commitment to openness. Bourne claimed as the essential task of "the younger intelligentsia of America" the pursuit of a "Beloved Community" which would rise above any restricted viewpoint. "Trans-national America" was rooted in Bourne's experiences in New York—his personal relationships with men and women of relatively diverse origins and his larger contacts with the city of immigrants. But if the immediate issue was ethnicity, the essay concluded with a bold call for intellectual disinterestedness. "Bourne," Hollinger has written, "was moved by the idea of a community of intellectuals, a complex yet unified, single discourse to which a variety of contingent particularisms would make their distinctive contributions." No particularism was valuable unless it contributed to "a more comprehensive outlook on the world." For Bourne's generation, the convergence in the Village demonstrated an ability to cast off every parochial concern that interfered with the expansion of understanding—to forge the broad perspective necessary for a vibrant and effective criticism.[11]

2.

Despite New York's importance in shaping and reinforcing a sense of involvement and expansiveness, its hold on intellectuals was incomplete and short-lived. The characteristic attitude toward the city became one of profound ambivalence by the late 1910s, as the metropolis continued its growth into megalopolis and critics began to consider more thoroughly the connections between New York and intellectual production. While

Edmund Wilson expressed his "great hope for New York as a cultural center" in 1921, he complained two years later that he felt "harassed" in the city and wondered "if it is possible to live there" and "produce anything serious at the same time." One did not have to be so studied an observer of urban life as Mumford to see in the course of the city's development the consolidation of corporate capitalism at the expense of a healthy culture. Crossing from Jersey City "on a gray morning of November" in 1919, Wilson looked in disgust at skyscrapers "of the drabbest and most grimy colors and of a square machine-made architecture which excluded imagination." Here was the "dingy, crude and colorless material life" of modern America—evidence written in stone of the enormous obstacles to creative expression. In the capital of finance and greed, Wilson explained, the "tendency is for all writers to be driven the way of Heywood Broun—into an enormous mass production of diluted intellectual goods." [12]

This idea of the megalopolis as a threat to culture served as the basis for Mumford's life's work. As early as 1921, he used the city as a text for revealing the pathologies of American civilization, particularly the blight of materialism and the devaluation of art and intellect. The urban landscape stood as a symbol of "the goods life rather than the good life"—the prevalence of accumulation over thought. From Mumford's perspective, the "highest achievements of our material civilization—and at their best our hotels, our department stores, and our Woolworth towers are achievements—count as so many symptoms of its spiritual failure." With its gridiron design, New York north of the Village set the pattern for the twentieth-century city as a paean to commercialism and a symbol of "intellectual anaesthesia." [13]

Mumford found an alternative to the anti-intellectual metropolis in the New England culture city of the mid-nineteenth century. His contribution to the Stearns symposium began with the regrettable decline of the "Concord culture," and in subsequent work he undertook a full-blown discussion of this lost place and moment. *Sticks and Stones* and *The Golden Day*, as John Thomas has observed, located in nineteenth-century New England and its Puritan background the ideal conditions for the creative life. The New England town became for Mumford a "model in the mind signifying community, permanence, and continuity—a benchmark for measuring subsequent backslidings." [14] Not least of all, he discovered an environment which nurtured artists and thinkers and reconciled the "breach between art and life." These towns were themselves works of creative imagination, products of "genuine community planning" in which all work delighted the producer and enhanced the community as a whole. When "the town itself was an omnipresent work of art," as Mumford said of all medieval cities in 1938, there could be no fundamental antagonism between the artist and society and only a minimal potential for intellectual alienation. Everybody was an artist; society was the collective product of creative minds.[15]

If Mumford was exceptional in the depth of his historical search for the ideal culture city, he was hardly alone in looking backward for the kind of landscape best suited to the intellectual life. In many ways, Greenwich Village itself was a holdover from the nineteenth century, and by the 1920s, the prewar Village had passed into the realm of pleasant memory. "The Village," Leslie Fishbein has written, "was an oasis in an industrial desert, a place in which remnants of a craft tradition could survive, a community with the closely knit social relations reminiscent of small-town life."[16] Insulated from the cash values of the twentieth-century metropolis uptown, it preserved a human scale that complemented its inhabitants' common quest for fulfilling work and intellectual camaraderie. For a moment, young writers found themselves suspended in time and space between the provincial city and the financial megalopolis, living in a latter-day version of the artisanal villages of the old Northeast.

As Mumford came back repeatedly to the regional moment of the New England town, others of his generation returned to the idyllic Greenwich Village of 1910–17. It was here that George Cram Cook found temporary satisfaction for his longing "to live with beauty-loving, expressive people," "to draw around us a community—a less visionary Brook Farm." It was here too that Brooks received an answer to the plaintive question he asked in his solitude in England, "oh, don't we *deserve* some fellowship, some community of ideals in life?" Dell and Eastman both contrasted the Village's tranquillity to the "noisy waves of enterprise" outside the "island paradise," and both invoked the memory of "a gentler pace" more conducive to the life of letters than the "Swift-hurrying" of modern New York. Eastman remembered the Village as "still almost rural, for Seventh Avenue had not yet crashed down through it, biting the very houses in two. That roaring north-and-southbound monster was still confined above Eleventh Street, and below there was quietness and quaintness, there were neighbors who knew each other, there was sauntering in the streets."

Dell recalled that the "rents were cheap because the rush of traffic could not make its way through the little twisted streets that crossed and recrossed each other and never seemed to get anywhere else," and he also dated the end from 1917, when Seventh Avenue was "ruthlessly and efficiently cut through as the West Side subway was extended southward."[17]

By 1920, Dell's paradise had surrendered to the forces of commercialization that constantly threatened artistic and intellectual integrity. "I loathed what the Village had now become," he wrote in 1933. "It was a show-place, where there was no longer any privacy from the vulgar stares of an up-town rabble." For Randolph Bourne, the enemy appeared in slightly different form; pseudo-intellectuals, fake artists, an assortment of faddists and hangers-on had corrupted the Village by introducing a new kind of conformity and disrupting the work of its more serious inhabitants. Bourne was so disturbed by this that he made up his mind to leave New York—a decision he never carried out. "It would seem strange to turn my back on New York and our network of people, and definitely closing a chapter in my life," he confessed to his fiancée in August 1917, "but such things have to be done. I am coming to think of Greenwich Village as a poisonous place which destroys the souls even of the super-villagers like ourselves." Irresistibly, it seemed, the acquisitive city extended its grimy hand down into the Village, shattering the calm, raising rents, and imperiling the genuine artists and intellectuals.[18]

The depth of nostalgia for the prewar Village suggests something of the growing hostility many intellectuals felt toward New York as it subsumed their community. With H. L. Mencken, who never liked New York, they came increasingly to view the city as a drain on their energies, a temptation into hack writing and selling out, and a series of distractions from the important work before them. Mencken's editorial responsibilities for the *Smart Set* and the *American Mercury* forced him to make frequent visits to Manhattan, and these prompted him to reflect on the city's limitations as a home to critics. In Baltimore, he found, he could "live through three or four days on end without being bothered," while in New York he was "beset day and night." Mabel Dodge offered a similar assessment from the serenity of Taos. "In New York," she remembered, "the hastening, frantic stream of traffic flowed through the streets, sometimes overflowed them into the apartment."[19] What Dodge condemned were precisely those features of the city—its ceaseless activity, its crowds, its air of importance, its modernity—that had attracted so many of her acquaintances in the first place and furnished them with a sense of meaningful presence. But their other concern, their quest for an expressive life free of encumbrances and annoyances, led them to look askance at New York and to explore alternatives that might still allow a reconciliation of independence and involvement.

3.

In the intellectuals' search for a home, the claims of modernity competed with the model existence of the nineteenth-century literati. Walter Lippmann, one of those least burdened by living in New York, conveyed this impression to Bernard Berenson, the older American art historian who had set himself up as a Renaissance man of letters in a villa outside Florence. "Living in the country redeems much," Lippmann wrote. "One gets so good a sense of things that do not matter and a decent relief from the feverish factionalisms of the city. But I'm afraid it's a long time before any considerable number of us can cultivate our gardens. Sometimes I think we are a damned generation. I suppose we are in comparison with the late Victorians."[20] Bourne experienced a similar tension between the peace and leisure of the country and the action of the city; his preferences alternated dramatically during summers spent in Dublin, New Hampshire, and at Elsie Clews Parsons' farm in Lenox, Massachusetts. "Just now it is the country that appeals to me," he told a friend at the beginning of June 1915. "The city is incredibly dusty and acts like a huge sounding board for all the din and children's cries." Six weeks later, he complained that the "country does not seem to agree with me . . . There is obviously nothing but Europe. If you can't go there, it is New York you must stay in." Within three days, his mood had changed again. Now he was "enjoying the calm country, and the freedom from noise and distractions. I think I ought to live in the country, for I work very well, there seems to be plenty of time, and I delight in the colors of the hills and meadows and the passage of the summer day."[21] This was the dilemma of Lippmann's "damned generation": stay in the city and risk compromise and diversion; or move away and jeopardize effectiveness and a grasp on contemporary reality.

Bourne's solution was to establish an intellectual colony—a community of the disinterested within striking distance of New York yet far enough removed to maintain its integrity. He imagined a cooperative farm in Westchester, "an old house with ten acres of land," "an expensive cook and perhaps a community auto." The "nucleus" was to be Bourne and Esther Cornell, Van Wyck and Eleanor Brooks, and the critic Ordway Tead and his wife, all of whom he took to be "keen for it." According to Bourne, he and Brooks "did a lot of enthusiastic talking" about the project, "and it seems to be our salvation." He may even have looked at a few rental properties in White Plains, but after rejoicing that his "imagination takes wings" at the thought of such a community, Bourne quietly abandoned the effort.[22]

Without Bourne's deliberateness, other colonies did begin to take shape after 1915, and here again it was Mabel Dodge who served as pathfinder. In 1915, Dodge discovered the rustic Westchester town of Croton-on-Hudson, where she bought Sharkey Cottage and then Finney Farm on Mount Airy Road. "My life was thus divided for a while between New York and the country," she recalled, but not for long. Dodge gave up her famous Fifth Avenue apartment in 1916 for the "lovely, quaint country-side" and "the truer living in its deep pulse." Several of her friends followed her to Croton. She sold the Sharkey Cottage to Reed in November 1916, the same month in which, to Dodge's dismay, he married Louise Bryant. Eastman had arrived even earlier, putting twenty dollars down on a fifteen-hundred dollar house that he would share with his sister. Dell, several of the *Masses* artists, and Stuart Chase also staked their claims in Croton, so that by the time the radical English socialite Clare Sheridan visited in May 1921, she could observe that "there is a sort of Colony at Croton, and every house is inhabited by someone one knows, or who knows the other."[23]

The Mount Airy residents did not leave Sheridan with any sense of their retreat's real importance. Her impressions of the physical landscape —Croton was "real country and luxuriantly green, with the fresh immaturity of impending summer"—were keener than her comprehension of its inhabitants. In her view, these were all "work-worn journalists, artists and Bohemians generally, who came there with their children for a rest." But it was work that drew Reed, Bryant, Eastman, Dell, and Chase to Croton. It was the yearning for freedom from distraction that prompted Reed to tell Bryant, "I wish I could stay out in the country awhile, instead of this terrible rushing about the city!" Bryant set out most clearly the desired relation between Croton and New York, which was the inverse of what Sheridan later imagined. "I think it will be so fine to do *work* out here, uninterrupted, and play in town," she wrote Reed just after moving into Sharkey Cottage. "We can't put off real work year after year."[24] This semi-rural environment, where intellectual and artistic fellowship combined with contemplative solitude, was the proper place for free expression. Eastman, recently liberated from the bonds of marriage, explained that "I could enjoy my freedom better in my own house and in the country." From his "uncovered porch," he "could look down through forest trees to the river. Beside the porch, and overarching it almost like a roof, was an Osage orange tree some twenty feet high, the only one I ever saw in our part of the world." For "further isolation," Eastman built "a little study in the barn." He lived and worked in the Croton house on and off for twenty-five years.[25]

Dodge was also one of the pioneers in the settlement of Provincetown by artists and intellectuals, but in this she was preceded by Susan Glaspell and George Cram Cook, who bought a house there in 1915. In the summer of 1915, they and their friends began to put on informal plays on Mary Heaton Vorse's fish wharf, and by the summer of 1916, Reed, Bryant, Eastman, Hutchins Hapgood, Neith Boyce, and Robert Edmond Jones were helping Cook write, design, and act in the productions of the Provincetown Players. Provincetown may have been more a place of respite than of work, but like Croton, it took on meaning as a home to unobstructed creativity. Vorse's recollections of the first years of the Players emphasized the group's freedom from commercial pressures and connected this freedom to the theater's transforming influence. "We were bound by no conventions," she wrote. "We didn't have to think of box-office or what the public wanted and so we knew what the public wanted better than did the hard-boiled producers who were bound by a thousand conventions and a thousand fears."[26] Glaspell described the colony as a fulfillment of Cook's wish for a "Beloved Community of Life-Givers," committed to an existence away from the cash nexus and the non-productive values of the city:

[I]t seems to me we were a particularly simple people, who sought to arrange life for the thing we wanted to do, needing each other as protection against complexities, yet living as we did because of an instinct for the old, old things, to have a garden, and neighbors, to keep up the fire and let the cat in at night. None of us had much money, these were small houses we lived in . . .[27]

The dispersal of the original group of Provincetown artists and intellectuals by the early 1920s did not end Cape Cod's attraction for writers in search of rusticity. "Ever since I've been here," Waldo Frank wrote from Truro in 1933, "I have realized how much I needed a place in the country. New York is the body of our social disease: I can see the disease here, as elsewhere, but the body—concentrated—is the city, and to live *in* it does strange, secret, terrible things to one's perspective." Edmund Wilson began to spend summers on the Cape in 1927 with a stay at Eugene O'Neill's house, and after a winter in Connecticut in 1936 convinced him that he "ought to live in the country," he settled more or less permanently in Wellfleet. Though he was younger than Eastman and Dell, Wilson shared their longing for the small communities of the past. In a remarkable chapter in *Travels in Two Democracies*, a book that also praised the Soviet Union and heralded the coming of socialism to America, he revisited his ancestors' home in Talcottville, New York, and reflected on the passage of the nineteenth-century communal life. Soon, he mourned, there would "be little left but our house confronting the hotdog stand and the gas station," while the near bank and "little falls" of the Sugar River had been destroyed "to get stone for the new state highway." His ancestors, he noted, had been "very impressive people, the survivors of a sovereign race who owned their own pastures and fields and governed their own community." But this sovereignty and satisfaction belonged to the past. "Today their descendants perform minor functions in a machine which they do not control."[28] Much as Wilson was drawn to modernity —and he was certainly more of a modernist in literary taste than Eastman, Dell, and Brooks—he too craved the life of the nineteenth-century man of letters: independence, authority, leisure, rusticity, community. Wellfleet was the closest he could come.

Through the 1920s and 1930s, an intellectual constellation formed around New York in places near enough to maintain frequent contact with the metropolis yet far enough away to preserve a sense of autonomy. Brooks commuted from Westport, Connecticut, to his office at the *Freeman* from 1920 to 1924 and only returned to live in New York for a short period in the 1940s. The Westport community soon came to include Paul Rosenfeld, the theater critic and designer Lee Simonson, the intellectual journalist and popular historian Hendrik van Loon, and the regionalist painter John Steuart Curry. Charles Beard lived nearby in New Milford, as did Scribner's editor Maxwell Perkins and the Irish-born critics Padraic and Mary Colum in New Canaan. By 1930, Malcolm Cowley, Matthew Josephson, and Slater Brown had all staked claims in Sherman, where, as Josephson remarked, "within a radius of twenty to thirty miles of our house, in Connecticut or rural New York, practically everybody we might enjoy was available." According to Brooks, the Connecticut landscape of "rolling hills . . . seemed to favour those who cared more for the state of their minds than the state of their fortunes." In the spring of 1924, he boasted to a New York friend that he was building a wall—a kind of wholesome labor unavailable to city-dwellers, and he told another friend that he counted "every mile blessed" that removed him from the city.[29] But what Brooks and his contemporaries had really done was to strike a compromise between New York and the country, assuring them of both freedom and connection, distance and proximity. They wished to avoid what Mumford called "a metropolitan civilization which baulks our natural, creative impulses at every turn and sends them into the various channels of dissipation which are associated with luxury, display, conspicuous expenditure, and sexual adventure." At the same time, however, they were unwilling to abandon it entirely. Their geographical solution allowed them the claim of integrity and the closeness to reality necessary for critical assessment and prescriptions for social change.[30]

4.

Almost every intellectual at some point contemplated a third option beyond the city and the country. Expatriation became a more acceptable choice for younger critics such as Malcolm Cowley and Matthew Josephson, a method of liberation from the Philistinism of the 1920s. But Brooks' end of the generation had wrestled with the issue earlier and continued to mull it over as some of its own and more of its successors made their way to Europe in the period of normalcy. The debate over expatriation was part of the larger discussion of the intellectual's place in American civilization.[31]

For Brooks, Lippmann, Bourne, Reed, Stearns, and others, the first mature exposure to Europe came in the form of a trip after college. Seeing Europe as cultured young men still awed by Ruskin, Morris, Shaw, Wells, Nietzsche, and Anatole France, they inevitably found themselves confirmed in their belief that the Old World valued its thinkers infinitely higher than the United States valued or even recognized its own. While still at Harvard, Brooks made the common observation that "all Americans are born Philistines, and whatever they may acquire that is anti-Philistine comes from contact with Europe." This was the assumption that he spent the rest of his life trying to disprove. Bourne struggled in his year abroad to reconcile his "American intellectual patriotism" with a sense of cultural humility and envy at the way Europeans respected and listened to their writers. From Paris in 1914 he wrote, "Our 'intellectuals' will have to sharpen up their knowledge, and stiffen their fibre a good deal, it seems to me, before they can take the commanding place of leadership which they fill in France." Bourne's report to Columbia's trustees, written to fulfill the terms of his fellowship, noted the absence in Europe of the highbrow/lowbrow gap. "In fact," he declared, "the distinction between the 'intellectual' and the non-intellectual seems to have quite broken down in France." Five years before Mumford admired at first hand Patrick Geddes' accomplishments in Edinburgh, Bourne wrote with approval of the British and German experiments in "modern town-planning" that demonstrated the reality of intellectual leadership outside the United States. Harold Stearns pointed out the glaring contrast between Europe and America as he pondered the question "Where Are Our Intellectuals?" According to Stearns, the sad fact remained "that in France and England this group has exercised, and is exercising to-day, enormous influence; it is also the fact that in America to-day it is exercising no influence at all."[32]

Europe's other great attraction for American intellectuals, and the one that ultimately led some to expatriate, was its tolerance for free expression. In Europe, writers could distance themselves from Comstockery, conformity, and commercialism and achieve the cosmopolitan perspective essential for great criticism and art. This is what Brooks had in mind when, at twenty-two, he "supposed that the only chance an American had to succeed as a writer was to betake himself there with all possible speed."[33] This was also the guiding idea in the social criticism and personal behavior of Stearns, the most notable expatriate of Brooks' generation. Like Brooks, Stearns repeatedly enumerated the obstacles to intellect and art in America: the "iron repression of the free spirit," the "monotonous standardization of everything" that was creating "a civilization of the commonplace and the second-rate." In what became his manifesto of expatriation, "What Can a Young Man Do?" Stearns offered both arguments as to why America was unsuitable for the intellectual life. It allowed neither freedom nor influence; "there is no flexibility, no colour, no possibility for adventure, no chance to shape events more generously than is permitted under the rules of highly organized looting." By 1921, he had reached the conclusion that "in twentieth-century America the chances are becoming slimmer and slimmer every day of leading any other kind of life than the monotonous majority-ruled, unimaginative existence of the great average." Fortunately, he noted, there was an alternative. In Europe, "life can still be lived." [34]

Stearns' reasons for leaving were both personal and public. The death of his wife from complications in childbirth in 1920 left him shattered, and he spent most of three months drunk, lingering at the Hotel Brevoort and the Boni Brothers' Bookshop in the Village. His loss and his drinking habits fueled a general sense of outrage at Prohibition which, according to Gilbert Seldes, prompted him to launch "an individual bootlegging concern." Befriending the stewards on the French ships docked in New York, Stearns bought liquor from them and distributed it to his friends on a non-profit basis. Seldes testified that Stearns' "work against Prohibition was purely inspired by principle." Brooks offered the more perceptive observation that Stearns "was beginning to identify his likes and dislikes with cultural standards, and so he understood Prohibition to be a sign of the decadence of American life." Organizing and editing the *Civilization in the United States* symposium brought temporary relief, and there is evidence that he intended to go abroad for the summer and then resume "cooperative" work along the lines of *Civilization*. But after turning over the manuscript to Harcourt, Brace, he made a ceremonious departure on July 4, 1921, and did not return for more than a decade. [35]

What is most significant about Stearns' expatriation is not that his immediate motivation was personal grief. Nor is it, as Seldes, Ernest Hemingway, and Malcolm Cowley were the first to reveal, that Stearns' life in France was a downward spiral into intellectual stagnation, poverty, and illness. The remarkable fact about his departure and his time abroad is that he consistently referred to his behavior in impersonal terms—that he chose to present his personal experiences as an intellectual problem. Long after he had entered his decline, he persisted in defending expatriation as the best choice available to an American intellectual. In a letter to F. Scott Fitzgerald dated October 1, 1928 and published several months later in *Scribner's* magazine, Stearns freely admitted that he had "few friends, no family or amorous life," that he was "bored, often hungry, seldom well clothed, and never happy." Yet, he wrote, "I continue to stay." He stayed because an "articulate mediocrity, armed with self-assurance, a full stomach, and a tenacious determination to destroy anything better than itself" still held sway in America. In France, even if he had no place "in the successful and vital currents," he possessed the freedom that was a precondition for the creative life. "If America left you free—free to work, to create, to make a fool of yourself or a success—where would a rational man rather live?" he asked. "But the point is, in the United States you are not free." Although his existence in France had not been intellectually productive, Stearns reasoned, at least he had been allowed to fail as an autonomous human being, instead of being destroyed by the "thoroughly doctrinated herd life" of America.[36] Stearns had opted for a place that granted intellectual independence, even if nothing socially valuable came of it.

While the logic of living in New York had been the immersion in lowbrow reality, it did not always follow that expatriation meant a flight into the highbrow. Brooks admitted as much when he remarked that "I have always found when abroad that the thought of America becomes a kind of obsession. One keeps perpetually searching for an 'explanation.' "[37] Distance increased the risk of losing touch, of course, but it could also provide a superior perspective. This was the reasoning of Ludwig Lewisohn, the Berlin-born drama critic for the *Nation*, who returned to Europe from 1924 to 1933. Lewisohn styled himself an advocate of "the critical spirit which is also the creative spirit" and aligned himself with Brooks and Mencken against the "aimless business" and "sapless pleasure" of American civilization. Before leaving the United States, he offered an explicit restatement of Bourne's "impossibilist élan." Critical literature was reaching only "a handful of people," he admitted, and to claim that any change was imminent would have been to indulge in the national vice of "professional optimism." Recognizing that the "hour is dark," however, would "not prevent us from working and striving for a better one that may come hereafter." Lewisohn did not abandon this faith when he sailed for Europe. Instead, he linked expatriation to greater effectiveness, arguing that "a perspective of both time and distance" would let him view the "American scene with that detachment which draws an interpretive order out of reality and re-creates life by making it intelligible." Europe would give him "more peace and equilibrium," free him from a "hectic inner involvement" in American life, and allow him "to exercise the shaping imagination" that America needed. Unlike Ezra Pound, who had turned his back and retreated into a private and unintelligible world, Lewisohn would keep his eyes focused on America and return a better critic. As it turned out, Europe bolstered Lewisohn's sense of social commitment even as it helped reorient it. The specific motivations for his trip had been both personal and public. The immediate occasion was an unhappy marriage and a love affair with a professional singer, which he could pursue more freely overseas. But he was also responding to Chaim Weizmann's invitation to observe the resettlement of Polish Jews in Palestine for a series of *Nation* articles—an experience which made him a convert to Zionism. Settling in Montparnasse, Lewisohn spent much of his time there studying the history of Judaism. He returned to the United States a passionate spokesman for the Zionist cause, certain that his removal had opened the way to a new understanding and a clearer social purpose.[38]

Two additional cases confirm the diversity of expatriate experiences. George Cram Cook, disturbed by the Provincetown Players' drift toward commercial success in New York, gave up the directorship and moved to Greece with his wife Susan Glaspell in March 1922. The problem, as Cook saw it, was that the theater had abandoned its mission of social regeneration and become a mere collection of egos. "Our individual gifts and talents have sought their private perfection," he complained. "We have not, as we hoped, created the beloved community of life-givers." Cook's journey to Greece was not a flight from social concern to creative freedom. His obsession with the Periclean age was part of a recurring dream of a creative community at the center of society, defining and transforming it. In ancient Greece, poets, playwrights, and philosophers had been leaders, not marginal men. Dressed in peasants' clothes and letting his white hair and beard grow long, Cook imagined a new Athens, populated by American youth redeeming the world through their expressive gifts: "With young earth-born richly vital Americans, from here we could once more conquer the world. They are so damned insignificantly shallow where they are. From here, what couldn't they do? What couldn't we have done from here?"[39] His dream came no closer to realization than the creation of a peasant theater called the Delphic Players. Cook died of a fever at Delphi in 1923.

Max Eastman's expatriation was based on a less bizarre mission of redemption. In 1922, Eastman turned over the *Liberator* to Claude McKay, Michael Gold, and Joseph Freeman and traveled to the Soviet Union. There, as Reed had done earlier, he would learn the science of revolution; to secure "a better entree among the ruling circles of Moscow," to gain access to the successful engineers of the Russian Revolution, he even joined the Workers' Party. Eastman undertook his journey in the interest of fortifying his qualifications for intellectual leadership at home. His goal was to gain a first-hand knowledge of revolution which he could then apply to American circumstances. Between 1922 and 1924, he tried to keep to this goal, studying the New Economic Policy, meeting Bolshevik officials, planning a biography of Trotsky, attending the Fourth Congress of the Comintern and the Twelfth and Thirteenth Congresses of the Communist party.[40] But Eastman's plans for "practical" work—the social side of his expatriation—quickly ran into a competing urge. In the autumn of 1923, he moved from Moscow to the quiet Soviet town of Sochi and began to write an autobiographical novel. Soon he found himself wrapped up completely in this decidedly non-revolutionary endeavor, casting off any public obligation that interfered with it. "I have no intention of coming back to Moscow this winter," he wrote his future wife Eliena Krylenko. "I have no desire and no purpose in this world now but to finish this book—finish it without ever stopping." At one point he confessed to feeling "ashamed" that he was "running away from Trotsky," but after a cup of coffee and thinking about the novel he "didn't care so much." Always extremely self-conscious, Eastman knew that he was caught up in a struggle between independence and social responsibility, and for the moment he resolved it in favor of self-expression. He was not going to "fight the *influences* of other personalities and other lives" while he was writing his book; he was "*not* going to finish Trotsky, . . . not going to do anything else" until he completed the novel.[41] From 1924 to 1927, Eastman lived in France, socializing with other American expatriates, alternating between revolutionary and personal writing. Through his friendships with Fitzgerald, Hemingway, Gerald and Sara Murphy, he understood the lure of separation. But he also feared the loss of influence and social involvement in American life, even though he had been studying and publishing on the subject of revolution. "I feel I'm *out of it* now for a long time," he wrote Crystal in 1926. "Nobody will read my book."[42]

The overplayed themes of a "Lost Generation" and art for art's sake,

which served polemical purposes in the thirties, failed to account for
much of the intellectual travel literature of the previous decade. Malcolm
Cowley's *Exile's Return*, as Warren Susman suggested, was more a rallying
cry to social commitment than an accurate description of what most
intellectuals were doing abroad from the late 1910s to the early 1930s.
Published in 1934, *Exile's Return* confined its focus to the expatriate avant-
garde in Paris and excluded those writers who viewed their travels as a
form of social engagement rather than a retreat into irresponsibility.
Cowley had no place for Eastman or Lewisohn; his plea for intellectual
involvement and his construct of flight and return could not accommodate
the expatriates and travelers who used their observations and experiences
to criticize America's bungled civilization and to offer alternatives.

In Spain, the Near East, Central and South America, traveling intellectuals found living cultures that valued craftsmanship, play, and spirit
over money, machinery, and material goods—models in one form or
another of a non-acquisitive way of life. John Dos Passos' romance with
Spain began in 1916 and continued through the Civil War, and the record
of his visits stands as one of the most compelling statements of the socially
responsible style of expatriation of the 1920s and 1930s. Among the
Spanish peasants, Dos Passos discovered what he called "the life for a
man"—a pre-urban, pre-industrial existence rooted in "the village community." In contrast to the standardized, centralized civilization of the
"Anglo-Saxons," Spain had managed to retain a "local" or "regional"
orientation. This, according to Dos Passos, made for a more natural,
more essential, more human way of life in which individuals achieved
genuine self-fulfillment within an authentic community. The "social
cohesion" that he observed in Spain came from a shared "love for place"
and an unspoken commitment to expression—"the gesture"—rather than
acquisition. Here, in short, was the expressive community that stood out
against compulsory work and the "dynasty of Things." When he traveled
through the Near East in the early twenties, Dos Passos once again
grasped the possibility of "a life bare and vigorous without being savage,
a life naked and godless where goods and institutions will be broken to fit
men, instead of men being ground down fine and sifted in the service of
Things."[43] *Journeys between Wars* was the story of a search, not an escape;
American civilization was Dos Passos' constant frame of reference, the
target of his criticism, and the intended beneficiary of his discoveries.

The line between expatriates and others is further blurred by the fact that writers who had no intention of permanently relocating also traveled abroad in search of better ways of life. Like Dos Passos, Stuart Chase admired the peasants' pre-industrial conception of work and their "want-lessness" with regard to consumer goods and conspicuous wealth. Mexican Indians, Chase claimed, "punch no time clocks, prepare no job tickets, visit no employment office, receive no welfare work, say yessir to no boss. They work when they feel like it, sleep when they feel like it." Chase freely conceded that he envied such a "formula"; through "the meshes of a New England upbringing," he was "striving" to adopt a similar attitude. *Mexico: A Study of Two Americas* explicitly compared "the way of life in the free villages"—Mexico's surviving "handicraft economy"—to the machine civilization of the modern United States. Using the Lynds' *Middletown* and Robert Redfield's *Tepoztlan* as his basic sources and building in observations from his own five-month visit, Chase wrote a kind of hortatory travelogue in which he urged the people of North America's Middletowns to learn from their southern neighbors "the art of living." By this he meant the liberation from "essentially meaningless" material goods and the substitution of a handicraft mentality for Middletown's "over-commercialized, mechanized, standardized," and largely passive style of work and play. What Chase appreciated most about the Mexican village—what made its inhabitants artistic rather than acquisitive—was that it had remained "an economically independent community." Odd as it might seem, he had found among the semi-literate Indians of Oaxaca and the Yucatan not only some general lessons about regional self-sufficiency but also a source of inspiration for independent intellectuals in the United States. Another traveler, Waldo Frank, similarly observed in the "traditional life" of Hispanic America the "true concept of the person" as a self-fulfilled "integer" in "an organic whole." In his ponderous fashion, Frank described an alternative sense of self and society among the Spanish-speaking peoples to pit against the exploitative outlook of the Anglo-Saxon world.[44]

5.

The varied character of expatriation and the uncertain distinctions between escape and search, and between traveling and uprooting, did not preclude sharp attacks on writers who stayed away too long. For those who resisted and condemned the flight to Europe, the prospect of marginalization served as the focus of concern. Images of writers cast adrift, out of touch with their native land and without a legitimate subject matter, dominated the criticism of expatriation. While Bourne insisted on a cosmopolitan outlook, he also warned against deracination. "The American has to work to interpret and portray the life he knows," Bourne argued in the autobiographical "History of a Literary Radical." "He cannot be international in the sense that anything but the life in which he is saturated, with its questions and its colors, can be the material for his art." Brooks' second cautionary tale, *The Pilgrimage of Henry James* (1925), expanded on this theme of the rootless writer. Brooks used the example of James to instruct Stearns and the younger intellectuals about the ultimate gains and losses of expatriation: the winning of an empty independence at the expense of substance. As long as James could draw on his store of American material, he succeeded in his art. But the longer he stayed abroad, the more disconnected he became from any "immediate sense of life and character." In his later novels and stories, "he was drifting very far from the world of 'reality,' from the common earth to which, to renew his strength, the artist, like Antaeus, must ever return." Finally, James retreated into a kind of art for art's sake—a private, internal mode of expression that represented an abandonment of the writer's interpretive and redemptive role. He died "the minor artist for whom his own perplexities and the caprices of the imagination" took "the place of the knowledge and experience of life."[45]

As much as it was a warning to his fellow writers, *The Pilgrimage of Henry James* was also an indication of Brooks' own state of mind. The Henry James who sees America as "a wilderness," signifying "nothing but calamity, destruction, oblivion," speaks for Brooks himself. So does the James who views the United States as "a country that certainly provided one with opportunities for making money, but in which it remained to be seen whether the higher human faculties would be able to survive at all." Brooks shared with his subject a sense that "Europe was the land where great men came into their own," and he too possessed "a nostalgia for that far-away paradise" of creative freedom and intellectual authority.[46] His friend Mary Colum recognized the autobiographical dimension of the James study and the attraction to Europe against which Brooks struggled through the 1910s and 1920s:

He had an odd though, perhaps, not so unusual way of reading into his subjects his own characteristics and problems, and he was sometimes aware of this, especially as regards Henry James. He thought actually that he was attacking Henry James for the things he had wanted to do himself, such as living abroad on an independent income, and he got so worried about this at one time that he withdrew the manuscript, though later he sent it back to be published as it stood.

These anxieties very likely contributed to the breakdown Brooks suffered shortly after the publication of the book; at its onset he found himself haunted by nightmare visions of Henry James. Later he acknowledged the "lingering fears of expatriation" and the "ambivalence" that shaped his outlook in the 1920s.[47]

Many of Brooks' contemporaries experienced a similar ambivalence. Bourne had discussed New York as an inadequate substitute for Europe in 1915. The widely shared impression of America as a sterile place for creative growth emerged out of a contrary view of Europe as intellectually tolerant and culturally superior. H. L. Mencken frequently announced his plans to relocate, to "get away from visible America" as he phrased it to Theodore Dreiser in February 1919. "I have five or six books to write, wholly unlike anything I have yet done," he said in contemplating a move to Germany. "Trying to write them while in active contact with American life would be like trying to read in a nail-factory." A month later he confessed his readiness to "depart these shores more or less permanently on the restoration of free seas." But even Mencken, who constantly protested against the idea of the writer as reformer or revolutionary, resisted expatriation. Despite his hatred of Comstockery and his disgust at America's hostility to culture, he knew that his own writing thrived in the "active contact with American life" against which he occasionally railed. "There is nothing more charming than to sit among dunderheads and watch them at their idiotic sports," he wrote in 1920. "This, in fact, is the one thing that makes life bearable."[48]

In the literature of intellectual flight and return, it is the sense of marginalization and the desire to participate in the reconstruction of America that draws expatriates back to their homeland. When Stearns returned from France in 1932, he joined his one-time critics in characterizing expatriation as a "flight from reality" and urging American writers to contend for a place in the thick of things. "I have found that a real world exists after all—," he proclaimed, "and that real world is my own country, from which I have been away far too long." As with his departure, the circumstances of Stearns' return were primarily personal; he was dangerously ill and destitute. But he presented his repatriation as part of an intellectual odyssey, in which the hero returns emboldened in his commitment to society and social change. "If things go badly at home," he wrote in the midst of the Depression, "there is only one thing to do—to hang on, to fight, to work as intelligently and diligently as one can until they go better." In more ways than one, Stearns confirmed Waldo Frank's warning that "to save his life" the expatriate "must return to his own country."[49]

The generational conflicts of the early twenties over the location of the literary life had subsided by 1930, when Matthew Josephson anticipated his friend Cowley in celebrating the exiles' return. "We turn back after the lapse of a whole misled generation," Josephson wrote; "we return, literally, to face again the American scene with our hopes and demands." While he continued to insist that Europe had always been "an excellent vantage-point from which to study American character," he now saw that the "salvation and strength of artists" as a "potential force for Humanism" resided "in their ability, hereafter, to incorporate themselves within the actual milieu." Josephson disputed Brooks' assessment of Henry James, whose later work was "among the finest literature of his time" and whose expatriation therefore seemed "a very successful adventure." He also observed that Brooks' predisposition toward a hortatory literature, "one that acts directly upon public opinion by *advocation* rather than indirectly by example," made him hostile toward formal experimentation. But Josephson's apologies were overshadowed by his Brooksian conclusion that the "phenomenon of exile persists, today, as one of the secret maladies of American society."[50] By the 1930s, American critics had come to a consensus in their debate over expatriation. The search for independence that lured creative minds to Europe carried the enormous costs of involvement and efficacy. Striking a balance between freedom and participation proved difficult enough at home. Expatriation made it impossible.

CHAPTER 5

Women and the Critical Community

Some remarkable women converged in Greenwich Village in the 1910s and became a central presence in the radical politics, artistic flowering, and feminist insurgency of the period. Margaret Sanger, Mabel Dodge, Emma Goldman, Elizabeth Gurley Flynn, Henrietta Rodman, Mary Heaton Vorse, Crystal Eastman, Freda Kirchwey, Susan Glaspell, and Edna St. Vincent Millay, to name a diverse few, were all a part of the larger milieu in which the community of critics took shape. Friendships, temporary alliances, and lasting admiration linked together women and men of many different talents and aspirations into a more extensive network of social and vocational relationships than that with which I am primarily concerned here. It is striking, therefore, that so few of the women whose careers began or flourished in the same general environment that produced a Lippmann, Bourne, or Max Eastman chose criticism as their major line of work. In 1921, the novelist, playwright, and folklorist Mary Austin noted that whatever the term "intellectuals" meant abroad, "in the United States it stands for a small group of determinedly young and preponderately male persons, for the most part engaged in retrieving from the sum of human knowledge such facts as tend to show that we would all be much better off if society were quite other than it is. In the current periodicals where our American Intellectuals are actively in evidence," she continued, "it is noticeable that there are few women's names, and none that stand out as convincingly, femininely original."[1]

Why, as a rule, did women opt for imaginative literature or social and political activism instead of intellectual journalism, literary criticism, and related forms of expression? To raise this question is not to deny the contributions of full-time women critics such as Kirchwey, Elizabeth Shepley Sergeant, Edna Kenton, and Constance Mayfield Rourke, nor is it to deny that women poets, novelists, and activists produced important critical literature of their own. Rather, it is to inquire further into the concerns that pervaded the independent intellectual life, to ask how issues of gender came into play, and to investigate the role of women in the formation and character of the critical community.

1.

While male intellectuals rebelled against the universities for their failure to promote either self-expression or the proper forms of social engagement, their female counterparts had another target: the settlement houses. The settlement pioneers had rallied around the idea that their movement fused the individual's quest for a fulfilling life with the mission of what Jane Addams termed "social progress." In her famous lecture of 1892 on "The Subjective Necessity for Social Settlements," Addams argued that self-fulfillment came through self-sacrifice and drew the logical conclusion that "social and individual salvation" were identical. "We have in America a fast-growing number of cultivated young people who have no recognized outlet for their active faculties," Addams said. This waste of "young life," including the tendency of many to "dissipate their energies in so-called enjoyment," appeared to her "as pitiful as the other great mass of destitute lives." Meaningful work in the settlements seemed to answer the subjective need for gratification while harnessing self-fulfillment to the greater good of the community. Because "social obligation" was instinctual—"it begins with birth itself"—individual happiness and social concern were one and the same, subjective impulses served objective ends, and the settlement worker found joy in reaching out to humanity.[2] Here was the classic articulation of the intellectuals' ideal of unselfish self-expression.

Addams, of course, was particularly concerned with finding a path to fulfillment for women, for remedying the problem of "restricted and unhappy" female lives, and the generation of women that followed her continued Addams' search while redirecting it in significant ways. In contrast to many of the settlement pioneers, these younger women were less willing to forgo heterosexual relationships, marriage, or children for public involvements. The educational reformer Margaret Naumburg was married to Waldo Frank from 1916 to 1924. Crystal Eastman, Margaret Sanger, Mabel Dodge, and Freda Kirchwey all had children. Mary Heaton Vorse, one of the *Masses* circle and a friend of Naumburg, Sanger, and Dodge, was widowed twice by 1915 and supported her children by supplementing her labor articles with popular fiction. As Dee Garrison has written, "feminists of Vorse's age claimed the right to career, marriage, *and* motherhood. Unlike their older models, they did not want to purchase independence at the price of celibacy or childlessness."[3] The notable women of Addams' generation, it seemed to Vorse and others, had sacrificed their biological fulfillment—the genuine side of womanhood—in the quest to break free from the social and psychological restraints that barred women from experiences outside the domestic sphere. In challenging false constructs of femininity, they had repressed their essential femaleness. Crystal Eastman, Max's older sister, conveyed the generational distinction in 1918: "Feminists are not nuns. That should be established." Eastman had the example of a mother who successfully combined a career in the ministry with marriage and family. "I was just as passionately determined to have children as I was to have a career," Crystal explained in a 1927 *Nation* series of feminist reminiscences. "And my mother was the triumphant answer to all doubts as to the success of this double role." Susan Glaspell, who had stepchildren but no children of her own, spoke regretfully about this absence in her life: "Women say to one, 'You have your work. Your books are your children, aren't they? And you look at the diapers airing by the fire, and wonder if they really think you are like that.' "[4]

The decision to attempt this double role produced strains that the settlement generation had not generally experienced. "How to reconcile these two desires in real life, that is the question," Eastman wrote in an unpublished essay entitled "Pandora's Box, or What Is Your Trouble?" Sanger recorded in her diary a dream in which she saw her daughter playing and described her "sadness" that because of her work she "could not hold her" or "at least get closer to her." Freda Kirchwey, whose feminism was shaped by Eastman, Vorse, Marie Jenney Howe, Mary Simkovitch, and Henrietta Rodman at the famous Heterodoxy Club in Greenwich Village, agonized over the difficulty of splitting her time between her children and her work at the *Nation*. According to her biographer, Kirchwey "admitted" by the early 1930s "that her generation had not discovered the means to achieve the tenuous balance of career and family." Vorse, in a public confession titled "Why I Have Failed as a Mother," discussed the "terrible conflict" between the "basic need" for "love, a home, children" and "the passionate desire for independence." The commitment to motherhood, she argued, threatened both the freedom and the public commitments of the woman writer. Women "crave the experience of adventure as much as men," yet they are checked by domestic responsibilities, particularly toward their children. "All I want is to be let alone," Vorse explained. "I often dread to leave my workroom to meet their never-ceasing demands. They seem to me like a nestful of birds, their yellow beaks forever agape for me to fill."[5] In an atypically pessimistic conclusion to an article in the popular *Cosmopolitan* magazine, Vorse wondered whether the attempt to carve out a place in the world of adventure and experience while trying to raise children would condemn both efforts to failure. Despite moments of doubt, however, women who shared Vorse's outlook held to the belief that theirs was a more natural ideal of female self-fulfillment—one that recognized a distinction between artificial notions of what was properly feminine and the apparent realities of sex.

Addams and her contemporaries had failed on a second count as well, according to the next generation. By the 1910s, the social settlements no longer seemed to meet women's "subjective necessity" for a public role. They had hardened into a conventional channel for women's energies and now functioned to reinforce rather than upset the old ideology of separate spheres; they had merely recreated domestic havens in urban neighborhoods. Margaret Naumburg, recalling her decision to open the experimental Walden School, explained that any genuine "transvaluation of values" required a "fresh start, outside of all accepted institutions." No longer were the settlements suitable either to women's quest for self-fulfillment or to the complementary task of social reconstruction. They were stagnant and insular, concerned more with their own preservation than with developing productive ties to the community. "Well," Naumburg wrote, "like most pioneer organizations that have become institutionalized, their spirit has died. They belonged to a previous generation."[6] Implicit in this critique was the belief that the women of Addams' generation had sacrificed their biological fulfillment while neglecting to challenge in any meaningful way traditional conceptions of women's affectional and nurturing orientation. They had missed women's total experience while being at the same time too conventionally feminine in their ostensible rebellion against accustomed roles. Theirs was a false start.

2.

The rejection of the Addams model initiated the effort to define new modes of public involvement, but here again "women rebels" (as Margaret Sanger called them) encountered men's misgivings, including those of the young male intellectuals. Some of these misgivings took the familiar form of doubts about women's ability to transcend the emotive and intuitive. Yet male intellectuals had distinctive anxieties of their own about welcoming women into their fellowship on equal terms.

Women first had to overcome institutional obstructions to their full inclusion in the evolving intellectual community. For the most part, critical careers originated in the all-male Ivy League colleges, where intellectual camaraderie and identity centered around the literary magazines and socialist clubs. Apprenticeships in journalism depended on the patronage of established writers, editors, and publishers, most of whom were men and many of whom considered serious journalism a male career. The doctrine of spheres had an institutional incarnation in the bifurcated world of men's and women's publications, and men continued to control even such staples of domesticity as the *Ladies' Home Journal.* Louise Bryant needed the help of John Reed to obtain her first press credentials, and it was only through extraordinary persistence and courage that she made herself into a successful syndicated correspondent. Dorothy Day remembered that even Reed's *Masses* colleagues refused at first to grant that Bryant had "brains" of her own and "were constantly minimizing her." It was her daring frontline coverage of World War I and the Russian Revolution, along with the inspiration of her Russian friends Alexandra Kollantai and Maria Spiridonova, that finally allowed Bryant to emerge, in her biographer's words, "from the shadow of her famous poet-reporter husband."[7]

Joan Shelley Rubin, discussing Constance Rourke, has described the obstacle facing all women critics in the 1910s and 1920s—"the difficulty of being taken seriously at the outset." For the most part, "the literary woman's vocation" was confined to "scribbling 'women's books,' " "editing ladies' magazines," and "teaching at women's colleges." It may have been Rourke's Vassar teaching experience that gave her the confidence and the credentials needed for a woman to break into free-lance criticism.[8] The female support networks that historians have recently begun to explore represented in one sense an effort to counter the "old boy" networks through which Lippmann, Reed, Bourne, Stearns, Wilson, and other male intellectuals began their careers.[9]

Beyond these traditional disadvantages, women inclined toward criticism also confronted the ambivalence—and, at times, opposition—of their male contemporaries. Strong ties to feminists, women activists, poets, and novelists did not translate into a readiness on the part of male critics to encourage women to join their ranks. With their own pressing concerns about marginalization, they had an ideological predisposition against permitting women to discover new modes of self-fulfillment in the world of criticism. Whether or not the process of feminization was as real or complete as Ann Douglas has suggested, the idea that American culture was dangerously feminine had wide resonance among intellectuals in the early twentieth century. In describing women as obstacles to genius, H. L. Mencken sounded a common theme of his generation:

Women not only do not inspire creative artists to high endeavor; they actually stand firmly against every high endeavor that a creative artist initiates spontaneously. What a man's women folks almost invariably ask of him is that he be respectable—that he do something generally approved—that he avoid yielding to his aberrant fancies—in brief, that he sedulously eschew showing any sign of genuine genius. Their interest is not primarily in the self-expression of the individual, but in the well-being of the family organization, which means the safety of themselves.[10]

When women controlled the creative process, Mencken reasoned, either through their influence over men or by direct involvement, the usual result was respectable and therefore irrelevant art.

George Santayana made the first explicit association between women and an irrelevant American culture in "The Genteel Tradition in American Philosophy," given as a lecture at Berkeley in 1911 and published in *Winds of Doctrine* in 1913. Santayana anticipated Brooks in dividing the American mind into two parts, one "occupied intensely in practical affairs" and the other "float[ing] gently in the backwater." The failure of the intellect to make a difference in American life had to do with the fact that the "American Will" was "the sphere of the American man," while the "American Intellect" was "predominantly" the sphere "of the American woman." Brooks altered this into his idea of the two publics—"the cultivated public and the business public, the public of theory and the public of activity," the highbrow and the lowbrow. Again the dichotomy was phrased in terms of sex, with one public "largely feminine, the other largely masculine."[11] Socializing the intellect would involve defeminizing the life of the mind.

Brooks' followers, while endeavoring ultimately to subvert it, extended the use of this sexual metaphor to separate their own intellectual generation from the peripheral thinkers of the immediate past and to justify their pursuit of criticism as something new and meaningful. Lewis Mumford condemned William Dean Howells for his "prudence," "checks," and "elegances," which were "the marks of the spiritual castration which almost all his contemporaries had undergone." Noting the negative connotations of the term "intellectual," Harold Stearns asked, "[W]hy should it carry with it a faint aura of effeminate gentility?" He and his contemporaries, Stearns suggested, were living in an "Intellectual Eggshell Period" and were trying to free the American mind from "the anaemic, the feminine, and the fearful."[12] The belief that women and intellectuals were similarly cut off from genuine experience and social influence did not lead, in most cases, to a sense of common struggle. It is possible, as James Hoopes has suggested, that Brooks' "revolt" might have been "complementary rather than antagonistic to feminism."[13] But for Brooks, Mumford, Stearns, and many critics of their generation, the need to rescue the intellect from the taint of effeminacy took precedence over the effort to create an equal place for women. Feminization devalued the intellectual life as a path toward self-fulfillment for men; only its defeminization could make the critical endeavor wholly satisfactory.[14]

One did not have to be such an arch anti-feminist as Mencken to display a profound ambivalence about women's fight for equality. Mencken did women the service of granting them intelligence—"independent thought and resourcefulness," he called it—but proceeded to argue that they used this intelligence to ensnare men "for a lion's share" of their earnings: "The very ease with which she defies and swindles him in several capital situations of life is the clearest of proofs of her general superiority." He also dismissed the myth "that women are devoid of any sex instinct" while labeling birth-controllers and suffragists "pseudo-males" who ran

"no more risk of having unwilling motherhood forced upon them than so
many mummies of the Tenth Dynasty." As more women took up careers
outside the home, Mencken predicted, many would "begin to wonder
why they didn't let well enough alone."[15] Randolph Bourne, hardly the
acerbic opponent of social movements that Mencken was, took an equally
dim view of feminism in a portrait of an aspiring writer named "Karen."
Karen's "fling of feminism," Bourne wrote, destroyed her femininity.
The "stress of public life" made her "fierce and serious," and she now
appeared "hideous in mannish skirts and waists." Sacrificing her friendship with Bourne, she became "intimate with feminists whose feminism
had done little more for their emotional life than to make them acutely
conscious of the cloven hoof of the male."[16] Bourne's cosmopolitanism,
the spirit of toleration captured in "Trans-national America," ran aground
on the question of sexual equality; despite his attachment to feminism in
the abstract, he could endure neither the feminized culture he associated
with his New Jersey childhood nor the apparent effects on women of
participation in a different kind of culture. According to Bourne, the
intellectual life simultaneously ran the risk of emasculating men and
defeminizing women; while the sphere of the intellect had to contend
with the threat of feminization, women who tried too hard to liberate
themselves from the sphere of domesticity faced the danger of masculini-
zation.

Floyd Dell, another self-styled feminist, suggested the ambivalence of
a male intellectual confronting the women's movement. Unable or unwilling to conceive of women as a self-directed social and historical force,
Dell offered the strange claim that "the woman's movement of today is
but another example of that readiness of women to adapt themselves to a
masculine demand." In Dell's reasoning, men were "responsible for the
movement" because they now wanted "to find in woman a comrade and
an equal." The outward hostility of many men toward feminism Dell
explained as a device for making women work for their freedom. Men
had set the movement in motion and then opposed it because "what men
desire are real individuals who have achieved their own freedom," even if
in reality it was men who were the decisive actors on both sides of the
struggle.[17] For Dell, an idea that spilled over into decisive action was a
masculine idea, and the only imaginable kind of female self-fulfillment
was one that would be determined by and thus compatible with male
demands.

Max Eastman's feminism, which was shaped in large part by his sister, was never quite as peculiar as Dell's. Certainly his work for women's suffrage and his admiration for Crystal's public activism were sincere. But Eastman entertained curious ideas about women's place in the literary and artistic fields. His ideal woman, and Reed's as well, was what Lois Palken Rudnick has called "the embodiment of a male Oedipal fantasy" and what Eastman himself labeled the "mother postulate"—one who would nurture the creative talents of the male artist. Eastman gave this ideal its fullest expression in the portrait of Mabel Dodge, or "Mary Kittridge," in his 1927 novel *Venture*. Mary lives to love and inspire the novel's hero, Jo Hancock—an amalgam of Eastman and Reed—whose "overbearing impulse to attack the world with his own ego" grows and matures through her encouragement. In Eastman's view, Jo's need to plunge into the world is "the masculine principle—assuming for the moment that there is a masculine principle," while Mary is supposed to find sufficient satisfaction in serving as lover, mother, and muse. She ultimately acquiesces in the "time-honored female role" of being "a mother-premise to Jo's lively experiences" and sends him off more confident and secure into "real life."[18] Many intellectuals, including Mumford, Brooks, and Eastman himself, brought these conventional expectations into their marriages, even if their ideas and behavior were unconventional in other ways. They looked to their wives to provide the domestic support for their intellectual adventures. "More often than not," observed Matthew Josephson, "the sort of fellow who was ridden by his ambitions or anxieties about his writing or painting proved to be uxorious, needing the constant solace of some maternal female and frequently a woman older then [*sic*] himself."[19]

James Hoopes has said of Brooks that the purpose of gender stereotyping among male intellectuals was not to exclude women but to make culture a legitimate endeavor for men in a business civilization. As critics, they did encourage and praise the work of women poets, playwrights, and novelists. Yet the association of women with extraneous and ineffective ideas did not make the new community of critics a particularly inviting one for women. Dell admitted as much when he reflected on a decade of intellectual life in 1926. No longer so pleased that men were setting the terms, and aware that his generation had not entirely departed from its predecessors with regard to the equality of women, he wrote, "It was simply the old situation over again—we were running things, as usual."[20] The obsession of male critics with social impact made them noticeably nervous about inhabiting a feminine and correspondingly de-valued realm, and produced the conviction that their community, if not the larger literary world, should be a masculine one.

3.

The sense of generational passage implicit in the dissatisfaction with the settlements encouraged a variety of attempts to locate a new basis for women's self-fulfillment and social involvement. Margaret Sanger specifi-cally pointed to the equal participation of women in "the intellectual, artistic, moral and spiritual life of the world" when she delineated the social possibilities of birth control in 1920. Women freed from the bur-dens of involuntary motherhood, she predicted, would have "the oppor-tunity to keep abreast of the times, to make and cultivate a varied circle of friends, to seek amusements as suit their taste and means, to know the meaning of real recreation."[21] Sanger herself had traded a domestic sub-urban existence for the ferment of Greenwich Village, where she became an important presence in Mabel Dodge's salon and began to live the free and fulfilling life she anticipated for all women with the popularization of birth control. In 1914, Sanger followed the impulse toward independent journalism by launching the *Woman Rebel*, a magazine that even Max Eastman found too wildly radical.[22] Though the *Woman Rebel* was quickly suppressed by Anthony Comstock and his anti-vice crusaders, this was a crucial experience for Sanger, who moved on to discover more effective ways of spreading her ideas and changing the sexual practices of the American masses.

Women such as Sanger, who participated in the formation of the new intellectual community, shared with their male contemporaries the desire to reconcile thought and action, to do work that was fulfilling because it was both self-directed and socially meaningful. For these women, how-ever, the danger of marginalization was twofold. They faced exclusion from the center of American life not only as intellectuals but, more significantly, as women. "Not an infrequent temperament of the times," Nancy Cott has noted, the "longing of the pampered or the intellectual to be in touch with vital things was found among men as well as women and expressed in reactionary as well as rebellious politics, but for educated women in particular it was an expression of their alienation from the restricted genteel world conventionally allowed them." Sanger's early careers as a nurse and a suburban housewife gave subjective force to her observations about "woman's instinctive urge to freedom and a wider development."[23] It is possible that the stridency which Eastman condemned in Sanger grew out of a sense of this double exclusion, and it is certain that Sanger's yearnings for decisive influence drove her into kinds of practical activities that male counterparts like Eastman generally shunned.

The women with connections to the intellectual community recognized that the shared goals of independence and influence were even more elusive for them than for their male counterparts. Still confronting the doctrine of separate spheres and a range of obstacles to full participation in American society, women intellectuals fashioned their own methods of public involvement. Within the traditionally "feminine" field of imaginative literature, they crafted forms of expression that would break through the conventions of the Victorian cult of domesticity. And while male writers struggled against the limits of criticism, many women grew sufficiently impatient that they refused to confine themselves to literary pursuits as the preferred means of reconciling thought and action. Literature, like the settlements, after all, threatened to keep them within the bounds of the acceptable.

Sanger's advocacy of birth control quickly moved beyond the *Woman Rebel* and mere publicity; her initial confidence that the repeal of the obscenity laws would guarantee the movement's success gave way to more concrete projects. "I could no longer look upon it as a struggle for free speech," she recalled of her revised views after 1915, "because I now realized that it involved much more than talks, books, or pamphlets." The journalistic phase of her career represented a "feeble" effort "built on dreams and ideals." Though she founded the *Birth Control Review* in 1918 and ran it until 1928, and though she published several books about the movement in the 1920s and 1930s, Sanger's writing became a secondary part of her work. She expended much greater effort on organizing and sustaining the American Birth Control League, conducting conferences, accumulating data, opening clinics, mounting legal challenges, and lobbying legislatures. As early as 1919, she disavowed "drifting and waiting" in favor of "The Current of Activity."[24]

Crystal Eastman displayed a similar willingness to throw herself into organizational activities and political agitation—kinds of participation that engaged her brother only sporadically. Writing, which for Max was the essential pursuit, was only one phase of Crystal's involvements. A lawyer, she served on the New York Employer's Liability Commission and wrote a model workers' compensation law for the state in 1910. In addition to her constant work for women's suffrage, she was president of the New York Woman's Peace Party and helped organize the national party and the American Union Against Militarism. During the war, Crystal, Roger Baldwin, and Norman Thomas initiated the AUAM's Civil Liberties Bureau, predecessor to the ACLU.[25] It was not until 1918, when she and Max launched the *Liberator*, that Crystal dedicated most of her energies to intellectual journalism. After the magazine shut down in 1924, she wrote articles for the British and American feminist press— but largely because her husband, Walter Fuller, had moved to England and she was almost commuting between New York and London. According to Blanche Wiesen Cook, the five years before her death in 1928 were "marked by illness and an inability to find the steady and satisfying work for which she thirsted."[26]

The careers of two students of John Dewey capture the divergent concerns of the men and women who came to intellectual maturity in the Greenwich Village of the 1910s. Randolph Bourne's admiration for his teacher's educational theories inspired him to produce several important educational writings of his own, including *The Gary Schools*, a book based on observations about Deweyan ideas in practice in Indiana. It is significant, however, that Bourne did not extend this admiration beyond theory and observation into practice. Margaret Naumburg extended Dewey's influence in a different direction, creating her experimental school in 1914 and directing it as it grew into a complete elementary and secondary program. Naumburg recognized the limits of the seemingly endless expenditure of words on educational ideas if these words failed to penetrate the world of real children and real schools. In one of her few published writings, a series of dialogues between people observing or associated with the Walden School, she made a university student remark that "we're sick and tired of being fed so much on the theory of new education in our courses at the university, and then to see so little of it put into actual use anywhere."[27] When Paul Rosenfeld, who knew and wrote about both Bourne and Naumburg, reflected on Naumburg's work in *Port of New York*, he concluded, "The young directress is a sort of poet among the educators."[28] Every other essay in *Port of New York* discussed a writer, artist, or composer. For one as predisposed against institutional involvements and administrative responsibilities as Rosenfeld, it was both a great compliment and a revealing choice of words to call Naumburg a poet. He clearly admired her activism and the non-literary, yet still somehow poetic, direction of her work.

Among the stories of women's search for alternative forms of self-fulfillment and influence, the odyssey of Mabel Dodge, a significant figure in twentieth-century American cultural history, is one of the most intriguing and bizarre. In 1912, Dodge consciously took on the role of community-builder for people of ideas, putting together her "Evenings" at 23 Fifth Avenue to create a "sense of a spiritual home" for intellectuals. Dodge conceived of her salon as a place where the free exchange of ideas would encourage a sense of common identity and stimulate the transformation of thought into action. "When I came to New York to live last winter," she wrote in 1913, "it seemed to me that there were a great many interesting men and women, all thinking and doing different things, but there didn't seem to be any centralization, any place where all sorts of people could meet under one roof and talk together freely on all subjects."[29] In her mixing and matching of people, Dodge literally fused the intellect with the active life, thrusting writers and publicists into contact with radical activists. Sanger, Reed, Lippmann, Steffens, Hutchins Hapgood, Robert Edmond Jones, Mary Heaton Vorse, and Carl Van Vechten found themselves embroiled in discussions with Big Bill Haywood, Alexander Berkman, and Elizabeth Gurley Flynn. Dodge later recognized that the Evenings were part of a personal search for place and power following "several nervous crises" and the collapse of her first marriage; she even suggested that a case of tonsillitis "was testimony either to some lack of aspiration or of failure to achieve."

Moving and shaking the "movers and shakers" became a path toward meaningful experience. Her own role, however, remained conventional in the sense that she was primarily a facilitator of others' ideas and activities and that she engaged only secondarily in her own work. Dodge proudly recalled that in living with Reed she was able "to stimulate him to greater achievement in that world where men *do* things in order to prove themselves powerful to themselves." In both Reed and herself she recognized a thirst for influence that took precedence over the content of ideas; "I really didn't care much for his ideas," she admitted, "and neither did he in any ultimate way." Yet her preferred mode of influence, as Lois Palken Rudnick has documented, was indirect and frequently damaging

to herself and others—an influence over and through men like Reed.
D. H. Lawrence, who visited Dodge in 1922–23 after a period of correspondence, came to believe that a "terrible will to power," a need "to
compel life," was the driving force in her personality. Lawrence accused
her of using her patronage and hospitality to manipulate people, to engage
in "bullying and mischief." "I don't care a straw for your money and the
things you 'give'—," he wrote her after their falling-out, "because after
all it is on these you finally take your stand."[30]

In the winter of 1917, Dodge's search for a decisive place in the real
world drew her away from the intellectual community she had helped to
construct in New York. Earlier she had sent her husband, the artist
Maurice Sterne, to New Mexico; now he urged her to join him, appealing
to her desire for purpose. "Do you want an object in life?," he asked her.
"Save the Indians, their art-culture—reveal it to the world!"[31] In Taos,
Dodge came to repudiate intellection entirely, seeing it now as an insu-
perable barrier to direct experience. Her memoirs, a four-volume work of
extraordinary self-consciousness, reached the conclusion that thought was
an obstacle to life. The final volume, *Edge of Taos Desert*, began with
Dodge's declaration that she had "entered into a new life" and that she
"was done with reading any books for a long time." She subtitled the
book "An Escape to Reality," suggesting that her life in New York had
been unreal and hinting at the book's theme: that a "genuine and down to
rock-bottom" existence was possible only by willing away the intellect.
At last she had freed herself from the "ruthless, restless wordmongers"
who represented the "doom of our race." The purpose of the memoir,
Dodge announced, was to celebrate "this life of natural beauty and clarity
that had never been strained into Art or Literature," to proclaim her
discovery to those who persisted in "looking at life, not living it" and
"telling about it, not being it." Dodge's departure from the "dying world"
of excessive thinking and her long-awaited plunge into real life coincided
with her separation and divorce from Sterne and her marriage to Antonio
Lujan. Sterne, though younger than Lujan, "seemed old and spent and
tragic," a symbol of "the pretence and the artificialities" she "had always
lived with." Lujan, an American Indian, represented Dodge's realization
of the external world "with his power unbroken and hard like the carved
granite rock." Here was a man who "had a kind of direct knowledge,
unhindered by the need to think out things." Mabel Dodge's search for
an object in life and a guiding hand in the outside world ended in Taos

with Tony Lujan and the belief that the future lay with him, herself, and those "unworried by thinking." [32] The attempted annihilation of the intellect was certainly an extreme solution to the problem of marginalization, but Dodge's "escape to reality" was only an exaggerated version of a common endeavor; many women of her generation acted on the same sense of an enormous distance between themselves and the essence of American life.

Among those who did establish themselves as intellectual journalists, the thirst for experience led to encounters with reality as dramatic as any of John Reed's. Like Reed, Louise Bryant gave up poetry for direct contact with the major events of her time: the Great War and the Russian Revolution. In her account of the revolution, *Six Red Months in Russia*, Bryant portrayed herself as a humble reporter who unexpectedly witnessed an epochal moment and now assumed the task of conveying its significance to an uninformed or misinformed American public. "I who saw the dawn of a new world," she wrote, "can only present my fragmentary and scattered evidence to you with a good deal of awe. I feel as one who went forth to gather pebbles and found pearls." Elizabeth Shepley Sergeant experienced the war more viscerally than she could have ever imagined when she temporarily abandoned literary criticism to serve as a *New Republic* correspondent in France. Sergeant was badly injured on a tour of the battlefield at Mont Bligny when a companion picked up a live hand grenade; the explosion shattered both of Sergeant's ankles, and she spent the next six months in French hospitals. In her diary account of the experience, published in 1920, she observed her sudden entry into the masculine world of war: "I am lying on another mud floor, surrounded again by men, men. Perhaps I am the only woman in the world." Despite the pain, Sergeant confessed that she was "actually enjoying the adventure" and feeling that she had broken through to a deeper, more elemental reality than she had known before. "Mine is not more than a pin-point of sharp experience in the vast catastrophe. Yet its stab unites me to millions of other human beings." Later, when she had been installed in a special room at a Neuilly hospital, she regretted her removal from raw experience. She was now "aware what a vicarious version of 'life' " she was getting. "I am impatient to touch life again," she admitted, "to feel it swirling hard against my own body." Unlike Bryant, however, who spent the rest of her life looking for experiences as compelling and real as those of 1917–18, Sergeant returned to the United States and to literature. [33]

Yet it is Sergeant's equivalent of Dodge's "escape to reality," not her return, that seems to capture so vividly the urgent effort of women intellectuals to overcome the confines of conventional gender roles. Such urgency shaped the careers of those whose direct and sustained commitments to political and social causes made writing a secondary activity. It also entered into the work of women who were writers first and foremost. Describing the competing pulls of motherhood and career, Mary Heaton Vorse wrote, "The truth was I lusted for new experiences and new forms of work." In Vorse's case, the lust for significant experience produced a lifelong involvement with the cause of American labor; she was present as both sympathetic observer and union activist at almost every major strike from Lawrence in 1912 to Henderson, North Carolina, in 1959—reporting, speaking, and organizing. Freda Kirchwey, perhaps the most notable example of a woman of this generation for whom intellectual journalism was the primary activity, acknowledged the lure of tangible commitment when she reviewed Emma Goldman's autobiography in 1931. "She is contemptuous of any intellectualizing that stands in the way of faith and action," Kirchwey noted. "Always she feels first and thinks later—and less. . . . We may reject such satisfactions as immature, but some part of our being remains envious, feels itself 'petty and unblest'—and unfulfilled."[34]

There was an ironic convergence between Kirchwey's concerns about her distance from the life of action and the complaints of her male counterparts that literature carried the taint of effeminacy. Starting from extremely different positions, men and women intellectuals ended up in basic agreement that the literary life was too feminine. When men intellectuals voiced or otherwise conveyed their fear of being emasculated in a feminized realm, they were simultaneously speaking to the anxieties of the "New Woman" about remaining trapped in what they too perceived as an objectionably feminine sphere. The socially activist careers that many women intellectuals pursued—some permanently, others only briefly—reflected the impulse to reach beyond the merely literary into the traditionally masculine sphere of making things happen or at least experiencing them deeply and directly. While the male intellectuals sought to purge literature of its feminine connotations by participating in a more forceful, socially engaged, and realistic kind of criticism, their women contemporaries tended to favor non-literary pursuits, or non-literary journalism, in an attempt to free themselves from the confines of traditional feminine roles; the women who wrote criticism agreed that it needed the savor of reality and social fact to be worth the effort. In a curious way, then, an accommodation of purposes was achieved.

There was, however, an additional irony in the attempt to defeminize the intellectual life. By committing themselves to a more immediate public role than that occupied by most of the professoriate, independent intellectuals opened themselves up to the criticism that they were popularizers rather than original thinkers. The fear of being mere journalists was, as we have seen, omnipresent. What could the generalist be but a popularizer when specialized research was becoming increasingly synonymous with innovative knowledge? The charge of unoriginality is one with which women intellectuals, from both inside and out of the academy, have long had to contend. In describing what she calls "the class system of the intellect," Berenice A. Carroll speaks of the "workers, male and female, who labor in the fields doing the dirty work of so-called 'routine,' 'derivative' research and scholarship, teaching the masses, and 'popularizing' the great ideas."[35] If the effort to be public intellectuals was in some sense an attack on a detached, impotent, effeminate intellectual life, then what the male critics constructed as an alternative represented an escape only into a different "feminine" trap. For the labels of popularizer and journalist created an unanticipated and unseen bond between them and the many generations of women intellectuals who have been dismissed or ignored according to political and gender-based criteria.

CHAPTER 6

Education and the
New Basis for Community

The difficulty of reconciling free expression and socially productive endeavor—the difficulty that defined the independent intellectual life and
gave coherence to the community of free-lance critics—was more than a
private problem for intellectuals. In this and the next two chapters, I
want to suggest some of the connections between the critics' conceptions
of their own communal project and their pronouncements on more general issues of education, morality, and the American past. My intention
is not to argue that their vocational concerns were the sole determinant of
their public positions. But it is my contention that their analyses of the
place of the intellectual and their projections of a more viable intellectual
life intersected with their broader critique of American institutions and
traditions. To say that they brought personal interests to bear on public
matters is not to question their motives or raise doubts about their integrity. If anything, the sense of a personal stake made their writing more
passionate and their search for alternative institutions and traditions more
sincere.

The centrality of education in the critics' definition of their own
vocation made their interest in the subject a natural one. They fashioned
a role for themselves that was essentially pedagogical in that they resisted
the direct exercise of power as administrative experts and chose instead to
engage the public in a kind of collective learning process. Meanwhile,
their critique of higher education led some independent intellectuals deeper

into the problem of American schooling, and while they despaired of the universities, they held out hope for reform at the lower levels. This was particularly true of Randolph Bourne, who managed to maintain through most of his career an uneasy balance between generationalism and hero-worship of John Dewey.[1] In much of their work, Bourne and his contemporaries sought a non-coercive means toward establishing an alternative individualism and a communal sensibility in modern America at large. Educational reform was an attractive possibility, since it offered the opportunity to catch children before they were corrupted by the attitudes and demands of a Puritan-capitalist-industrial civilization.

1.

As America's outstanding educational philosopher at a time when education was the prescription for almost every social ill, Dewey was certain to gain a degree of notoriety. But Bourne contributed to Dewey's growing reputation as a spokesman for social renewal. Lawrence Cremin has noted Bourne's role at the *New Republic* in generating a "nationwide interest" in Deweyan education, and it was Bourne's phrasing of his mentor's educational philosophy that set forth most forcefully the redemptive potential of the new education.[2] So taken was he by this vision of ideas as catalysts for social change that Bourne did not subject Dewey's assumptions to critical scrutiny until their differences over the war led him to reassess his earlier infatuation. When he collected his education essays for publication in 1917, Bourne wrote of his "enthusiasm for the educational philosophy of John Dewey" and frankly conceded that his own role had been that of popularizer rather than critic. What, he asked, was "a good philosophy for except to paraphrase?" Bourne's awestruck response to the sight of theory blossoming into meaningful action also helps to explain the uncritical manner in which he reported on the Gary, Indiana, schools. He marveled at William Wirt, the Gary superintendent and an older Dewey disciple, who had managed to be "at once a social engineer and educational philosopher." In Bourne's lucid prose, Dewey's belief in the vast possibilities of educational innovation received its most dramatic statement. "To decide what kind of school we want," Bourne declared, "is almost to decide what kind of society we want."[3]

The vital task of education for Bourne, as it had been for Dewey since 1895, was to engender a social sensibility while engaging the interest of the pupil. Traditional education, they agreed, stifled self-expression without fostering any compensatory devotion to communal well-being. But Bourne's version of the critique of the old education was characteristically more personal and visceral than Dewey's. His first piece for the *New Republic* recounted a visit to his old high school, where he found a young teacher and a bored class suffering under the burdens of bankrupt methods. Bourne faulted the system rather than its victims, who cooperated in "making the best of a bad bargain" and in "slowly putting the hour out of its agony." The teacher and most of the students placidly accepted "the ritual of education" as something "inevitable," to be endured rather than challenged. The only resistance Bourne observed was the desperate behavior of the so-called " 'bad' children," such as the boy who sharpened his pencil down to nothing for want of better stimulation. This action, said Bourne, "had a sort of a symbolic quality; it was assertion against a stupid authority, a sort of blind resistance against the attempt of the schoolroom to impersonalize him." From Bourne's perspective, the environment of the classroom conspired to "demagnetize" the students, to divert healthy curiosity into meaningless activity or "inert" obedience.

"In a Schoolroom" echoed Dewey in dismissing traditional education for erecting artificial barriers to self-expression and in arguing that these barriers, in turn, undermined education's socializing function. Like Dewey, Bourne lashed out at the formal arrangement of the classroom as an emblem of this anti-social orientation. Seated at "stiff little desks, equidistantly apart, and prevented under penalty from communicating with each other," the students "existed for the teacher alone" rather than operating as "a network or a group." The results of such a warped environment were docility, "bumptiousness and diffidence," and the real harm was that these "great enemies" of a social sensibility were cultivated in the "most impressionable years." Foolish educational methods contaminated American society, producing stunted human beings incapable of thinking and acting in a socially responsible manner.

As always, Bourne reflected on his own position in rejecting the accepted rules of pedagogy: "Was I a horrible 'intellectual,' to feel sorry that all this animation and verve of life should be perpetually poured out upon the ephemeral, while thinking is made as difficult as possible, and the expressive and intellectual child made to seem a sort of monstrous pariah?"[4] His answer was no: that self-expression was not merely an intellectual problem, that nobody profited from an antiquated system which discouraged individual initiative and defeated social progress, and that everybody would benefit from educational reform in the Deweyan mode. Whatever was happening in his old school and in others like it, Bourne concluded, was not education. According to Dewey's criteria, this kind of schooling was a complete failure. Its inattention to the psychological imperatives of childhood and its concomitant disregard for the needs of society meant that solving the fundamental problem of modern education demanded new theories and new methods. By linking the repressive atmosphere of the traditional school with its apparent failure to promote social improvement, progressive theorists were prepared to offer an alternative pedagogy that denied the incompatibility of self-fulfillment and social good.

2.

The key word in the progressive educational vocabulary was "natural," and any method that ran counter to nature was an obstruction to genuine education. Under the biosocial conception of mind, the mere imparting of information could not produce knowledge. Learning could not occur through the external presentation of facts by the teacher to the student. Only when the student had a direct interest in a problem, only when ideas arose out of natural circumstances could it be said that learning was taking place.[5] Education, therefore, required a recognition of the interests of the individual. Bourne followed Dewey in arguing that natural interest rather than compulsion had to serve as the basis for learning. "Anything else," he bluntly put it, "may produce, at its best, a trained animal." Only when the school cultivated these interests did the child stand a "chance of being more than a nerveless mediocrity." Bourne treated discipline as an element of self-expression, parroting Dewey's pronouncement that "[i]t is hardly necessary to press the point that interest and discipline are connected, not opposed." As Bourne phrased it, "It is meaningless to talk of interest *vs.* discipline when all real interest has an organizing effect on one's activity, and any real discipline is built up on a foundation of interest."[6] The only effective discipline was self-discipline —and in a particularly benign form, since it functioned in the service of self-fulfillment.

Attention to the child's instincts and impulses covered the personal dimension of the educational process but left unresolved the problem of coordinating the personal and social components. The concept of interest, however, seemed to preclude self-expression from veering off in anti-social directions. Genuine interest existed only as a relation between individuals and their world and was not a finite quality; it could not stop with ephemeral satisfactions. Once a goal was realized, it became the means toward further accomplishment. Interest engendered more interest and led the individual deeper into the world.[7]

In this sense, even a child's interests naturally tended toward social knowledge. In the pristine preschool years, children began to investigate the relations of their social environment through play, testing in a rudimentary manner the results of their own actions on their surroundings. From Dewey's theories of knowledge and interest, Bourne concluded that schools must not intrude upon children's "pushing wills and desires and curiosities." Through trial and error, by "following their curiosities," they learn "as their life makes demands upon them." School should not interrupt a process which, Bourne agreed, was already under way in infancy. "All their education," he wrote, "is really acquired in the same random way that the baby learns to control his movements and respond to his environment." All genuine learning occurred as children's impulses carried them further and further out into social situations, where their minds and interests developed in a continuing effort to solve problems in a manner that would most benefit themselves and others. In short, interest could be trusted to foster discipline and to stimulate social awareness.[8]

3.

If learning was a natural process, if discipline and self-fulfillment were complementary, if interest automatically guided children into social concern, what then were the functions of the school and the educator? Though their dictatorial roles had evaporated under the logic of an interest-based education, progressive teachers and administrators still faced an enormous task. Odd as it might seem, the natural process of learning could no longer occur naturally. At one time, children had been assured of satisfying their curiosity by engaging in a variety of concrete communal activities. In a smaller world, where opportunities to satisfy interests emerged out of the child's immediate experience, it was easier to follow the connections between the self and society; the child had to comprehend a relatively limited sphere of social relations. With specialization and the separation of children from regular contact with the productive work of their society, the modern world had reduced the chances for learning in the course of daily life. Meanwhile, individuals functioned now within a greatly enlarged social universe. Once upon a time children had received a natural education through the experience of living as members of a small-scale productive community. On the farm, nature rather than human authority determined the tasks at hand; the land itself produced the impetus to work. But there was no use in bemoaning the loss of something unrecoverable, and alternatives would have to serve. As Bourne pointed out, "Life can no longer be trusted to provide this education; the school must substitute."[9]

Since the child's environment was no longer natural, schools had to step in and compensate. Bourne took from Dewey the idea that the *creation* of a natural environment was the primary concern of progressive education. Their ideal teacher was both a scholar and a psychologist, capable of constructing a course of learning that was compatible with the interests of the individual child and that produced a natural accumulation of valuable knowledge. "Let the teacher cleverly supervise and coordinate," Bourne summarized, "see that the children's interests are drawn out, and that what they do contributes to their growth." In an essay entitled "The Self-Conscious School," Bourne made clear the challenge of generating an environment in which spontaneous interests could grow in their normal social direction. Natural development required a self-conscious school in which "the child's own curiosity sets the cue, and the school's work is to provide manifold opportunities for the satisfaction of that curiosity."[10]

The problem with imagining an activist role for progressive educators was that the creation of the self-conscious school not only had to appear natural but had to *be* natural. Otherwise, the school would fall into the old practice of trying to impose interest instead of encouraging it. To avoid the appearance of intrusiveness, Bourne joined Dewey in using language that minimized the authoritative role of teachers even as they insisted on their importance. No longer the "direct preceptor," said Bourne, the teacher became the "helper," the "guide and mentor" who provided the "best possible environment" for "freedom of expression and spontaneity." While the school became a "controlled environment," this control emanated from the perceived interests of the children and served merely to "strike the electric contact of curiosity and response" and to "get experiences that thrill with meaning for them." There was, Bourne took pains to point out, a middle way between rigid, artificial methods and a random, laissez-faire approach. At the Gary schools, for example, "Things are neither forced" on the student "nor aimlessly selected." Dewey considered it a fallacy "that we have no choice save either to leave the child to his own unguided spontaneity or to inspire direction upon him from without." By observing the child, the teacher could choose the means by which self-expression would develop in ways that were natural but that nonetheless demanded the wisdom of the trained educator. "A sympathetic teacher is quite likely to know more clearly than the child himself what his own instincts are and mean," Dewey wrote. "But the suggestion must *fit in* with the dominant mode of growth in the child; it must serve simply as stimulus to bring forth more adequately what the child is already blindly striving to do." This notion of guidance allowed Dewey and Bourne to reconcile the radical innovations of progressive education with an unimpeachable commitment to self-expression. Their call upon teachers was "by indirection to direct," to furnish the conditions necessary for children to achieve the "culmination of themselves."[11]

Bourne gave educational theorists the job of teaching the teachers how to guide the child's interest "so that it will be purposeful" and how to make the school "a sifter where children unconsciously as they live along from day to day are choosing the ways in which they can best serve both themselves and their community." Conscious planning for unconscious choices was a precarious proposition, but Dewey's and Bourne's unwillingness to dictate specific educational agendas did not prevent them from suggesting in broad outline the ways in which schools could facilitate the process of natural growth. Directing children's interests into the normal social channels required the removal of all barriers between the school and community; schools, Dewey insisted, had to "reproduce the conditions of real life." By reconstructing the school as a "child-community," by making the school environment a natural one, progressive educators would accomplish the twofold task of engaging the spontaneous interests of the children and guaranteeing that these interests were socially constructive. When the school became society in miniature, children would have the "chance to test all impulses and tendencies in the world of things and people" and thus to develop those impulses that were socially beneficial while weeding out, on their own, those that were not.[12] The responsibility of the progressive school was both simple and enormous: to introduce, in step with the individual's evolving interests, a series of concrete situations that would bear out an expanding network of social relations. Education meant a growing sense of the wholeness, the interrelatedness, of all knowledge and all life.

Bourne's report on the Gary schools, in a case-study approach that could not fully conceal the author's enthusiasm, traced the flowering of spontaneous interest into social concern from early childhood to young adulthood. Bourne praised the combination of elementary and secondary education under one roof for impressing upon the students the "unity in length" of their "school life." Without the disruptive and artificial breaks between grammar school, junior high, and high school, learning flowed forward smoothly, and children gained a healthy "disregard for boundaries" that complemented their sense of the unity of knowledge and the connection of self and society. Unity "in breadth" came from the scrapping of traditional subject matter and a new emphasis on the organic quality of learning and knowledge. History and geography were taught together. Physiology went with zoology. English and math came in everywhere—physics, history, carpentry, home economics—with English teachers roving from class to class as their tools were needed. Bourne found significance in the physical arrangement of Wirt's schools, taking his readers on a tour of the second floor of the Froebel School and pointing out the juxtaposition of classrooms, a pottery studio, laundry, physics laboratory, drawing room, "music and expression studios," conservatory, and botany laboratory. This, according to Bourne, served to draw out the students' latent interests and to get them to see for themselves, through their school environment, the interconnectedness of all their studies and activities. For the younger children, windows and glass doors helped arouse "their curiosity" and their "ambition to work at these interesting activities in which they see the older children engaged."[13]

The vocational orientation of Wirt's schools did not evoke from Bourne his usual pronouncements on a spiritless, materialistic, acquisitive America. The wonderful spectacle of a city putting John Dewey's ideas into practice led him instead toward an admiring interpretation of this vocational emphasis. He saw the Gary experiment not as an early training of children for work in American industry but as "a sort of unconscious prevocational school in which the child tries out his interests and powers." Here, Bourne believed, the child rather than the industrial regime determined the course of education. Here, too, vocational education shed its connotations of narrowness. Students came to their callings after exposure to a wide range of activities, and they left school, therefore, with a clear idea of the place of their work in the larger social scheme. By erasing the distinction between what Dewey and Bourne called "cultural" and "utilitarian" education, moreover, the Gary schools removed the possibility of dividing students and arranging curricula along class lines. "All the subjects are taught, as far as possible, in concrete ways which shall draw upon familiar experience and teach the child by making him do something," Bourne remarked in language that implied a degree of force that he actually believed unnecessary and abhorrent. Reconstituting the school as a "self-sustaining community" which attempted to replicate the productive work of "the outside world" did not imply the perpetuation of a competitive society built upon unfulfilling lives. The Gary schools, as Bourne presented them, created opportunities for the unimpeded expansion of "self-activity" into kinds of work that would "enhance the life of the social community."[14] An environment that put children together in activities that attracted and enlarged their interests, that allowed them to learn the social meaning of these and other activities, that broke down the boundaries between the child and the world and between the school and society, was something worthy of celebration. Bourne had looked for and found proof that free expression was the way toward social redemption, though it took a considerable amount of unconscious finesse to make Wirt's innovations appear natural and unintrusive.

4.

Had Bourne brought his critical skills to bear on the Gary schools, he might have foreseen some of the problems of Dewey's ideas in practice and anticipated his wartime critique. Instead, he succumbed to the same kind of wishful thinking that he later derided in Dewey's pro-war stance; in Gary, he saw what he wanted to see and ignored the rest. For example, Bourne praised Wirt's "platoon" system for its apparent flexibility and attention to individual needs and interests. Yet the system, which shuttled children between rooms to maximize the use of facilities, was designed as much for efficiency as for natural growth. Wirt conceived of himself as an expert administrator in charge of an "improved school machine" which would cut costs, eliminate waste, and maximize production.[15] Bourne's conclusion that the Gary Plan was antithetical to corporate-industrial values simply glossed over the scientific management side of Wirt's agenda. Moreover, his claim that the Gary schools had closed the gap between cultural and utilitarian education and risen above class discrimination was patently false. A General Education Board report that came out in the same year as Bourne's book found that the predominantly immigrant student body of the Froebel School (the school which Bourne praised unabashedly) was "consistently channeled into manual training and industrial education." Froebel "offered substantially fewer academic courses" than the schools with native-born majorities. It is remarkable that Bourne, the critic of Anglo-Saxon domination and the theorist of cultural pluralism, withheld comment on Gary's program for the rapid assimilation of immigrants to middle-class Anglo-Saxon norms. According to Ronald D. Cohen and Raymond A. Mohl, there were competing impulses at work in Gary, but Wirt himself was devoted to "elitist purposes—Americanizing immigrant children and adults, molding docile workers and citizens, manipulating students for the purposes of an orderly society." Recognizing only the benign aspects of the system, Bourne missed an early opportunity to examine the consequences of a skewed or half-baked application of Dewey's theories. In this case, he neglected to apply pragmatic standards of judgment and ended up presenting the wish as fact.[16]

Bourne also failed to provide a critical assessment of Dewey's *Democracy and Education*, which appeared in 1916 and marked a subtle but important shift in emphasis. While Dewey's call for an environment that would "organize" impulses did not necessarily signal a departure from his previous educational writings, his repeated warnings about the anti-social possibilities of unchecked spontaneity did represent a new twist to his thought. He had never trusted "the accidents of circumstance." He had never advocated leaving "everything to nature," except in the sense that purposeful human intervention could be a part of the evolutionary process. But Dewey now wrote much more forcefully of the importance of guiding children away from negative habits of mind and destructive patterns of behavior. He placed increased emphasis on the school as a "*simplified* environment," charged with the task of "weeding out what is undesirable." This would complement its more positive function as a broadening environment which offered the "opportunity to escape from the limitations" of narrow social groupings such as family, religion, race, and ethnicity. He also invoked the word "control" with greater frequency, careful to avoid any implications of external force but equally concerned about the potential for disorder. Control was the process of discouraging the wrong interests while encouraging the right ones by manipulating the child's surroundings. "The basic control," he observed, "resides in the nature of the situation in which the young take part." A "social direction of disposition" required the provision of the kinds of "joint or shared situations" that would prevent the formation of anti-social dispositions. Dewey could continue to call this "internal control" by claiming its compatibility with the dominant social interests of the individual.[17]

Throughout *Democracy and Education*, Dewey tried to minimize what was, after all, an extraordinary grant of power to educators. His use of the passive voice helped to conceal this fact; he may have employed it unconsciously as a way of avoiding uncomfortable confrontations with the authority he was placing in the hands of educators. In the end, however, his faith in an enlightened pedagogy was the only check on abuse. Dewey was capable, too, of obscuring the unpleasant implications of his ideas by resorting to understatement. "In last analysis," he said in a remarkable example of the language of minimization, "*all* that educators can do is modify stimuli so that response will as surely as is possible result in the formation of desirable intellectual and emotional disposi-tions." Significantly, he spoke now of education as "*re*-direction" rather than "indirection."[18]

The point here is not to suggest that Dewey was a latent authoritarian. He was not.[19] Yet the ambiguities in his prose and his deepening concerns about "capricious" expression raised the possibility of a more coercive kind of progressive pedagogy that placed efficient technique ahead of the critical determination of ends. Of all Dewey's disciples, Bourne was the best prepared to point out and clarify these ambiguities and to suggest the dangers implicit in Dewey's less lucid remarks about social control. *Education and Living* came out after *Democracy and Education*, in the same month that the United States entered the war. Aside from minor revi-sions, however, Bourne published his education essays as they had origi-nally appeared. He introduced the collection with his spirited tribute to Dewey, referring to the master's ideas as "truisms" which needed adver-tisement and nothing more. Even in 1917, Bourne mentioned neither the problem of anti-social interests nor the potential distortion of Dewey's ideas into a technique for efficient assimilation. In "Class and School," first published in that year, he held to his belief in a natural spilling-over of curiosity into social good—in an automatic progress from personal interest to communal welfare, given a more natural school environment. Out of schools and curricula dedicated to "interest and intelligent enthusiasm" would "issue the self-sustained discipline by which all good work is done in the world."[20] For the time being, Bourne clung to the faith that Dewey's educational theory was as much a program for personal freedom as for social reform.

Only after Dewey announced his support for American participation in the war did Bourne come to see the evasions in his theory and the propensity of his followers to adopt dangerous means to vacuous ends. "Dewey, of course," Bourne commented in October 1917, "always meant his philosophy . . . to start with values. But there was always that unhappy ambiguity in his doctrine as to just how values were created, and it became easier and easier to assume that just any growth was justified and almost any activity valuable so long as it achieved ends." Retrospectively, Bourne found that Dewey had unwittingly created a carte blanche for social engineers to operate as if in compliance with individual interests and genuine critical discussion. It took the war for him to discover Dewey's vagueness about what constituted social aims and the potential dangers in his determination to direct individuals toward such ambiguous goals, even though these problems had already surfaced in Dewey's *Democracy and Education*. It also took the war for Bourne to realize that his true sympathies lay with William James rather than with John Dewey. Finding himself pitted against the engineers of war, he returned to "the spirit of William James"—to James' belief that the good society could only be built upon "freedom of speculation," a "gay passion for ideas," and "creative desire."[21] Bourne never came to believe that free expression and social regeneration were mutually exclusive. But the war brought the realization that without a full and clear determination of purpose the quest for social good ran the risk of stifling individuality. His intellectual alliance with Dewey had rested in large part on their shared desire for harmony between the individual and society. Bourne's unwillingness to criticize Dewey before the war meant that the disagreement, when it came, was especially traumatic. Without his earlier idolatry, the "Twilight of Idols" would not have been so sudden and painful.

5.

After the war, several writers of Bourne's generation who took on the subject of education tried again to establish the confluence of self-fulfillment and social good. Often this entailed a continued evasion of the conflicts and contradictions experience had exposed in the progressive gospel. In *Were You Ever a Child?*, first published as a series of articles in the *Liberator*, Floyd Dell made a "plea for the New Education" that largely rehashed the old ideas of Dewey and Bourne. Once more the re-creation of "the real world on a smaller scale" was the key to the conjunction of an unbounded individuality and a regenerated society. The new school would be a place for children to "observe, touch, handle, take apart and put back together again, play with, work with, and become master of"—a place in which they would "learn to be efficient and happy human beings" who could then venture forth "into the great world outside without any abrupt transition." Dell, too, treated books as servants and adjuncts which entered the child's education only when direct contact with reality was impossible. But *Were You Ever a Child?* went beyond Dewey and Bourne in its articulation of what Lawrence Cremin has called a "sentimental pedocentrism." In contrast to the Deweyan faith in growth, Dell posited a kind of stasis as the end of education. "The object of a genuine democratic education," he announced, was to allow the student "to remain always a child." Childhood was a time of expansiveness, spontaneity, and curiosity which, if preserved indefinitely and universally, would produce a society of creative, expressive, fulfilled individuals. By enabling the realization of "one's own creative wishes, one's own dreams," by permitting the "natural expressions" of the child's "creative impulses," the new education would lay the foundation for a new world of the "free and happy."

For Dell, education was less a process of redirection or indirection than of non-direction; he completely minimized the role of the educator. "We no longer seek to educate the child," he wrote. "[W]e only attempt to give him the opportunity to educate himself." Dell offered a scheme of self-realization and social renewal that willed away the tensions between individual freedom and communal welfare by conceiving of every individual as an artist—the ideal citizen for whom work was play, for whom free expression was constructive labor, for whom natural instincts and social purpose were identical. Much more romantic than any of Bourne's writings on education, *Were You Ever a Child?* had to go to extreme lengths to salvage the connection that the war had unravelled between the individual's interests and society's demands.[22]

Others were not as willing as Dell to proclaim absolute faith in the goodness of instinct and impulse, but neither were they willing to accept any trace of coercion in the educational process. Harold Rugg, a professor at Columbia's Teachers College and a friend of Waldo Frank, Paul Rosenfeld, and others in the old *Seven Arts* group, included among the "articles of faith" of the new education the "[f]reedom to develop naturally, to be spontaneous, unaffected, and unselfconscious." On the other hand, he pointed out in *The Child-Centered School,* few would advocate that "the entire work of the school be based solely upon" the "naive and spontaneous interests of children." Rugg's solution was to reassert the efficacy of group activities in bringing out the inevitable social interests of the child. "The new school bridges the gap . . . between the development of individuality on the one hand and successful social participation on the other," he wrote, "by insisting that the true development of the individual and the fulfillment of personality are best attained as one expresses himself most successfully and adequately *with* others and *toward* others."[23] This kind of rhetorical finesse, however, was as evasive as anything Dell had to say about creative impulse and a society of liberated individuals. The advocates of child-centered education failed to deepen their analysis of the connections between self-fulfillment and social good, and repeated instead the phrases of prewar theorists who had not had occasion to confront the strains in their ideas.

It was this same wish to preserve the old harmony between "the expansion of many-sided individuals" and a "vital and varied social group" that led Margaret Naumburg in 1928 to criticize Dewey's educational work even as she borrowed his terminology. Naumburg concluded that her mentor's methods ultimately ignored the individual; they had "gradually been transformed into an effort to train children into a realization of their social responsibilities for citizenship" instead of functioning to encourage "the individual capacities and tastes of the children." Because Dewey viewed the emotions, the subjective impulses, as the product of action and objective fact, Naumburg argued, he ignored the significance of these personal impulses and "always subordinated" individual preferences "to a social plan." What she called "the reconstruction of education" had to take as its premise the importance of "each personality" and of "independent growth and expression." She was certain that "spiritual renewal" would come from "some creative expression of personalized values." But Naumburg, like Rugg, qualified her enthusiasm for the unrestricted freedom of the child. She dismissed "the extremists of uncontrolled self-expression" as naive reincarnations of Rousseau and blasted educators who tended "to exaggerate the aspect of self-expression and forget that in full creation significant standards must also be maintained."[24] Here again was the dilemma. Committed to protecting "the values of the individual rather than those of the herd," convinced that this commitment held the key to "a transformation of the American scene," Naumburg also believed in the need for direction. Her way out was the familiar one of imagining a kind of guidance so benign, so beautifully attuned to each individual, that it seemed at last as if free expression flowed automatically into socially productive channels. Among the experiments in enlightened pedagogy at Naumburg's Walden School was to bring in Lewis Mumford, Hendrik Van Loon, and Ernest Bloch to teach English, history, and music.[25]

The war diverted Bourne's attention away from education, and it is impossible to know how he would have rephrased his ideas had he survived into the 1920s. Those of his associates who did write on education after 1918 held to the belief that coercion was not an inevitable part of the educational process. Bourne, too, might have moved to the child-centered view, with its willing-away of institutional intrusions; certainly his discoveries of 1917–18 only bolstered his faith in the fully developed personality as the vital component of a healthy society. More likely, he would have attempted to connect his educational theories to a broader set of ideas about the nature of decision-making and the need for a revitalized public discourse. For Dell, Rugg, and Naumburg, the war may have strengthened the resolve to shield the individual from external control, but it did not lead them to pit self-expression against social renewal. Even after such a jarring experience, to admit the incompatibility of the needs of the individual and the best interests of society was inconceivable. The control necessary for a revived sense of community had to originate in an education defined as the growth of creativity and the blossoming of self-fulfillment into social sympathy.

Progressive education's future, at any rate, did not really belong to generalists like Bourne and Dell, or Greenwich Village free spirits like Naumburg. It belonged instead to a new kind of educational expert, trained in the latest theories and eager to put them into practice on a wide scale. In 1919, with the founding of the Progressive Education Association, a movement that had begun as a revolt against institutions created its own central organization and embarked on the paradoxical enterprise of setting guidelines for teachers and schools while continuing to insist on complete flexibility. Even as it tried to remain open in its statements of principles and procedures, the PEA by the late 1920s was an established professional body governed by an executive board and subdivided into a number of commissions and committees.[26] What Bourne would have thought of these developments can only be a matter for speculation. But given his sharp sense of irony and his angry critique of Dewey, it is likely that he would have found in the PEA another example of values and vision subordinated to technique. For Bourne's type of intellectual, the idea of fostering self-expression and social cohesion through systematic or bureaucratic innovation was too contradictory to be taken seriously. Naumburg wrote in 1930 of the "dull and gloomy picture" that Dewey's "technological utopia" suggested "to those of us who still hope for a richer and socially balanced individualism—the flowering of a more equitable society." From the fringes of the movement, she refused to abandon the belief that the "process of correlating the individual and society" could be "an opportunity for mutual sustenance" rather than an acceptance "of conflict and opposition."[27]

Eight years later, Lewis Mumford indicated that progressive education still had not become the exclusive province of the professionals. Mumford placed the progressive school at the physical and cultural center of his new regional city. "The School as Community Nucleus" was the title he gave to the section of *The Culture of Cities* in which he argued that the "reawakening of purposive group life" demanded a "full-time school taking stock of and taking part in the whole life of the neighborhood, the city, the region." Mumford's concept of education, although tempered by a more critical view of human nature and defined as part of a larger regional reorientation, matched Dewey's and Bourne's in its expansiveness. The "instruments of modern education," he wrote, "are continuous with life itself." The school had to transcend the "mere building" and extend outward into participation in the "industrial processes" of the community and region, and into "visual and tactile explorations of the environment." Meanwhile, to combat mere vocationalism, Mumford called for a reordering of the industrial processes and the environment themselves. An "effort must be made," he argued, "to develop the flexible and many-sided personality of the amateur, rather than the vocationally nar-rowed capacities of the specialist." Education, therefore, had to be seen as an organic process by which the school expanded into the city and the city itself functioned as "the wider school of the young and the university of the adult."[28] Mumford's own life and work stood as the implicit model for the free-ranging amateurs of the regionalized world, while the city had been the real university of his young adulthood.

Recasting education as organic, continuous, participatory, and trans-generational meant that the cultivation of a truer individuality and the regeneration of society were once again complementary rather than antag-onistic. Mumford placed educational reform within a richly detailed prophecy of social, economic, and political transformation. Yet he clearly saw education as the vital mechanism for change—the natural process by which "open inquiry and co-operative discipline" combined "to make over reality in conformity with purpose and ideal." In 1938, with fascism and Stalinism looming in the background, education resurfaced in the work of an independent intellectual as a non-coercive path toward social cohe-sion and renewal.[29]

CHAPTER 7

An Alternative Morality

As the concerns about education suggest, the problem of constructing an autonomous yet socialized intellectual life spilled over into discussions of the larger question of reconciling individualism and community. To what extent did social responsibility require constraints upon the free play of ideas and creative impulses or upon personal behavior? Younger intellectuals offered a response based on the shared assumption that the Victorian moral code had neither enhanced the life of individuals nor served the collective welfare. Few terms appeared in their writings of the 1910s and 1920s with such urgency and frequency as "self-fulfillment" and its synonyms "self-realization," "self-expression," and "self-development." In rejecting conventional careers, including the academy, Randolph Bourne's generation of critics recognized personal satisfaction as the basic ingredient of the good life and denounced an older morality that condemned individuals to miserable lives of self-denial and thwarted expression. "We have surrounded ourselves with so many moral hedges," Bourne observed in 1913, "have imposed upon ourselves so many checks and balances, that life has been smothered." The choice of the free intellectual life implied the substitution of what Van Wyck Brooks called "self-fulfillment as an ideal" for the sacrifice of happiness that a job in business or the university inevitably entailed. Bourne and his contemporaries generalized the free expression that they considered indispensable to the intellectual life into a "new morality" based on "giving our good impulses full play" instead of clinging to "the rigid mastery which self-control implies."[1] Demanding and articulating a new morality became one of the central pursuits of this generation.

The ideal of self-fulfillment, however, was not intended as a justification for private indulgence or short-lived gratification. It would have been impossible for critics so deeply concerned about forging a social role for themselves to posit an anti-social morality—a morality that placed individual well-being in opposition to the public good. When Brooks spoke of self-fulfillment, he contrasted it to "self-assertion," the competitive individualism at the heart of an irresponsible business civilization, and made it abundantly clear that self-fulfillment held the greater promise of social renewal. As we shall see, those who discussed the new morality saw no incompatibility between personal satisfaction and social welfare. In part, this was made possible by the extreme vagueness of their terms. Self-fulfillment could mean anything from sexual gratification to sublimation and unalienated labor, and their failure to speak with greater precision left them open to a range of criticisms. They have variously been branded bohemians, Rousseauian romantics, biological determinists, bourgeois adventurers, and apologists for a therapeutic consumerism. Yet none of these labels recognizes their sincere belief that an alternative kind of individualism was the essential criterion for the good society and, as Casey Blake has observed, the most perceptive among them defined self-fulfillment as the development of the whole personality through involvement in a communal project.[2]

1.

Brooks and Bourne were both extremely reticent about sex and phrased their ideas about the transformation of morality in a manner that tended to emphasize artistic creation rather than sexual freedom. Even privately, Bourne was no more explicit than to invoke "genuine comradeship and healthy frank regard and understanding" between men and women. Brooks' 1926 affair with fellow critic Mary Colum—which he claimed never went beyond a single kiss—helped precipitate his nervous breakdown.[3] But others, particularly those who gathered around the *Masses* before the war, were considerably more forthright. Certainly one aspect of the ideal of self-fulfillment was a concern for sexual freedom, and it was in the formulation of a more liberal sexual code that male critics and female activists and writers forged their strongest bonds. In this formulation, the providential harmony between individual satisfaction and social good received its fullest elaboration. Popular lore about Greenwich Village and free love has obscured the fact that the intellectuals who wrote about the new morality and experimented with sexual relationships attached a social meaning to their ideas and behavior. Free love did not mean hedonism; it did not mean personal gratification at the expense of the communal good.

Margaret Sanger, the American intellectual most responsible for creating out of Freud, Havelock Ellis, and Ellen Key an ideology of sexual liberation, spoke frankly of "the force of the sexual instinct" and rejected "the traditional inhibitions concerning the discussion of sexual matters." In general, Nancy Cott argues, feminists of Sanger's generation fought against the sexual double standard not in favor of chastity but for "a single standard balanced in the direction of heterosexual freedom for women" as well as men. Yet Sanger emphatically denied "that sex should be reduced to the level of sensual lust," never publicly advocated promiscuity, and always insisted that the ultimate value of birth control was public, not private. Voluntary parenthood would eradicate poverty by decreasing the glut of laborers, eliminate urban overcrowding and improve the general health, allow parents to concentrate their resources on fewer children and raise the level of education, reduce the "burden of the imbecile and moron" by containing the reproduction of "transmissible taints," and end war by stopping international overpopulation. With typical hyperbole, Sanger described the birth control movement as "the third and most important battle for general liberty upon American soil," ahead of the American Revolution and Robert Ingersoll's fight for free thought.[4]

The myriad social possibilities of birth control were rooted in women's desire for "self-development" and "self-expression." But when Sanger spoke in these terms, she did not envision a self-indulgent freedom. Rather, she argued that "individual regeneration," built upon "complete freedom," would lead to "social regeneration." The older code of repressed sexuality, "imposed" by "self-appointed and self-perpetuating masters," fraudulently assumed a conflict between personal fulfillment and "the interest and well-being of the race," while the real obstruction to social progress was this antiquated morality itself:

There is no antagonism between the good of the individual and the good of society. The moment civilization is wise enough to remove the constraints and prohibitions which now hinder the release of inner energies, most of the larger evils of society will perish of inanition and malnutrition. Remove the moral taboos that now bind the human body and spirit, free the individual from the slavery of tradition, remove the chains of fear from men and women, above all answer their unceasing cries for knowledge that would make possible their self-direction and salvation, and in so doing, you best serve the interests of society at large.[5]

Like her mentor Havelock Ellis, Sanger viewed an honest and liberated sexuality as the means to something greater. Through open discussion and birth control, sex could be guided beyond lust toward love—the essence of "a liberated and abundant life." Women, who always assumed the responsibility for contraception in Sanger's scheme, "must elevate sex into another sphere, whereby it may subserve and enhance the possibility of individual and human expression."[6] Sanger's repeated invocation of such phrases as "self-expression," "self-fulfillment," and "self-development" did not serve, at least in her own mind, to advance a morality that turned its back on the mission of social redemption. For her, self-realization, through the instrumentality of birth control, was the building block of revolution.

How ideas about self-realization were to translate into actual behavior and real relationships Sanger did not fully specify. Her own marriages, first to architect William Sanger and then to 3–in–1 oil magnate J. Noah Slee, were decidedly open; she had a number of lovers. But Sanger's pronouncements on sexual freedom did not include any mention of extramarital affairs, and many in sympathy with the movement argued that birth control, by allowing two fully developed human beings to enter into an equal partnership based on love, would strengthen the institution of marriage.[7] Some admitted they were confused. Indeed it was confusion that prompted Freda Kirchwey's *Nation* symposium, *Our Changing Morality*, published as a book in 1924. In her introduction, Kirchwey wrote of "chaos," "tangled, conflicting codes," and "moral disorder." The breakdown of traditional sanctions, she observed, had left people floundering amid "the changing standards of sex behavior" that had largely resulted from women's demands for freedom and equality. Privately, Kirchwey and her husband Evans Clark agreed that extramarital affairs were necessary for independence and fulfillment. The symposium was Kirchwey's attempt to make morality into a problem demanding intellectual inquiry, to lift the problem to the level of disinterested investigation. *Our Changing Morality* would avoid "dogmatic conclusions" while recognizing that "guidance and interpretation are deeply needed, if only to take the place of the pious imprecations of those who fear life and hate the dangers and uncertainties of thought and emotion."[8] In short, Kirchwey asserted the leadership of intellectuals in the realm of morals, where narrow-mindedness had too long prevented independent evaluation. The open discussion of morality might serve as a bridge from private concerns to public influence.

Several of the contributors joined Kirchwey in implying a parallel between the ideal intellectual life and the new morality. Independence and unfettered expression, however difficult to achieve, were the proper goals of all human endeavor. If thinking and writing were tasks reserved for the few, the intellectual life might serve as a model for the conduct of life in general. Bertrand Russell set the tone for much of the symposium by rejecting all external constraints upon individual development. "The ideal to be aimed at," he wrote, "is not life-long monogamy enforced by legal or social penalties. The ideal to be aimed at is that all sexual intercourse should spring from the free impulse of both parties, based upon mutual inclination and nothing else." In a passage that must have resonated with his American counterparts, Russell applied the gospel of anti-institutionalism to the moral sphere, contending that the "cramping of love by institutions is one of the major evils of the world."[9] Floyd Dell suggested that extramarital friendships between women and men represented the artistic and intellectual life writ large—"a poignant fulfillment of those profound impulses which we call curiosity and candor" and "in some sense an art" like any other. Elsie Clews Parsons contrasted the ideal of "social independence" with "[w]ifely parasitism" and "integral satisfaction" with "constancy, fidelity, and duty." Parsons had contributed to the *Masses*, the *New Republic*, the *Dial*, and Harold Stearns' *Civilization in the United States*, and had been a friend of Randolph Bourne. As early as 1906 she wrote in favor of trial marriages, and by 1915 was discussing sex as "a factor in the enrichment of personality and of contacts between personalities"—a means toward full development and a more expansive humanity. In *Social Freedom*, Parsons predicted a future when "passionate love will forget its shameful centuries of degradation to spread its wings into those spaces whereof its poets sing." One of the first to demand the destruction of all artificial barriers to self-fulfillment, she continued in Kirchwey's symposium to treat love and sex as private concerns with important social implications. The crux of *Our Changing Morality* was that free love and personal fulfillment were vital to a healthy society and that, as Dell put it, conventions were "inevitably a shackle upon the free motions of the soul." Only Joseph Wood Krutch, Kirchwey's colleague at the *Nation,* dismissed as naive the assumption that freedom from external prohibitions and inner inhibitions would usher in a new age of fully developed individuals and idyllic love.[10] Admittedly more tentative than Sanger, Kirchwey and most of her contributors agreed that self-realization, a different kind of individualism from the competitive materialism of a business civilization, must be the universal aspiration of modern men and women. Artists and intellectuals might be the first to explore this alternative individualism, but the life of free expression was available to everyone.

In much the same spirit of the middle-twenties that animated Kirchwey's symposium, V. F. Calverton took up the task of explaining the new morality and its connection to an emerging communal order. Calverton was a younger critic who identified closely with the *Masses* style of cultural radicalism, considered himself a member by common outlook of Eastman's generation, and sought, as Leonard Wilcox has shown, to point the way to a synthesis of Marx and Freud. Such a synthesis, he believed, would help to channel irresponsible and thoughtless rebellion into intelligent social revolution; sexual liberation would be an important component of a classless society. Calverton predicted the demise of "bourgeois monogamy" once private property, inheritance, and grasping individualism had been abolished, and envisioned "the growth of social emotions in a more communal life." In place of the "destructively individualistic" tendencies of the bourgeois family, which centered "around a little group instead of the entire community," modern men and women would cultivate "expansive" (as opposed to "ingrown") affections. Meanwhile, however, the revolt of youth "against the old traditions" was haphazard and anti-social, extravagant and excessive. Sex had become "maximized and advertised," "[e]xtreme inhibition" had "given place to extreme exhibition" in the current period of "class decay and social disintegration." The "present chaos in modern morals" demanded "wide and intelligent consideration" in order that confusion might yield to a stable and healthy morality for the modern world.[11]

Yet Calverton's vulgar Marxism undermined the critical project of delineating the new morality as a social alternative to be consciously pursued. In his attempt to reconcile sexual and social revolution, he veered toward a view of morality as epiphenomenal. "Sexual ethics," he argued, "are more of an effect than a cause in the progress of social relations. They reflect rather than determine the nature of advance." No effort on the part of critics to describe a less repressive code of behavior or to clear up the present confusion could have any noticeable effect until the social and economic foundation had been transformed. At times, Calverton spoke as if the two revolutions were complementary and worthy of equal emphasis; social revolution was necessary for the success of a "[m]oral revolt" which had already commenced. Ultimately, though, he refused to allow any real power to ideas or codes of conduct and, by implication, made his own work pointless: "The new morality has brought us to a new cross-road in the history of morals in our civilization. Yet its actual realization can only be achieved in a new economic order." For Calverton, then, the function of *Sex Expression in Literature* (1926), *The Bankruptcy of Marriage* (1928), the discussions in his magazine the *Modern Quarterly*, and his own symposium *Sex in Civilization* (1929) was merely to demonstrate the evolution of morality along the lines of a crudely deterministic historical analysis. Until 1929, he could look to Soviet Russia as the culmination of this process—the place where "early exaggerations and excesses dwindled, and the basis of the new morality, organized about the new code, was begun." He specifically described Soviet experiments in birth control, companionate marriage, relaxation of divorce laws, and communal childrearing as evidence of a liberated yet socially productive morality under communism.[12]

Calverton's attempt at a synthesis of Marx and Freud foundered as much upon a thin foundation of psychology as upon a hollow economic determinism. He was not alone in the poverty of his psychological understanding. Wilcox has said of Calverton that he "displayed an interest in psychoanalysis in so far as it could be appropriated to the cause of instinctual liberation and cultural renewal." Like Sanger, Eastman, Dell, Bourne, and most of his older models, he favored Ellis and a cheery interpretation of Freud which made for a simple equation of self-fulfillment and social good and left out "the rich tragic vision of Freud" that the Frankfurt School later brought to bear upon Marxism. The American critics who discussed the new morality in the 1910s and 1920s lacked the well-developed "intellectual matrix" needed to produce anything more than the wishful projection of a vital general community based on a freer individuality. This might help explain the gap between public celebrations of a liberated sexuality and a great deal of private unhappiness. As

Nancy Cott observed of the feminist "pioneers of heterosexual freedom," they "were far from acknowledging publicly the potential for submergence of women's individuality and personality in heterosexual love relationships, or the potential for men's sexual exploitation of women who purposely broke the bounds of conventional sexual restraint. In private they saw, inevitably, travesties of their ideal."[13]

The stakes were too high to question seriously the notion that the unfettered self and the regenerated community were providentially connected. Ideas about sexual and intellectual expression were too tightly bound together in the minds of critics like Waldo Frank, who insisted in Calverton's 1929 symposium that there can never be a "mature" art "where the artist is sexually restrained," and that "[s]piritual obtuseness is the result of biological repression." The closest Calverton came to voicing doubts was to acknowledge that freedom, like repression, would have its "costs." "If freedom as a theory is perfect, and as an aspiration is ideal," he admitted in one of his more thoughtful moments, "it is foolish of us, however, to imagine that in practice it will be accompanied by a complete absence of discord." Even so, he did not doubt the fundamental compatibility of communism and "the ineluctable demands of the sexual impulse" for "[c]hange, variety, newness."[14]

2.

The effort to give coherence and social meaning to unconventional private behavior produced some remarkable connections between love lives and intellectual lives, and for a few critics who tried to explain their behavior, the problems of modern love became synonymous with the dilemma of the modern intellect. Facing a crisis in his marriage to Ida Rauh in 1914, Max Eastman first went through psychoanalysis with the New York Freudian Smith Ely Jelliffe and then a summer of intensive self-analysis in Provincetown. Rauh's departure left Eastman with "a real upspringing in solitude of the old enthusiasm for the free realization of all life," which had been his "religion" before marriage. Monogamy, he decided, was an obstacle to this free realization and stood in opposition to his "love of ideas" and "love of the whole world." He may have shared this notion with his friend John Reed, who made a plea to Louise Bryant for free expression without stating whether his release from "repression" would take sexual or sublimated form. Reed simply said that "no one I love has ever been able to let me express myself fully, freely, and trust that expression." Eastman wrestled with the possibility that he was constructing elaborate intellectual justifications for hedonism but managed to convince himself that his resistance to monogamy had a greater purpose than unrestricted sexual pleasure. At the beginning of August, he stated this possibility: "I am *not happy with Ida because I want to be free to satisfy other sexual desires*. There! I have said it. Now the question remains: is it the essential truth?" Two days later came the answer: "no, it is not."[15] After he and Rauh separated in 1916, Eastman entered into an extended relationship with the actress Florence Deshon, who left him for Hollywood in 1920, became involved with their friend Charlie Chaplin, and committed suicide in 1922.

Eastman continued to have affairs during his second marriage, to the Russian artist Eliena Krylenko, sister of the Bolshevik commissar of justice. At work on a novel and a biography of Trotsky in the Soviet Union in 1923–24, he suffered a breakdown over his writing and his commitment to Eliena, two problems which he explicitly linked together. "O yes I am mad," he wrote her in January 1924. "I am so mad and so weak . . . a little desperate quivering heart-broken child." But now, he believed, the conflict between commitment and intellectual independence was not as simple as it been with other women. In previous cases, the solution to what he variously called his "demon," his "complex," and his "divided condition" had been "my going gradually away, and finally getting in love with somebody else, and *doing it again*." It had been evident that "those loves were not helpful to my work, to my egotism, which is the real force in me." With Eliena, however, the split between monogamy and creative freedom was not clear. "*There is no conflict between you and my writing*," Max told her. "You both fight on the same side and my neurosis fights on the other side—and I? I am a field of battle and I have a headache!" His choice was to try "to conquer the feeling that I can't write unless I am alone" by "going entirely back to you in my heart," or "to leave you forever" and fall in love with somebody else. "Then I might have another little period of clarity, before the conflict began again." If he could not find resolution soon, he wrote, he would go to Vienna and see Freud.[16]

Candid in his autobiography about his affairs before marrying Eliena, Eastman was not as revealing about those that came after. But it appears that he and Eliena reached some understanding about the necessity of freedom in love for his emotional and intellectual well-being. They discussed their attractions for other people and spoke of at least some of their affairs. "I did kiss a girl a few times last night," Max wrote on his way to Europe in 1929, "and she was a nice girl too." When Eliena wrote back that she had refused someone, Max advised her, "Don't kiss anybody you don't want to—and kiss everybody you do want to (if you can)—this is the first and great commandment." While Max was on a lecture tour in 1932, Eliena became involved with a mutual friend, Scudder Middleton. Eastman's happy response to this news was in keeping with his belief that married love had to be free to be healthy. "I haven't a single flicker of anything but joy in your feelings about Scudder and your being with him," he declared. "It makes our love so much more four-square and perfect for me, and I hope you love him. But it would make me so tragically sad if you stopped loving me right now when I am so happy in continual thoughts of you." He concluded, "Thank you, my darling, for your sweet midnight letter which made me so happy—All my deepest love."[17] Eastman's second marriage survived more than thirty years, until Eliena's death in 1956. Whatever the precise nature of their understanding, it seems to have succeeded in reconciling Max's dilemmas about the connection between sexual and intellectual freedom, allowing him to roam the world of people and ideas while maintaining a deep emotional involvement with one person. It would be impossible to describe Eastman's arrangement as typical, but the magnitude of his concerns about independence and commitment in his private life, and his association of these concerns with those of the intellect in America, speaks to the pervasiveness and depth of the conflict between freedom and engagement among American intellectuals.[18]

Familiarity with Freudian or Jungian psychology may have contributed to the tendency to discover larger patterns or meanings in personal conduct. Edmund Wilson played out the conflict between the highbrow and the lowbrow in his private life in the twenties and then worked it into a novel at the end of the decade. Wilson's relationships with Edna St. Vincent Millay and a working-class woman called "Anna" in his published diaries seemed to personify the gap between ideas and reality that served as the theme for most of his important writing of the period. Millay, the model for Rita Cavanagh in *I Thought of Daisy*, represented Wilson's aspirations to creative freedom, his desire to turn his back "on all that world of mediocre aims and prosaic compromises" and to be "set free to follow poetry." In contrast, "Anna," Daisy Meissner in the novel, had an "organic-animal-human look." She was "frank, vulgar, humorous, human!" and Wilson's vital link to the common life of America. Torn between the two women, Wilson and his narrator sought some means of fastening upon literature while saving themselves "from that dreadful isolation," those "impregnable solitudes with the creation of impossible worlds" that Millay and Rita represented. Finally, frustrated in his pursuit of Millay-Rita and convinced that the highbrow world was undesirable in any case, Wilson sought what Sherman Paul has called "a mystical Whitmanian communion with the body of America," symbolized by Daisy and "Anna." The solution in the novel prefigured Wilson's journey into reportage, as the narrator determined to "make some sketches of Daisy," to "hit off, in prose, her attitudes, her gestures, her expressions, the intonations of her voice." In this manner, "by the way of literature itself" and by throwing in his literary lot with the common people, he would "break through into the real world."[19] Doubtless Wilson had been involved with Millay and his working-class mistress before he attached any general significance to these affairs. But, as with Eastman, it is revealing that he conjoined problems of love with problems of the life of art and ideas. He, too, found social meaning in intimate matters.

In Lewis Mumford's case, extramarital affairs seemed necessary for personal growth, both sexual and intellectual. When he and Sophia Wittenberg were married in 1921, it was she who wanted an open marriage and he who did not. By 1930, Sophia could tell him, "You see, my darling, I've kept your 1922 morality, and you left it behind." Mumford had at least two affairs that year—one with Helen Ascher, an old friend and the wife of a colleague from the Regional Planning Association of America, and the other with Catherine Bauer, a talented urban planner. Earlier he had been drawn to the poet Josephine Strongin, though they apparently never had a sexual relationship. ("Happily," he recalled, "it was her mind, not her barely pubescent body, I fell in love with.") Mumford's justification for his involvement with Bauer was not unlike Wilson's explanation of his relationships with Millay and "Anna." According to Donald Miller, Strongin had represented "intellectual passion"; she was what Mumford called "the daughter of the sky." Ascher, "the daughter of the earth," had conveyed sensuality. Bauer combined the two. Mumford believed that she was vital to the reawakening of his mind and his grasp of life. "[A]t some point the appearance of another person on the horizon comes like the first flapping of sails on a becalmed boat," he wrote later, "when an offshore breeze breaks through the sleepy torpor and drives it again out on the open sea." He was convinced that Bauer played a role in his life akin to that of Hilda Wangel in Ibsen's *The Master Builder*, who encourages the hero to attempt greater forms of expression, which for Mumford became *Technics and Civilization* and *The Culture of Cities*. Like Eastman, he also associated sexual freedom with the freedom to follow his intellectual inclinations unobstructed. In some ways, he reasoned, the latter was even less compatible with marriage: "I am more of a brute when I am writing a book" than engaging in an affair; "and the hurt to Sophie's ego is quite as great, too: because no person has ever held me as firmly as my own thoughts, at least over a long period." If Mumford experienced some guilt over this, it took a direct statement from Sophia to make him aware that his independence had been purchased at the expense of her own. When they had met, she was working at the *Dial*. Now she had no outside work and had abided by his decision against an open marriage. "You cut . . . that end of my life off," she wrote in the midst of his affair with Bauer, "and I am left with no proper place of my own. I'm a hanger-on to you."[20]

Mumford's marriage survived, but Waldo Frank's linkages of sexual and creative freedom, extramarital affairs and intellectual growth produced irremediable strains. Frank spent a good part of his marriage to Margaret Naumburg traveling alone, in the belief that this would simultaneously liberate his creative powers and bring him closer to the common life of the American people. Naumburg indulged his impulse to roam; though she told him that he would ultimately "face the fact that the real problem lay within," she "realized" that he "had to go through the 'vagabonding' in the outside world." In the winter of 1920, she agreed to join him in Alabama only if it was "really true, as you now insist, that there is no conflict between me and your work." But when Frank claimed that his intellectual development demanded that he have an affair with the writer Evelyn Scott, Naumburg became noticeably less tolerant of his egotism. She derided his "elaborate phantasy about my being completely identified with you in this Jewish thing as opposed to the Pagan in Evelyn Scott." Frank's attempts to broaden his experiences and achieve creative fulfillment had numbed him to her needs, Naumburg observed: "I realize perfectly well that at bottom *no one* has really any other function in your life except as a function of your own creation." If he intended to go ahead with the affair, he needed to have "the honesty to accept the responsibility for the consequences" of his acts, "whatever they may be." The marriage lasted from 1916 to 1924, with many separations in the interim. By the beginning of 1923, however, Naumburg was convinced that Frank had "driven" himself "up a blind alley in placing" his "work before life." For him, she noted, human relationships were merely a means toward producing the "work that is the pivot and justification of your life." Yet even his writing had suffered for its lack of "a clear and purely functioning human being as its base." She urged that his next trip be to Vienna for psychoanalysis with Freud.[21]

Frank coupled his insistence on the freedom to roam with the demand that his wife sustain him in his work through complete devotion. His second marriage, to the educator Alma Magoon, was strained from the beginning by his repeated accusation that she did not love him sufficiently and that this "lack of deep feeling" was making him physically ill and destroying his ability to write. In 1929, five years after they became involved and two years after they were married, Frank told her that her failure to love him left separation as "the one course that is not cowardly and fatal." Despite such episodes, and though they were apart for much of the time, they did not legally separate until 1943. Meanwhile, Frank continued to remind Alma that her purpose in life was to make his life wholly conducive to intellectual production by loving him unconditionally and understanding his need for extramarital adventures. "It is highly right that people should rejoice in their function in life," he reminded her in 1932. "And enabling me to live and to do my job is a very crucial function, and it is yours: and I hope you are free enough of new-fangled nonsense to be glad. I need you profoundly, and I know it." A year later, he told some friends "how wonderful" Alma was about his "occasional 'amours.'" When one of these friends asked Frank if he would "permit" Alma "the same liberty," he replied that he "would suffer profoundly, be hurt much," but "bear it" and not abandon the marriage if she still loved him. Then, in recounting the conversation for Alma, he explained why he "would suffer so much more than you seem to: because of man's traditional 'proprietorship'; because of man's traditional sense of his beloved's body as his sanctuary, his 'holy place'; and (in my case) because of my terrific visual imagination which would make me *see* the love-act—as compared with your lack of that kind of imagination."[22] Frank was unaware of or unconcerned with the costs to his wives of his chosen path

toward self-fulfillment and creative expression. There is no more trans-
parent instance of the failure to perceive the limits to self-fulfillment as a
code of conduct—to recognize its capacity to spill over into self-impor-
tance and self-indulgence, to produce conflict and suffering, and to undermine women's own quest for fulfilling lives.

3.

A generational consciousness shaped the new morality from its initial
formulations, with youth clamoring for liberation from outworn conventions. One of Bourne's first significant essays, "The Two Generations,"
was a response to a 1911 *Atlantic* article attacking the younger generation
for its vapidness and irresponsibility. Sanger considered the task of "moral
house cleaning" a fight for freedom "from the grip of the dead hand of the
past."[23] But in the late twenties, challenges to the ethos of self-fulfillment
began to come from within the generation to which Bourne had helped
give identity. As early as 1926, Dell examined "that generation of intelligent, sensitive and more or less creative young people to which I and
most of my friends belong" and found that it had failed to transcend self-
indulgence and "a super-vagabondish point of view." In both love and
art, his generation was prone to "irresponsible self-expression" and a
"laissez-faire, do-nothing selfishness."[24] *Intellectual Vagabondage*, Dell's
jeremiad, was a far cry from his earlier celebrations of free love and free
expression and a significant departure from the belief in the inevitable
social value of spontaneity and impulse. Dell continued to view his
generation as "young" even as he approached forty, but the passage of
years and the failure of the good society to materialize out of the gospel
of the liberated self led to a process of reevaluation.

Nothing better symbolized this reaction than the convergence of several critics of Dell's generation with Irving Babbitt, Paul Elmer More,
and the amorphous New Humanist movement. Gorham Munson, the
friend of Waldo Frank who had written for Albert Jay Nock and Van
Wyck Brooks at the *Freeman*, contributed a scathing attack on his fellow
critics to Norman Foerster's 1930 symposium *Humanism and America*.
Labeling Brooks "a charming minor critic," branding Lewis Mumford
"impractical because of his credulity as to what modern letters can actually effect in modern society," dismissing Joseph Krutch as a victim of
"weak despair" and Mencken as self-satisfied and second-rate, Munson

censured American critics for being both complacent and utopian. At the heart of his critique was a denunciation of the faith in self-expression. " 'Self-expression' is simply a magical catchword of the black variety," Munson wrote, and "advice to be spontaneous, to let oneself go without check, to follow one's impulses is necessarily advice—to do what?—*to live as unconsciously and mechanically as possible.*" Vague about his alternative, Munson called for an American Matthew Arnold who would combine good taste, restraint, and objectivity, and replace excess and lack of discrimination with "a burning unquenchable indomitable love of perfect things." The New Humanism did not accept a more limited function for the critic. Rather it viewed the critic as the model of moderation who would educate the public to the proper level of moral and aesthetic standards. As Babbitt wrote in the same symposium (still attempting "An Essay at Definition" of Humanism after more than twenty years), "if the humanistic goal is to be achieved, if the adult is to like and dislike the right things, he must be trained in the appropriate habits almost from infancy." Munson followed his new leader in suggesting that it would be both words and deeds, ideas and examples that would serve the American Arnolds in elevating the masses.[25]

The one contemporary critic for whom Munson reserved at least some praise was Walter Lippmann, who published *A Preface to Morals* in 1929 and articulated a "new asceticism" which Munson admired. Never a full adherent to the faith in self-expression, Lippmann had in his earliest books argued the need "to fit institutions to the wants of men, to satisfy their impulses as fully and as beneficially as possible." A more sensitive reader of Freud than some of his Greenwich Village friends, he had written of sublimation and borrowed William James' theory of moral equivalents, acknowledging that not every impulse would produce positive effects. But Lippmann had also been caught up in the assault on "empty taboos" and pointed out the constructive possibilities in "the ideals of human feelings." By the late 1920s, Lippmann was moving away from his old hero James and gravitating toward another Harvard professor, Babbitt. While declining to participate in Foerster's symposium and critical of Babbitt's dogmatism, he expressed interest in the project and noted that he was "in sympathy" with the New Humanism. Lippmann's ever-growing distrust of an irrational public and his own unhappy marriage contributed to the new ideology of self-denial developed in *A Preface to Morals.*[26]

It was now evident, he observed, that the promise of even individual happiness through the destruction of taboos had proven false. Lippmann denied the "major premise of modernity," that "the human passions, if thoroughly liberated from all tyrannies and distortions, would by their fulfillment achieve happiness." The cult of impulse was yielding to the "discovery that our wishes have little or no authority in the world"—to the realization that there was no inherent connection between individual desire and either personal or social regeneration. But it was also clear that traditional moral codes had ceased to carry any weight. Lippmann distinguished modernity as the first time in which "any fixed and authoritative belief" had become "incredible to large masses of men." External codes could not compel obedience without a complete faith in God and church, and with the dissolution of "the ancient order of things," the only available solution was to turn to what Lippmann called a "morality of humanism." This he defined as "the re-education of desire," the maturation of individuals to a level at which they outgrow "naive desire" and can begin to cultivate a "disinterestedness" in place of dangerous passion and "authoritative morality." Clinging to the ideal of the disinterested self, Lippmann no longer viewed "detachment, understanding, and disinterestedness" as the inevitable result of the absence of compromising institutions and external demands on the individual. Through a process of self-denial, individuals could make themselves "transcend the immediacy of desire" and "live for ends which are transpersonal." The willing away of destructive impulses would produce the objectivity necessary for confronting the problems of the modern world, and it was the pure scientist and the modern manager who best lived up to this desideratum. In the realm of love, the mere indulgence of passions threatened enduring and meaningful relationships. Borrowing from Krutch's critique of hedonism in *The Modern Temper*, Lippmann did not share Krutch's view that the reduction of love to mere physical attraction by modern psychology had permanently destroyed its spiritual possibilities. "If you start with the belief that love is the pleasure of the moment," Lippmann agreed, it is not "really surprising that it yields only a momentary pleasure." But here, too, once lovers experienced the "personal anguish" of recognizing the limits to a love based exclusively on sexual passion, they would learn "to transcend naive desire and to reach out towards a mature and disinterested partnership with the world."[27] Self-discipline in love, art, politics, and business became for Lippmann the alternative to both self-indulgence and outside authority, and functioned in opposition to statism and anarchy as the key to the "Good Society."

The brief and bitter debate over the New Humanism culminated in 1930 with Foerster's symposium and a response entitled *The Critique of Humanism* which included pieces by Wilson, Mumford, Cowley, Kenneth Burke, Allen Tate, Yvor Winters, R. P. Blackmur, John Chamberlain, and others. The editor of this symposium, C. Hartley Grattan, recognized that there was little agreement among the participants; there were deep differences between Wilson, Mumford, and Cowley on one side and the slightly younger critics who argued that aesthetics and ethics were ontologically separable, while Tate stood alone in his embrace of religion. Grattan viewed the diversity of opinion as a positive sign "that the non-academic critics of this country will not march under any single banner, no matter how pretty the device it displays." To this extent, perhaps, the anti-Humanism symposium did defend the cause of unobstructed individual expression.[28]

Yet the responses hardly celebrated self-fulfillment with the same enthusiasm as that which charged Bourne's attack on More in 1916. Bourne had written approvingly of "an incalculable and importunate stream of desire" and its unimpeded flow "into creative channels" in place of "its suppression or even control by that reason which is so often a mere disguise of another and more acceptable desire." In *The Critique of Humanism*, Wilson repeated the old charge that Babbitt and More were prone to "the unexamined prejudices of a Puritan heritage" which they had "never outgrown." He also commented sardonically that since "negative behavior" or the will-to-refrain was the whole of the Humanist philosophy, then Americans were almost "all Good Humanists"; they seemed "to refrain from most of the enjoyments." Cowley characterized the Humanist outlook as the "heights of chaste absurdity." Mumford argued that "if living well were only a matter of restraint and a limitation of 'expansiveness' a chronic invalid would be the supreme type of an ethical personality."[29]

While they condemned the New Humanism for its narrow morality and excessive negativism, however, none of these critics countered with simple calls for the liberated self. Whether the Humanist critique forced them to abandon their earlier assumptions, or the refrain of self-fulfillment had come to seem stale and naive, they were increasingly hesitant about claiming that the mere obliteration of traditional strictures was the path to the good life for either the individual or society. When Wilson's onetime friend Seward Collins presented his defense of the New Humanism two months after the appearance of Grattan's symposium, he asked of Bourne and Brooks' gospel of self-fulfillment, "Was there ever a vaguer or more mawkish program for the revolution?" Wilson, whom Collins accused of "malevolence," "ignorance," "obtuseness," and a "complete abdication of conscience" for his contribution to the anti-Humanist book, was by no means in complete disagreement with his adversary's verdict on self-fulfillment as a social program.[30]

Rather than answering the charge that their generation had adopted a naively rosy view of human nature, Wilson, Cowley, and Mumford attacked the Humanists for their reliance on an ahistorical morality which they tried to disguise as an "inner check" but which really relied on outworn external rules of conduct. The anti-Humanists, Wilson implied, were the genuine exemplars of the inner check; they were the ones who chose the difficult course of self-discipline rather than the easy path of obeying authority. More, according to Wilson, "apparently believes that the only way in which it is possible for a writer to discipline himself in these bad days is to write literary criticism like his own and Babbitt's, which, though it is distinguished by thorough reading and sound writing, has obviously not required a discipline a fifth as exacting as that which has gone to produce some of the works of which it so superciliously complains." Henry Hazlitt, the *Nation* literary critic and another contributor to Grattan's symposium, conceded that "we need to direct and harmonize our affections, desires, and purposes" but contended that "we can learn to do this through knowledge and good-will" instead of "supernatural sanctions." Mumford accused the Humanists of making a fetish of morality, of treating it as an end and a program in itself when discipline should merely serve as a means to a fuller life, "growth and renewal." "[W]hat a truly human life demands," Mumford insisted, "are positive channels of effort, useful and dignified tasks, fine and significant actions, and quiet states of beatitude, which by their very pursuit or enjoyment provide, incidentally, such checks and restraints as may be necessary to their success."[31] In these invocations of self-discipline was a tempering of the earlier faith in release, spontaneity, and impulse and an acceptance, in a general way, of Lippmann's call for "the re-education of desire." Lippmann viewed this reeducational process as a necessary condition for social renewal; Mumford believed that self-discipline would come with

the commitment to larger purposes. Indeed, the response to the Humanists hinged not on a defense of self-fulfillment, but on the argument that
they had failed to provide a substantial vision of social change. Cowley
rebuked Babbitt for "confusing morality in general with the one virtue of
chastity." For the most part, however, he seemed to accept the validity of
self-control when it appeared as an adjunct to genuine social commitment.[32]

Perhaps the most telling event in the process of moral reevaluation was
Dell's publication in 1930 of *Love in the Machine Age*, an open celebration
of monogamy and family life that he had been working toward since the
early twenties and that he hoped would stir up some controversy among
his contemporaries. Dell was quick to alert his readers that this was not a
defense of tradition, not a return to the ideas of a patriarchal society in
which love, sex, and marriage were subordinated to "the property motive." But, he insisted, "modernity" itself "re-establishes family life on
the basis of romantic love." While Dell never approached Lippmann and
the New Humanists in arguing the social merits of self-restraint, he did
join them in pointing out the excesses of free love. Placing the movement
toward sexual freedom in historical context, he treated promiscuity as an
ideological overcompensation for the purposeless repressions of a vanishing civilization. Conventional morality was the vestige of a society based
on the transmission of landed property and thus parental restrictions on
mating and marriage. Yet the idea of "Sex as Amusement" that came in
reaction to this cultural lag was responsible for defeating "the mating
impulse" and "repudiating the goal of sex." Modern society, by tolerating
the early interaction of the sexes, by abandoning outmoded obstacles to
adolescent courtship and early marriage, by providing "not only knowledge of birth-control methods but an education in general for matehood,"
could make the adjustment to happy marriages and stable families. Dell
still used the term "self-realization," but this now denoted the process of
finding a permanent mate and having children. "The question is," he
asked, "do we want to train young people for—we need not hesitate to
use the phrase—living happily ever after in heterosexual matehood, or
for living tormented and frustrated lives of homosexuality, impotence,
frigidity, and purposeless promiscuity? We have our choice." Unwilling
to concede that monogamy and family life demanded the denial of desires, Dell decided that these were, after all, the natural outcomes of
desires.[33]

Whatever impact Dell hoped to have with his elaborate defense of marriage as the apotheosis of personal satisfaction and the key to social good, he was greeted instead with the scorn of old friends and admirers. By 1930, discussions of self-fulfillment seemed increasingly anachronistic to many of Dell's contemporaries. The kind of commitment Dell advocated was not the kind that his former associates on the *Masses* and the *Liberator* came to favor. To them, the intellectual preoccupation with love and sex and self-fulfillment was essentially inward-looking, part of "the cult of the sacred ego" that Joseph Freeman identified as an obstacle to revolutionary fervor. Freeman rejected the "passion for 'self-expression' " as a reflection of "the bourgeois world" intellectuals thought they had escaped "but whose cult of rugged individualism they retained." When Dell resigned from the *New Masses* in 1929, Michael Gold accused him of "writing cheap sex confession" instead of engaging in the literary fight for social justice. Where once it had been "considered daring" to advocate and "indulge in free love," now this was an emblem of middle-class decadence; according to Gold, "every Babbitt goes in for 'affairs.' " The hero of the old *Masses* remained "centred [*sic*] in the female anatomy," repeating "the same adolescent clichés that once seemed so Gallic, so adequate and charming."[34]

It hardly mattered that Dell was now advocating a relatively conservative program of freely chosen yet permanent monogamy that might have complemented a revolutionary politics. Nor did it matter that he too had argued against a vagabondish freedom and in favor of "organized social activities involving all the customary personal virtues, including such dull matters as honesty, sobriety, responsibility, and even a sense of duty." Not long after Gold's attack on Dell, Malcolm Cowley used a review of the Calverton-Schmalhausen symposium to argue that critics who believed in "the importance of sex and the high value of the books they write about it" were thoroughly detached from the vital realities of American society; they were "sex boys," adrift "in their balloon of rhetoric." Calverton, who had criticized Dell in 1926 for failing to give the social revolution a prominent enough place in his discussions of sex, found that in the new climate of opinion they were lumped together and dismissed as playboys.[35]

To many of those who denounced or ignored Calverton and Dell, the attempts to revise morality that had seemed so vital now appeared effete and anti-social, a reminder of the drift and self-indulgence they came to associate with American intellectual and artistic life in the twenties. Never intended as an excuse for excess and selfishness, the ideology of self-fulfillment, when not under attack after 1929, became merely super-fluous. During the Depression, sacrifice seemed the more proper public code of conduct, and among American intellectuals, freedom from repression ceased to be the preferred path toward a new society.

CHAPTER 8

Uses of the Past

From their adversarial position toward modern America, young critics also confronted the nation's past. Casually at first, then more directly, they took on American history in an attempt to explain their own situation and to discover strategies for change. Ten years before he issued his famous call for a "usable past," Brooks had already begun to explore the legacy of Puritanism and the historical conditions behind the present crisis in America's intellectual life. Mencken, Bourne, Lippmann, Stearns, Willard Huntington Wright, and others joined him in the search for the causes of intellectual marginalization, and for a time they found themselves united in an effort to expose history as a conspiracy against the present. But the characteristic critical attitude toward the American past was one of ambivalence. No matter how often they sneered at it and how hard they tried to turn away from it, the writers of Brooks' generation returned repeatedly to the problem of history. While they were capable of making light of American myths, heroes, institutions, and values, they also recognized that there were serious issues at stake in their struggle with the past. In large part, their historical sensibility reflected the tensions they experienced as intellectuals, and their shifting attitudes toward the past mirrored the continuing effort to discover a secure basis for the intellectual life in contemporary society. The desire to belong in America without compromising placed Brooks' generation in a precarious relationship with the American tradition.

The central problem of history for independent critics was the question of predecessors. Were there previous generations to which they could look for guidance? Had there ever been a viable intellectual community in the United States? The answers to these questions, which changed over time, say a great deal about intellectual aspirations and self-image in the period between 1910 and the end of the Second World War. Without doubt, Brooks' generation was presentist in its conception of history; it never attempted to conceal its assumption that the past had value only insofar as it served the purposes of social and cultural criticism. And if history carried lessons, nothing was more important than what it could tell about the conditions and possibilities for an effective intellectual community in twentieth-century America.

1.

There had to be an explanation for America's undervaluation of the intellect. As he scanned the past for clues to the predicament of young writers, Brooks came to the conclusion that epitomized the historical understanding of his generation in the 1910s. "American history," he declared in *The Wine of the Puritans* (1909), "is so unlovable!" The tone of American life had been established early on, according to Brooks, by people obsessed with "the machinery of life" at the expense of spirituality and art. For the Puritans—a label that came to include not only the settlers of Massachusetts but all the heirs to their alleged materialism— the exigencies of settlement precluded any attention to culture. But this exploitative outlook had long outlasted necessity; it had become the dominant feature of the American character. One could trace a linear descent from Puritan to pioneer to robber baron to modern captain of industry. John D. Rockefeller was not out of place in Brooks' discussion of the legacy of Puritanism. "Will anybody be honestly able to deny that the world would have been much better if he had never lived?" he wondered. What had once been "virtues" were now "obsolete" by any intelligent assessment, yet the concern with the economic side of life had developed into a fetish. "Puritanism" was a concept which minimized historical complexity by collapsing a variety of American types into a kind of materialistic archetype. For Brooks and his contemporaries, it helped explain why they found themselves consigned to the periphery.[1]

Young intellectuals could take some comfort in this conception of the past as weighing them down in their efforts at creativity. Their own insignificance, the difficulties they faced in assuming a position of influ-

ence, had deep historical roots. In an essay that began as a joint review of
Edgar Lee Masters and Theodore Dreiser, Brooks tackled the subject of
America's barren past. The "absence both of an intellectual tradition and
a sympathetic soil" explained the "stunted, starved, thwarted, embit-
tered" artists, writers, and thinkers who populated Masters' "amazing
microcosm of our society." An anti-intellectual tradition had molded a
civilization that "saps away at those vital elements" out of which intellectual leadership and an intellectual community might have grown.[2] Waldo
Frank also drifted toward a deterministic explanation for intellectual
failure. He, too, used a discussion of Masters and Dreiser to launch into
a rumination on the burdens of the American past. The "vehemence" of
these writers' attacks on the past, Frank argued, corresponded to the
oppressive force of the pioneer tradition on the creative mind. "They
attack," he said, "because the Past is still so emotionally real; because it
holds them back from full bestowal upon the Present." The struggling
writer had to cope with the presence of a "materialistic, unaesthetic"
tradition and the absence of any alternative tradition—with a history
both heavy and hollow. "The Past is still with us in this land," Frank
observed in 1919; and this was far from beneficial, for the "stride of
America was fatefully economic."[3] At times, especially to Brooks, history
appeared as something insurmountable. In Stearns' symposium, he complained of a "racial compulsion" toward the practical, a history that
conspired to produce only "sharp-witted men of business" and left a "long
list of spiritual casualties" in its wake. Stearns himself pointed out that
"the real America" had been and still was "in the heart of the pioneer"
who was free "of any common heritage or tradition which might question
his values."[4] At these pessimistic moments, history served as more than
an explanation; it became an excuse as well. Who could blame the writer
who failed to assume a position of leadership in a civilization that had
consistently stifled expression in favor of acquisition?

2.

For the most part, however, the negative assessment of the past functioned not as an apology for resignation and paralysis but as a call to
action. America's lack of a meaningful cultural heritage had less to do
with the strength of the Puritan-pioneer tradition than with the weakness
of the artistic-literary alternative. The inability of past generations of

creative minds to capture the nation did not represent the inevitable triumph of the acquisitive instinct; rather it indicated a failure of nerve by artists and writers. Brooks' peculiar use of the terms "highbrow" and "lowbrow" suggests something of his commitment to the idea of literary free agency and his opposition to historical determinism. In Brooks' usage, "highbrow" and "lowbrow" referred first and foremost to the orientation of the writer and only secondarily, if at all, to the tastes and composition of audiences. "Highbrow" connoted abstraction, an unwillingness to experience and address reality, a self-imposed isolation. "Lowbrow" implied materialism, an acquiescence in business civilization, the refusal to accept responsibility for altering the status quo and moving "the soul of America away from the accumulation of dollars." According to this definition, audiences were largely the passive recipients of culture, and whether or not they were challenged to adopt non-commercial values depended on the integrity and the will of the artist. In both the content of their work and the conduct of their lives, writers and artists made choices; if they flew off into detachment and idle speculation or compromised themselves as apologists for greed and exploitation, the fault was theirs. Brooks urged a path between these two extremes—one that would combine a grasp of real life with a transforming vision.

Unfortunately, no example of such a middle course was to be found in the American past. *America's Coming-of-Age* (1915) blamed Emerson, Poe, and Hawthorne for dwelling in an "immense, vague cloud-canopy of idealism," for drifting into vacuous abstraction and leaving the practitioners of self-interest unchallenged. Waldo Frank, who eagerly embraced Brooks' terms, engaged in a similar kind of Emerson-bashing. "He and his followers starved on the crass food about them: their stomachs spewed it up. So they concocted air-brews for substitutes." With their heads in the clouds, the writers of Emerson's time removed the only potential obstruction to the pioneering impulse. "If the pursuit of beauty took one to these chill Emersonian heavens," Frank reasoned, "why then of course the earth was safe for the pursuit of money."[5] Those, on the other hand, who had capitulated to the lowbrow also bore the blame for their own corruption. Despite its deterministic tone, Brooks' *Ordeal of Mark Twain* (1920) challenged the writer to resist the destructive forces of an acquisitive society. Twain should have fought off his wife's efforts to make him into a mere breadwinner; he should have battled more vigorously against the pioneer and "Calvinistic tradition" that threatened his art. "Only if the artist in him" got "the better of the pioneer" could Twain have succeeded, and in the end he gave up the struggle. "Mark Twain," Brooks concluded, "had failed to rise to the conception of literature as a great impersonal social instrument."[6]

The highbrow/lowbrow construct was Brooks' major contribution to his generation's literary and historical understanding. For modern readers, it seems a hazy and facile method of categorizing and criticizing American literature, but dismissing the American pantheon in this way had a liberating effect on young critics. The dismal record of America's most celebrated writers, ultimately attributable to nothing but their own weakness, meant that the new generation held the key to its own fate. Furthermore, this generation believed that it possessed the insight that would save it from repeating the mistakes of the past; the highbrow/lowbrow scheme explained why others had failed and thus provided a set of caveats to guide creative work in the future. Brooks, Frank, and their followers were able to divide the entire roster of American literary and artistic figures into "those who gained an almost unbelievable purity of expression by the very violence of their self-isolation, and those who, plunging into the American maelstrom, were submerged in it, lost their vision altogether, and gave forth a gross chronicle and a blind cult of the American Fact."[7] Here was the historical consciousness that allowed young critics to proclaim their independence and distance themselves from the ineffectiveness of their predecessors.

In this sense, iconoclasm went hand in hand with generationalism. When Stearns announced that "We have no heritages and traditions to which to cling except those that have already withered in our hands and turned to dust," he was placing his own generation at the beginning of a new time.[8] Stearns and his contemporaries were prepared to avoid the flight into the highbrow and the submersion in the lowbrow that had characterized the American past because they had reached a critical understanding of history. The past was useful insofar as it served as a warning and a point of departure. Equipped with the negative lessons of history, young writers could break away from America's highbrow/lowbrow tradition and at long last rescue the intellectual life from the periphery. A little-noticed corollary to the iconoclasm of the 1910s was a positive sense of mission—a generational declaration of independence infused with the spirit of social renewal.

Tales of frustration and defeat, then, ultimately functioned to help define and embolden a new generation. After railing against the Puritan legacy, Brooks told his readers that they "must put aside anything" that tended to make them "self-conscious in this matter of American tradition and simply *be* American," to extract from America's "vulgarities and distractions and boastings" the "elements of a gigantic art." He called on his generation to bridge the highbrow and lowbrow by bringing vision to American life without surrendering to it or fleeing from it. This hopefulness connected with the denial of the past received its fullest expression in the pages of the *Seven Arts*. Romain Rolland's contribution to the first issue reversed the usual logic by making Europe appear to be burdened with history while America was free for innovation and redemption. "There is in you no weariness of the Yesterdays; no clutterings of the Pasts," Rolland told his American admirers in Waldo Frank's translation. When the *Seven Arts*' editors announced that "[w]e have no tradition to continue," it was in the same spirit of possibility. The rejection of history allowed them to make sweeping claims about the originality of their efforts. Nobody had ever tried to steer America away from the cult of materialism; nobody had rooted prophecy in reality. What Paul Rosenfeld said of Alfred Stieglitz could have served as a larger generational credo: "So he would put his foot through all the past that hinders man from reaching life."[9]

For young writers seeking to establish a new foundation for the intellect, a conviction of their own uniqueness was essential. Iconoclasm provided this sense of exceptionalism. Writing about Dreiser, Bourne conveyed an image of a generation poised on the brink of an alternative history. "He expresses an America that is in process of forming," Bourne explained. "The interest he evokes is part of the eager interest we feel in that growth." A valid American tradition was starting now, with writers looking forward to a potential America rather than backwards at a useless past. "The only substitute for dependence on the past," John Dos Passos observed in an argument taken straight from Brooks, "is dependence on the future."[10] At very least, the conception of American history as a wasteland allowed Bourne and his contemporaries to believe that they were attempting something new—that they had distanced themselves from the legacy of failure.

Perhaps the clearest statement of the virtues of iconoclasm came from Walter Lippmann. In *A Preface to Politics*, Lippmann's target was neither the American literary canon nor the American political tradition per se;

he directed his attack at all bankrupt ideas and institutions. At the top of his list of moribund ideas, in fact, was the narrow conception of politics as a sphere apart from social life. From Lippmann's perspective, a thorough reorientation of American culture had to precede political reform. "Without a favorable culture," he contended, "political schemes are a mere imposition." When he chose the title "Some Necessary Iconoclasm" for one of the book's pivotal chapters, he suggested the importance of a critical attitude toward the past in any plan for cultural renewal. "If only men can keep their minds freed from formalism, idol worship, fixed ideas, and exalted abstractions," he advised, then the creative work of social change could proceed unobstructed. According to Lippmann, tradition diverted attention from the needs of the present. The danger of slipping into fetishistic modes of thought was so formidable as to warrant a kind of constant iconoclasm. "Without an unrelenting effort to center the mind upon human uses, human purposes, and human results," he warned, "it drops into idolatry and becomes hostile to creation." To what Morton White described as a transgenerational "revolt against formalism," Lippmann added a generational dimension. A youthful spirit—a consistently critical posture toward anything old and established—served as Lippmann's key to meaningful reform. His image of the Inventor versus the Routineer placed a slavish "historical sense" in opposition to a belief in "the deliberate, conscious, willing individual." The backward-looking intellect doomed itself to failure by losing contact with the conditions of modern life, and Lippmann scorned the "idle dream" of returning "to the imagined glories of other days" or trying to "recover what is passed [sic]." The liberated intellect, the mind in touch with the real world, discarded the past as it asserted its capacity for effective and disinterested leadership.[11]

3.

If, in hopeful moments, iconoclasm pointed toward intellectual engagement, it was equally capable of producing isolation. The break with the past threatened to cast intellectuals adrift by removing them from the course of American experience. Without a valid literary or critical tradition, without the example of a successful intellectual community, they faced estrangement not only from the present but from the entire background to modern America; in this perspective, intellectuals had never been anything but outsiders or yea-sayers. The likelihood of continued detachment was just as great as the possibility of asserting a more meaningful presence, and with the whole weight of history pushing against a vital intellectual life, alienation was a real danger.

For these reasons, even the most outspoken iconoclasts grasped the inadequacies of a blanket condemnation of history. Lippmann himself resisted a complete repudiation of the past by offering a tentative suggestion as to its uses for the present. While nothing from history had any immediate application, modernity could look back for inspiring examples of the creative will in action. "What will fascinate us in the past will be the records of inventions, of great choices, of those alternatives on which destiny seems to hang," Lippmann allowed.[12] As long as they resisted imitation and idolatry, modern thinkers could find some sustenance in the fact that there had been innovative minds in other times and places. But Lippmann stopped short of advocating a concerted effort to uncover a tradition of intellectual originality and effectiveness, and he did not point to any particularly inspiring American minds.

The call for a usable past came from elsewhere. Unlike Lippmann, Bourne conceived of an inspirational history as the product of conscious creation and recovery rather than something that intellectuals might accidentally stumble upon in the course of their work. While Lippmann and others were assaulting tradition indiscriminately, Bourne distinguished between an official past and possible alternatives. "It is not tradition in itself that is dangerous," he argued, "but only dead tradition that has no meaning for the present and is a mere weight on our progress. Such is the legal and economic tradition given to us by our raucous, middle-aged leaders of opinion, adopted by them through motives of present gain, and not through sincere love of the past." Bourne's distinction, perhaps inspired by his teachers James Harvey Robinson and Charles A. Beard, allowed him to envision a competing history that would anchor and sustain young writers. Part of the creative task of his generation would be to rescue the past from the grip of businessmen and politicians, and to make it something more than an apology for the acquisitive present. Paraphrasing the Belgian playwright and essayist Maurice Maeterlinck, Bourne proclaimed that there was nothing "irrevocable about the past. On the contrary, we are constantly rearranging it, revising it, remaking it." Instead of discarding it, critics could shape history to serve their needs; they could redirect America's historical sensibility so as to bolster the creative life and devalue the acquisitive life. Bourne recognized that control over the past determined control over the present—that history would either vindicate the intellect or defeat it. "For the Past is really the child of the Present," he wrote. "We are the authors of its being, and upon it we lavish all our thoughts, our interest and our delight."[13] To surrender history to the forces of modern-day Puritanism would be to admit the marginality of the creative mind in America. Establishing a tradition of intellectual engagement, on the other hand, would in itself demonstrate the power of young intellectuals to challenge the rule of the narrow-minded.

Bourne's historical vision was considerably more expansive than that of Brooks, who remained convinced that the usable past consisted of little more than negative examples. Brooks' famous essay of 1918, "On Creating a Usable Past," began by restating Bourne's distinction between a conservative and a redemptive history. In keeping with his feelings about the universities, Brooks blamed the professors for placing "a sort of Talmudic seal upon the American tradition" which rendered it "sterile for the living mind." He now admitted that this sterility was not inherent in the past but the result of the "typically non-creative habit" of the professorial mind. As apologists for a business civilization, academic men interpreted the American tradition in a manner that corresponded to their subservient position: "Now it is obvious that professors who accommodate themselves without effort to an academic world based like ours upon the exigencies of the commercial mind cannot see anything in the past that conflicts with a commercial philosophy." Brooks, therefore, was able to join Bourne in urging his contemporaries to snatch history away from the timid. "[T]he spiritual past has no objective reality," he conceded; "it yields only what we are able to look for in it." This allowed him to begin to edge away from the condemnatory stance he had taken in *The Wine of the Puritans* and *America's Coming-of-Age* and to conceive the outlines of an alternative tradition. "If, then, we cannot use the past our professors offer us," Brooks asked, "is there any reason why we should not create others of our own?"[14]

Brooks, however, stopped short of claiming that the freedom to "invent a usable past" permitted critics to discover an American tradition of creative success. He remained unwilling to give his literary predecessors credit for accomplishing what he wanted his own generation to achieve: the reconciliation of the highbrow and the lowbrow and the establishment of a legitimate community. The American past could be scoured for noble attempts, but the present generation had to retain its right to improve upon history. "To approach history from the point of view not of the successful fact but of the creative impulse," argued Brooks, "is to throw it into an entirely new focus. What emerges then is the desire, the aspiration, the struggle, the tentative endeavor, and the appalling obstacles our life has placed before them." By knowing the record of heroic failures, writers could assume a place within a tradition, see themselves as the potential victors in a long struggle, and ultimately triumph over the past. Brooks' compromise meant that he and his contemporaries could simultaneously belong to and alter the American experience, stand in a line and stand out at the same time:

Knowing that others have desired the things we desire and have encountered the same obstacles, and that in some degree time has begun to face those obstacles down and make the way straight for us, would not the creative forces of this country lose a little of the hectic individualism that keeps them from uniting against their common enemies? And would this not bring about, for the first time, that sense of brotherhood in effort and in aspiration which is the best promise of a national culture? [15]

In the shared belief that history progressed toward themselves and their success, writers might discover a source of strength and a basis for community. Brooks approached his books on Twain and Henry James with the conviction that he was realizing the agenda set forth in the essay on the usable past. These were to be stories of aspiration and defeat that would convey the idea of historical continuity even as they fostered a sense of generational uniqueness.

While Brooks temporized, others believed it imperative to find writers in the American past who had succeeded in preserving their critical integrity while immersing themselves in real life. John Macy, the socialist writer who contributed to the *Masses*, the *New Republic*, and later to the *Freeman*, the Stearns symposium, and the *Nation*, went about rescuing the American canon from the professors as early as 1913. Macy was concerned with establishing an adversarial tradition to which modern writers could look for models. In *The Spirit of American Literature* (1913), he worked his way through the nineteenth century and sorted out the worthy from the unworthy on the basis of their independence and their grasp of contemporary social problems. Thus Hawthorne was "a delicate detached artist" in the "fanciful, dainty," and "feminine" line who "looked upon social conditions at home and abroad with melancholy indifference." Poe was "another impoverished dreamer" with "his head in the clouds." But there was also Thoreau—"our own spiritual liberator" with whom "we remain unacquainted"—who "did not shrink from facts like some other poets who have fled stricken to the shadow woods." Macy identified a string of writers that represented the creative intelligence engaged with society and demanding change. In them, he located an alternative past that could root and inspire their twentieth-century heirs. "The more powerful writers, Emerson, Thoreau, Whitman, Whittier, Mark Twain," Macy observed, "are *in opposition* to things as they are; they are men of radical convictions, which they try to impress on the reader through satire, sermons, inspired journalism, intense occasional verse." William James, unlike his aloof brother Henry, carried this line forward to the younger generation by relating his philosophy "to popular meanings, to the experiences of common humanity."[16] By Macy's analysis, contemporary writers were not completely cut off from all sources of sustenance; proof existed that they could practice their craft on American soil without drifting off into abstraction or crumbling under the pressures of Puritanism.

Even those most scornful of America's literary heritage found one notable exception; Walt Whitman was a flicker of light out of the nation's dark past. Paul Rosenfeld offered a strange blend of hero-worship and iconoclasm when he celebrated Whitman for having been an iconoclast himself. "We must go where Whitman led," Rosenfeld exclaimed, "casting from us our past, joyously sure that where the wizard power of faith goes, there life follows after." Yet to idolize Whitman as a prototypical iconoclast was a rather limited use of the past, and Brooks had already interpreted him more expansively in *America's Coming-of-Age*. Whitman, Brooks discovered, represented "the rudiments of a middle tradition, a tradition that combines theory and action." Here was a writer who had rooted himself in the realities of American life and worked with organic materials, who had begun to express "a national ideal" yet avoided the highbrow, who had come down from the lofty plane of Emerson and claimed a place for literature among the common people. But Brooks, in keeping with the wish to establish the importance of his own generation, refused to grant Whitman complete success. Whitman was, after all, "undiscriminating, confused and a little fatuous"; he was "lost on the plane of ideas" and relied too much on emotion at the expense of intellect;

he embraced America to the point of affirming everything, and he was insufficiently critical.[17]

To some of Brooks' followers, however, Whitman demonstrated the possibility of reconciling the highbrow and lowbrow. Dos Passos celebrated the poet for having "shouted genially, fervidly his challenge to the future" even if he had "failed to reach the people he intended to." At least he had shown the ability to fuse vision with experience, and in this he served as an inspiration to those who were arriving at a better time for rousing the nation. Waldo Frank similarly identified Whitman, along with Lincoln, as the prophets of a new America. Together they heralded "the break from the materialistic culture of pioneer America" and "the emergence from it of a poetic and religious experience based on the reality of American life." In 1919, the same year in which Frank recognized these heroes, Dell wrote of Whitman as the spirit behind the younger generation's mission of transforming America's crude realities into a beautiful society—as the originator of the impossibilist élan. It was Whitman who had expressed his faith in turning the "sow's ear of prose" into the "silk purse of his poetic prophesy."[18] Slowly, Dell's generation came to identify a rudimentary prophetic tradition—a heritage of creative minds in touch with society and demanding its redemption. Earlier Americans, it seemed, had taken critical stands in the faith that their judgments would ultimately prove true and their words inspire change. Modern critics could begin to view themselves as the successors in a line of independent and socially aware writers and artists. Bourne understood the importance of belonging to such a line and reinforcing a sense of purpose in communion with the heroes of the literary past. Looking perhaps to his friend Brooks, he called for a "new classicist" to "rescue Thoreau and Whitman and Mark Twain and try to tap through them a certain eternal human tradition of abounding vitality and moral freedom, and so build out the future."[19]

4.

The real work of constructing a sustaining past commenced in the 1920s, but Brooks was not among the builders. His conception of the intellectual as adversary prevented him from embracing a tradition that had belonged for so long to the professors and the businessmen. "I agree with the poet who says: 'To write in favor of that which the great interests of the world are against is what I conceive to be the duty and the privilege of the intellectual,' " he stated in 1921; and he might have added the corollary that it was the intellectual's responsibility to repudiate everything that the "interests" revered.[20] Expanding on the themes of *America's Coming-of-Age* and "On Creating a Usable Past," Brooks devoted himself in the first half of the twenties to a kind of redemptive debunking. His cautionary tales, he hoped, would embolden modern writers in their spirit of opposition and inspire them to transcend the limits of the past. While Mumford would later insist that Brooks had taken the lead in "awakening American interest in the unsuspected richness of our literary past," his influence appeared more in the form of exhortation than example.[21] Others initiated the positive attempts at recovery.

Mumford's friend Paul Rosenfeld is the forgotten figure in the effort to establish a viable alternative tradition. Rosenfeld's *Port of New York* (1924) was a transitional work between iconoclasm and a new historical understanding. The usable past that he discovered extended back only a few years; the creative heroes of *Port of New York*, with only one exception, were members of his own generation. Yet Rosenfeld discussed them as if they represented a substantial heritage—a foundation on which to build the culture that would regenerate America: "These creators, independently, through different mediums, and in different manners, had nevertheless all of them given me the sensation one has when, at the close of a prolonged journey by boat, the watergate comes by, and one steps forth and stands with solid [ground] under foot." In the artists Albert P. Ryder, Marsden Hartley, Kenneth Hayes Miller, John Marin, Arthur G. Dove, Georgia O'Keeffe, and Alfred Stieglitz, the poets and novelists Carl Sandburg, William Carlos Williams, and Sherwood Anderson, the musician Roger H. Sessions, the educator Margaret Naumburg, and the critics Brooks and Bourne, Rosenfeld believed he had located the beginnings of an indigenous culture which combined a sense of place with a transforming vision. "For the first time," he rejoiced, "among these modern men and women, I found myself in an America where it was good to be."[22]

Like all of Rosenfeld's non-fiction books, *Port of New York* was a collection of essays. But here there was a clear sense of movement, chronological to some extent and progressive in that the subjects of the essays appeared in increasing order of creative success. Thus the book began with Ryder, a classic case of the rootless American artist who could not quite manage to bring his fine spirit to bear upon earthy realities. "The upper spiritual reaches of the body were singing flesh to him," Rosenfeld wrote. "The lower he could not fit into his scheme of beauty." Then came Brooks, the critic whose insistence on "the life of expression, the disinterested existence" showed the way for creative minds to bring themselves to bear upon American life. "For an entire population," Rosenfeld argued, "Brooks has begun the creation of an [sic] 'usable past.' " But his more recent work suggested the kind of acquiescence and defeatism that he had always condemned in others. In *The Ordeal of Mark Twain*, Brooks seemed to delight in showing the inescapability of "an unfavorable environment," even to the point of minimizing the triumph of *Huckleberry Finn*. By harping on failures rather than accomplishments—in his assessment of Whitman, for example—he undermined the usable past he claimed to desire. Brooks' apparent belief in the inevitable corruption of the creative mind by a business civilization demonstrated "the very want of sympathy for art and the artistic life of which he accuses society."[23] From such stories of failed will, Rosenfeld moved toward the heroic figures of Bourne and Stieglitz, the prophetic critic and photographer who neither shied away from nor acquiesced in the harsh substance of American experience. Bourne's "fighting papers" on the war used the brutalities of the present to show "a beautiful unrealized world" and "to make that hidden sphere more real and visible." Stieglitz's photographs of New York, "full of strange brazen human emptiness," were also "full of a marvelous potential life." This form of presentation allowed Rosenfeld to preserve a degree of generational exceptionalism while also contributing to the creation of a usable past. His occasional homage to Whitman or Twain did not seriously contradict the placement of his own generation in the vanguard of an alternative tradition. America now had a usable past, Rosenfeld told his contemporaries, and they were it.[24]

Mumford's first investigations into American cultural history dug deeper than Rosenfeld's instant tradition. Not only did *Sticks and Stones* (1924) revalue the New England village, but it also recovered a hero from amid "the barbarism of the Gilded Age." H. H. Richardson, according to Mumford, had "pitted his own single powers" against the vicious materialism and debased architecture of his time without retreating into the nostalgia of Morris and Ruskin; he had resisted the "sloppy workmanship and quick turnover" that characterized the period, yet "he did not turn his back upon the excellences of industrialism." In Brooks' terms of creative integrity, Richardson had managed to merge an ideal of the good life with the materials he found nearby.[25]

For Mumford, however, the resurrection of Richardson was only a tentative step toward creating a whole roster of inspirational figures. His next project was to reclaim the writers of 'The Golden Day"—Emerson, Thoreau, Whitman—from both the professors and the iconoclasts. Emerson, it turned out, was not the pathetic highbrow that Brooks had portrayed. Instead, he was a man with a hearty grasp of real life as well as a man of ideals—one who "recognized the formative role of ideas" when they were rooted in experience:

For Emerson, matter and spirit were not enemies in conflict: they were phases of man's experience: matter passed into spirit and became a symbol: spirit passed into matter and gave it a form; and symbols and forms were the essences through which man lived and fulfilled his proper being.

Thoreau and Whitman also took "America as it was" and out of it produced writing that envisioned "a better order of society." In a passage that summarized the prophetic tradition for which he was searching, Mumford described "the smell of reality" and the "largeness of comprehension" in Whitman's poetry; "to transcribe for him was in the highest sense to *translate*." The Golden Day writers were at home in their time and place even as they imagined "a new world" and a "deeper life." At last, Mumford announced, American writers could claim a meaningful heritage, not for purposes of imitation but for inspiration. From the Golden Day's "example," the present generation could find its "own foundations" and discover its "own particular point of departure." Meanwhile, there was security in the knowledge that the prophet was not an anomaly in America and that the creative individual was not automatically an outcast.[26]

Between 1926 and 1931, Mumford filled out his usable American past. *Herman Melville* (1929) and *The Brown Decades* (1931) bridged the gap between the Golden Day and the twentieth century, and in the latter book Mumford provided his most explicit statement of the value of a continuous tradition. The "danger" that the "Buried Renaissance" of the Gilded Age would "vanish" before it had been "properly evaluated or fully assimilated" made it imperative that he describe the contributions of Ryder, Richardson, Louis Sullivan, Thomas Eakins, Winslow Homer,

Frederick Law Olmsted, George Perkins Marsh, and John and Washington Roebling. "If these artists and poets and thinkers are imperfectly remembered," Mumford wrote, "our own generation may perhaps pride itself a little more completely on its 'uniqueness,' but it will lose the sense of solidity that a continuous tradition, actively passed on from master to pupil or disciple, supplies."[27] Nobody had made a clearer assessment of the limits of iconoclasm than this. The sense of liberation that came from a break from the past was hardly worth the sacrifices in knowledge, culture, and rootedness.

Edmund Wilson made a similar observation in discussing the same period. Henry James and Stephen Crane, "though their ideas were less 'emancipated' " than those of the present generation, "possessed a sounder culture than we." They were "better craftsmen"; they were "professional men of letters, and they had learned their trade." The "illusion of a stronger vitality and a greater intellectual freedom" among "our race of writers today" could not obscure a lack of grounding. In a stab at "the recent renascence" of the mid-1920s, Wilson suggested that the repudiation of all tradition had left modern writers detached and intellectually impoverished, "polyglot, parvenu, hysterical and often only semi-literate."[28] Without a sense of tradition and continuity, the risk of lacking direction and squandering talent increased dramatically. Writers could easily find themselves speaking to no one and gravitating even further toward the periphery.

5.

When Brooks shifted definitively to a positive assessment of the American past, particularly with the publication in 1936 of the first book in his five-volume cultural history, *Makers and Finders*, he heard few words of praise from an intellectual community increasingly enamored of Marx and doggedly in pursuit of the class struggle in history and literature. One exception was Wilson, who recognized the merits of *The Flowering of New England* and *New England: Indian Summer* and tried to explain the critical backlash against Brooks. "Beginning as an opposition critic, read by a minority of the people," Wilson wrote, "he has lived to become a popular author, read by immense numbers of people and awarded a Pulitzer Prize —with the result that the ordinary reviewers are praising him indiscriminately and the highbrows are trying to drop him."[29] Whether for this reason or others, Brooks' work of the 1930s and beyond has been the repeated target of dismissive phrases and negative comparison. In 1981, Jackson Lears characterized Brooks' second phase as "the tired reiteration of nineteenth-century optimism," and Thomas Bender recently referred to Brooks' "undiscriminating, fact-laden, and intellectually vacant multivolume celebration of American literary culture."[30] While the division between Brooks' two phases is sharp, to write off his post-breakdown work as wholly uncritical and accommodationist is to misunderstand this later period. To gain a better conception of what Brooks believed he was accomplishing in the *Makers and Finders* books, it is necessary to look back to the mid-1920s, when he first began to formulate his reinterpretation of the American tradition.

By the time he published *The Pilgrimage of Henry James*, Brooks was already struggling to write the tale of success that would round out the story he had begun with the Twain book in 1920. After an initial nervous collapse in the summer of 1925—punctuated, significantly, by nightmares about Henry James—he believed he had reached a new understanding of Emerson and was prepared to use him as the subject of his next study. In response to a letter from Mumford which had laid out the argument of *The Golden Day*, Brooks announced his new awareness "of the value and meaning of all the things" Mumford had been "turning over" lately. He agreed with Mumford's ideas about "the 'mission'—what other word is there?—of literature, and the necessity of re-asserting the idealistic point of view, with an energy and a faith our good country has not *known* for many years." To this end, Brooks was prepared to create an Emerson who represented the integration of the highbrow and the lowbrow, the reconciliation of the competing pulls that had destroyed James and Twain. "Everything I have done so far has been a kind of exploration of the *dark* side of our moon," he confessed, "and this blessed Emerson has led me right out into the midst of the sunny side." With Twain as thesis and James as antithesis, Emerson would be the synthesis that pointed the way to a viable intellectual and artistic life. "These stories of 'failures' are only by the way," Brooks told Sherwood Anderson after the appearance of the James book, "and I am working now along quite another line—or rather as I hope, finishing that line with a story that is written the other way around."[31]

Before he could complete *The Life of Emerson* to his satisfaction, Brooks suffered another, more serious breakdown. Though the full Emerson study was not published until he had emerged from his "Season in Hell" in 1932, he agreed to the publication of six chapters as essays in 1927. *Emerson and Others* established the themes that Brooks would develop more fully after his recovery; in rough form, it presented his revised version of the nation's literary and intellectual past. Brooks' new Emerson was no longer the aloof Transcendentalist of *America's Coming-of-Age*. Instead, he was a man of intellect entirely at home in the world of reality—a thinker who loved "to exchange ideas with artists and teachers" but who "learned from his country neighbors too!" Thoroughly rooted in the life of the region, Emerson escaped the threat of abstraction. Among the farmers and craftsmen of Concord and the merchants and laborers of Boston, he studied "the low tone, and he never forgot in their presence that the roots of the great and high must be in the common life." But Emerson's close contact with reality did not drag him down into a lowbrow acquiescence in the status quo. He remained independent; he stood firm against the crackpot reform schemes of his friends and the conformist tendencies of American life. Brooks called him "the greatest heretic of them all" and celebrated him for persisting "in his own native choices against all argument and example" and defending them "against the multitude" and "against the wise." Emerson was, in short, the outstanding figure in an American prophetic tradition that combined independence and involvement, letters and leadership. According to Brooks, Emerson absorbed the materials of the common life and used them to transform the public consciousness by making people aware of their "latent power and knowledge."

In this "prophet of the new age," Brooks had discovered his model intellectual. Brooks' Emerson was a central presence in his place and time, a writer and lecturer who "energized" his audiences and inspired them to realize the beauties of self-expression. "What had been vague in their minds became suddenly clear, doubts were transformed into certainties, half-hearted hopes into vigorous resolutions." In "the minds of his listeners he separated all that was active, creative and fine from the slothful remainder. Life, at the sound of his voice, sprang out of apathy, and faith out of unbelief." Here, at last, was proof of the possibility of an unalienated, influential intellectual life in America, and Brooks made certain to bring out the parallels between past and present. Emerson had chosen to work outside the ministry and the college; he published in and helped run a little magazine; he supplemented his income and reached a larger public by lecturing; he recognized self-expression as the basis for social renewal; and, of course, he set the example for where intellectuals should live—far enough away from the city for freedom, close enough for a "periodical raid." "He could do his thinking alone," Brooks noted, "but he had to go to market to get his facts."

This revised Emerson vindicated the efforts of Brooks and his generation by confirming that the independent thinker could also be a vital force for social change. When Brooks announced to Mumford his discovery of a positive example in the American past, he also indicated that a celebratory history could point toward an alternative future: "Emerson was right when he said that it only needs two or three men to give a new turn to the public mind." When Brooks' judgment of the past began to shift, it did not signal a new affirmation of the present. The reconstruction of an American literary tradition could be as much a work of social criticism as the rejection of the past had been.[32]

While Brooks was incapacitated, others carried on the challenge of creating a usable past. Constance Rourke, a friend of Brooks from the *Freeman* days, made it her life's work to disprove what she took to be the thrust of his early criticism: that creative minds had never really been at home in America. In 1931, she published her most important book, *American Humor.* Rourke's concern, as Joan Shelley Rubin has perceptively argued, was to find the popular roots of American literature and thus to place artists and intellectuals "at the center of American life." If it could be shown that high art grew out of folk culture, then artists and intellectuals could escape a sense of alienation. By claiming, for example, that "self-conscious reflection" was a common trait of the figures of American folklore, Rourke rescued intellectuals from the periphery and recast them as versions of the national type. There could be no validity to Brooks' highbrow/lowbrow dichotomy when high culture and popular culture were parts of a continuum and when intellectuals epitomized the American character. Rourke wrote of a unity between "popular fancies and those of genius" and brought together intellectuals and the folk in a "homogeneous world of the imagination."[33]

Brooks respected Rourke's work and recognized her as an ally in the search for a past that would nurture creative expression. But they differed in one crucial respect. Rourke was content to erase the division between the intellectuals and the common people by establishing the folk origins of all culture. In her attempts to show how a national literature followed the patterns set by folklore, she was not particularly interested in demonstrating how intellectuals and artists then influenced the folk, nor was she concerned with tracing out the contours of intellectual communities. She succeeded in making intellectuals belong without making them into leaders; Rourke's first goal was to connect writers to the masses, not to delineate the connections between writers that made for communal identity. Brooks, however, demanded more than a knowledge of common origins. Like Waldo Frank, who noted in 1929 that the folk represented conformity and a leveling downward as much as intuitive wisdom, Brooks insisted on asserting the intellectual capacity for public leadership and the integrity of artists and intellectuals as members of distinctive communities. In *The Re-discovery of America*, a more cryptic book than its title suggests, Frank argued that the "Golden Day" provided an example of thinkers "drawing and distilling and forming the energy of the folk-bodies."[34] This was an image more in keeping with Brooks' treatment of Emerson and with the massive cultural history that he began in the 1930s.

 The Flowering of New England (1936) expanded *Emerson and Others* (1927) and *The Life of Emerson* (1932) into a full discussion of the Golden Day in which the villains of *America's Coming-of-Age* reappeared as intellectual and artistic heroes. Brooks followed Rourke in reintegrating writers such as Longfellow, Lowell, Whittier, and Hawthorne into the American mainstream; he, too, insisted on their connections to the land and the folk. Lowell, Brooks claimed, had the "Yankee tongue" in "his blood." Oliver Wendell Holmes was "a good Yankee jockey, rejoicing in his own vernacular." Whittier's mind "was steeped in local associations, tales of witches, tales of the Indian wars, the gossip of wandering farm-hands and gypsies." Writers who had once seemed aloof from the common life now appeared as the spokesmen "of the folk point of view," the voices of the region and the nation. Their roots in lowbrow reality, in turn, allowed them to clarify and shape this point of view. In Longfellow, for example, "the poet had become the skald again, the bard, the singer and the story-teller, the moulder and hierophant of the national life, the people's aspirations." Not only did the Golden Day writers speak for the public; they also spoke to it. Brooks' objective in *The Flowering of New England* was to recover an authoritative intellectual community—one that refined common experience into forms of expression that would then inspire the public to seek a more expansive life. When he returned to Concord and Boston in *New England: Indian Summer* (1940), Brooks described the region's men of letters as both the "voces populi" and the rulers of the national mind. Boston, he declared, "possessed authority in every sphere," and the *Atlantic Monthly* "set the tone of American speech."[35]

In part, it was the discovery of a middle tradition that accounted for the celebratory tone of the *Makers and Finders* volumes. Brooks rejoiced at the New England Renaissance because he saw in it the reconciliation of the highbrow and the lowbrow. Here were writers who had managed to immerse themselves in reality and still preserve their integrity; here was a generation that had conveyed a vision based on what Brooks called "the simple, essential values" of creative labor, attachment to place, individual autonomy, and communal purpose. Brooks did not intend for his usable past to affirm the acquisitive present or to lure writers to adjust themselves to the world as they found it. Rather, he sought to recover a series of moments when artists and intellectuals seemed to have led the public into a consciousness of the good life and a commitment to its preservation or recovery. Returning to Emerson, Brooks noted his conception of the scholars' role: "They would be the world's eye and heart, resisting the vulgar prosperity that retrograded to barbarism." The past that Brooks presented in these books was an alternative tradition of intellectual engagement and leadership, self-expression and simple living rather than materialism and exploitation; the heroes he discussed were at once realists and prophets. His most sympathetic critic, Edmund Wilson, came closest to comprehending what Brooks was trying to accomplish. *The Flowering of New England*, Wilson commented, "brought home even to people who had already some acquaintance with the subject as no other book had done what post-revolutionary New England had meant to the America of its day as a cultural spokesman for the new humanity that was going to be built in the United States." Malcolm Cowley saw Brooks' revised assessment of the "New England Legacy" as part of a larger movement toward finding an alternative heritage. "[T]oday," he observed, "many sensitive men like Brooks are turning back to the great past in order to see the real nature of the traditions that we are trying to save and to gain new strength for the struggles ahead."[36]

In *The World of Washington Irving* (1944), Brooks offered his clearest picture of the middle tradition. Irving, Cooper, Audubon, Bryant, and Simms were all central rather than marginal figures in the young republic; "they were extroverts, generally speaking, at home with men of enterprise and action." Their orientation was both regional and cosmopolitan, and they were able to maintain a feeling for "local types" and "characteristic scenes" while avoiding narrowness and provincialism. Brooks down-played Irving's Anglophilia in presenting him as the quintessential man of the world whose strong regional ties prevented him from going the way of the later expatriates. "As a young New Yorker," Brooks wrote, "he shrewdly observed the ways of the town, for he was in temperament urban and always remained so." But Irving's deep roots in what Mumford called the valley-section kept him in touch with the regional landscape even during his years in Europe. He "liked to wander and dream on the banks of the Hudson" and to explore "the old Dutch farms and pastoral valleys," and he derived from his explorations subjects that would reso-nate with American audiences. Audubon, Cooper, Bryant, and Simms were also worldly writers with a sensitivity to place that gave their work the "authenticity" essential for a public literature.[37]

The greatness of Irving's generation lay not simply in its grasp of native materials, but in its ability to transform these materials into an image of "the nation of the future." Brooks hedged when it came to delineating the content of this national vision, yet he made clear that what these writers saw was not a future of rapaciousness and competitive individualism. They looked instead to a nation of enlightened craftsmen and cosmopolitan communities in which culture rather than acquisition would be the standard of living. *The World of Washington Irving*, though the third book to appear in the series, was the first volume chronologi-cally, and here Brooks was able to set out the central theme of the entire history—"what might be called the American prophetic tradition, of Whitman's *Pioneers*, the 'Trust thyself' of Emerson and Lincoln's mystical faith in the wisdom of the people." The heroes in this tradition affirmed the possibilities of democracy without abandoning the critical responsibil-ities of the creative intelligence. The fact that they were not alienated from American life—that they were, in Wilson's words, "many-sided in their interests and talents" and "men of the great worlds of society, geography, and nature"—did not mean that they surrendered their re-generative role. They were, as Brooks wrote of Aububon, the spokesmen "for the future of the race" and the pioneers in establishing a place for thinkers as awakeners and redeemers. "Thanks to these writers, acting together," he concluded, "the nation wakened rapidly to a sense of its own imaginative and mental resources." The recovery of this prophetic tradition would sustain modern writers in their efforts to comprehend

American life and transform its values. America's line of worldly prophets extended back to the beginning.[38]

Brooks' most significant achievement in *Makers and Finders* was captured in the phrase "acting together." As he abandoned the cursory glimpses into the past that had characterized his earlier books and immersed himself in the major and minor literature of entire generations, he came to see not only the existence of heroic individuals but the ties that bound these individuals into authentic literary communities. In the New England of the Golden Day, in the New York and Philadelphia of the early republic, Brooks discovered that writers and artists had known one another, communicated with and sustained one another, come together outside the established institutions of the ministry and the colleges to speak with an independent voice and to make contact with the social life of the region and the nation. The exhilaration of drawing connections and seeing communities in their full complexity accounts for the attention he paid to obscure figures and forgotten books; it also helps explain the density of his prose—his weaving into a single fabric excerpts from the lives and work of hundreds of people. Wilson recognized that much of the hostility to the *Makers and Finders* books had to do with Brooks' apparent inability to exclude any individual or piece of literature, no matter how mediocre or trivial. But Wilson also knew that this inclusiveness, this attention to "so many intertwined destinies," represented Brooks' great contribution.[39] He had managed to reconstruct in painstaking detail, not merely in broad outline, an American tradition of independent artistic and intellectual communities. It was this discovery rather than any embrace of the status quo that gave the work of Brooks' second phase its positive tone.

6.

The search for an alternative tradition gained a sense of urgency from national and international events in the 1930s and the early 1940s. In praising *The Flowering of New England* and thanking Brooks for laying "a cornerstone to the America of our dreams," Mumford placed the book in the context of world affairs. "A half dozen of us," he said in true prophetic form, "firing steadily from behind our book-barricade, may yet keep off the fascist hordes!"[40] For Brooks and others, the American past provided alternatives to the modern world, specifically to the evils of totalitarianism. A number of Brooks' contemporaries joined him in scouring American history for a society and politics to compete with fascism, communism, and corporate capitalism and made it their task to convey this competing vision to the American public.

In some cases, the specter of totalitarianism produced a kind of vacuous populism and nationalism that completely repudiated the earlier iconoclasm. Harold Stearns urged a return to "our old pioneering American spirit" as a solution to the Depression and allied himself wholeheartedly with "the common man" against the intellectuals and their "patronizing" schemes. Stearns' *Rediscovering America*, published in 1934, solved the problem of the intellectual's place by dismissing the idea of the intellectual as an independent social type. The writer who had once asked plaintively "Where Are Our Intellectuals?" now spoke derisively of "this curious monastic order" with its "romantic nostalgia for distinction." The best hope for America was to trust in common sense, to encourage a "feeling of nationalistic self-sufficiency," and to ignore the advice of those who insisted on standing apart. Stearns returned from Europe with a new target for his criticism and a new faith in American progress, democracy, and the melting pot which amounted to a strident anti-intellectualism and an uncritical Americanism. In the symposium he assembled sixteen years after *Civilization in the United States*, he juxtaposed an American tradition of skepticism and humor with the bombast of intellectuals. According to Stearns, "the soundest and most native aspect" of "the American stage-setting" was the folk's "keen sense of the ludicrous and absurd"—"our surest disinfectant against doctrinaires, language-wreckers, ideologists, and all the rest of the motley crew who carry over into manhood the nursery habit of playing with alphabet blocks."[41]

Gilbert Seldes also blasted the intellectuals in his search for a usable past and blamed the critics themselves for the absence of a worthwhile American tradition. Seldes actually attributed the confusion and loss of confidence that had exacerbated the Depression to the iconoclasm of the intellectuals. In a perverse claim for intellectual influence, he argued that American critics had "prevented us from understanding ourselves" by engaging in "a long-sustained attack on the outcome of a century and a half of American life." Instead of trying to find a usable American past, writers such as Brooks, Mumford, Mencken, Dell, Lewisohn, and Stearns had indulged in "the old assumption, the old propaganda, that literature is the standard by which a nation must be measured." This insistence on the value of an artistic tradition had effectively cut Americans off from their roots and left them unprepared to cope with modern problems. Seldes' *Mainland* (1936) was even more vehement in its anti-intellectualism than *The Seven Lively Arts* (1924) had been. Only self-important artists and critics believed in the value of art, according to Seldes, and in asserting the centrality of art, these elitists by implication supported autocracy. There had always been a "connection between artistic productiveness and national degeneration," he wrote; art presupposed "concentrated and centralized authority" and "political and economic slavery." Unlike Stearns, however, Seldes made a concerted effort to unearth a tradition that might guide the nation away from dangerous "isms" while reforming it in significant ways. American history was "not a record exclusively of robber barons triumphant, establishing the rugged individual," nor was it "the story of a nation developing remorselessly to the moment at which it is ripe for Communism." The tradition that Seldes discovered was a democratic capitalist heritage exemplified by William Jennings Bryan, the Populists, and Henry Ford. Bryan had stood for "a bourgeois-democratic system of ownership" which Ford had updated with his idea of the worker as consumer—his "democratic-capitalist method of avoiding the failure of buying power." What Americans needed to recover from the past was "their sense of freedom, their sense of endless possibilities, their right to work for what they want," in short, their pioneer spirit. The point to which this alternative tradition led, Seldes announced, was the New Deal. Franklin Roosevelt was the modern-day pioneer, the adventurous democrat who was breaking up plutocracy and restoring individual opportunity: "Bound to no single theory, capable of entertaining all ideas as possible and most of them as workable, he has a temperament which would be more appropriate in an era of exploitation and pioneering."[42] In his role as the anti-intellectual intellectual, Seldes sought to alert the American people to their pioneer past—now safely wrested from the highbrows—and to make this past serve as the basis for social, economic, and political reform. Despite his hostility toward intellectual pretensions, he did not hesitate to take on the responsibility of determining what was valuable in American history and explaining its applications for the present and the future.

If Seldes' version of the usable past pointed toward the New Deal as the alternative to plutocracy and autocracy, Lippmann's did just the opposite. *The Good Society* (1937) attacked all forms of bureaucratic statism and drew a connection between iconoclasm and arbitrary authority that signaled Lippmann's repudiation of the politics and historical sensibility of his youth. By rejecting all "tested truths," iconoclasts "made their own impulses the highest authority." Lippmann now embraced "the classical heritage" and "the liberal tradition" as the only alternative to the oppressive state, and he celebrated "the deep wisdom of the original Constitution" in checking excessive concentrations of power. A fuller appreciation of the rule of law as "the moral heritage of western society" and an understanding of the Constitution as a document intended to limit authority were necessary at a time of massive consolidation. Lippmann's own reform scheme, he insisted, was "deeply consistent" with this heritage. In place of bureaucracy, he would employ anti-trust and taxation policies to restore a more decentralized and competitive economy. The crisis of the Depression had combined with the iconoclasm of the 1910s and 1920s to displace the essential American tradition of limited government. Americans, it seemed, were now prepared to turn their backs on "a thousand years of struggle to bring the sovereign under a constitution." Lippmann faulted himself and his contemporaries for their disservice to history. "[O]ur generation has misunderstood human experience," he wrote. "We have renounced the wisdom of ages to embrace the errors the ages have discarded." Political, social, and economic reform demanded a renewed commitment to the liberal tradition; to stave off the triumph of "the Providential State" required an understanding of the historical fight "to extricate conscience, intellect, labor, and personality from the bondage of prerogative, privilege, monopoly, authority."[43] Part of the purpose of *The Good Society* was to rescue and restore this forgotten heritage.

The problem with celebrating alternative traditions, especially in the midst of New Deal and wartime nationalism, was that celebration often obscured criticism. When the critique of modernity was buried in the reverence for a lost moment or a hidden strand, the risk of reinforcing myths was as great as the likelihood of conveying a sense of dissatisfaction. Attempts to find indigenous alternatives to foreign ideologies in order to reform American society frequently sounded more like flag-waving than criticism. John Dos Passos' rejection of communism impelled him to search for an American radical tradition that could serve as the basis for social and political change. In 1942, he published *The Ground We Stand On*, a collection of historical portraits intended to lay out a democratic substitute for fascism, communism, and what he called "the baby-eating Moloch of monopoly capital." Dos Passos claimed that he was looking to history not as "an ornamental art" but "to find answers to the riddles of today," and he titled his introductory chapter "The Uses of the Past." Like Brooks, Mumford, and even Seldes and Lippmann, he came to value tradition for its emboldening effect on the present—its implication of shared involvement in a long struggle. In dangerous and unpredictable times, he wrote, "a sense of continuity with generations gone before can stretch like a lifeline across the scary present and get us past that idiot delusion of the exceptional Now that blocks good thinking." Dos Passos tried to use the republican tradition, best represented by Roger Williams and Jefferson, as a weapon against privilege in the fight for genuine social democracy. Yet his stale version of progressive history —"liberty" against "oligarchy," the people versus the interests—came out as a kind of tepid paean to American "selfgovernment." By the end of the book, the critique of modernity was lost in a celebration of Anglo-Saxon institutions, and the call for change was submerged in a generic statement of American destiny. "It was a commonplace of our fathers' and grandfathers' thought that men of Anglo-Saxon training and tradition know how to govern themselves better than other men," Dos Passos concluded. "Even through the shames and hypocrisies of the age of money rule which is now coming to an end it was not entirely an empty boast. Today our lives depend on it."[44] To sanctify any tradition, even as an implicit challenge to the status quo, made it difficult to avoid the impression of patriotic boasting. It was not easy to balance the desire for continuity and belonging with the need to dissent.

Nowhere is this more evident than in the case of Brooks, whose historical writings were significantly more cogent and thorough than the sketchy work of Dos Passos and others. His celebration of literary communities, of the middle tradition, of America's realist-prophets, of the balanced landscape and the cosmopolitan region, and of values other than accumulation continued to imply a critique of modern American life even in the midst of the Second World War. It is ironic, therefore, that Brooks found himself on the cover of *Time* magazine, the centerpiece of modern American mass culture, in October 1944. He was pleased to have broken through to a general audience and content with his financial independence. But the cost of popularity was a misinterpretation of his work— the imputation of an unabashed Americanism that made *Time* look kindly upon him and permanently clouded his image among critics and historians. *Time* transformed *The World of Washington Irving* into a proof of American destiny, without noting anything of its critical dimension. While the review recognized that Brooks was attempting "nothing less than to recreate the whole intellectual and artistic atmosphere of the period," it used his discoveries to gloat over America's ability to measure up to Europe and saw nothing to challenge the status quo in either the form or the content of America's "lively, vigorous and original" intellectual life. It even told the "plain reader" not to be "scared away by Author Brooks's reputation as the nation's most distinguished literary critic."[45] The adversarial mentality that informed all of Brooks' writing failed to come through in the *Makers and Finders* books, not because he emerged from his breakdown fully adjusted to modern America but because he believed that extolling the usable past was itself a potent form of criticism. Brooks' mistake was to imagine that very many readers would see in his glowing descriptions of an engaged and respected intellectual life a model for change rather than an apology for complacency. Unlike Lippmann, Dos Passos, Seldes, and Stearns, however, he had done more than simply pay homage to a democratic, republican, or liberal tradition and a handful of its heroes. With remarkable precision and in extraordinary detail, he had written an alternative history of intellectual communities that extended from *The World of Washington Irving* and the early republic to *The Confident Years* of his own generation.

CHAPTER 9

Versions of Marx

The "Red Decade," a label first applied by Eugene Lyons in 1941, misrepresents the intellectual attraction to Marxism. While it is true that writers embraced the ideologies of the Left in unprecedented numbers in the 1930s, the most committed leftist intellectuals began to explore Marx long before the Depression. Even the discussions that recognize antecedents insist on a dramatic reorientation of American intellectual life after the Crash and thus isolate intellectual Marxism from its broader and deeper context. The Depression no doubt had a serious impact on independent intellectuals. It made them much more aware of poverty and much more sensitive to economic conditions and processes. It also threatened their own precarious sources of income. But the effect of the economic crisis in "socializing" intellectuals can also be exaggerated. The effort to bring the life of the mind into significant contact with the life of society defined an entire intellectual generation that had embarked upon the task as early as 1910. Many members of this generation never came to Marx at all. Others identified themselves as Marxists only in the most general ways—by announcing their concern for the working class, by acknowledging the importance of economic relations in history, by voicing their agreement with the need for social transformation. Some drifted toward Marxism after exhausting some other method of socializing the intellect. Intellectual Marxism is best understood as part of a diverse and continuous struggle to find the connection between ideas and action and to make literature and criticism serve the purposes of social change. This was how Joseph Freeman characterized his own journey toward communism. "I wanted to be neither a businessman [father] nor a scholar [grand-father], but something else," he wrote in 1936, "something American which would combine action and thought."[1] Freeman's *American Testament*, published when he was still taken with communism, presented the discovery of Marx as an episode (the ultimate episode, according to Freeman) in a lifelong quest for engagement. Malcolm Cowley, whose *Exile's Return* helped foster the view of a distinct shift in intellectual concerns after the Crash, acknowledged an essential continuity when he wrote of his contemporaries' outlook in the 1920s: "So far from being an expression of their privileged position in society, their literary opinions were essentially a protest against society—in those days it seemed quite useless to protest by political action."[2] The "Red Decade" was a chapter in a much bigger story.

Above all, Marxism promised an end to intellectual isolation and marginalization. It offered visions of an expanded community of opposition in which intellectuals and workers would join together as historical agents. Communism, Waldo Frank recalled, "seemed to offer a *community;* and to belong to a community was what I needed." No matter how much sustenance an intellectual community provided, it had to link up with a larger social group; genuine belonging meant the integration of intellectuals into what Freeman called "the objective world." Maxim Gorky's phrase "the proletariat and the intellectuals," said Freeman, "indicated for us a social unity which alone pointed toward a new life."[3] Community, criticism, and effectiveness all seemed possible within Marx's framework—a framework which suggested the progression from the critique of bourgeois society to an active participation in its overthrow. While the precise nature of the intellectuals' role in bringing about social transformation was the subject of extensive debate, Marxism furnished a perspective from which intellectuals could work to make themselves matter. Here at last was the perspective that would solve the central problem of American intellectual life: how to reconcile free inquiry with importance. The only apparent certainty about Marxism was that it pointed in the right direction because it was hard-headed and realistic. The rest of the solution needed to be discovered or worked out, and this was the task of the critics.

1.

Until the Russian Revolution, Marxism had to compete as one among many possible paths toward regeneration and intellectual engagement. The writers for the *Masses* possessed at least a superficial familiarity with Marx, but as Leslie Fishbein has argued, his ideas merely blended into an eclecticism that offered "no coherent theory of social change." From the beginning, however, Marxism had one advantage over competing perspectives: an aura of realism. Max Eastman was introduced to Marx and Engels by his wife Ida Rauh in 1911. Suddenly, he remembered, his inclination "toward a kind of pastoral utopia where people would be more free and equal, more friendly, more given to dwelling in truth and reality" than they were "in this money-getting world" yielded to a body of ideas that seemed to consider "the hard facts of human nature" and the real forces at play in the material world.[4] Eastman's discovery of Marx was probably more gradual than the epiphany he described in his autobiography, but he could only welcome a philosophy that paid so much attention to economics and identified so clearly the mechanisms for change. The claim of realism was essential to those like Eastman who wanted to distance themselves from the ivory tower.

With the October Revolution, the appeal of Marxism grew dramatically. There could be no greater confirmation of Marxism's realism than the fact that it had worked. As John Reed saw it, the Revolution had not come "as the *intelligentsia* desired it; but it had come—rough, strong, impatient of formulas, contemptuous of sentimentalism; *real* . . ."[5] Reed's reaction represented an everpresent strain in intellectual Marxism. The identification of the working class (or its organized party) as the only genuine force for revolution produced a denigration of the "intelligentsia" as possessing any useful knowledge or any unique social role. One side of Reed—and of many of his contemporaries—was so eager to become socialized and to join the course of history that he veered into a sometimes strident anti-intellectualism.

In the immediate aftermath of the Revolution, Eastman displayed this anti-intellectual side as he engaged in several exchanges over the proper position for intellectuals to take. By way of an open letter to the French novelist and critic Romain Rolland, published in the *Liberator* in December 1919, Eastman insisted that Marx's division of society into "the capitalists and the proletariat" precluded all other social groupings.

"[M]orally it is distasteful to me to treat of myself, and to see you and those associated with you treat of yourselves, as 'intellectuals,' and conceive of yourselves as thus forming a separate class," he told Rolland. There was, according to Eastman, "no independent intellectual class, any more than there is an independent class of drygoods merchants." The only matter of choice for the so-called intellectuals was to merge into one class or the other, and historically "the most eminent wholesalers and retailers of intellectual goods" had tended to be "capitalist-nationalistic in their position." Eastman's prescription was to drop all claims to an independent standing in society and to work against the natural tendency to side with the capitalists. After the decision to enlist with "the wage-laborers of the earth," intellectuals should acquiesce in their leadership. "I would put more trust in the ignorant," advised Eastman, for the ignorant were not biased by "culture and wealth of knowledge" toward conservatism.[6] The class struggle seemed to demand that intellectuals abandon their identity as such and reemerge as workers who happen to labor with their minds and pens; they were not to think of this kind of work as being in any way superior to other forms of labor. Eastman did not specify the value of literary production in the class struggle.

He returned to this theme several months later, when it was suggested that the *Liberator* join the international movement *Clarté*, led by the French writer Henri Barbusse. Responding to this call, Eastman announced his "humble respect" for *Clarté*'s roster of intellectuals but confessed to feeling "alien and opposed" to the whole idea of the organization. In what was the most serious indictment a student of John Dewey could make, he said that the movement smacked of "bad science—or complete lack of science" because it failed to recognize Marx's substitution of material forces for ideas as "the real motor forces in social evolution." Once again Eastman dismissed the notion that intellectuals could occupy a special place in the real world of class conflict; the word "intellectuals" itself had always seemed to him more useful "as a missile with which to knock over a prig, than as a tribute of praise to a sincere man in humble contact with reality." Those who clung to the Hegelian fantasy that ideas could have any impact per se were merely trying to assert an impossible claim for themselves as "natural leaders and light-bringers in a revolutionary age." Against *Clarté*'s conception of a role for thinkers as illuminators of reality, Eastman urged a sober surrender of "the pretense of revolutionary and intellectual leadership":

It is not intellectuality, reason, "the power of thought," that will fight and win the battle for liberty and international peace. It is the self-protective will of the exploited classes that will do it. And if there really is such a thing as an intellectual —a person whose will attaches with a single devotion to abstract and impersonal truth—he will be distinguished by his *knowledge of this very fact*.[7]

When he heard in June 1921 that *Clarté* had "purged its ranks of reformers and amateur socialists" and "accepted the principle of the class-struggle in its full meaning," Eastman was able to treat the movement more kindly. He may also have begun to recognize that he was writing himself into a corner—that his attacks on intellectuals were a form of self-immolation; he was now willing to concede writers a unique place in the revolutionary ranks. Propaganda and education (which were synonymous in Eastman's view) were best left to the party and its publications. So then what could writers contribute to the cause? "There is no single word for it," he explained, "but in my own vocabulary I call it poetry." As he had argued in *Enjoyment of Poetry* in 1913, "literary and artistic people" were "distinguished" by their "ability to realize—to feel and express the qualities of things." These "experts in experience," by conveying reality, could contribute "something indispensable to the practical movement"—"something that we might call *inspiration*."

Whatever concessions Eastman had made to intellectual independence, however, were not sufficient to satisfy those who insisted on a freer and more decisive role for writers. Van Wyck Brooks, whose professed socialism was never anything more than vague, chafed at Eastman's ambiguous statements about the leadership of the Communist party and rejected the secondary status that writers continued to hold in Eastman's scheme. An inspirational role was not enough, Brooks argued, if autonomy and leadership had to be surrendered to others. Eastman was wrong to suggest that "literary and artistic people have no grounds for setting themselves up as leaders." After all, it was the artists and intellectuals—the Pushkins, Tolstoys, Dostoyevskys, Shaws, Wells, Webbs, Morrises, and Ruskins—who made "the statesmen, the economists and the scientists" possible by creating the "desire" that "precedes function." "If Pushkin had never existed," Brooks stated, "it is absolutely certain that Lenin would never have existed either." Neither the working class nor its politicians could ever be aroused except for the words and thoughts conveyed in literature and criticism; without literary leadership the masses would remain "so unconscious as to behave almost as if it were automatic." And for this leadership to assert itself required nothing "less than absolute freedom." From here the Eastman-Brooks debate devolved into an argument over semantics. Eastman's response, titled "Inspiration or Leadership," granted that literature might "sometimes in great hands inspire the workers in a practical movement towards a richer and more universal life for all." If Brooks wanted to call this leadership rather than inspiration, that was fine. But the workers were still the true agents of change, and the presence of artists and intellectuals was probably incidental to the success of any revolution.[8] For all his concessions and the much gentler tone of "Inspiration or Leadership," Eastman refused to admit what the whole exchange had made abundantly clear: that Marxism had not yet done anything to clarify the intellectuals' social function.

2.

Against the tendency toward anti-intellectualism, a competing strand of intellectual Marxism affirmed rather than denied the motive power of the creative intelligence. The Russian Revolution, according to this affirmative vision, did not point to the submergence of the intellect in the class struggle; instead, announced Floyd Dell, it offered writers "the possibility, in the nature at present of a religious hope, of shaping the whole world nearer to the heart's desire." In Dell's view, the Revolution signaled the end to a century of intellectual and artistic resignation that had followed in the wake of the French Revolution and persisted in the climate of determinism produced by Darwin and the theory of evolution. Even Marx's philosophy, when rigidly interpreted by resigned intellectuals, had served until 1917 as another excuse for "fatalism." But the Bolsheviks, Dell explained, had exploded the narrow determinism of the nineteenth century and restored the belief "that the Great Change was to be effected by a sweeping conversion of men's minds."[9] In other words, the Russian Revolution had demonstrated the place of human volition—and the centrality of intellectual leadership—in the historical process.

Lenin was the figure who seemed to confirm these beliefs and came to function as a particular kind of hero and model for Marxist intellectuals in America. Even as he was scoffing at the idea of intellectual leadership in his responses to Rolland and *Clarté*, Eastman apotheosized Lenin for his ability to guide and shape the Revolution. In a 1918 poem entitled "To Nicolai Lenin," Eastman celebrated his hero for bringing "light" (precisely what he mocked in his attacks on *Clarté*) and "mountain steadiness of power" to the cause. "You to the dreadful depth of change descend," the poem concluded, "And with its motion, moving it, you blend/ Your conquering purpose, as blue rivers roll/ Through all the ocean's waters toward the pole." Eastman's Lenin was no utopian; he did not move against the currents. But within the limits set by circumstance, he introduced purpose and steered the course of history toward a desired end.[10]

Eastman returned repeatedly to Lenin in the 1920s as an example of what he termed "a statesman of the new order," whose supreme trait was that he knew how to think. "He has the habit of defining a problem before he enters it," Eastman observed, "and he enters it with the trained equilibrium of one who knows the true relation between facts and ideas in scientific thinking." Lenin was, in short, the quintessential pragmatist —a thinker constantly aware of the "concrete situation" and able "to refocus his powerful will, and to readjust his wealth of ideas, to new states of fact" in order to produce results. As Lenin applied it, Eastman argued, Marxism was flexible rather than dogmatic and permitted the kind of intellectual freedom necessary to insure its efficacy. In fact, Lenin was so complete a pragmatist—so independent in his thinking because so committed to translating ideas into action—that he did not even consider "the Marxian theory as anything other than a scientific hypothesis in process of verification." What his critics called his "dogmatism" was really the pragmatist's clear identification of an end to be pursued, and what they called his "opportunism" was simply the flexibility needed to reach this end. When Lenin died, Eastman eulogized him as "the first great historic engineer"—"the first leader of mankind who, instead of unconsciously expressing the dominant social forces of his time, analysed those forces and understood them" and guided "the one he believed in to its goal." He was the supreme example of the free but focused intellect as a force for social change. "Lenin," Eastman summarized, "was the first man who ever consciously and in a profound sense, made history."[11]

In less elaborate form, Eastman's intellectual associates joined him in the cult of Lenin. John Reed, who in some places minimized the importance of any leadership, celebrated Lenin as "the locomotive of history" and a "strange popular leader—a leader purely by virtue of intellect." Like Eastman, he took particular notice of the Bolshevik leader's willingness to experiment. Floyd Dell, in a review of Reed's *Ten Days That Shook the World*, focused almost exclusively on the "towering" figure of Lenin. "Not by eloquence but by knowledge he becomes the prime mover of revolutionary events," Dell wrote; because of a thorough understanding of reality gleaned from calm and open-minded investigation, everything "is done as he says—for he is right." Clearly borrowing from Eastman, Dell described how "the scientifically daring, mathematically confident social-engineering genius of Lenin carried a distraught faction-torn nation to the right conclusion in the nick of time." As late as 1936, when Eastman was irretrievably out of favor with Stalinists such as Joseph Freeman, Freeman still paraphrased Eastman on Lenin: "He was a man who had aroused a class, an entire country to the meaning of scientific knowledge."[12] For American intellectuals, part of the mystique of the Russian Revolution lay in the decisive role that Russian intellectuals, with Lenin in charge, had played. Here was proof that the critical, creative, and socially conscious intelligence could assert its presence in the thick of vital events.

While no American writers were so hubristic as to see themselves as potential Lenins, many derived from the example of Russia's revolutionary leadership the conviction that they could participate meaningfully in the work of social transformation.[13] Dell joyously proclaimed a new "era" that would stand out "among all others in the history of the world for its gigantic conscious effort at political reconstruction." Within this broad effort, intellectuals and artists, combining "high philosophic calm" with a "warm and rich humanity," could take on the responsibility for stating "the nature of the task which mankind may accomplish." In its content, as Michael Gold also insisted in his early advocacy of proletarian literature, revolutionary writing could teach the masses "courage and confidence," lead them "to scorn the ideals of bourgeois and capitalist society," strengthen the "sense of community" among workers, and contribute to "an indomitable will to victory and freedom."[14]

More importantly, the *act* of literary expression could provide glimpses into the life of fulfilling work and human freedom that would emerge from the revolution. Dell poked fun at Gold's "romantic delusion that he belongs to the working class" and his apparent shame at "not being a workingman" as signs of a self-defeating and socially unproductive kind of anti-intellectualism. In April 1922, Gold had publicly refused to review Harold Stearns' *Civilization in the United States* on the grounds that even in skimming the book he had smelled "the faint, acrid aroma of intellectual irony" and aloofness. The proletariat, he argued, had "no time to think or lead full-orbed lives," and so the intellectuals, in urging a life of "Art and Culture," were guilty of bourgeois sympathies. Dell retorted that, like it or not, "Comrade Mike" was "a literary man, an intellectual," and that there was "nothing to be ashamed of in that." The writers' revolutionary task of explaining, encouraging, and teaching could only be accomplished if they were "free from the necessity of toiling eight to fourteen hours a day." It was only with "leisure," Dell instructed Gold, that artists and intellectuals could make their contributions; and it was in demonstrating the creative possibilities of both work and leisure that they made their most substantial contribution to the revolution. The free life of the artist-intellectual was the only existing model for the life of all in the classless society. "He has come back from the stoke-hold talking about how beautiful Strength and Steam and Steel and Noise and Dirt are," Dell remarked of Gold. "If so, I say, why abolish capitalism?"[15]

Such conceptions of the writer's relation to the revolution continued to form a subtheme of intellectual discourse through the 1930s. A manifesto prepared by Edmund Wilson, Lewis Mumford, Waldo Frank, and John Dos Passos in 1932 expressed the belief that "in imaginative works, in philosophic thought, in concrete activities and groups, the nucleus and the framework of the new society must be created *now*." The purpose of "the social-economic revolution," these writers contended, was to "release the energies of man to spiritual and intellectual endeavor"—a point which Eastman made somewhat differently when he wrote in 1934 that "Art is what the proletarian has taken weapons in his hands to win." In his speech to the First Congress of American Writers in April 1935, Frank announced that "[w]e must have poets to sing the image of the new and truer person: the person who knows his integration with group and cosmos; the person through whom the whole speaks—conscious cell of the conscious Communist order." Through the practice of their craft, writers could see to the other side of the revolution, where self-interest has surrendered to self-expression and community, and could pass this vision on to the masses.[16]

3.

The belief not only that criticism and free inquiry were possible within a Marxist framework but that they were essential to revolutionary progress informed the efforts of American intellectuals to publicize and interpret the class struggle in the middle and late 1920s. By the fall of 1922, with Max and Crystal Eastman living abroad, the *Liberator* had exhausted its funds, and Michael Gold expressed his concern that it would have to be turned over "to some individual or some party that can put it on its feet." Despite their wish "to maintain the independent character of the Liberator," Gold, Dell, and Freeman failed to find an alternative source of income and finally agreed to surrender control to the Communist party. Almost immediately after the disappearance of the *Liberator*, its former staffers and contributors began to perceive the need for a new magazine of independent radicalism.[17]

To rally support behind the venture, the organizers made explicit reference to the *Masses*—a name certain to resonate among American intellectuals as a symbol of free expression. The aim was to put together as diverse and impressive a roster of contributing editors as possible and to make clear from the start the new magazine's commitment to open discussion. It was a wise strategy. Lewis Mumford expressed his enthusiasm by exclaiming "perhaps The Old Masses hasn't been killed yet!" and offering the use of both his name and his "good right arm." John Dos Passos wrote that "I'm absolutely with you and would gladly do anything to help. The *Masses* was the only magazine I ever had any use for." By March 1925, the project had a tentative (and long) name—"Dynamo: A Magazine of Arts and Letters, Interpretive of American Life: Interested in the Social Struggle, and in the Stimulation of Imaginative Works Created Out of the New Civilization." Among those who worked actively to launch the publication were Waldo Frank, Freeman, Gold, and Dos Passos; the list of less active supporters included Mumford, Eastman, Van Wyck Brooks, Stuart Chase, Susan Glaspell, Edmund Wilson, Claude McKay, Gorham Munson, Sherwood Anderson, Jean Toomer, Carl Sandburg, Eugene O'Neill, Walter F. White, and Art Young.[18]

In the prospectus for "Dynamo," all the themes of the *Masses, Seven Arts, Freeman*, and the early *New Republic* were restated: the need for indigenous art and ideas; the importance and efficacy of free inquiry; the revolutionary potential of creative expression; the dangers of aloofness; the evils of institutionalization and affiliation. The magazine would "espouse no special party of social reform or revolution" but would "be open to the creative messages of all of them." (According to the prospectus, the problem with the *New Republic, Dial, New Yorker, American Mercury*, and other publications was that they were too "limited.") "Dynamo" would forgo narrowness and propaganda for "deeply human interpretation" in the knowledge that "true literature and art alone" could bring "the values and significance of life" into "the general consciousness of a people." It would "strike its roots strongly into American reality" and remain free from any infatuation with European ideas. The prospectus managed to convince Freda Kirchwey and the other directors of the radical American Fund for Public Service (known as the Garland Fund after its benefactor) that the project was a worthy one; in May 1925, the Fund agreed to a grant of $30,000 for three years of operations if the magazine raised $20,000 of its own.[19]

By December, the name had been changed to the *New Masses*, but the commitment to openness and expansiveness remained. The official announcement placed the *New Masses* firmly within a tradition of intellectual independence by claiming, under the heading "Our Inheritance," a direct descent from the old *Masses*. "Its sympathies," the editors declared, "will be frankly radical, but it will have no affiliations with any political party and be committed to no special propaganda." The first issue, which appeared in June 1926, seemed to confirm the announced policy by featuring an enormous list of contributing editors and a debate between Dos Passos and Gold on the meaning of intellectual independence. Dos Passos stated his concerns about "phrases, badges, opinions, banners imported from Russia or anywhere else." As he saw it, "imported systems" had always been "the curse of this country." The *New Masses* had to be "a highly flexible receiving station," "full of introspection and doubt," rather than "an instruction book." Gold did not disagree. He merely accused Dos Passos of wanting to "revolt blindly" rather than with "full, bold, hard consciousness." He was not, he insisted, urging slavishness; it was absurd to think that American intellectuals would "take their 'spiritual' commands from Moscow." But neither would he "deny that Soviet Russia and its revolutionary culture" formed "the spiritual core" around which all genuinely committed artists and writers were "building their creative lives." For Gold, the Marxist framework was broad enough to allow for flexibility and indigenous expression while providing the "scientific" perspective without which all artistic and intellectual efforts were doomed to insignificance.[20]

Events in the Soviet Union—and their ramifications within the American intellectual community—soon forced Gold to define more clearly how much independence Marxism permitted before the cause of revolution was jeopardized. It was his old friend Max Eastman, back from Europe and openly siding with Trotsky against Stalin, who tested the sincerity of the *New Masses*' commitment to open discussion. Eastman's name had appeared on the masthead from the beginning, not because he was making any direct contribution to the magazine but because he, more than anyone else, could lend the prestige of the old *Masses* to the effort. When he returned to the United States in 1927, Eastman looked to the *New Masses* as a forum for his views, only to find that his critical opinions of the Stalin government were unwelcome. The editors, he complained, would only allow him to write "an innocuous 'literary' book review." He protested by resigning from the magazine's board. In his letter of resignation, Eastman argued that he had "joined" the *New Masses* on the "understanding" that it would be "independent of all dictation—a 'free revolutionary magazine.'" He had discovered, however, that "through fear of the loss of patronage or circulation, or through mere fear of stating the facts of life," the editors were either directly or indirectly obeying "the dictation of party heads." In Eastman's view, "this confused and pussy-footing policy" showed a "lack of intellectual force and courage" and was "harmful to the advancement of a genuinely revolutionary culture in America." By excluding criticism and dissent, the magazine was abandoning its function of interpreting American conditions and fashioning a revolutionary course in keeping with these conditions. The *New Masses*, or more appropriately "the Yellow Masses," was repudiating science; it was "worse than useless."[21]

Apparently, Eastman's opinions reached the Garland Fund and produced at least some concern among the magazine's editors that their income was in danger. One of the editors, Egmont Arens, felt compelled to write to Roger Baldwin (a director of the Fund) "to correct a rumor which has gained wide currency, namely, that the New Masses is more or less of a Communist organ." Arens directed Baldwin to "glance over the names of the members of our executive board" and to note that only a minority were party members. In fact, the magazine was not an official party publication, but the editors drew the line at any views that might threaten its place within the revolutionary movement. The inclusion of anti-Soviet opinions would put the *New Masses* outside the realm of influence. While it remained "dedicated to the job of drawing together the progressive radical elements, not widening their differences," there were limits to what was genuinely progressive or radical; independence must not interfere with effectiveness. Michael Gold's dismissal of the Trotskyites in 1930 summed up this line of reasoning. "They are," he wrote, "separated from the main stream of history," and nothing was more distasteful to Gold than the thought of being relegated to the periphery.[22] While Eastman now believed that a critical Marxism was the only path toward meaningful change, Gold and his *New Masses* colleagues were reaching the conclusion that the commitment to free discussion stopped short of permitting ideas that endangered the revolution or went against the apparent course of history.

Whether or not Eastman's complaints were directly responsible, the Garland Fund was much less enthusiastic about the *New Masses* after 1928. At one point, Baldwin indicated that he wanted Eastman to take over the magazine (he never did), and the Fund refused to grant a request for an additional appropriation in April 1928. By the end of 1929, Floyd Dell had also resigned and earned Gold's eternal enmity. In October 1933, the Communist party took control of the *New Masses* and thus brought a conclusive end to the experiment in independent Marxism.[23]

Eastman carried on his pursuit of a scientific Marxism despite the opposition of the *New Masses*. In V. F. Calverton's *Modern Quarterly* and in his books, Eastman produced a critique of Marxist orthodoxy that would, he believed, serve as the first step toward the creation of a more legitimate alternative. He was guided in this task by a hostility to Stalin which extended as far back as Lenin's death. Eastman had, in effect, declared his independence in 1925, when he published Lenin's testament —a document that suggested Lenin's dislike for Stalin and his wish to be succeeded by Trotsky. The crisis in the Soviet Union compelled Eastman to search out its causes, which he discovered to be intellectual in nature; there had to be something wrong with Marx's *ideas* to produce such unfortunate results. In a curious interpretation of political developments, Eastman insisted that flaws in philosophy were responsible for Stalinism, and this, in turn, implied that a revision of Marx was necessary to produce a true socialism. By an intellectual tour de force, Eastman made his own work the key to revolution.

Marx and Lenin: The Science of Revolution (1927) was the fullest and most intelligent discussion of Marxist philosophy produced to date by any American intellectual of Eastman's generation. The book did not offer a new assessment of Lenin, whom Eastman still presented as the leader of a corps of "scientific revolutionary engineers." But Eastman was no longer prepared to view Marxism as an inherently scientific framework. Rather, he argued, Lenin was heroic precisely because he had gone against the essentially religious thrust of Marx's thought. Marx had never been able to cure himself completely of the "mental disease" of Hegelianism, described by Eastman as "an unintelligible mixture of emotional mysticism and psychological half-truth." In retaining the dialectic, even after substituting materialism for idealism, Marx and Engels perpetuated the belief that history was unfolding "in a congenial direction." Marxism thus possessed "the essential features of a religious psychology"—the faith "that the universe itself is producing a better society" and that people need "only to fall in properly with the general movement of this universe." In short, wishful thinking—what Eastman called the "animistic habit"—lay at the heart of Marxist orthodoxy. Dialectical materialism identified the goal of a communist society with the inevitable course of history.[24]

Eastman was most disturbed by the apparently fatalistic quality of Marxist metaphysics. There was no recognition by Marx and Engels that human purpose, not "History," was what really produced social revolution; there was no conception of "true science," of "defining a purpose and compelling the external world into its service." Eastman could not tolerate any system that seemed to deny the creative potential of thought, and the rigid economic determinism that he attributed to Marx and Engels implied such a denial. Their failure to differentiate between conditions and causes had produced a false view of history as a process beyond human control, shaped solely by unmanageable economic forces. In reality, Eastman contended, economic forces merely suggested the boundaries of human intervention, and if properly understood, contributed to the kind of scientific outlook that allowed people "to control history to the fullest possible extent." This was Lenin's genius. Lenin, according to Eastman, had no real interest in the dialectic; if he believed in it at all, he managed to escape from its deleterious effects by disguising his experiments in "practical engineering" as parts of some inevitable historical process. Without letting it be known, in other words, he was "heretical," and the Bolshevik Revolution—a product of scientific thinking—"was a violation of Hegelian Marxism." Lenin temporarily transformed Marxism from a religion into a science, which, as Eastman described it, met all the criteria of Dewey's instrumentalism:

It defines the structure of human society and determines the forces which control it, and upon the basis of those given facts which are not changeable, it proposes a method by which human society can be changed.[25]

After Lenin's death, however, Soviet Marxism turned back toward religion. Eastman concluded *Marx and Lenin* by connecting the bureaucratic statism of Stalin's Russia with a return to dialectical materialism. Either through his own ignorance or in a conscious effort to consolidate his power, Stalin was using Marx's belief in the inevitable progress of history toward communism (the withering away of the state) to justify his counterrevolutionary actions. As Eastman viewed it, "animistic mysteries have always been employed by an aristocracy to befuddle the masses," and in this case, they were being used to postpone or avoid the building of true communism.[26] In its orthodox form, Eastman was suggesting, Marxism could justify any evil. The salvation and extension of the revolution demanded that Marxism be revised from a religion into a science. *Marx and Lenin*, presumably, was the first step.

By the late twenties, Eastman had completely abandoned his earlier assumption that intellectuals would do best to blend inconspicuously into the proletariat. He now insisted that intellectual independence was crucial, not so much for its own sake as to provide intelligent guidance to the processes of social change. Though isolated from many of his old colleagues, Eastman could take solace in the apparent fact—by his own reasoning, at least—that he still had an important role to play in the revolutionary movement. It was the critical Marxist, the scientific Marxist, who was the sole hope for the revolution.

While he succeeded in pointing out some of the dangers of orthodoxy, Eastman failed to see the problems in his "scientific" alternative. His belief in a vaguely defined "science of revolution" itself verged on religious faith; at times, he was as dogmatic about science as others were about dialectical materialism. When Claude McKay, an editor of the *Liberator* after Eastman's departure, insisted that the magazine carry articles on black issues in closer relation to the proportion of blacks in the American population, Eastman blasted him for abandoning "the habit of practical thinking." "Where is your training as a political engineer?" he asked. "Do you live in the age of Lenin or Tom Paine?" Later, Eastman told McKay that it was a "tragedy" for "the leading revolutionary in the Negro world" to express doubts "that the race problem will be solved by the proletarian revolution."[27] Why Eastman believed that he was thinking scientifically on these issues is not clear. But if his self-image as a scientist of revolution led toward questionable judgments on certain matters, it also served to sustain him in his work. The revolution needed realists; it needed minds that could define purposes and chart courses of action. Opposition now—independence, hard-headedness, skepticism—could mean leadership later.

4.

The Depression, which pushed more of Eastman's contemporaries toward Marxism, did not alter the basic terms of the intellectual life. While Marxism savored of reality and revealed, it seemed, the hidden springs of social change, it also indicated a special place for those who were willing to explore, develop, and publicize its meanings and possibilities. The shift toward an explicitly Marxist critique of capitalism did not signal the repudiation of the goal of intellectual autonomy. Appealing as they were in providing context and structure, Marx's ideas were equally attractive for their apparent incompleteness and flexibility. In explaining his move to the Left after 1929, Waldo Frank confessed that the desire "to play a role of action" was paramount. But Frank and others responded to the promise of involvement in the belief that this need not preclude independence. The Communist movement required the "vision" that only writers could provide; the function of the intellectual as fellow traveler was "gradually to win" the Communists "to a deepening of their doctrine." Frank approved of Edmund Wilson's demand that American writers "take Communism away from the Communists"—that they take the lead in producing an independent Marxism better suited to American conditions. In the first half of the 1930s, there was reason for intellectuals to hope that they were on the verge of creating an autonomous yet decisive social role for themselves.[28]

Amid such hopes, independence was a persistent matter of concern. Though he felt drawn to the Left as early as 1930, Wilson resisted what he saw as the alien, religious character of communism. He had tried, he told Allen Tate, "to become converted to American Communism in the same way that Eliot makes an effort to become converted to Anglo-Catholicism." But there was something artificial about communism as it was currently constituted in the United States; it was somehow "unrelated to real life"—foreign rather than indigenous and ritualistic rather than adaptable.[29] He was not convinced, however, that these problems were insurmountable. In the *New Republic*'s "Position of the Progressive" symposium of 1931 in which he called upon intellectuals to rescue communism from the Communists, Wilson pressed for a resurgent opposition that would "not be afraid to dynamite the old shibboleths and conceptions and to substitute new ones as shocking as possible." Presumably, this would differ from the previous iconoclasm by substituting the sharper knowledge of society gleaned from Marx for a vague discontent and by recognizing that it was the "social system" itself that was responsible for America's lack of a "common purpose" and "common culture." With a clearer focus and a potential audience shocked into the realization that life in capitalist America was "meaningless," criticism stood a better chance than ever of becoming an authentic social force. The key to effectiveness, however, was intellectual integrity; there was no room for hackneyed phrases and borrowed ideas. "Who knows," Wilson asked, "that if we spoke out now with confidence and boldness, we might not find our public at last?"[30]

The articles that followed Wilson's in "The Position of the Progressive" series continued to insist on the necessity of intellectual independence. Matthew Josephson argued that intellectuals were uniquely capable of feeling and exposing the ills of capitalism. "I have always believed that the intellectual classes combat the profit-making order," he wrote, "not only because of their increasingly small part in it, but also because of the moral nightmares it gives them. The moment you are disinterested, as scientist, artist or teacher, you are hemmed in, jostled and harassed on every side by the stupefying principle that determines the whole environment: buy cheap and sell dear." By Josephson's reasoning, the fact that capitalism conspired against disinterestedness automatically placed intellectuals in opposition to bourgeois society and meant that disinterested thinking was by its very nature of service to the revolution. The writer's function was twofold: to agitate and convert. Through "the method of moral indignation," writers aroused the public; daring ideas, conceived by minds that functioned outside the profit-making order, possessed "psychological appeal" and "practical force." As a class apart, neither interested in the preservation of capitalism nor beaten down by it, "dissenting thinkers" were equipped to attack the status quo and to "imagine and picture the new state in all its forms."[31]

Benjamin Ginzburg went even further in defending the autonomy of intellectuals while insisting on the practical value of "cultural activity." Ginzburg warned against the tendency among "professional intellectuals" toward "a depreciation of their intellectual crafts in favor of a mysticism of social action" and criticized "the anti-intellectualism of the American intellectual, who is overawed by the practical sweep of American life." In one of the most perceptive self-analyses produced by an American critic in these years, he observed that "in no country is the intellectual so preoccupied with affecting the course of politics to the exclusion of his intellectual interests. The less power he has of determining conditions, the more passionate, it would seem, is his will-o'-the-wisp quest of political influence." The alternative to this "messianic inversion of values" was to recognize that the "real connection" between intellectual endeavor and social change could occur only when the autonomy of "intellectual and cultural activities" was absolute. These were the activities that "form the cradle of values, from which emerge the forces of spiritual generosity, freedom and disinterestedness that become crystallized, however slowly, in politics." From Ginzburg's perspective, preserving "intellectual values" —maintaining the intellectual community as an independent entity— was a vital precondition for "intelligent action."[32] On this point, at least, the participants in Wilson's forum were in agreement. No matter how great the allure of commitment, few among Wilson's contemporaries were willing to sacrifice their identities as critics to the cause of revolution; nor, as their hopeful statements suggested, did such a sacrifice seem necessary. The revolution would not only tolerate, but in fact seemed to demand, independent voices.

The idea that Marxism was pliable, that it lent itself to adaptation and revision for purposes of efficacy, surfaced often in the writings of intellectuals for whom Marx was a relatively recent discovery. Waldo Frank, for example, trumpeted his independence at the beginning of *Dawn in Russia*, an account of his Soviet travels published in 1932. His observations, he wrote, "may fully please no party. But perhaps, since they have satisfied a human need in me, they may satisfy a similar need in others who, like myself, are members of no party." Frank insisted on the role of "intelligence and will" in shaping revolution and thus felt an obligation to improve upon Marx; the book was a combination of reportage and Frank's own version of Marxism—the somewhat formless theory he later termed "integral Communism." Enamored of Russia, he was concerned nevertheless that its "militant ideology" would harden into dogma. "What," he asked, "may become of the relative truths of great men like Marx and Lenin—men who were the first to disclaim dogma and to stamp their doctrines as a method of action bound to shift as the scene of action shifted?" Like Eastman, Frank identified dialectical materialism as the troublesome component of Marxism. Frank's concern, however, was not with the dialectic but with materialism. Because Marx had been forced to wage war upon traditional religion, Frank argued, he had adopted a terminology which emphasized the hard facts of existence and the mechanics of life. The danger was that once the "first battles" to alter material conditions had been won, there was little in Marx to guide the revolution away from material values, "from the economic stage of proletarian dictatorship into the cultural stage of Communism." Somebody had to supply "a vision of life as deep and broad and flexible as growing life itself" to carry the revolution beyond the "mechanical and lifeless." Frank took it upon himself and his generation to add this spiritual dimension to Marxism: "to make it the religious movement for which the world is passionately crying." In contrast to Eastman, whose revisions were intended to make Marxism less rather than more religious, Frank believed that what was lacking in Marx was the mystical sense of the wholeness of life that he had tried to define in *The Re-discovery of America* (1929). To reach the "cultural stage of Communism," writers and artists would have to devise a "new philosophy" of "personal growth" and "*true* individualism." The greatest possible betrayal of the revolution would be for intellectuals to stop interpreting and to accept Marxism as a closed system. "To be a good Marxian," Frank bluntly put it in the September 1932 *New Masses*, "is to be creative enough to go beyond Marx." He clearly conceived of *Dawn in Russia* as an effort in this direction and concluded the book with a vindication of work such as his own:

The American intellectual above all must beware of a false emulation, which in accepting the letter destroys the spirit. We must be loyal to the social aims of Russia; loyal to the soldiers in the revolutionary ranks, and ready to take their side in every feasible way. But above all, we must be loyal—like the men of Russia—to our own needs and intuitions. We must forge our part of the world future in the form of our own genius.[33]

If intellectuals brought long-standing concerns about autonomy into their considerations of Marxism, direct observation of Communist party activities and troubling information about Soviet attempts to control the literary sphere deepened these concerns. After Wilson witnessed party organizers at work during the miners' strike in Harlan County, Kentucky, he "came back convinced that if the literati want to engage in radical activities, they ought to organize or something independently—so that they can back other people beside the comrades and so that the comrades can't play them for suckers." By June 1932, he was willing to agree with Dos Passos and to advise Frank, who had also been to Harlan County, that their proposed intellectual manifesto had to avoid following "the Communist formulas too closely." Wilson veered between the belief that "serious revolutionary work" was "impossible" without "obedience to central authority" and the sense that nothing valuable could be accomplished by "mere parrots of the Russian party and yes-men for Stalin." The furthest he would go in submitting to party "discipline" was to vote the Communist ticket in the November 1932 presidential election.[34]

A more detailed statement of the threats to independence came from the embattled Max Eastman, a party member for a short period in the early twenties who now emphatically rejected any such compromises of autonomy. In *Artists in Uniform* (1934), Eastman returned to his favorite theme of the evils of dialectical materialism—the "veritable theological bludgeon with which men of independent thought and volition are subdued to silence and conformity." Although he distinguished elsewhere between science, which was immediately concerned with practical results, and art, which conveyed life's experiences and possibilities, both were forms of "critical truth-seeking" and both demanded "honesty of mind" to be genuine and valuable. Because the "success" of the "soviets and of the proletarian class struggle" depended upon an "inflexible integrity of vision and speech," the spectacle of writers and artists slavishly submitting to the commands of the Comintern was profoundly unsettling. Eastman's specific target was the staff of the *New Masses*, whose "enthusiastic approval" of its own "dressing-down" by the International Union of Revolutionary Writers was the most disturbing example yet of "the dwindling dignity of the literary mind" and of "political (and financial) abjection parading as leadership in the creation of a new culture." Writers like Michael Gold were "sickly and unsound," Eastman wrote; "they do not believe either in science or art or in themselves." Their subservience represented a betrayal of their calling and ultimately of the revolutionary cause. "No man possessing the mind and will to revolutionize America," Eastman insisted, would "express it by wallowing at the feet of someone who helped, or has got into a position where he seems to have helped, to revolutionize Russia." If the purpose of revolution was to set people free, the surrender of artistic and intellectual freedom was pointless at best and counterrevolutionary at worst. By 1934, the critic who had blasted Rolland and Barbusse for their bourgeois delusion that writers were a class unto themselves was instructing his colleagues to refuse to join any "practical organization" and to "assert with self-dependent force" their "own sovereignty." [35]

Those who attended the first American Writers' Congress in April 1935 did not heed Eastman's advice about organizations, but they did conceive of the Congress as an effort to establish writers as a sovereign force in the revolutionary struggle. While the Communist party viewed the Congress and its offshoot, the League of American Writers, as components of the new Popular Front strategy to create a broad anti-fascist coalition, many of the participants used the occasion to advance the cause of intellectual independence under the Marxist rubric. Joseph Freeman may have acted cynically when he spoke in only the most general terms about writers being "an integral part of the working-class movement" and argued that their best work would emerge "out of active identification with it." But he had Eastman's *Artists in Uniform* specifically in mind and knew that he had to contend with questions about autonomy. What is most striking about the proceedings of the Congress is the amount of attention paid to issues of free expression. There was, of course, considerable discussion of the subject of Malcolm Cowley's address: "What the Revolutionary Movement Can Do for a Writer." Cowley and others celebrated the movement's value in carrying writers "outside themselves, into the violent contrasts and struggles of the real world." There was also, however, frequent discussion of the participants' other major concern. Cowley himself touched on the problem of independence when, in the vein of Eastman (persona non grata at the Congress for being too outspoken on Stalin and the party), he referred to Marx and Lenin as "scientists of action" and thus implied the value of flexibility and critical inquiry. [36]

The most direct comments on this matter came from Dos Passos, Frank, and Kenneth Burke. Dos Passos warned against "letting the same thuggery in by the back door that we are fighting off in front of the house" and urged openness in place of "minute prescriptions of doctrine." "A man can't discover anything, originate anything, invent anything," Dos Passos argued, "unless he's at least morally free, without fear or preoccupation insofar as his work goes." Frank, who was elected chairman of the League, spoke again of the "evil" of turning Marxism "into a dogmatically, mechanically *shut* philosophy." In his first address to the Congress, Frank referred to literary work as "*an autonomous kind of action*," and he repeated this claim in his acceptance speech for the League chairmanship: "We have to believe in our own work and in the necessity of the autonomy of our own work as craftsmen and writers." Burke's paper, with its controversial claim for the importance of symbols as well as economics and its call to replace "workers" with "people" in revolutionary discourse, was itself an example of intellectual autonomy. "Revolutionary Symbolism in America" spoke simultaneously to the issues of independence and efficacy by contending that a formulaic "proletarian" approach would unnecessarily constrain writers while alienating "the unconvinced," who could be enlisted only by using "*their* vocabulary, *their* values, *their* symbols." Burke even tried to rescue the term "propaganda" from its negative connotations of rigidity and uniformity: "The complete propagandist, it seems to me, would take an interest in as many imaginative, aesthetic, and speculative fields as he can handle—and into this breadth of his concerns he would interweave a general attitude of sympathy for the oppressed and antipathy toward our oppressive institutions." The function of revolutionary intellectuals was to "propagandize by inclusion, not confining themselves to a few schematic situations, but engaging the entire range of our interests." Generalists rather than dogmatists, as Burke saw it, were the most effective propagandists.[37]

Despite the later belief among many of those who attended the Writers' Congresses and joined the League that they had been "duped," the decision to participate was usually made in the same spirit as the decision to stay out. Participation did not necessarily indicate a lapse in judgment or a capitulation for the sake of a sense of involvement. Burke, Frank, Dos Passos, Cowley, Matthew Josephson, and writers such as Van Wyck Brooks who joined the League somewhat later, believed that their presence would help give the organization an independent stature and that this, in turn, would bind the intellectual community together as a sovereign social entity. It was such a conviction that allowed Brooks to belong to the League while lashing out at doctrinaire Marxist criticism for denying "the independence of the literary mind." Cowley agreed that the League would "certainly encourage writers to think of one another not as rivals, but as partners in the same undertaking."[38] Edmund Wilson, on the other hand, chose "to keep as far from the whole business as possible" in the belief that writers were best off avoiding all chances of getting dragged into petty party squabbles and doctrinal disputes. Wilson's advice to Dos Passos, whose address to the Congress he admired, was to leave "political controversy" to the Communists and merely do the important work of the independent writer. To denounce obstructions to free expression, within the context of such an organization, was "to enter into politics oneself and to have to take political responsibilities." Why not function outside the League and write on one's own terms? Wilson declared his own independence by resigning "from everything that I was aware of being associated with" and by writing to the officials of the Writers' Congress "that they either ought to include the members of heretical groups or change the wording of the sentence in their program about inviting 'all revolutionary writers.' "[39] For both Wilson and Dos Passos, however, the desideratum was the same: critical discussion in the service of social reconstruction.

Even the Party members among Wilson's contemporaries felt compelled to wrestle with the issue of intellectual and artistic freedom. Perhaps Michael Gold's statement at the first Writer's Congress that there was "room in the revolution" was merely lip service to attract a wider range of writers under the Popular Front program. But Gold, for all his willingness to advance the Party line, was also a product of the old *Masses* and an intellectual culture that placed a high value on independence. Lewis Mumford, who had attended City College with Gold, spoke even after being vilified by his old friend of "something vehement, defiant, deeply human . . . that made his conversion to communism and his acceptance of its regimentation of mind deeply foreign to his character."[40] In his own effort to reconcile thought and action, Gold no doubt came down on the side of action—often to the point where he verbally liquidated writers who struck him as bourgeois or counterrevolutionary. Yet he too was trying to discover a role for the "revolutionary intellectual" and the "activist thinker" that would allow for the preservation of intellectual identity while also promoting the class struggle. Thus he admired John Reed, who had succeeded, in Gold's view, in combining the careers of "active revolutionist" and "pioneer revolutionary writer." For Gold, "proletarian literature" was a broad enough rubric to permit a maximum of artistic freedom and still fulfill a revolutionary purpose. "The man with a revolutionary mind and approach," he told his colleagues at the first Writers' Congress, "can write a revolutionary book." Gold was certain that this offered plenty of leeway to include personal experience, opinion, and observation, as long as they did not cut against the grain of the revolution. Writers did have a unique part to play; they could and should maintain their communal identity even as they allied themselves with the proletariat and expanded their membership. "I think all of us must learn to become teachers of the working class," Gold urged. "We must assemble around ourselves a group of talented workers who wish to write, just as Gorky did it twenty-five years ago in Russia."[41]

Gold's friend Joseph Freeman similarly noted that the sole constraint upon the revolutionary writer was not to be "remote from the revolution" and not to write about "the self-indulgences of the philistine." Art, Freeman said in a direct attack on Eastman, was not sovereign if this meant speaking "from above the battle." But "[n]o one says the artist should cease being an artist; no one urges him to ignore experience." The vital question was what constituted valuable experience, and the answer was anything that pertained to the class struggle—including the writer's personal experience of coming to the revolution. "It is when the intellectual describes his own conflicts sincerely that he can create revolutionary art," Freeman wrote; "it is when he has transformed his life, when his experience is in the ranks of the advanced proletariat that he begins to create proletarian art."[42] Gold, Freeman, and others who were more willing to link their fortunes with the Communist party did so in the belief that what Freeman referred to as the fusion of art and life demanded it. In their minds, this choice did not represent a repudiation of intellectual independence so much as a channeling of independence into socially productive channels. It was only the freedom to be irrelevant that they despised.

5.

After 1935, in what was more a gradual dawning than an epiphany, American intellectuals abandoned the conviction that Marxism lent itself to revision and criticism. Revelations about the Moscow trials, Communist activities in the Spanish Civil War, the vilification and assassination of Trotsky, and the Nazi-Soviet pact functioned to undermine the assumption that Marxism permitted dissent and invited intellectual autonomy. By 1941, Gold and the remaining Stalinist intellectuals in the

United States were forced to give up the pretense of flexibility and to declare emphatically that writers were best off when they submitted to the direction of the party. In an attempt to rewrite recent American literary history in light of the Hitler-Stalin agreement, Gold credited the "strong, able, and culturally developed" Communist movement with saving "the majority of American intellectuals" from the fate of becoming "fools, dupes, and fascists" and giving "these groping intellectuals a form and philosophy for their inchoate disillusionments and rebellions." If it was "a Communist 'dictatorship' " that had "forced the writers out of the bourgeois caves of class blindness and despair," then he was all for it; the alternative, it seemed, was "lackeyism to capitalism."[43]

Most of Gold's contemporaries agreed with him only to the extent that they too came to see Marxism as incompatible with intellectual independence, and few accepted his conclusions about the benefits of submission. The literary production that best embodied this shift in understanding was Wilson's magnum opus of the 1930s, *To the Finland Station*. Though he did not complete the book until 1940, Wilson published the first chapters in the *New Republic* as early as 1934 and conducted part of his research on a Guggenheim Fellowship in the Soviet Union in 1935. Before departing, he confided the purpose of his work to Dos Passos. "What is needed," he wrote, "is to see Marx and Lenin as a part of the humanistic tradition which they came out of"—the tradition of the Enlightenment and the French Revolution that had divided in the nineteenth century into the bourgeois pessimism of writers such as Taine and the revolutionary hopefulness of Marx and Engels.[44] Wilson conceived of the project as a necessary recontextualization of Marxism to save it from the dogmatists and party officials and to demonstrate, as he put it in *Travels in Two Democracies* (1936), that "the socialist ideal is more natural to us than to the Russians."[45]

An important step in the recasting process was to demonstrate that Marx and Engels themselves were not doctrinaire when it came to explaining the place of writers in society. Marx, Wilson wrote in his essay "Marxism and Literature" (1938), never "worked out a systematic explanation of the relation of art to social arrangements," and he did not treat literature as "wholly explicable in terms of economics." Rather, he and Engels tended to see these as activities that worked "to get away" from their "roots in the social classes" and to develop their own "discipline" and "standards of value, which cut across class lines." Set free from narrow economic and social determinants, literature and art might then "reach a point of vitality and vision" where they could "influence the life of the period down to its very economic foundations." It was Wilson's contention that Marx and Engels recognized the possibility of ideas acting as independent historical forces and that, true to the spirit of the founders, Lenin and Trotsky had "worked sincerely to keep literature free." Stalin, on the other hand, had corrupted "every department of intellectual life, till the serious, the humane, and the clear-seeing" were forced to "remain silent." Yet in offering this expansive version of Marxism, Wilson insisted so vehemently on the autonomy of writers that little remained to identify him as a Marxist. As an interpretative framework, of course, Marxism could still "throw a great deal of light on the origins and social significance of works of art." But Wilson spoke now in only the most general terms about revolution—terms that were at best barely identifiable as Marxist. Paraphrasing Trotsky, he did refer to "society itself" under communism becoming a "work of art," and he celebrated the "efforts of the human spirit to transcend literature itself" in building a better society. Beyond his continued allegiance to the idea of "social engineering," however, there was nothing particularly Marxist about Wilson's prescriptions (or hopes) for change; in his preoccupation with the problem of intellectual freedom, he virtually ignored the class struggle.[46]

To the Finland Station further wrestled with the problem of the "superstructure"—the independence and motive force of ideas—that Wilson had begun to explore in "Marxism and Literature." In the spring of 1938, Wilson read Eastman's *Marx and Lenin*, which he praised as "the best critical thing" he had encountered on the "philosophical aspect of Marxism," and began to reconsider his assumptions about the humanistic character of Marx's thought.[47] While he still admired Marx and Engels for their attempts "to make the historical imagination intervene in human affairs as a direct constructive force" and for their "sense of a rich and various world," he recognized in the dialectic a competing element of "mysticism" and German intolerance. Following Eastman's argument, Wilson discovered a dangerous religious tendency in Marx's effort "to harness the primitive German Will to a movement which should lead all humanity to prosperity, happiness and freedom." The "disguise of the Dialectic"—"a semi-divine principle of History"—had made it possible to evade "the responsibility for thinking, deciding, acting." Wilson continued to distinguish between Marx and Engels and "the crude pedants and fanatics" who claimed to be their followers, but he also found in the dialectic a component of Marxism that "lends itself to the repressions of the tyrant."[48]

Because it was written over a six-year period, *To the Finland Station* turned out to be an ambiguous book. The admiration for Marx, Engels, and Lenin was tempered by Wilson's arrival at the conclusion that the dialectic was a built-in excuse for autocracy. His method of resolving this dilemma was consistent with the implications of "Marxism and Literature." Wilson argued, in effect, that Marx, Engels, and Lenin were heroic figures precisely because they ignored one of the principle features of Marxism; in other words, they were sufficiently flexible to transcend Marxism itself. Stalin and Trotsky were not. Trotsky was "far from the exploratory spirit" that characterized Marx, Engels, and Lenin, and his work revealed a "dogmatic Marxism" that contrasted starkly with the ideas of these other men. Wilson managed to salvage something of his original purpose by claiming that, for a moment, in the person of Lenin, "history acted and history written" had converged to a positive end. But what Wilson had begun as a celebration of ideas becoming social and historical forces finally emerged in a much more ambivalent form. An individual who believed that he "was carrying out one of the essential tasks of history" could do more harm than good if he lacked the exceptional qualities of a Marx or Lenin; and Marxism, as a body of ideas capable of influencing the historical process, was to be feared as much as admired—especially now, in its period of "decadence."[49]

If Wilson hedged on whether Marxism tended inevitably toward dogmatism and autocracy, Eastman did not. By the mid-1930s, his disillusionment had grown to include Trotsky, whom he had looked upon since 1924 as the leader of a more democratic and scientific communist movement. After spending some time with Trotsky at Prinkipo in July 1932, Eastman came to the unpleasant conclusion that the exiled Bolshevik represented no real alternative at all. Eastman's initial impression, written early in the visit, was that Trotsky was a humble man who had to employ "enormous self-discipline" to overcome "the childlike charm of the artist" and transform himself into "a man of action." Twelve days later, Eastman recorded that his "mood" had "changed utterly." He was hurt by Trotsky's "inward indifference to my existence, my interests, my opinions." Trotsky was a complete dogmatist, certain "that he is the truth, that other people are merely to be judged and instructed" and unwilling to listen to suggestions or criticisms. Eastman left Prinkipo thinking that his former hero was "as cold as poultry" and that "his gift of friendship" was "about upon the level of a barn-yard fowl." Though he did not express these sentiments publicly until after Trotsky's death in 1940, Eastman had privately come to see yet another confirmation of the dangers of the dialectic: a belief in divine providence that excluded the free discussion of alternatives.[50]

When he published a revised version of *Marx and Lenin* under the title *Marxism: Is It Science?* in 1940, Eastman included Trotsky and Lenin in his condemnation of the "dialectic religion." Much of the book was identical to the 1927 edition, and Eastman continued to link the "scientific attitude" to "the general aim of a more free and equal society." But his answer to the question posed in the new title was a resounding no. By 1940, Eastman no longer saw Marxism as a flexible system of thought which could be saved from Marx and purged of its religious orientation. A note added to the old section on Lenin as a scientist of revolution captured Eastman's change of mind: "Lenin's faith in the dialectic philosophy was more vital to his thinking, and more disastrous, than I realized." Eastman now believed that Lenin's embrace of the dialectic had allowed him to equate the dictatorship of the party with progress toward communism, when in reality it had led to Stalin. In a companion volume, *Stalin's Russia and the Crisis in Socialism*, also published in 1940, Eastman repeated the charge that Lenin had "trusted too much in the benign intentions of a dialectic universe." Marxism's ability through the dialectic to justify everything as a step toward the withering away of the state and the triumph of socialism had, according to Eastman, permitted Stalin to construct a totalitarian regime and purge his enemies in the name of socialism; the dialectic had allowed Stalin to portray "etymological" finesse as real social change.[51]

Eastman intended the last section of *Stalin's Russia* to lay the foundation for a revised socialism. After condemning Michael Gold and the intellectual fellow travelers ("Totalitarian Liberals," he called them) for seeking "a substitute for God," Eastman repeated his time-worn plea for a scientific approach to social change. Without Lenin as a model, however, his alternative was even less substantial than before, and the most he could suggest was the substitution of the word "radical" for "revolutionary" to indicate that "the attitude of experimental science" had replaced "an

imported revolutionary metaphysics." Eastman explained his vagueness
by claiming that "of the two main ingredients of wisdom, practical action
and detachment," he had "for some years cultivated only the latter." But
he could say with certainty that what was needed now was "a movement
of hard minds, loyal to the oppressed," and "disillusioned" with "evangel-
ism" and "self-consoling ideologies." Most of all, they had to know the
"errors as well as the truths in Marxism" and "the lessons of the Russian
revolution and the fate of the Third International." What truths remained
in Marxism Eastman did not say. *Marxism: Is It Science?* and *Stalin's Russia*
seemed to suggest instead that Marxism and "honest intelligence" were
fundamentally incompatible and that, at most, Marxism could point to
underlying historical conditions—not causes or solutions.[52]

By 1941, Wilson was able to perceive the end of a phase of American
intellectual history. In a tribute to Eastman, Wilson argued that the
intellectual attraction to Marxism had been little more than desire mas-
querading as realism:

The fact that Marx and Engels combined an unexamined idealism with real
and great intellectual genius has made it possible for American intellectuals to
whoop it up for the Marxist religion, under the impression that they were
applying to the contemporary world a relentless intellectual analysis; and strong
in the reassurance of standing right with the irresistible forces of History, the
Marxist substitute for old-fashioned Providence, they have felt confident that
History would see them through without further intellectual effort on their
part . . .

If this was primarily an attack on the Stalinists, it was also a piece of self-
criticism—a recognition that the conception of Marxism as expansive and
non-dogmatic was based more on a wish than on critical thought. Like
Eastman, Wilson found Marxism salvageable only as an interpretative
tool, not as a prescription for change. Marx and Engels had provided a
"technique" for studying historical and contemporary problems with reference to their social and economic context, but because of their German
background, they had "tended to imagine socialism in authoritarian terms."
The "desire to get rid of class privilege based on birth and on difference
of income" remained noble. Yet Marxism's claim to offer the means for
realizing this desire was wholly unfounded. "The formulas of the various
Marxist creeds," Wilson wrote, "including the one that is common to
them all, the dogma of the dialectic, no more deserve the status of holy

writ than the formulas of other creeds."[53] Intellectuals, he implied, would have to be more skeptical, more vigilant about preserving their independence, in the future. They had to know the risks involved in the quest to assert their social presence and foster change, even if this meant modifying their expectations in the interests of autonomy.

Epilogue:
Defending the Intellectual Life

Totalitarianism and the approach of war brought a reorientation of the intellectual life for the surviving members of a generation that had once defined itself by youth. By the 1940s, Eastman and many of his contemporaries had found some of the security of middle age: dependable incomes, stable marriages, adult children, solid reputations, young disciples. Some turned toward reminiscence and the writing of memoirs; two significant figures, Harold Stearns and Paul Rosenfeld, died in 1943 and 1946. While the rapid shift of Eastman and Dos Passos toward the political right is well known, these dramatic changes were only the most extreme examples of a larger generational movement toward an intellectual conservatism that did not always manifest itself in conventional political terms. With the apparent exhaustion of Marxism and the looming presence of fascism and Stalinism, a tone of pessimism and a dampened sense of possibility began to emerge. Even where the redemptive impulse remained, it was tempered by a revised concept of the intellectual as the preserver of humane values in a world run amok.

When Malcolm Cowley told Edmund Wilson that "I want to get out of every God damned thing," he was reaffirming the necessity of non-affiliation. The repudiation of politics that Cowley urged was actually a response to what many intellectuals came to see as a disruption of the delicate balance between independence and public involvement during the 1930s. Politics, in this view, meant the sacrifice of a more expansive critical sensibility to trivial "feuds and vendettas." Intellectuals who played at politics were dangerous because a lust for power replaced a genuine concern for ideas and debate. "A world run by them would be a very unpleasant place," Cowley imagined, "considering all the naked egos that would be continually wounding and getting wounded, all the gossip, the spies at cocktail parties, the informers, the careerists, the turncoats." The best course was one of retrenchment and reevaluation, with a strong commitment to a "higher level" of discussion at which arguments would be conducted "impersonally" and with respect for the "good motives" of the opposition. The intellectual community felt compelled to focus now on its own integrity—and on intellectual freedom generally—to correct the recent imbalance.[1]

1.

One result of the world situation was a recasting of the relationship with America, especially after the United States entered the war. Older critics were willing to make a provisional peace with America in taking on fascism; the adversarial impulse, in wartime, became a kind of common ground when it focused on an external enemy. This was the context in which Brooks proclaimed his "break with the intellectuals" and his integration into the common life. With the United States "fighting not nations but evil itself," Brooks could fuse patriotism and opposition. "Paris has lost its charm," he wrote in 1941, "and Moscow is fast losing its charm with our growing sense of what Washington has come to stand for." Waldo Frank also cast his lot with America against Europe. "There is a bloom within our land which Europe lacks," he observed; "a generosity and the faith and good will which flower from it, long lost in England, France, Germany, Italy. This gives us a glow of promise which Europe for all its cathedral towns and men of genius does not have . . ."[2] The notion of America as a particularly inhospitable place for the artistic and intellectual life, which had already been undermined by the reassessment of the American past, could not bear the weight of comparison to an occupied Europe or a Stalinist Soviet Union.

Yet the reconciliation with America remained only partial. Brooks' announced break with the intellectuals was more a condemnation of literary modernism and dogmatic Marxism than a genuine embrace of the American status quo. Frank similarly castigated the intellectuals who had succumbed to shallowness and facile thinking in the 1930s, but he did not couple this criticism with any celebration of popular wisdom or common sense. Instead, Frank argued that the seeds of fascism were planted in America as well as Europe—in the frustrations, ignorance, and distorted values of Americans living in a depressed machine civilization. "Consult your own life: the stifled good in you, the starving strength, the thwarted dream," Frank advised in 1940. "In your character, and your brother's, you will find fears, confusions, dwindling faiths and values which, in the transmutation of crisis, become the fuel and the traits of Fascism." The greatest threat to "the culture of the individual" that represented the best in "Western civilization" existed "at home" and "within."[3]

Even as they insisted on America's duty to combat fascism, anti-isolationists such as Frank and Mumford rejected any complacent notion of American superiority; at most, they conceded that the American public and its government were not irretrievably corrupted. Mumford joined Frank in characterizing the American people as potential fascists whose lack of "ethical content or ideal purpose" made them highly susceptible to the "grizzled, pock-eaten, warped, dehumanized visage of the power personality." It now appeared to Mumford that the cult of power, the machine, and accumulation which had been the subject of most of his work culminated in totalitarianism on the Nazi or Stalinist models. If the Germans were "active barbarians," most Americans were their "passive" allies—different only in that they were less advanced along the same road. "Those who have already lost their manhood and their self-respect," Mumford wrote of these passive barbarians, "who value their shabby little selves, regardless of what sort of life they pass on to their children, are the chosen accomplices of fascism: they are ready for its more boisterous denials of freedom, justice, and truth."[4] In his judgment of the American public, though not in his proposed remedies, Mumford was moving closer to what Walter Lippmann had been saying since 1922.[5]

After Pearl Harbor, Mumford toned down the attack on his compatriots in the spirit of common engagement, but he continued to warn against any sense of America's immunity to fascism. During war especially, Americans were prone to the cult of power, the surrender of vital freedoms, and the pursuit of victory for its own sake rather than humane purposes. In 1939, Mumford himself had advocated severe restrictions on civil liberties—fascist means to anti-fascist ends—in order to combat internal subversion. "With a free society as our goal," he had written in *Men Must Act*, "we must restrict freedom to those who would destroy it. These are bitter paradoxes. Like the necessity for arming briskly against fascism, they imply a temporary defeat for our common civilization. It is only, however, by making the best of this temporary defeat that we can avoid a more permanent one: the victory of fascism."[6] By 1944, Mumford recognized that the defeat of Germany and Japan would be no more than a Pyrrhic victory if winning the war became the exclusive end of the struggle: "Without a deep regeneration and renewal, the external triumph of American machinery and arms will but hasten the downfall of the Western World." Edmund Wilson made the same point after the American bombing of Berlin in 1944. "I have felt for the first time," he noted in his diary, "that we were sucked into the spiral of our society going, as Dos [Passos] says, down the drain."[7]

The idea that the war had to be waged against an internal as well as external threat of fascism prefigured the critique of mass society that became such a prevalent strand of intellectual discourse in the 1950s.[8] The submission of the masses to the machinery of war and to the power of the state, without a compensatory articulation of larger purposes, was a source of deep concern to intellectuals who strongly supported America's war effort. When Eastman published *Heroes I Have Known* in 1942, he described the book as an example of "civilized hero worship" and an alternative to "the god-hatching demonic infatuation with heroes" that seemed to characterize the current age. By contrast, Thomas Carlyle's famous nineteenth-century book on heroes was "evil"—"an evangel of irresponsible surrender to blind force, a veritable induction of Christians to Hitlerism." Eastman situated his portraits, which included his mother, Eugene Debs, John Reed, Charlie Chaplin, and John Dewey, within a discussion of the masses' tendency to acquiesce in their own dehumanization. He insisted on an understanding of the war as "a struggle against a passion and a habit of mind to which all men are susceptible—a frenzy of allegiance to a Leader and his gang and pronunciamentos taking the place of self-reliant loyalty to mankind, the nation, and the people, and the truth."[9] If intellectuals saw the necessity of fighting the Second World War, they did not view it as a clear-cut conflict between fascism and democracy. In the most optimistic terms, it was a war between the certainty of totalitarianism and the possibility of democracy.

2.

Against the rampant power-lusts of fascism, Stalinism, and total war, maintaining the integrity of the intellectual life assumed a new importance. Critics no longer conceived of themselves as the vanguard of imminent social transformation; instead, intellectual independence became a defensive measure against social decay. The preservation of humane culture, critical discussion, free speech (even if this required curbs on those who threatened it), and an immunity to the allure of power took precedence over more expansive visions during the war. Ultimate renewal depended on the survival of the disinterested intellect and the values it embodied, and therefore the immediate concern was to shield the intellectual life from the danger of extinction. Dissent itself, regardless of influence, was the essential responsibility of intellectuals. Edmund Wilson's homage to Max Eastman in 1941 emphasized Eastman's "conviction that there is a part to be played in human society by persons who make it their business to keep clear of the standards of the world and to stick by certain instincts of thinking and feeling whose value is not measured by their wages, and which it is always to the immediate interest of some group to mutilate, imprison or suppress." A deepened commitment to independence was the most important service critics and artists could perform in the face of ubiquitous threats. In Eastman's case, this commitment spilled over into red-baiting and an obsessive fear of a Communist conspiracy to destroy intellectual, artistic, and human freedom.[10]

As Eastman's generation came to reflect on its own history in the 1940s, integrity and strength of conviction served as the critical measures of success. Waldo Frank argued that resistance to specialization and dedication to the creative life, more than a discernible impact, were the essential qualities. The "function of the intellectual and artist" was to keep alive "the values that underly the organic sense of life and man's individual and holy share in it"—to make certain that these values remained "present" in the culture and formed a background to the lives of "public leaders and rank and file." The intellectual's "specialty is the whole," Frank insisted, and the intellectual who "embodies any smaller purpose" than the preservation and transmission of values "is a traitor to his ancient priesthood." If Frank continued to insist on a vital social function for intellectuals, his primary concern was that they not betray their integrity. By 1940, his discussion of social alternatives had reached new levels of vagueness, and his most substantive suggestion was that intellectuals remain true to their calling.[11] When Van Wyck Brooks characterized the entire American literary tradition as "Jeffersonian," he too revealed that the best alternative he could offer after the war was a sketchy kind of civic republicanism.[12]

Reflection and protection rather than the articulation of new approaches to social change dominated Wilson's outlook as well. "He was putting the affairs of his life in order, straightening out his relation to his children and friends and relatives on his bit of enchanted ground at Cape Cod," Leon Edel has written of Wilson in the 1940s. Wilson's plot for an unwritten autobiographical novel captured his reorientation. He planned three episodes, each of which would correspond to a decade of his life. The first episode Wilson summarized in his notes with the phrase "swimming, lovemaking, gin." The second would take him to the Soviet Union and through the period of political commitment. In the last part, he finds resolution through self-examination and reflection on his personal history. As Wilson envisioned this final episode, his alter-ego "comes to U.S.A. and goes up to see [Max] Eastman, John Dos Passos at Provincetown. Enjoys the writers' and artists' freedom, thinks of living in such a place, sitting down and writing about what has happened to him, trying to get to the bottom of it and find out what it really means." At the novel's conclusion, he is reconciled to the life of letters as an inherently worthy occupation; "he realizes what he is, what he has learned, what he represents now as a type of the thinking human being, independent of class (?) or nationality, at this point of man's progress."[13]

Paul Rosenfeld's death in 1946 prompted further reflection on the meaning and value of the critical intellect. Rosenfeld had not fared well in the 1930s. The stock market crash and Depression reduced his income, and his resistance to Marxism made it more difficult to publish in the intellectual magazines. In 1933, he directly attacked his fellow critics for sacrificing their independence in an ill-advised quest for political power.[14] A memorial volume published in 1948 included essays by many of those whom Rosenfeld had implicitly condemned, and one of the unifying themes of the volume was Rosenfeld's integrity in standing up to intellectual and political fashions. Wilson now viewed his friend as a victim of the 1930s:

The persecution of the Jews by Hitler came later to weigh upon Paul and to become overpoweringly identified with the difficulties he was facing at fifty. The times had not brought to fulfillment that creative and enlightened era of which they had seemed to be witnessing the dawn when the *Seven Arts* was founded: totalitarian states and class pressures were closing down the artistic elite. The independent American journalism that had flared up for a while in the twenties had given way to the steamlined commercial kind, and the non-commercial magazines were composed for the most part by this time of second-rate academic papers and the commentaries of Talmudic Marxists.

Waldo Frank called Rosenfeld one of America's "martyrs" for opposing both "the pseudo-humanism of the neo-Babbitts and Eliots" and "the sterile economisms of the *New Masses*, the *Nation*, [and] the post-Croly *New Republic*." Mumford also celebrated Rosenfeld's "resolute opposition" to the demeaning of the intellectual and artistic life.[15]

Paul Rosenfeld: Voyager in the Arts was an extended tribute to the preservation of intellectual independence in the face of political, economic, and ideological dangers. If Rosenfeld's vision of an America redeemed by art had not materialized, at least he had not compromised for the sake of money or power. It was sufficient, the volume's editor wrote, that he had remained "unsullied"—"one of the inviolate beings of American literature."[16]

Perhaps the best indication of the changing self-image of Rosenfeld's generation in the 1940s appeared in Eastman's tribute to his long-dead friend John Reed. Reed had been revived in the 1930s as an American Communist hero; the young artists and intellectuals who joined the "John Reed Clubs" knew him as a symbol of the writer as man-of-action who had given his life to the Bolshevik Revolution. Granville Hicks' 1936 biography emphasized his service to the Comintern and his submission to the discipline of the Party. When Eastman returned to Reed in 1942, he made his friend's politics—his "Bolshevik convictions"—a secondary matter. More important were his "rugged personal honor," his "impetuous truth-telling," and his "prior consecration to poetry as real living." In contrasting the genuine Reed with Hicks' party-line Reed, Eastman cast him as an intellectual whose fundamental commitment was to creative expression rather than political action. He "would have come back to his gay and various self," Eastman ventured, "to those whims and multicolored interests which were an essential part of his endowment as a creative writer." As with Rosenfeld's eulogists, Eastman's predominant concern was to show that his friend had not bent with the prevailing winds, had not flung away his intellectual integrity in an obsession with influence.

"John Reed was a thinking man," he declared. He had "an original, independent, very swift, and very brilliant mind." Most of all, he was willing to "speak his own thoughts and defend them against anybody from Lenin down to the sergeant-at-arms." Here was the intellectual whose heroism lay not in identifiable results but in his defense of intellectual freedom against the forces that would destroy it.[17]

3.

The beauty of the impossibilist élan was that visions of regeneration could survive even the bleakest scenarios. Some, of course, abandoned their commitment to social transformation and lapsed almost completely into a defensive posture. Eastman's fight against internal and external enemies after 1940 signaled the end to any positive idea of change. Wilson moved toward an increasingly dark perspective on history in which the world seemed to be locked into "a competition for power for its own sake." In the introduction to *Patriotic Gore*, his 1962 study of the literature of the American Civil War, Wilson created a dismal picture of unchecked expansionism and argued, in effect, that Lincoln had thrust the United States on a catastrophic and inevitable course toward the Cold War and the national security state. He did not think it out of place to connect the events of 1861–65 to the atomic bomb, chemical weapons, the FBI, CIA, and urban blight. Only the "insufferable moral attitudes that appeared to us first to be justified by our victory over the Confederacy in 1865" prevented "us from recognizing today, in our relation to our cold-war opponent, that our panicky pugnacity as we challenge him is not virtue but at bottom the irrational instinct of an active power organism in the presence of another such organism, of a sea slug of vigorous voracity in the presence of another such sea slug."[18] Wilson's best hope was not for sweeping regeneration, but simply for a wider awareness of this downward spiral into decay. After World War II, he no longer spoke of the redeemed America he had dreamt of in the 1930s.

Those who clung to their faith in renewal surrounded their affirmations with equally bleak impressions of the postwar world. "As for our own society," Mumford wrote Frank in 1940, "no matter whether Hitler conquers or loses, it seems to me that we are in for another Dark Ages." He described the context for *The Condition of Man* (1944) as "a period of rapid social disintegration." Any remaining "hope for the future" represented "what is left after one has faced the worst." In this climate of disintegration, the depth of the required transformation was greater than ever; Mumford demanded "a reorientation of our whole life, a change in occupation, a change in regimen, a change in personal relationships, not least, a change in attitude and conscious direction: fundamentally, a change in religion, our total sense of the world and life and time." Donald Miller has detailed the increasing pessimism of Mumford's postwar outlook and his deeper reliance on religious conversion as the basis for social change. Like Wilson, he was profoundly unsettled by the expansion of the national security state, the threat of nuclear war, and the continued decline of the cities. "In the present posture of the world," he confessed to Frank in 1957, "I feel oddly irresponsible, feeling that no immediate act or idea could possibly have any effect in changing the grim course of things." Two years later he spoke in the same catastrophic terms that Wilson would employ in *Patriotic Gore:* "I see so many evidences of a deep and pervasive irrationality, a true will to annihilation, that I no longer have the faintest belief that any real changes will be effected [by] argument, persuasion, example. If a change comes it will come only after such an inner disruption and disintegration as that which ushered Christianity into the world." [19]

Yet Mumford did not relinquish the vision that had sustained his generation for more than thirty years. Perhaps because he had never staked much on Marxism and sudden transformation, he could continue to speak of regeneration even as his view of the modern landscape grew bleaker. After all, he had written as early as 1930 that renewal was "not a task for the next ten years, but for the next two hundred." *The Condition of Man* ended with a reaffirmation of the impossibilist élan, with the assertion that "everything is possible." Mumford's consistent articulation of a regionalist alternative, his call for decentralization and redistribution rather than bureaucratization and destructive growth, his demand for the humanization of technology made him less prone to the exhaustion that characterized other critics after 1940. In the twenties and thirties he had looked to the greenbelt town-building projects of the Regional Planning Association and the community development schemes of the Tennessee Valley Authority and the Resettlement Administration as the experimental beginnings of a wholesale social reconstruction. But he had also established the prophetic voice that would sustain him and his work after these experiments collapsed and "the regional moment" had passed. If the

intrusion of events led Mumford to conclude that he had been too optimistic in *The Culture of Cities* (1938), nothing ever told him that he had
been wrong. He never doubted that the region was the "basic configura-
tion in human life." He never felt compelled to repudiate his claim that
"regionalism belongs to the future," although after the war this was no
longer a statement of imminent possibility and hope, but rather a warning
that human survival depended on it.[20]

Defending the "dream" of personal and social regeneration in 1950,
Mumford held to the conviction that "it is better to sink one's last hopes
in such a dream than to be destroyed by a nightmare." The most vital
task facing the individual in the second half of the twentieth century, he
continued to insist, was to think and live not as "the specialist" but as
"the whole man."[21] This had been the essential struggle of Mumford's
intellectual generation. As one of its longest surviving members, Mumford carried into the last quarter of the century the dual dream—perhaps
never fully reconcilable—of intellectual independence and a role in creating a more humane world.

4.

Certainly the most potent social criticism after 1940 came from the pens
of the so-called New York Intellectuals, most of whom had cut their
literary teeth at the *Partisan Review* in the 1930s. As death, exhaustion,
and dispersal depleted the ranks of the older generation, the voices of
William Phillips, Philip Rahv, Lionel Trilling, Mary McCarthy, Dwight
Macdonald, and others matured and grew in strength. This generational
passage expressed itself most starkly in Macdonald's attack on Brooks'
Opinions of Oliver Allston in 1941—an attack that began by questioning the
older man's intolerance for modern fiction and blew up into the ridiculous
claim that Brooks was "our leading mouthpiece for totalitarian cultural
values."[22] Macdonald's criticisms, despite the essential truth in treating
Brooks as hostile toward literary modernism, failed to credit him for his
role in staking out the terrain in which independent critics could function
in modern America. Alfred Kazin, who also disparaged *Oliver Allston*,
corrected this omission in 1942 by recognizing in Brooks "the spiritual
conviction that had been so indispensable to the modern movement in
America."[23] For Kazin, the previous generation was now part of an

extended usable past that grew organically out of the nineteenth century and could serve to energize his own youthful contemporaries.

Whether acknowledged or not, Brooks and his coevals bequeathed to the New York Intellectuals the concerns with independence and influence that would guide the younger critics as well. The fact that this generation came in large part to reconcile itself with the expanding universities does not diminish its debt to those who had tried to define and construct a public intellectual life earlier in the century. The generations shared an attachment to the essay as their characteristic form of expression; both used book reviews or discussions of specific texts as points of departure for freewheeling excursions into American culture; and neither believed that political commentary precluded considerations well beyond particular events or policies. The older generation also passed on some of its deficiencies: hurried and occasionally superficial work under financial pressures; a defiant generalism that at its worst produced glibness and imprecision; a tendency to speak in terms of rigid cultural categories such as highbrow and lowbrow; an overall lack of concern with issues of race and gender. Perhaps the most important intergenerational bond was the commitment, however flawed in practice, to a common language—to the ideal of an inclusive critical conversation that would transcend limited perspectives and narrow interests.

As a rule, perhaps, the New York Intellectuals were better able to achieve the security necessary for the production of fully realized work. Their return to the universities gave them the resources for sustained research and writing. For their predecessors, the essay may have taken precedence over the completed book more as a matter of necessity than choice. What has been said of Walter Lippmann applies more legitimately to others—that he never succeeded in writing anything beyond prefaces. Yet Lippmann's generation did produce books that were more than prefaces and more than essay collections, despite the effects of the market on its collective output; the five volumes of Brooks' *Makers and Finders* and Mumford's *Renewal of Life* series are only the most dramatic examples. Moreover, it bears repeating that there was compensation for the lack of reliable support in the freedom not to play it safe. Randolph Bourne never wrote a whole book, but several of his essays are among the most important American writings of the twentieth century.[24] Independent intellectuals consistently ventured beyond matters of technical problem-solving to address issues of value and purpose.

The passage of generations, for all its continuities, also signified a deep shift. Through their many conflicts and vicissitudes, the older critics had shared a view of culture that emphasized change. At times they imagined dramatic, even cataclysmic transformations; at others they thought of gradual but equally vital processes of decay and renewal. Much of their faith in themselves and their work, indeed the impossibilist élan itself, depended upon a belief in the necessity and possibility of bold redirection.

After World War II, the dominant outlook of American intellectuals underwent a thorough reorientation. Ironically, however, the shift that Fred Matthews has described—from a "processual" to a "structural" framework of understanding—undermined the perspective of the older critics.[25] Their successors increasingly concentrated on the intransigence rather than the malleability or linearity of culture. Members of the end-of-ideology school—Daniel Bell, Arthur Schlesinger, Jr., and Daniel Boorstin, for example—spoke of the postwar United States as if all the important issues had been addressed and all that remained to be done represented minor adjustments within a permanent social and political structure. While insisting that the "genius" of America was its freedom from intellectual and political systems, these intellectuals celebrated what they took to be optimal and unalterable American forms and institutions. As Richard H. Pells and Robert Booth Fowler have argued, the end-of-ideology formulation was itself a powerful ideology which fetishized "the tenets of realism, pragmatism, pluralism, the two-party system, the mixed economy, and social stability." Other postwar intellectuals, including Richard Hofstadter, Louis Hartz, David Riesman, and C. Wright Mills, recognized and criticized liberalism as an ideology but were even more likely to identify the structures that precluded anything beyond adjustment or minimal change. The liberal tradition, the other-directed culture, the power elite seemed virtually immutable. By describing and evaluating these structures, intellectuals offered some hope for living more fully and autonomously within modern institutions. They agreed, however, "that the nation's institutions were now too stable and too imposing to be altered" in any significant way.[26]

Under these circumstances, the processual orientation seemed hopelessly simplistic and old-fashioned. John L. Thomas has noted the differences in language between the two generations—the shift from such metaphors as "streams, currents, seasons, diurnal cycles" to a terminology of "equilibrium, patterning, stability, form, limits."[27] The implications for the role and self-image of intellectuals were enormous. Postwar critics became influential in large part by avoiding the prophetic voice and by soberly explaining the realities of modern life to their sophisticated audiences. The claim of realism bolstered the case for influence, while the goal of explication permitted greater complexity than had the exhortations and prophecies of the prewar years. What was lost in the change was the pervasive sense that the critical intelligence could step in and alter the course of history—that independent intellectuals could shape and transform as well as dissect and analyze. The idea of the truly purposive intellect was submerged after 1945, and when it returned, it appeared in the ideas and actions of another generation of young intellectuals in the early years of the New Left.

Notes

Introduction

1. H. L. Mencken to Max Eastman, quoted in Eastman, *Love and Revolution*, 195; Mencken to Ernest Boyd, Oct. 9, 1916, and Mencken to Theodore Dreiser, April 22, 1915, in *Letters of H. L. Mencken*, 91, 68; Max Eastman, ms. tribute to Mencken [n.d.], Max Eastman Papers. Eastman quotes the letter slightly differently in this tribute: "You boys are bringing out the best magazine in the country —not once in a while, but right along, every month." The epigraph before the introduction is from a letter from Van Wyck Brooks to B. W. Huebsch [n.d., ca. 1916], Huebsch Papers.

2. Bender, *Community and Social Change*, 8, 11.

3. Ibid., 7.

4. Jacoby, *Last Intellectuals*, 5, 7.

5. Ibid., 3.

6. Bender has made the point that the peak influence of public intellectuals came in the late 1940s and early 1950s, when there was "a rapidly intellectualizing middle class that needed and welcomed guidance on cultural matters." Jacoby, he argues, ignores the fact that the "public sphere" has become more "contested and fragmented" since the age of consensus—a period that should not be idealized. See Bender, "Lionel Trilling and American Culture," esp. 340–44.

7. Jumonville, *Critical Crossings*, xii.

8. The most sensitive discussion of predecessors is in Cooney, *The Rise of the New York Intellectuals*, chap. 1. Other recent studies include Alexander Bloom, *Prodigal Sons: The New York Intellectuals and Their World* (New York: Oxford University Press, 1986) and Alan M. Wald, *The New York Intellectuals: The Rise and Decline of the Anti-Stalinist Left from the 1930s to the 1980s* (Chapel Hill: University of North Carolina Press, 1987).

9. Lewis A. Coser uses the terms "independent intellectuals" and "unattached intellectuals" in *Men of Ideas*, esp. chap. 20.

10. The literature on the emergence of professional communities and organizations is extensive. The general causes and dimensions of professionalization and specialization are treated in Wiebe, *The Search for Order, 1877–1920*, esp. chap. 5; John Higham, "The Matrix of Specialization," in Oleson and Voss, *The Organization of Knowledge*, 3–18; Burton J. Bledstein, *The Culture of Professionalism: The Middle Class and the Development of Higher Education in America* (New York: Norton, 1976); and Magali Sarfatti Larson, *The Rise of Professionalism: A Sociological Analysis* (Berkeley: University of California Press, 1977). Specific professions and disciplines are considered in Haskell, *The Emergence of Professional Social Science;* John Higham, *History: Professional Scholarship in America* (Baltimore: Johns Hopkins University Press, rev. ed., 1989); Novick, *That Noble Dream;* Kuklick, *The Rise of American Philosophy;* Paul Starr, *The Social Transformation of American Medicine* (New York: Basic Books, 1982); Daniel J. Kevles, *The Physicists: The History of a Scientific Community in Modern America* (New York: Alfred A. Knopf, 1978); and Edwin T. Layton, *The Revolt of the Engineers: Social Responsibility and the American Engineering Profession* (Cleveland: Case Western University Press, 1971).

In speaking generally of professionalization, I collapse some important distinctions. I do not mean to imply that the process occurred at the same pace or with identical results in every field or discipline. For example, success in achieving autonomy varied widely among the professions.

11. Higham, "The Matrix of Specialization," 6–7.

12. This kind of categorization is particularly evident in Pells, *Radical Visions and American Dreams;* Nash, *The Nervous Generation;* and Wertheim, *The New York Little Renaissance*. An otherwise excellent treatment of the *Masses* group, Fishbein, *Rebels in Bohemia*, applies anachronistic and irrelevant political criteria to its subject. Superior and less rigid group studies are Forcey, *The Crossroads of Liberalism*, and Blake, *Beloved Community*. Blake's book is an extremely thorough and intelligent discussion which salvages its subjects' ideas from the dismissive category of the "lyrical left," found, for example, in Abrahams, *The Lyrical Left*. In designating my work a cultural history of intellectuals, I am distinguishing it from studies such as Blake's.

13. David A. Hollinger, "Historians and the Discourse of Intellectuals," in Higham and Conkin, *New Directions in American Intellectual History*, 43. The essay is reprinted in Hollinger's collection, *In the American Province*, 130–51.

14. Novick, *That Noble Dream*, 9–10.

15. Walzer, *The Company of Critics*, 20.

16. Lasch's pioneering social history of intellectuals involved a series of biographical chapters. See Lasch, *The New Radicalism in America*. There are, of course, a number of fine biographies of individuals who figure in my discussion. I would particularly point to: Clayton, *Forgotten Prophet;* Hoopes, *Van Wyck Brooks;* Miller, *Lewis Mumford;* Rosenstone, *Romantic Revolutionary;* Rudnick, *Mabel Dodge Luhan;* and Steel, *Walter Lippmann*.

17. On European generational thought, see Robert Wohl, *The Generation of 1914* (Cambridge: Harvard University Press, 1979). Late in his career, Malcolm Cowley attempted a theory of American generations along the lines set out by

Ortega y Gasset, but even this remained quite informal and impressionistic. See Malcolm Cowley, " 'And Jesse Begat . . . ': A Note on Literary Generations," in —*And I Worked at the Writer's Trade*, 1–20.

18. The assault on the genteel tradition is discussed most thoroughly in May, *The End of American Innocence*. Arthur Frank Wertheim sees his four groups— socialists, "apolitical iconoclasts," cultural nationalists, and aesthetic modernists —as united in "common cause . . . against the genteel tradition." See Wertheim, *The New York Little Renaissance*, xii.

19. Cain, *F. O. Matthiessen*, 209. On Mencken's relationships with African-American writers, see Scruggs, *The Sage in Harlem*. The question of Mencken's racism long predates the publication of his diary in 1989. Charles Angoff raised the issue as early as 1956. Scruggs argues that, despite Mencken's frequent use of racial epithets and his belief in racial differences, to label him a racist "is not only wrong but irrelevant" given his support for the Harlem Renaissance (p. 51). The fact that Mencken wrote so much more than other white critics about African-American literature and life has opened him up to criticisms that cannot be leveled against those who remained relatively silent.

1. The Repudiation of the University

1. On the connection between interdependence, the recession of causation, and the rise of the professions, see Haskell, *The Emergence of Professional Social Science*, esp. chap. 2. An excellent discussion of professional autonomy can be found in Eliot Freidson, "Are Professions Necessary?," in Haskell, *The Authority of Experts*.

2. Geiger, *To Advance Knowledge*, esp. chaps. 1–2; Hofstadter, *Anti-Intellectualism in American Life*, 204.

3. Adams, *Education*, 299, 304.

4. Adams, *Education*, 306; Hawkins, *Pioneer*, 62.

5. Phillips, "John Dewey," 16, 37.

6. Daniel Coit Gilman, "The Utility of Universities," in *University Problems*, 67, 58; Woodrow Wilson, "Princeton in the Nation's Service," in Hofstadter and Smith, *American Higher Education*, II, 685; Storr, *Harper's University*, 194.

7. Daniel Coit Gilman, "Higher Education in the United States," in *University Problems*, 297.

8. Quoted in Veysey, *Emergence of the American University*, 119, 61.

9. Dewey, "A College Course: What Should I Expect from It?" (1890), "The Angle of Reflection 2" (April 1891), and "The Scholastic and the Speculator" (December 1891–January 1892), in *Early Works*, III, 54, 199–200, 152.

10. Wilson, "Princeton in the Nation's Service," 694–95.

11. Phillips, "John Dewey," 98–134, 265–82. Phillips' dissertation gives a full account of the relationship between Dewey's philosophical development and his desire for involvement in the world of affairs.

12. Storr, *Harper's University*, 197, 209, 211; Gilman, "Higher Education in

the United States," 298; John Dewey, "The Angle of Reflection 3" (May 1891), in *Early Works*, III, 202; Phillips, "John Dewey," 149. On *Thought News*, see also Westbrook, *John Dewey and American Democracy*, 51–58.

13. Addams, *Twenty Years at Hull-House*, 430–36; Frederick J. Turner, "The Extension Work of the University of Wisconsin," in George Francis James, ed., *Handbook of University Extension* (Philadelphia: American Society for the Extension of University Teaching, 1893), 319; Alfred Lawrence Hall-Quest, *The University Afield* (New York: Macmillan, 1926), 16–17.

14. Veysey, *Emergence of the American University*, 107–108. Van Hise encouraged professors to assume the role of experts in government service. His conception of university extension was vocational and narrowly utilitarian.

15. John Dewey, "The Angle of Reflection 3" (May 1891) and "The Scholastic and the Speculator" (December 1891–January 1892), in *Early Works*, III, 149–51, 202.

16. Veysey, *Emergence of the American University*, 324; Hawkins, *Pioneer*, 112.

17. William James to Charles Renouvier, 1896, and William James to Henry James, 1903, quoted in Perry, *William James*, I, 441–42.

18. Santayana, *Character and Opinion*, 62, 42, 36.

19. Veblen, *The Higher Learning*, 166.

20. Veblen, *The Theory of the Leisure Class*, 368, 394, 372.

21. James, "The Ph.D Octopus" (1903), in *Memories and Studies*, 334, 343, 345–47; Stein, *The Autobiography of Alice B. Toklas*, 97–98; quoted in Dorfman, *Veblen and His America*, 308.

22. Santayana, *Character and Opinion*, 57; quoted in Veysey, *Emergence of the American University*, 77; Babbitt, *Literature and the American College*, 126, 148, 134, 149.

23. William James to Charles W. Eliot (1891), and Eliot to James (1894), quoted in Veysey, *Emergence of the American University*, 435, 438; Santayana, *Character and Opinion*, 57; Veblen, *The Higher Learning*, 220, 66, 104, 221, 224.

24. John Reed, "The Harvard Renaissance," unpublished ms., Reed Papers; William James, "The True Harvard" (1903) and "The Social Value of the College-Bred" (1907), in *Memories and Studies*, 354–55, 320. The emphasis is James'.

25. Lippmann, "An Open Mind: William James," 800–801. See also Steel, *Walter Lippmann*, 17–18.

26. Randolph Bourne to Prudence Winterrowd, Jan. 16, 1913, Bourne Papers.

27. Bourne, "Dewey's Philosophy," 154–56.

28. Eastman, *Enjoyment of Living*, 281–83. See also Max Eastman, "The Hero as Teacher: The Life Story of John Dewey," in *Heroes I Have Known*, 275–321.

29. Macy, *The Spirit of American Literature*, 298.

30. Edmund Wilson, "Christian Gauss as a Teacher of Literature," in *Shores of Light*, 5–6; Mumford, *Sketches from Life*, 220; Walter Lippmann, "George Santayana—A Sketch" (August 1911), quoted in Steel, *Walter Lippmann*, 21.

31. Bourne, "Dewey's Philosophy," 155–56; Wilson, *Shores of Light*, 24; Wilson to John Peale Bishop, Jan. 22, 1919, in Wilson, *Letters on Literature and Politics*, 41; Wilson, *I Thought of Daisy*, 213; Josephson, *Life among the Surrealists*, 27–28.

32. Bourne, "Dewey's Philosophy," 156; Lippmann, "Santayana," quoted in Steel, *Walter Lippmann*, 21–22.

33. Van Wyck Brooks, Diary, Nov. 30, 1904, Brooks Collection.

34. Bourne to Prudence Winterrowd, Jan. 16, 1913, and March 2, 1913, Bourne Papers.

35. Stearns, "Confessions of a Harvard Man" (December 1913), 820; Stearns, "Confessions of a Harvard Man—II" (January 1914), 79.

36. Van Wyck Brooks, "America's Coming of Age" (1915), in *Three Essays on America*, 28–29.

37. Mumford, "Fruit," esp. 890–92; Cowley, *Exile's Return*, 35, 37; Reed, "Almost Thirty," 269; Lippmann, *Liberty and the News*, 96. Mumford's story is reprinted in *Findings and Keepings*, 12–15.

38. Eastman, *Enjoyment of Living*, 290–91, 255.

39. Brooks to Frank J. Mather, Jr., Dec. 6, 1939, Brooks to J. S. Zelie, Sept. 7, 1921, Brooks Collection; Brooks, *Autobiography*, 191.

40. Brooks to Newton Arvin, March 5, 1922, Brooks Collection.

41. Ellery Sedgwick to Bourne, Dec. 13, 1911, Bourne to Alyse Gregory, April 10, 1914, Sedgwick to Bourne, May 9, 1914, Bourne Papers.

42. Lincoln Steffens to Frederick M. Willis, Dec. 8, 1889, Steffens to Reed, Oct. 8, 1909, Steffens to Laura Steffens, Dec. 24, 1911, in *Letters of Lincoln Steffens*, I, 30, 229, 284; Reed, *The Day in Bohemia*, 7. See also Rosenstone, *Romantic Revolutionary*, 83.

43. First announcement of the New School for Social Research (1919), quoted in Dorfman, *Veblen and His America*, 449.

44. Lippmann, *Preface to Politics*, 29; Mumford, *Sketches from Life*, 189; Mumford to the Editor of the Forum, [1916], Mumford Collection. Mumford did accept visiting professorships at Dartmouth in the 1930s, Stanford from 1942 to 1944, the University of Pennsylvania for ten years beginning in 1951, MIT in 1957, and Berkeley in 1961. In every case, however, he insisted on the most liberal terms of employment, directed his courses toward his own current interests, and resisted permanent appointments. See Miller, *Lewis Mumford*, throughout.

45. See Bourke, "Social Critics," 70. Lewis Perry has also made this observation: "The first decision facing a would-be intellectual between 1900 and 1945 concerned whether to pursue a career inside or outside the professoriate." Perry, *Intellectual Life in America: A History*, 291.

46. Bourne to Prudence Winterrowd, Feb. 5, 1913, Bourne Papers.

2. Making a Living

1. Brooks, *Ordeal of Mark Twain*, 85, 74, 104, 45, 50–51, 82.

2. Malcolm Cowley, "Introduction," in Brooks, *Ordeal of Mark Twain*, 7, 10.

3. Brooks, *Ordeal of Mark Twain*, 142.

4. Stearns, "Confessions of a Harvard Man," 81; idem, "La Peur de la Vie,"

and "What Can a Young Man Do?" in *America and the Young Intellectual*, 42, 164–65; idem, *The Street I Know*, 43.

5. Bourne, "The Virtues and Seasons of Life" and "The Dodging of Pressures," in *Youth and Life*, 273, 57, 271; Wilson, *A Prelude*, 158. See also Clayton, *Forgotten Prophet*, 21–22.

6. Hapgood, *Victorian in the Modern World*, 503; Brooks, *Wine of the Puritans*, 48; Brooks, "America's Coming-of-Age" (1915), in *Three Essays on America*, 33; Eastman, *Journalism versus Art*, 68; Mumford, *Golden Day*, 119; idem, *Technics and Civilization*, 177; Dos Passos, "Young Spain," *Seven Arts* (August 1917), 488; Anderson, "From Chicago," *Seven Arts* (May 1917), 43.

7. Brooks, Diary, Jan. 21, 1904, July 21, 1909, Brooks Collection; Bourne to Prudence Winterrowd, April 10, 1913, and Bourne to Dorothy Teall, July 9, 1915, Bourne Papers.

8. Rosenfeld, *The Boy in the Sun*, 162.

9. Bourne to Carl Zigrosser, Nov. 16, 1913, Bourne Papers.

10. Dell, *Moon-Calf*, 187, 167; idem, *Homecoming: An Autobiography*, 33, 57, 62.

11. Brooks, *Autobiography*, 498; Wilson to Stanley Dell, Feb. 5, 1919, in *Letters on Literature and Politics*, 42.

12. Wilson, "The Delegate from Great Neck: Mr. Van Wyck Brooks and Mr. Scott Fitzgerald," in *Discordant Encounters*, 54, 57.

13. Anderson, *Story Teller's Story*, 5; Luhan, *Movers and Shakers*, 54–55; Mumford, *Sketches from Life*, 43. See also Miller, *Lewis Mumford*, 132 and throughout.

14. Eastman, *Journalism versus Art*, 79; Mencken to Eastman, Nov. 6, 1936, Eastman Papers; Mumford to Frank, Jan. 19, 1938, Frank Collection. For a discussion of Eastman's general tendency to shrink from popular acclaim, see O'Neill, *The Last Romantic*.

15. Edmund Wilson, "Signs of Life: Lady Chatterley's Lover" (July 3, 1929), in *Shores of Light*, 405; Lee Simonson to Lippmann, Aug. 4, 1913, Lippmann Papers. The emphasis is Simonson's.

16. Dell, *Homecoming*, 91; quoted in Eastman, *Enjoyment of Living*, 160, 265, 330.

17. Vernon Louis Parrington, *The Beginnings of Critical Realism in America, 1860–1920* (New York: Harcourt, Brace, 1930), xxvii.

18. Anderson, *Notebook*, 147, 64.

19. Ibid., 148, 152, 49; Anderson, *Story Teller's Story*, 327, 81; Parrington, *Beginnings of Critical Realism*, 371.

20. Brooks, *Wine of the Puritans*, 46, 42, 142. For two excellent discussions of the ideology of productive labor, see Marvin Meyers, *The Jacksonian Persuasion: Politics and Belief* (Stanford: Stanford University Press, 1960 [1957]), esp. chap. 2, and Eric Foner, *Free Soil, Free Labor, Free Men: The Ideology of the Republican Party before the Civil War* (New York: Oxford University Press, 1970), esp. chap. 1. On some adaptations of this ideology in the late nineteenth and early twentieth centuries, see Thomas, *Alternative America*, and Diggins, *The Bard of Savagery*.

21. Anderson, *Story Teller's Story*, 320; Mumford, *Sticks and Stones*, 219; Ran-

dolph Bourne, "On Discussion," in *History of a Literary Radical*, 175; Brooks, *Ordeal of Mark Twain*, 56, 63; Wilson, *Discordant Encounters*, 55; Mumford, *Technics and Civilization*, 205.

22. Ludwig Lewisohn, on the staff of the *Nation*, remembered his "days of slavery" as an instructor at Ohio State University but also spoke of his need for "some sort of a regular basic job" in place of an academic position. Lewisohn to Huebsch, July 1, 1920, Huebsch Papers.

23. Steffens to Frederick M. Willis, Dec. 8, 1889, Steffens to Joseph Steffens, May 4, 1892, Steffens to Joseph Steffens, Jan. 26, 1893, in *Letters of Lincoln Steffens*, I, 30, 75, 90.

24. Kuttner to Lippmann, [1910], Lippmann Papers.

25. Steffens to Joseph Steffens, Jan. 18, 1893, Steffens to Harlow Gale, Jan. 13, 1895, Steffens to Joseph Steffens, March 18, 1893, Steffens to Joseph Steffens, Jan. 18, 1893, in *Letters of Lincoln Steffens*, I, 89, 110, 92, 88; Steffens, *Autobiography*, 313, 293.

26. Quoted in Wreszin, *Superfluous Anarchist*, 39; Hapgood, *Victorian in the Modern World*, 138, 141; Steffens, *Autobiography*, 314, 339.

27. Dell, *Homecoming*, 133, 190.

28. Dell, *Moon-Calf*, 352; Rosenstone, *Romantic Revolutionary*, 113–14; Reed to Louise Bryant, June 14, 1917, Reed to Bryant, June 28, 1917, Reed Papers; Frank, *Memoirs*, 57–69.

29. Rosenfeld to Philip Skinner Platt, Oct. 8, 1912, Aug. 7, 1913, Dec. 5, 1913, Jan. 11, 1914, Rosenfeld Papers.

30. Dell, *Homecoming*, 133.

31. Eastman, *Journalism versus Art*, 73, 23, 70, 53, 11, 74; Eastman, *Enjoyment of Living*, 551. Commenting on Upton Sinclair's *The Brass Check*, a scathing look at the popular American press, Eastman wrote: "American journalism is a monstrous and malignant growth, which if it continues uncured will destroy every honest and straightforward and hopeful thing in our civilization." Max Eastman, Draft Review of *The Brass Check*, Nov. 30, 1919, Eastman Papers.

32. Herbert Croly, unpublished proposal for the *New Republic*, 1914, Lippmann Papers.

33. Lippmann to Brooks, Feb. 5, 1914, Lippmann Papers.

34. Bourne to Alyse Gregory, April 10, 1914, Bourne to Gregory, Sept. 28, 1914, Bourne Papers.

35. "An Expression of Artists for the Community," *Seven Arts* (November 1916), 53; Reed to Louise Bryant, July 10, 1917, Reed Papers.

36. Back cover of the *Freeman*, March 17, 1920, quoted in Wreszin, *Superfluous Anarchist*, 52; Munson, quoted in Hoffman, Allen, and Ulrich, *Little Magazine*, 5.

37. Eastman, *Enjoyment of Living*, 540; quoted in Eastman, *Enjoyment of Living*, 440–41.

38. Bourne to Alyse Gregory, July 5, 1914, Bourne to Elizabeth Shepley Sergeant, Aug. 24, 1916, Bourne Papers; Lippmann to Graham Wallas, Jan. 14, [1915 or 1916], Lippmann Papers; Lippmann, Memorandum to *New Republic* editors, [n.d.], Lippmann Papers.

39. Huebsch to Brooks, Dec. 12, 1919, Brooks to Edward T. Booth, May 12, 1920, Brooks to Alfred Stieglitz, Nov. 29, 1921, Brooks to Sherwood Anderson, July 23, 1923, Brooks to Newton Arvin, July 17, 1921, Brooks to Arvin, June 27 or July 4, 1921, Brooks to *American Scholar*, Jan. 11, 1947, Brooks Collection. The emphasis is Brooks'. Mumford spoke similarly of "escaping mechanical routine as editor, literary hack, or what not that will stunt my development during a period in which I am still capable of growing." See Mumford to Sophia Wittenberg, July 4, 1920, in Mumford, *Findings and Keepings*, 48.

40. Lippmann to Bernard Berenson, Sept. 15, 1919, Lippmann to Berenson, Aug. 31, 1921, Robert Hallowell to Lippmann, July 27, 1921, Laurence Stallings to Lippmann, May 4, 1927, Carl Becker to Henry Seidel Canby, [1928], Lippmann to Berenson, June 25, 1930, Lippmann Papers.

41. Mencken to Ellery Sedgwick, Oct. 18, 1918, Mencken to Fielding Hudson Garrison, Nov. 17, 1919, Mencken to Theodore Dreiser, Feb. 2, 1920, Mencken to Dreiser, Sept. 13, 1920, Mencken to Albert G. Keller, Oct. 4, 1933, Mencken to Eugene T. Saxton, Oct. 9, 1933, in *Letters of H. L. Mencken*, 130, 161, 173, 196, 367, 368.

42. Mencken to Charles Green Shaw, Dec. 2, 1927, in *Letters of H. L. Mencken*, 307; Mencken, "On Being an American," in *Prejudices: Third Series*, 17; Bourne to Alyse Gregory, July 5, 1914, Bourne Papers; Chase, "The Luxury of Integrity," in *The Nemesis of American Business*, 45, 29.

43. Cowley to Wilson, Feb. 13, 1929, Wilson Papers.

44. Bourne to Alyse Gregory, early 1916[?], Bourne to Gregory, Feb. 1914, Bourne to Elizabeth Shepley Sergeant, Aug. 24, 1916, Bourne to Sergeant, Oct. 31, 1916, Bourne to Gregory, Jan. 3, 1916, Bourne to Gregory, Fall 1916[?], Bourne Papers.

45. Bourne, Diary, 1916, Bourne to Elizabeth Shepley Sergeant, Sept. 20, 1916, Bourne to Sara Bourne, Oct. 12, 1918, Natalie Bourne Fenninger to Esther Cornell, Jan. 7, 1919, Bourne Papers.

46. Bourne to Sara Bourne, Nov. 4, 1918, Bourne Papers; Brooks to Frank, Sept. 23, 1919, Brooks to Edward T. Booth, May 12, 1920, Brooks to Newton Arvin, Aug. 8, 1924, Brooks to Booth, Dec. 18, 1925, Brooks Collection.

47. Brooks to Henry Stimson, Feb. 28, 1937, Brooks Collection.

48. Reed to Bryant, July 15, 1917, July 18, 1917, Dec. 11, 1916, March 18, 1918, Reed Papers; Rosenstone, *Romantic Revolutionary*, 264; Reed, *Insurgent Mexico*, 40. The emphasis is Reed's.

49. Brooks to Newton Arvin, [n.d., ca. 1925], Brooks Collection; Wilson to Christian Gauss, March 4, 1924, and Wilson to Stanley Dell, Aug. 27, 1925, in *Letters on Literature and Politics*, 121, 127; Francis Hackett to Huebsch, May 14, 1921 and April 5, 1922, Huebsch Papers; Hackett to Mumford, March 26, 1922, Mumford Collection. The emphasis is Hackett's.

50. Max Eastman to Eliena Krylenko Eastman, Sept. 30, 1942 and Oct. 14, 1942, Eliena Krylenko Eastman Papers; O'Neill, *The Last Romantic*, 214, 256–58. The *Reader's Digest* paid Eastman a $10,000 annual retainer and $2000 per article —quite a leap from the $150 a month of the *Masses* days.

51. Sherman Paul, "Paul Rosenfeld," in Rosenfeld, *Port of New York*, x-xi.

52. Josephson, *Life among the Surrealists*, 25, 69, 373. Malcolm Cowley recalled that the first time he "felt at ease financially" was during the Depression, when he became literary editor of the *New Republic*. He dismissed the idea that there was any connection between the personal fortunes of writers and radicalism. Cowley, *Dream of the Golden Mountains*, 168.

53. Lippmann to Stearns, March 25, 1919, Lippmann Papers; Lippmann Federal Income Tax Returns, Lippmann Papers.

54. Wilson to Stanley Dell, Feb. 19, 1921, Wilson to Lippmann, Feb. 13, 1922, in *Letters on Literature and Politics*, 56, 78.

55. Wilson, *Cold War and the Income Tax*, 4–6.

56. Rosenfeld to Mumford, May 8, 1937 and Oct. 18, 1937, Mumford Collection; Rosenfeld to Wilson, Dec. 27, 1937, Sept. 10, 1940, Jan. 19, 1941, Wilson Papers. On the other hand, the fact that Rosenfeld and Cowley were not on good terms meant that Rosenfeld had difficulty publishing in the *New Republic* during the thirties. Financial pressures were also responsible for Wilson's decision to stand in for Cowley. After leaving the *New Republic* to do free-lance writing in the thirties, Wilson found himself $1141.25 in debt to his former employers. See Bruce Bliven to Wilson, Oct. 18, 1933, Wilson Papers.

57. Robert Edmond Jones to Lippmann, [n.d.], Reed to Lippmann, Feb. 23, 1913 and Sept. 1913, Marsden Hartley to Lippmann, [1916], Lippmann Papers.

58. Bourne to Everett Benjamin, Nov. 26, 1917, Bourne Papers; Van Wyck Brooks, Introduction, in Bourne, *History of a Literary Radical*, x.

3. From Expression to Influence

1. Eastman, *Enjoyment of Living*, 306, 313.

2. Eastman, *Enjoyment of Poetry*, 88, 15, 6, 11, 29, 78. Walter Lippmann claimed that he "gurgled with delight" reading Eastman's book. Lippmann to Eastman, April 24, 1913, Eastman Papers.

3. Eastman, *Enjoyment of Poetry*, 147, 54, 198, 197, 193.

4. Bourne to Alyse Gregory, Sept. 8, 1913, Bourne Papers; Randolph Bourne, "The Adventure of Life," "Some Thoughts on Religion," and "The Mystic Turned Radical," in *Youth and Life*, 187, 196, 208.

5. Randolph Bourne, "The Adventure of Life" and "For Radicals," in *Youth and Life*, 168, 308–9.

6. Brooks, *Wine of the Puritans*, 140, 121, 136. The emphasis is Brooks'.

7. Lippmann, *Preface to Politics*, 306, 244.

8. Croly, unpublished proposal for the *New Republic*, 1914, Lippmann Papers.

9. [Waldo Frank], "An Expression of Artists for the Community," Romain Rolland, "America and the Arts," Waldo Frank, trans., Peter Minuit [Paul Rosenfeld], "291 Fifth Avenue," *Seven Arts* (November 1916), 48–49, 53, 64; Alfred Booth Kuttner, "The Artist," *Seven Arts* (February 1917), 412; Van Wyck Brooks, "Our Critics," *Seven Arts* (May 1917), 112.

10. Luhan, *Movers and Shakers*, 204; Virginia Hunt or Edward Eyre Hunt to Reed, June 12, 1913, Reed Papers. A full account of Reed's involvement in the Paterson strike and the Pageant can be found in Rosenstone, *Romantic Revolutionary*, chap. 8. See also Green, *New York 1913*.

11. John Reed, "War in Paterson," *Masses* (June 1913), 14–17; Reed, *Insurgent Mexico*, throughout; Steffens, *Autobiography*, 739.

12. Reed, "Almost Thirty," 267–68; Reed to Bryant, July 15, 1917, Reed Papers.

13. Max Eastman, quoted in "Thousands Mourn Death of Reed, Rebel-Poet-Artist," *New York Call* (October 19, 1920), 2; Reed, *Ten Days That Shook the World*, 220, 125, 16.

14. Charles Forcey, *The Crossroads of Liberalism*, 5.

15. Lippmann, *Drift and Mastery*, 147; Lippmann, Diary, July 4–5, 1914, Lippmann Papers. These entries are the last substantial examples of self-examination in Lippmann's diaries and letters.

16. Lippmann to Norman Hapgood, July 20, 1917; Lippmann, Diary, May 13, 1918; Graham Wallas to Lippmann, Nov. 9, 1917, Lippmann Papers.

17. [James Oppenheim], *Seven Arts* (March 1917), 504–5. For a full discussion of the idea of war as an alternative to business civilization, see Lears, *No Place of Grace*, esp. chap. 3.

18. "American Independence and the War: A Supplement with the April Issue," *Seven Arts* (April 1917), throughout; John Dewey, "In a Time of National Hesitation," *Seven Arts* (May 1917), 6–7.

19. [James Oppenheim], *Seven Arts* (May 1917), 68–71.

20. Randolph S. Bourne, "The War and the Intellectuals" (June 1917), "Twilight of Idols" (Oct. 1917), "A War Diary" (Sept. 1917), "The State" (1918), all in Carl Resek, ed., *War and the Intellectuals: Collected Essays, 1915–1919* (New York: Harper & Row, 1964), 12, 62, 40, 73.

21. Bourne to Dorothy Teall, June 4, 1915, Bourne Papers; Bourne, "A War Diary," 47.

22. Bourne to Lippmann, Aug. 21, 1917, Lippmann to Bourne, Aug. 23, 1917, Lippmann Papers.

23. Bourne, "The War and the Intellectuals," "A War Diary," "Twilight of Idols," 14, 47, 64.

24. Bourne, "The War and the Intellectuals," 3, 5, 9.

25. Bourne to Brooks, March 27, 1918, Bourne Papers. Bourne's source for the idea of a vital myth is uncertain. Stanley M. Bligh, the British psychologist with whom Bourne later had an unpleasant visit in Wales, recommended the work of Hans Vaihinger to his young American correspondent in 1912. Vaihinger's *The Philosophy of "As If,"* published in Berlin in 1911, was not translated into English until 1924, although Bourne may have read it in German. For Vaihinger, however, fictions were most important as working concepts in experimental science, not as general articles of faith for intellectuals. Georges Sorel's *Reflections on Violence*, which appeared in French in 1908, came out in the United States in a B. W. Huebsch edition of T. E. Hulme's translation in 1912. But Sorel excluded

intellectuals, who were supposed to know better, from the myth of the general strike. In Bourne's version of the vital myth, intellectuals were to perform a kind of balancing act between skepticism and belief. He put "leaders" in quotation marks, presumably to suggest that the assumption of leadership was based on long-term faith, not direct fact. See Stanley M. Bligh to Bourne, Nov. 11, 1912, and Dec. 7, 1912, Bourne Papers.

26. Stearns, "Where Are Our Intellectuals?" in *America and the Young Intellectual*, 50.

27. Rosenfeld, *Port of New York*, 235–36; Van Wyck Brooks, Introduction, in Bourne, *History of a Literary Radical*, xxx; Mumford, *Golden Day*, 268. Acceptance of this vital myth did not imply naiveté or simple credulity. Brooks, for example, could hold onto his faith in criticism and still comment wryly on his own work's limited popularity. In reference to his *Letters and Leadership*—the book that had inspired Bourne's evocation of a vital myth—Brooks remarked, "I'm always eager for those large royalty-checks that show how much the American public admires me." Brooks to Huebsch, June 14, 1919, Huebsch Papers.

28. Wilson to Stanley Dell, Jan. 21, 1921, in *Letters on Literature and Politics*, 45; Stearns, Preface, in *Civilization in the United States*, viii, iii; Mumford, *Sketches from Life*, 368; Wilson, *Discordant Encounters*, 25. In questioning the validity of disillusionment as a useful description of intellectual attitudes in the twenties, Charles C. Alexander has argued that *Civilization in the United States* "expressed basically the same ambivalent but ultimately hopeful feelings about America that had characterized insurgent criticism for more than a decade." See Alexander, *Here the Country Lies*, 90–92.

29. Frank, *Our America*, 227–28.

30. Frank, *Our America*, 147, 135, 143, 186; Rosenfeld, *Port of New York*, 257, 288. See also Heller, "Paul Rosenfeld," esp. 36–38.

31. Freeman, *American Testament*, 323.

32. Lippmann, *Public Opinion*, 31, 375, 314, 384; idem, *The Phantom Public*, 150; Lippmann to Wesley C. Mitchell, Jan. 18, 1922, Lippmann Papers. For an excellent discussion of *Public Opinion*, see Tompkins, "Twilight of Idols," 199–210. It is worth noting that the arch-realist Lippmann called Mumford's *The Story of Utopias* "easily the most important book on politics we've had for a very long time." Lippmann's pronouncement came *after* the publication of *Public Opinion* and referred to a book which explicitly restated Bourne's vital myth. Mumford claimed to speak to "those who are stirring uneasily in their sleep, and beginning to dream . . . . We would give them courage to attack reality once more, by way of the dream." Lippmann to Mumford, March 30, 1923, Mumford to Horace B. Liveright, Jan. 21, 1922, Mumford Collection.

33. Soule, *The Useful Art of Economics*, Foreword and 242; Stuart Chase, "A Private Utopia," in *The Nemesis of American Business*, 190; idem, *The Tragedy of Waste*, 280, 23; Soule, *The Coming American Revolution*, 303. On Chase, see Westbrook, "Tribune of the Technostructure." For additional discussions of Chase and Soule, see Lawson, *The Failure of Independent Liberalism*, 67–84 and 226–37, and Pells, *Radical Visions and American Dreams*, 71–75 and 101–2. Lawson notes

the important fact that Soule turned down Rexford Tugwell's offer of a position in the New Deal and remained an independent critic (p. 70).

34. Soule, *The Useful Art of Economics*, 233, 222, 228; Chase, *The Tragedy of Waste*, 279; George Soule, "One Way to Begin" and "The Organizing Man," in *A Planned Society*, 252, 150; Stuart Chase, "The Abuse of Capital" and "Prometheus Enchained," in *The Nemesis of American Business*, 107, 104, 97; idem, *Men and Machines*, 239, 346–47; idem, *The Economy of Abundance*, 313–14.

35. George Soule, "An Unmanaged Civilization," in *A Planned Society*, 52; Chase, *Men and Machines*, 348; idem, "The Abuse of Capital," 96.

36. Soule, *The Coming American Revolution*, 68, 281; idem, "The Organizing Man," 152–53; Chase, *Men and Machines*, 216, 21; Gilbert, *Designing the Industrial State*, 290. Chase and Soule appear only briefly in Gilbert's book. The observation that I quote refers generally to intellectuals who looked to the corporation as their model for political society.

37. Irwin Granich [Michael Gold], "Towards Proletarian Art," *Liberator* (February 1921), 22, 23.

38. Rosenfeld, "James Oppenheim," *New Republic* (December 10, 1924), quoted in Heller, "Paul Rosenfeld," 39, 40.

39. Munson, *Waldo Frank*, 53–54, 58, 61.

40. Burke to Cowley, Jan. 14, 1921, and Jan. 18, 1923, in Jay, *Selected Correspondence*, 79, 133–34; Burke to Frank, Sept. 4, 1922 and Oct. 7, 1922, Frank Collection. The emphasis is Burke's.

41. Burke, "The Status of Art" and "The Poetic Process," in *Counter-Statement*, 92, 70; idem, *Permanence and Change*, 36, 69, 350; idem, "The Calling of the Tune," in *The Philosophy of Literary Form*, 233. Burke stood out even from his friends Munson and Malcolm Cowley with his densely analytical prose.

42. Burke, *Attitudes toward History*, I, 223, 180, 220; idem, "Foreword," "The Philosophy of Literary Form," and "The Virtues and Limitations of Debunking," in *The Philosophy of Literary Form*, vii, 130–31, 188. The emphasis is Burke's. In his concern for symbolic forms and his insistence on the writer's responsibility for engaging the public through the creation of resonant alternative symbols, Burke was involved in a similar project to that of Lewis Mumford in the 1920s. On Mumford's ideas of "symbolic interaction," see Blake, *Beloved Community*, 220–28.

43. Seldes, *Seven Lively Arts*, 303, 246, 207; Frank, *Our America*, 214; Eastman, *Love and Revolution*, esp. 190; Wilson, *Twenties*, xiviii.

44. Seldes, *Seven Lively Arts*, 48, 197, 265, 266, 295. Josephson, *Life among the Surrealists*, 191. Within a few years, Josephson would modify his Dada-influenced reverence for American machines and mass culture. By 1930, he was urging "a *rapprochement*" of intellectuals with the machine so that "in the end the force of mind in them may again leaven this society which has known only material preoccupations." Josephson, *Portrait of the Artist as American*, 308.

45. Casey Blake has observed in the cases of Bourne, Brooks, Frank, and Mumford that a commitment to public discussion competed with a vision of "prophetic inspiration." But even in their hopes for a democratic culture, they

essentially relied on exhortation and the example of their own criticism as the first step toward renewal. In other words, they saw prophetic inspiration as a means toward a more participatory alternative. See Blake, *Beloved Community*, 283 and throughout.

46. Wilson, *Twenties*, 312, 351; idem, *I Thought of Daisy*, 175.

47. Wilson to Allen Tate, May 20, 1929, Wilson to Christian Gauss, Nov. 12, 1929, in *Letters on Literature and Politics*, 164, 177.

48. Wilson, *Axel's Castle*, 266, 269, 292.

49. For a critical discussion of radical reportage in the 1930s, see Stott, *Documentary Expression*, esp. chap. 10. Stott builds upon Daniel Aaron's argument that non-fiction was the dominant form of expression in this period, even among writers who had already established themselves in fiction. Wilson later regretted that his reportage had been tainted by a naive acceptance of "the contemporary line of Marxism." See Stott, *Documentary Expression*, 177. But in 1936, he drew the praise of John Dos Passos, who noted: "It sure does pay to put down what happens just as it does happen — I'm not at all sure that it isn't all anybody can do that's of any permanent use in a literary way." Dos Passos added that to produce good reportage was "just as difficult an imaginative process as anything else," which implied that the reporter was not obliged to sacrifice creativity for utility. Dos Passos to Wilson, [1936], Wilson Papers.

Matthew Josephson saw his own experiences in reportage as an attempt to solve the lingering problem of the separation of intellect and society: "I was trying to get out of the Ivory Tower in which most American men of letters still confined themselves and learn at first hand what sort of country we were living in." Josephson, *Life among the Surrealists*, 362.

50. Eastman, *The Literary Mind*, 64, 102, 158, 216, 53, 26, 29.

51. Ibid., 122, 206, 254, 269–70.

52. Mumford, *Herman Melville*, 61, 184. See also Miller, *Lewis Mumford*, 272–74, and Richard Wightman Fox, "Tragedy, Responsibility, and the American Intellectual, 1925–1950," in Hughes and Hughes, *Lewis Mumford*, 323–37.

53. Mumford, *Technics and Civilization*, 435.

54. H. L. Mencken, "The Forward-Looker," in *Prejudices: Third Series*, 213; idem, "The Cult of Hope," in *Prejudices: Second Series*, 218, 211; idem, "Criticism of Criticism of Criticism," in *Prejudices: First Series*, 16.

55. H. L. Mencken, "Footnote on Criticism," in *Prejudices: Third Series*, 96, 85, 90–91, 92.

56. H. L. Mencken, "The National Letters," in *Prejudices: Second Series*, 70, 16; Mencken to Theodore Dreiser, Jan. 7, [1919], in *The New Mencken Letters*, 95. Mencken acknowledged a debt to Bourne in one of his most famous essays, "Puritanism as a Literary Force," in *A Book of Prefaces*, 237. Privately, and in the midst of the World War, he could offer only a backhanded compliment: "Bourne is horribly New Republican. But he is at least a cut above Lippmann, Hackett and the rest of those sophomores. We must thank God for every mercy, however slight. Bourne did a good article on Dreiser." Mencken to Burton Rascoe, [Oct.? 27?, 1917], in *The New Mencken Letters*, 77.

57. Mencken, "The National Letters," 69–70, 66–67, 65, 95.

58. H. L. Mencken, "The Genealogy of Etiquette," in *Prejudices: First Series*, 169.

59. Mencken, "Footnote on Criticism," 90–91, 103–4.

60. H. L. Mencken, "Preface," in *A Book of Prefaces*, [n.p.]; idem, "Criticism of Criticism of Criticism," 19; idem, "The American Novel," in *Prejudices: Fourth Series*, 282. For a thoughtful but excessively rigid categorization of the prewar New York intellectual milieu, see Arthur Frank Wertheim, *The New York Little Renaissance*.

61. Mencken's work as a "constructive" critic was most evident in his support for the Southern literary renascence of the 1920s. After debunking the South throughout the 1910s and in his famous essay of 1920, "The Sahara of the Bozart," he actively cultivated the Southern writers who responded to his indictments. See Hobson, *Serpent in Eden*.

62. Mencken, "Theodore Dreiser," in *A Book of Prefaces*, 98; idem, "Criticism of Criticism of Criticism," 18; idem, "From the Memoirs of a Subject of the United States," in *Prejudices: Sixth Series*, 78; idem, "The National Letters," 70; Mencken to Wilson, May 28, 1921, Wilson Papers; H. L. Mencken, "The Nation," in *Prejudices: Fifth Series*, 258–59. Some of the themes I am discussing here are developed more fully in Tompkins, "Twilight of Idols," chap. 5.

4. The Geography of the Intellectual Life

1. On the changing character of communities in American history, see Higham, "Hanging Together," and Bender, *Community and Social Change*.

2. Tebbel, *Between Covers*, 81, 85; Bruccoli, *Mitchell Kennerley*, 26; Mumford, *Sketches from Life*, 190. The belief that publishing was, in Huebsch's words, something more than "a way of making a living" contributed to a sense of "fellow feeling" among newcomers such as Huebsch, Kennerley, and Knopf. Knopf sent Huebsch a copy of his first book with a warm inscription, which prompted Huebsch to return his "earnest wishes" for Knopf's "success." Long after Kennerley's house had failed, Huebsch kept him personally afloat with loans and gifts. See Huebsch's 1952 tribute to Knopf, Huebsch to Alfred A. Knopf, Sept. 16, 1915, Mitchell Kennerley to Huebsch, Feb. 1, 1940 and Feb. 3, 1940, Huebsch Papers.

3. Bruccoli, *Mitchell Kennerley*, 34–35, 68; Miller, *Lewis Mumford*, 92, 94; Brooks, *Autobiography*, 163.

4. Eastman, *Enjoyment of Living*, 262, 266. Eastman was quoting a 1907 letter to his sister.

5. Miller, *Lewis Mumford*, chap. 5; Mumford, *Sketches from Life*, 3, 129.

6. Dell to Edna Kenton, [1912], Provincetown Players Papers, Harvard Theater Collection, Pusey Library, Harvard University; Dell to William Fineshriber, Oct. 1913, quoted in Tanselle, "Faun at the Barricades," 140–42.

7. Hackett, *American Rainbow*, 262, 286–88; Dell, *Homecoming*, throughout; Hart, *Floyd Dell*, 33–39; Colum, *The Life and the Dream*, 225. On Dell's move to

New York, see Kramer, *Chicago Renaissance*, 236–40. An intelligent account of the decline of the Chicago movement in literature—as opposed to the departure of its intellectual leaders—can be found in Duffey, *Chicago Renaissance*, 258–62.

8. Quoted in Hahn, *Romantic Rebels*, 180. The standard work on Greenwich Village as Bohemia is Parry, *Garrets and Pretenders*.

9. Brooks, *The Confident Years*, 475; Dell, *Love in Greenwich Village*, 22, 25, 27.

10. Randolph Bourne, "Trans-national America," in *History of a Literary Radical*, 291; David A. Hollinger, "Ethnic Diversity, Cosmopolitanism, and the Emergence of the American Liberal Intelligentsia," in *In the American Province*, 59.

11. Bourne, "Trans-national America," 299; Hollinger, "Ethnic Diversity," 65, 59. See also Bender, *New York Intellect*, 246–49. Terry A. Cooney has discussed the cosmopolitanism of Bourne's generation as the intellectual background to the *Partisan Review*. See Cooney, *The Rise of the New York Intellectuals*, chap. 1.

12. Wilson to F. Scott Fitzgerald, July 5, 1921, and Wilson to Christian Gauss, July 24, 1923, in *Letters on Literature and Politics*, 64, 109; Wilson, *Twenties*, 23, 26. Broun was a columnist with the New York *World* at this time.

13. Lewis Mumford, "The City," in Stearns, *Civilization in the United States*, 5, 8–9.

14. John L. Thomas, "Lewis Mumford, Benton MacKaye, and the Regional Vision," in Hughes and Hughes, *Lewis Mumford*, 82.

15. Lewis Mumford, *Sticks and Stones*, 234, 23; idem, *The Culture of Cities*, 51.

16. Fishbein, *Rebels in Bohemia*, 66. Kenneth S. Lynn has made the same point in his study of the backgrounds of the Greenwich Village "rebels" who, he argues, "acutely missed the personal associations of small-town life" and "turned to the Village in the hope of finding them again." See Lynn, "The Rebels of Greenwich Village," esp. 362–63.

17. Quoted in Glaspell, *The Road to the Temple*, 87, 132; Brooks, Diary, Aug. 6, 1909, Brooks Collection; Dell, *Love in Greenwich Village*, 15; Eastman, *Enjoyment of Living*, 266. The emphasis is Brooks'.

18. Dell, *Homecoming*, 325; Bourne to Esther Cornell, Aug. 10, 1917, Bourne Papers.

19. Mencken to Ernest Boyd, Aug. 30, 1925, in *Letters of H. L. Mencken*, 281; Luhan, *Movers and Shakers*, 344.

20. Lippmann to Bernard Berenson, July 16, 1919, Lippmann Papers.

21. Bourne to Elizabeth Shepley Sergeant, June 9, 1915, Bourne to Dorothy Teall, July 21, 1915, Bourne to Alyse Gregory, July 24, 1915, Bourne Papers.

22. Bourne to Agnes de Lima, Aug. 6, 1917[?], Bourne Papers.

23. Luhan, *Movers and Shakers*, 345, 425; Eastman, *Enjoyment of Living*, 537; Sheridan, *My American Diary*, 129.

24. Sheridan, *My American Diary*, 129; Reed to Bryant, July 1, 1917, Reed Papers; quoted in Rosenstone, *Romantic Revolutionary*, 255. The emphasis is Bryant's.

25. Eastman, *Enjoyment of Living*, 582; idem, *Love and Revolution*, 5.

26. Vorse, *Time and the Town*, 126. See also idem, *A Footnote to Folly*, 129.

27. Glaspell, *The Road to the Temple*, 252, 235–36.

28. Frank to Mumford, July 5, 1933, Mumford Collection; Wilson, *Thirties*, 18–19, 614; idem, *Travels in Two Democracies*, 72–74. See also Paul, *Edmund Wilson*, 4. The emphasis is Frank's.

29. Brooks, *Autobiography*, 253; Brooks to Alyse Gregory, March 30, 1924, and Brooks to Newton Arvin, [1925?], Brooks Collection; Josephson, *Infidel in the Temple*, 38.

30. Mumford to Delilah Loch, March 11, 1922, quoted in Miller, *Lewis Mumford*, 216. Mumford moved to Sunnyside Gardens, Queens, the attempt at a garden city he helped plan, in 1925. He spent his summers in Amenia, New York (a two-hour trip from New York City) beginning in the same year, and settled there year-round in 1936. See Miller, *Lewis Mumford*, 240–42.

31. Susman, "Pilgrimage to Paris," 63. Despite its focus on Paris and an overly restrictive generational perspective, Susman's study captures the complexity of expatriation in this period and argues convincingly that expatriation was one of several attempted solutions to the problem of being an American intellectual.

32. Brooks, Diary, July 2, 1905, Brooks Collection; Bourne to Arthur Macmahon, Jan. 30, 1914, Bourne to Prudence Winterrowd, March 11, 1914, Bourne Papers; Bourne, "Impressions of Europe, 1913–14," in *History of a Literary Radical*, 246, 261–62; Stearns, "Where Are Our Intellectuals?" in *America and the Young Intellectual*, 48. See also Susman, "Pilgrimage to Paris," 100–102.

33. Brooks, *Autobiography*, 150. In a marginal note he added to his 1909 diary in 1952, Brooks exclaimed, "What an ass I was at the age of 22!" The Irish-born Francis Hackett moved back to Europe permanently in the mid-1920s in the belief that there "our kind of people have all the means of a civilized life without engaging in the scuffle for money." The word "means" probably referred to the combination of the strong dollar and Europe's alleged appreciation of intellectuals. Hackett to Huebsch, March 30, 1924, Huebsch Papers.

34. Harold Stearns, "A Study in Docility" and "What Can a Young Man Do?" in *America and the Young Intellectual*, 37, 159, 164–65, 167. The latter essay originally appeared in the *Freeman* in August 1920. Part of Europe's promise of independence was its affordability. The favorable exchange rate linked expatriation to freedom from an excessive concern with money. Matthew Josephson, who distanced himself from Stearns because of the latter's behavior in Paris, nonetheless cited similar reasons for expatriation. He noted that "countries of an older civilization" offered "some quantum of individual liberty" and a chance for "the preservation of the individual type, the defense of the human self from dissolution in the horde." Josephson, *Portrait of the Artist as American*, xi-xiii.

35. All of these quotes are from Shaw, "Harold E. Stearns: Eternal Expatriate," 39. Shaw conducted interviews with Seldes and Brooks to help supplement the somewhat meager record Stearns himself left. See also Stearns, *The Street I Know*, and Ford, *Four Lives in Paris*. The evidence that Stearns did not plan an extended expatriation is in a June 3, 1921 letter to the participants in the symposium, located in the Mumford Collection.

36. Harold Stearns, "Apologia of an Expatriate," *Scribner's* (March 1929), 338–41.

37. Brooks to Huebsch, [n.d., ca. 1916], Huebsch Papers.

38. Lewisohn, *Up Stream*, 247–48; idem, *Mid-Channel*, 65–66, 54. For a brief discussion of Lewisohn's marriage and affair, see Lainoff, *Ludwig Lewisohn*, 16–17.

39. Quoted in Glaspell, *The Road to the Temple*, 309, 367.

40. Eastman, *Love and Revolution*, 272.

41. Max Eastman to Eliena Krylenko, Oct. 3, 1923, and two undated letters [Fall 1923], Eliena Krylenko Eastman Papers. The emphasis is Eastman's.

42. Quoted in Eastman, *Love and Revolution*, 454. The emphasis is Eastman's. The book he referred to was *Marx and Lenin: The Science of Revolution*.

43. Dos Passos, *Rosinante to the Road Again*, 30, 92, 185, 52; idem, *Journeys between Wars*, 86, 95.

44. Chase, *Mexico*, 187, 177, 327, 205, 16; Frank, *America Hispana*, 352, 316. See also Frank, *Virgin Spain*. Chase's *Mexico* was a curious book, given its author's general predilection for technocratic progressivism. Frank traveled incessantly in Europe and Central and South America, in part to discover how "to make living in America less disastrous to the nerves and the purse" and in part because he was better received abroad. Frank to Mumford, Feb. 4, 1927, Mumford Collection.

45. Randolph Bourne, "History of a Literary Radical," in *History of a Literary Radical*, 29; Brooks, *The Pilgrimage of Henry James*, 123–24, 140.

46. Brooks, *The Pilgrimage of Henry James*, 19, 17, 8–9.

47. Colum, *The Life and the Dream*, 343; Brooks, *Autobiography*, 256.

48. Mencken to Theodore Dreiser, Feb. 1, 1919, Mencken to Ernest Boyd, March 13, 1919, and Mencken to Louise Pound, Jan. 14, 1920, in *Letters of H. L. Mencken*, 137, 142, 169.

49. Stearns, *Rediscovering America*, 14, 23, 40; Frank, *The Re-discovery of America*, 5.

50. Josephson, *Portrait of the Artist as American*, 298, 92, 306, 292, 294. The emphasis is Josephson's.

5. Women and the Critical Community

1. Mary Austin, "American Women and the Intellectual Life," *The Bookman* (August 1921), 481. Austin (1868–1934) then praised the work of women fiction writers and reformers and theorized that women had not joined the ranks of the critics in large numbers because they were indifferent to "traditional methods of expression" and as yet had only an "incompletely realized sense of form." Meanwhile, she argued, they had created in the "federated and affiliated women's organizations" a "medium for intellectual exchange unparalleled in history" (pp. 484–85).

2. Jane Addams, "The Subjective Necessity for Social Settlements," in *Twenty Years at Hull-House*, 122, 120, 121, 118.

3. Dee Garrison, Introduction, in Vorse, *Rebel Pen*, 14. The emphasis is Garrison's. See also Vorse, *A Footnote to Folly*, throughout.

4. Crystal Eastman, "Birth Control and the Feminist Program" (1918) and "Mother-Worship" (1927), in *Crystal Eastman on Women and Revolution*, 46–47; Glaspell, quoted in Sochen, *Movers and Shakers*, 81. I am not suggesting here that the women of the settlement generation did not have fulfilling relationships. In many cases, they had enduring relationships with other women. I am merely arguing that the next generation perceived them as unfulfilled in this regard.

5. Crystal Eastman, quoted in Sochen, *Movers and Shakers*, 51; Sanger, Diary, May 1, 1926, Sanger Papers; Alpern, *Freda Kirchwey*, 97; Mary Heaton Vorse, "Why I Have Failed as a Mother," in *Rebel Pen*, 344–45. On Heterodoxy, see Schwarz, *Radical Feminists of Heterodoxy*; Cott, *The Grounding of Modern Feminism*, 38–40; and Garrison, *Mary Heaton Vorse*, 67–71. Garrison's biography discusses Vorse's lifelong difficulties with her children and her belief that she had failed as a mother.

6. Margaret Naumburg, *The Child and the World*, 36, 31–32, 38–39.

7. Day, quoted in Gardner, *"Friend and Lover,"* 16; Gardner, 96.

8. Rubin, *Constance Rourke and American Culture*, 24–25. For a provocative discussion of nineteenth-century women's roles in the creation and transmission of culture, see Douglas, *The Feminization of American Culture*.

9. See, for example, Blanche Wiesen Cook, "Female Support Networks and Political Activism: Lillian Wald, Crystal Eastman, Emma Goldman," in Cott and Pleck, *A Heritage of Her Own*, 412–44.

10. H. L. Mencken, "Appendix on a Tender Theme," in *Prejudices: Second Series*, 240.

11. George Santayana, "The Genteel Tradition in American Philosophy" (1911), in *The Genteel Tradition*, 39–40; Van Wyck Brooks, "America's Coming-of-Age," in *Three Essays on America*, 78–79. Many years later, Brooks himself would be criticized by John Dos Passos for showing too much "female enthusiasm" in *The Flowering of New England*, which Dos Passos found "disgusting." Brooks, he told Edmund Wilson, "was going to be God's gift to the women's clubs." Wilson liked the book, however, and urged Dos Passos to reread it. Dos Passos to Wilson, Feb. 9, 1937, and March 9, 1937, Wilson Papers.

12. Mumford, *Golden Day*, 168–69; Harold Stearns, "America and the Young Intellectual" and "An Intellectual Eggshell Period," in *America and the Young Intellectual*, 9, 68.

13. Hoopes, *Van Wyck Brooks*, xiv.

14. One recourse for defeminizing the intellect—involvement as experts in progressive-era politics—was unpalatable to those who wanted to remain generalists and unaffiliated. On expertise as an alternative mode of defeminization, see Hofstadter, *Anti-Intellectualism in American Life*, 191–96.

15. Mencken, *In Defense of Women*, 17, 66, 125–26, 161, 129, 59.

16. Randolph Bourne, "Karen," in *History of a Literary Radical*, 53–54. Bourne, it must be noted, developed a sympathy for feminism during his post-graduate year abroad. In England, he witnessed the hunger strikes surrounding the arrest

of Emmeline Pankhurst and returned to the United States, in Bruce Clayton's words, "nine-tenths a feminist." He also carried on several close friendships with feminists, including Alyse Gregory and Agnes de Lima. See Clayton, *Forgotten Prophet*, 102–5. But Bourne's feminist sympathies could not eradicate the competing need to purge the life of letters of its alleged effeminacy and did not alter his view of the ideal woman as gentle and deferential or maternal and nurturing.

17. Dell, *Women as World Builders*, 19–21.

18. Eastman, *Venture*, 173, 66, 200. This interpretation comes from Rudnick, *Mabel Dodge Luhan*, 114–20. It should be pointed out, without overstating the "mother postulate," that most of the women discussed in this chapter were older than the male intellectuals with whom they associated. Dodge was born in 1879, Sanger also in 1879, Vorse in 1874, Henrietta Rodman (whom Dell much admired) in 1878, Elizabeth Shepley Sergeant in 1881, and Crystal Eastman in 1881 as well.

19. Josephson, *Life among the Surrealists*, 49.

20. Dell, *Intellectual Vagabondage*, 141.

21. Sanger, *Woman and the New Race*, 70, 55.

22. Eastman criticized the magazine's "style of overconscious extremism and blare of rebellion for its own sake" and expressed concern that "those who incline to the life of reason will be the last to read it." Quoted in Kennedy, *Birth Control*, 23. See also Reed, *From Private Vice to Public Virtue*, 86. Commenting on the *Woman Rebel*, Sanger's mentor Havelock Ellis warned her about "being too reckless and smashing your head against a blank wall." Ellis to Sanger, [1915], Sanger Papers.

23. Cott, *The Grounding of Modern Feminism*, 33; Sanger, *Woman and the New Race*, 12.

24. Sanger, *An Autobiography*, 152; Sanger to Mabel Dodge Luhan, March 13, 1937, Sanger Papers; Kennedy, *Birth Control*, chap. 3; Reed, *From Private Vice to Public Virtue*, chaps. 8–9; Sanger, Diary, June 10, 1919, Sanger Papers.

25. Blanche Wiesen Cook, Introduction, in Crystal Eastman, *Crystal Eastman on Women and Revolution*, throughout.

26. Ibid., 2.

27. Naumburg, *The Child and the World*, 103.

28. Rosenfeld, *Port of New York*, 118.

29. Quoted in Luhan, *Movers and Shakers*, 95, 93.

30. Luhan, *Movers and Shakers*, 11, 20, 234, 251; D. H. Lawrence to Baroness Anna von Richthofen, Dec. 5, 1922, Lawrence to Mabel Dodge, Oct. 17, 1923, and Nov. 7, 1922, in Lawrence, *The Letters of D. H. Lawrence*, 351, 514, 337. The emphasis is Dodge's and Lawrence's. See also Rudnick, *Mabel Dodge Luhan*, ix–xvi and throughout, and Christopher Lasch, *The New Radicalism in America*, chap. 4.

31. Quoted in Luhan, *Movers and Shakers*, 534.

32. Luhan, *Edge of Taos Desert*, 6, 98, 301–2, 66, 221, 193, 276, 228.

33. Bryant, *Six Red Months in Russia*, xi; Sergeant, *Shadow-Shapes*, 15–19, 20, 26, 33, 111.

34. Vorse, "Why I Have Failed as a Mother," 344; quoted in Alpern, *Freda Kirchwey*, 95–96. Garrison, *Mary Heaton Vorse*, cited above, is a detailed account of Vorse's career as labor journalist, war correspondent, and social activist.

35. Carroll, "The Politics of 'Originality,'" esp. 138. Carroll argues against the emphasis on "eponymity" in intellectual history and urges an "interactive, egalitarian, and social vision of the process of creative change in ideas" (p. 157).

6. Education and the New Basis for Community

1. Studies of Bourne, including Clayton's *Forgotten Prophet* and Blake's *Beloved Community*, have tended to de-emphasize his educational writings because of their derivative character. In offering a more complete assessment of Bourne's theories of education, I am not suggesting any startling originality on his part. But in the context of the young intellectuals' struggle to reorient American values—to assert the claims of expression and community—the educational ideas of Bourne and his fellow critics deserve fuller consideration than they have received.

2. Phillips, "John Dewey," 254, 235; Cremin, *The Transformation of the School*, 119–20, 157. For a discussion of Bourne's educational ideas in terms of the tensions in progressive thought between democratic communitarianism and technocratic expertise, see Blake, *Beloved Community*, 93–99.

3. Randolph Bourne, Preface and "The Democratic School," in *Education and Living*, vi, 147; idem, *The Gary Schools*, 11.

4. Randolph Bourne, "In a Schoolroom," in *Education and Living*, 41–48. See also Clayton, *Forgotten Prophet*, 121. Dewey's early educational theories can be found in *The Child and the Curriculum*, and in the "Plan of Organization of the University Primary School" (1895), in Wirth, *John Dewey as Educator*.

5. Wirth, *John Dewey as Educator*, 22–23, 76, 79–81.

6. Randolph Bourne, "Class and School" and "The Democratic School," in *Education and Living*, 168–70, 152; Dewey, *Democracy and Education*, 152.

7. See Dewey, *Interest and Effort in Education*, esp. 14, 90–91, and Wirth, *John Dewey as Educator*, 93.

8. Randolph Bourne, "Education and Living" and "The Organic School," in *Education and Living*, 7, 101.

9. Randolph Bourne, "The Democratic School," in *Education and Living*, 151. Aside from the school, the other possible replacement for farm work was factory labor, and this was unpalatable to a progressive like Dewey or a radical like Bourne, both of whom knew the ills of child labor in industrial America.

10. Randolph Bourne, "Education and Living" and "The Self-Conscious School," in *Education and Living*, 10, 16–17.

11. Bourne, *The Gary Schools*, 132, 153, 163, 109; idem, "Education and Living," 7–8; Dewey, "The Child and the Curriculum," in *The Child and the Curriculum*, 30–31; idem, "Froebel's Educational Principles," in *The Child and the Curriculum*, 129. The emphasis is Dewey's.

12. Randolph Bourne, Preface, in *Education and Living*, vii; Dewey and Dewey, *Schools of Tomorrow*, 210, 102.

13. Bourne, *The Gary Schools*, 31–32, 125, 115.

14. Ibid., 109, 130, 56, 114.

15. Quoted in Callahan, *Education and the Cult of Efficiency*, 130.

16. Cohen and Mohl, *The Paradox of Progressive Education*, 90–91, 88, 29. Bourne's confusion of the ideal and the real is precisely what he criticized in Dewey during the war. See Westbrook, *John Dewey and American Democracy*, 202–8.

17. Dewey, *Democracy and Education*, 108, 24, 28–29, 47–48. The emphasis is Dewey's.

18. Ibid., 121, 115, 212, 31. The emphasis is Dewey's.

19. Robert B. Westbrook contends that *Democracy and Education*, true to its title, envisioned the classroom as "a community of full participation." While I agree with Westbrook's assessment of the general thrust of Dewey's thought as adversarial and radically democratic, I differ in my reading of *Democracy and Education*, in which I find inconsistencies, or at least evasiveness, on the role of educators and the processes of defining educational goals. See Westbrook, *John Dewey and American Democracy*, 167–73.

20. Randolph Bourne, Preface and "Class and School," vi, 172.

21. Randolph Bourne, "Twilight of Idols," in *War and the Intellectuals*, 60–61, 64.

22. Dell, *Were You Ever a Child?*, v, 25–26, 46, 90–91, 131, 123. Cremin describes a general split in the ranks of progressive educators after the war between a child-centered group and a social reform group. See Cremin, *The Transformation of the School*, 184–85. But Dell, as I have suggested, saw the child-centered school as a tremendous force for social change.

23. Rugg and Shumaker, *The Child-Centered School*, 56, 58, 65. The emphasis is Rugg's.

24. Naumburg, *The Child and the World*, 122, xviii, 11, 36, 15, 256. Dewey titled chapter XXII of *Democracy and Education* "The Individual and the World."

25. Naumburg, *The Child and the World*, xxiii. On Naumburg and the Walden (Children's) School, see Robert H. Beck, "Progressive Education and American Progressivism: Margaret Naumburg," *Teachers College Record* 60, No. 4 (January 1959), 198–208; Cremin, *The Transformation of the School*, 211–15; and Rosenfeld, *Port of New York*, 117–33.

26. Cremin, *The Transformation of the School*, 240–58.

27. Naumburg, quoted in Beck, "Progressive Education," 207. These remarks originally appeared in a *New Republic* symposium that also featured an essay by Dewey in which he criticized the "one-sidedness" of the child-centered approach.

28. Mumford, *The Culture of Cities*, 471, 477, 474–75.

29. Ibid., 476.

7. An Alternative Morality

1. Randolph Bourne, "The Virtues and the Seasons of Life," in *Youth and Life*, 87, 81; Van Wyck Brooks, "America's Coming-of-Age," in *Three Essays on America*, 34–35.

2. Blake, *Beloved Community*, 77, 124–26, and throughout. A previous generation's more systematic thinking about the social nature of the self receives attention in Wilson, *In Quest of Community*, and Quandt, *From the Small Town*. See also Bruce Kuklick's discussion of George Herbert Palmer's neo-Hegelian ethics of self-realization and Josiah Royce's philosophy of loyalty in Kuklick, *The Rise of American Philosophy*, 215–27 and 296–300. On Dewey and self-realization, see Westbrook, *John Dewey and American Democracy*, 43–44 and throughout.

3. Bourne to Prudence Winterrowd, April 28, 1913, Bourne Papers. On Brooks' "brief but intense" affair with Colum, see Nelson, *Van Wyck Brooks*, 182–86.

4. Sanger, *Pivot of Civilization*, 127, 212, 93, 115; Sanger, *Woman and the New Race*, 187; Cott, *The Grounding of Modern Feminism*, 42. Cott cites the example of Inez Milholland (1886–1916), a lawyer and suffragist who was romantically involved with Max Eastman before marrying Eugen Boissevain, later the husband of Edna St. Vincent Millay.

5. Sanger, *Woman and the New Race*, 28, 68, 3, 56; Sanger, *Pivot of Civilization*, 23, 239, 269–70, 232.

6. Sanger, *Pivot of Civilization*, 218, 212. See also Reed, *From Private Vice to Public Virtue*, for a discussion of Sanger's conception of birth control as a social necessity.

7. Reed, *From Private Vice to Public Virtue*, 85; Kennedy, *Birth Control*, 170.

8. Kirchwey, Introduction, in *Our Changing Morality, A Symposium*, v–ix; Alpern, *Freda Kirchwey*, 61.

9. Bertrand Russell, "Styles in Ethics," in Kirchwey, *Our Changing Morality*, 14–15.

10. Floyd Dell, "Can Men and Women Be Friends?," Elsie Clews Parsons, "Changes in Sex Relations," Joseph Wood Krutch, "Modern Love and Modern Fiction," in *Our Changing Morality*, 41, 44, 46, 193, 185, 174; Parsons, *Social Freedom*, 36–37. On Parsons, see Hare, *A Woman's Quest for Science*, and Rosenberg, *Beyond Separate Spheres*, chap. 6.

11. Calverton, *The Bankruptcy of Marriage*, 297–98, 19, Preface; idem, *Sex Expression in Literature*, 308; V.F. Calverton and Samuel D. Schmalhausen, Preface, in *Sex in Civilization*, 11; Wilcox, "Sex Boys in a Balloon," 7–26. On Calverton's career, see Gnizi, "V. F. Calverton."

12. Calverton, *The Bankruptcy of Marriage*, 307, 118, 267; idem, "Sex and Social Struggle," in Calverton and Schmalhausen, *Sex in Civilization*, 250, 282–84. Sanger took exception to Calverton's determinism in her contribution to his symposium: "I hope to show that birth control is a cause, not a mere effect." Margaret Sanger, "The Civilizing Force of Birth Control," in Calverton and

Schmalhausen, *Sex in Civilization*, 525. See also Wilcox, "Sex Boys in a Balloon," 14.

13. Wilcox, "Sex Boys in a Balloon," 19, 25; Cott, *The Grounding of Modern Feminism*, 45. On the optimistic interpretation of Freud in the United States, see Matthews, "The Americanization of Sigmund Freud," 39–62.

14. Frank, "Sex Censorship and Democracy," in Calverton and Schmalhausen, *Sex in Civilization*, 177; Calverton, *The Bankruptcy of Marriage*, 330, 301.

15. Quoted in Eastman, *Enjoyment of Living*, 496, 500, 506, 516; Reed to Bryant, July 5, 1917, Reed Papers. The emphasis is Eastman's.

16. Max Eastman to Eliena Krylenko, Jan. 8, 1924, Jan. 28, 1924, Feb. 5, 1924, Eliena Krylenko Eastman Papers. The emphasis in both cases is Eastman's.

17. Max Eastman to Eliena Krylenko, Sept. 1929, Feb. 13, 1932, Eliena Krylenko Eastman Papers.

18. Mencken, who certainly did not share Eastman's penchant for sexual adventure, may have similarly connected marriage to the restriction of intellectual freedom. Marion Bloom commented on why her long affair with Mencken ended in 1919: "I saw him, an individual, striving to attain some inner urge for what he called freedom. I discerned that he saw in me (the woman I believed he loved) an enemy to that freedom." Though there were certainly other reasons involved (including his attachment to his mother and his distaste for Bloom's "Christian Science fever"), Mencken chose not to marry until 1930, when he was almost fifty. His marriage to Sara Haardt lasted until her death in 1935. Marion Bloom, personal memo, August 2, 1923, quoted in *The New Mencken Letters*, 115; Mencken to Estelle Bloom Kubitz, Aug. 10, [1923], in *The New Mencken Letters*, 173.

19. Wilson, *I Thought of Daisy*, 43, 21, 308; idem, *Twenties*, 517; Paul, *Edmund Wilson*, 70. Paul's is an excellent discussion of *I Thought of Daisy*.

20. Quoted in Miller, *Lewis Mumford*, 310, 206, 308; Mumford, *My Works and Days*, 320, 302. Miller, who received permission from Mumford to examine his restricted correspondence, provides a complete account of Mumford's affairs to which my discussion is almost wholly indebted. Rosalind Williams has also found that "Mumford assumes a correspondence between the personal and the universal drama." See her consideration of the Bauer affair in "Lewis Mumford as a Historian of Technology in *Technics and Civilization*," in Hughes and Hughes, *Lewis Mumford*, 45–46. In the midst of his own turmoil, Mumford wrote of Herman Melville: "So closely were Melville's sexual impulses and his intellectual career bound up that I am tempted to reverse the more obvious analysis of Pierre, and to see in its sexual symbols the unconscious revelation of his dilemmas as a writer." Mumford, *Herman Melville*, 220.

21. Naumburg to Frank, Jan. 5, 1920, Dec. 5, 1920, Aug. 5, 1920, Jan. 4, 1923, Frank Collection. The emphasis is Naumburg's.

22. Waldo Frank to Alma Magoon Frank, July 4, 1929, July 9, 1929, July 20, 1929, Sept. 24, 1932, Jan. 3, [1934], Frank Collection. The emphasis is Frank's.

23. Sanger, *Woman and the New Race*, 171, 71.

24. Dell, *Intellectual Vagabondage*, ix, 190, 260, 175.

25. Gorham B. Munson, "Our Critical Spokesmen," and Irving Babbitt, "Humanism: An Essay at Definition," in Foerster, *Humanism and America*, 245–49, 242, 256, 51. The emphasis is Munson's. A fine study of the ideas of Babbitt, More, and their younger disciples is Hoeveler, *The New Humanism*.

26. Lippmann, *Preface to Politics*, 84, 51, 80, 9; Lippmann to Norman Foerster, Aug. 8, 1929, and Lippmann to Seward Collins, March 25, 1930, Lippmann Papers. See Steel, *Walter Lippmann*, for a discussion of the connection between the status of Lippmann's first marriage and *A Preface to Morals*, esp. 346.

27. Lippmann, *Preface to Morals*, 158, 187, 12, 139, 224, 238–39, 257, 304. See also Krutch, *The Modern Temper*. Krutch complained that "Love is becoming so accessible, so unmysterious, and so free that its value is trivial" (p. 101).

28. C. Hartley Grattan, Editor's Note, in *The Critique of Humanism*, [n.p.].

29. Randolph Bourne, "Paul Elmer More," in *War and the Intellectuals*, 168; Edmund Wilson, "Notes on Babbitt and More," Malcolm Cowley, "Humanizing Society," Lewis Mumford, "Towards an Organic Humanism," in Grattan, *The Critique of Humanism*, 49, 47, 77, 348.

30. Seward Collins, "Criticism in America: I. The Origins of a Myth," *The Bookman* (June 1930), 251; "III. The End of the Anti-Humanist Myth," *The Bookman* (October 1930), 163. Collins' long and vituperative essay appeared in three installments. Only five years earlier, Collins had been a devoted follower of Havelock Ellis, whom he described as "St. Havelock." Apparently, Margaret Sanger tried to help Collins fulfill his "closely cherished ambition" of meeting Ellis. Sanger and Collins had a "short talk" which left him "in a most childish state of elation." Collins to Sanger, July 31, 1925, Sanger Papers.

31. Wilson, "Notes on Babbitt and More," Henry Hazlitt, "Humanism and Value," Mumford, "Towards an Organic Humanism," in Grattan, *The Critique of Humanism*, 52, 102, 347, 359, 350. During World War II, Mumford reversed his earlier assessment of the New Humanism and praised Babbitt's attack on hedonism and his ethics of self-restraint. See Lewis Mumford, "Program for Survival," in *Values for Survival: Essays, Addresses, and Letters on Politics and Education* (New York: Harcourt, Brace, 1946), 125–29.

32. Cowley, "Humanizing Society," 77. The crux of Cowley's argument—and an indication of a tipping of the balance between self-fulfillment and social commitment—appeared in the following passage:

Economically, socially, [the New Humanists'] doctrine is based on nothing and answers no questions. Out of what society does Humanism spring, and toward what society does it lead? Has it any validity for the mill hands of New Bedford or Gastonia, for the beet-toppers of Colorado, for the men who tighten a single screw in the automobiles that march along Mr. Ford's assembly belt? Should it be confined to the families who draw dividends from these cotton mills, beet fields, factories, and to the professors who teach in universities endowed by them? Can one be a Humanist between chukkers of a polo match, or can the steel workers be Humanists, too—once every three weeks, on their Sunday off? Has Babbitt any social program? (Pp. 68–69)

33. Dell, *Love in the Machine Age*, 7–8, 178–79, 364.

34. Freeman, *An American Testament*, 290, 287; Michael Gold, "Floyd Dell

Resigns," *New Masses* (July 1929), 10–11. See also Aaron, *Writers on the Left*, 167–68n, 214–19.

35. Dell, *Intellectual Vagabondage*, 257; Cowley, quoted in Wilcox, "Sex Boys in a Balloon," 21. Eastman dismissed Dell's *Love in the Machine Age* on the grounds that it raised issues that had already been settled. He thought it was nothing more than a four-hundred-page justification of Dell's own marriage, "a pseudo-scientific after-birth of Puritanism" which was both self-serving and irrelevant. Eastman did not go so far as to repudiate his generation's concern for matters of love and sex, but he, too, seems to have believed that it was time to move on. Eastman, "Floyd Dell's Double Life," in *Art and the Life of Action*, 140 and throughout.

8. Uses of the Past

1. Brooks, *Wine of the Puritans*, 14, 51, 91. Warren Susman discussed the meaning of the Puritan and pioneer for American intellectuals in two brilliant essays, "The Frontier Thesis and the American Intellectual" and "Uses of the Puritan Past," both in Susman, *Culture as History*.

2. Van Wyck Brooks, "Toward a National Culture," *Seven Arts* (March 1917), 539.

3. Frank, *Our America*, 133, 14, 17.

4. Van Wyck Brooks, "The Literary Life," and Harold E. Stearns, "The Intellectual Life," in Stearns, *Civilization in the United States*, 185–86, 138, 140.

5. Van Wyck Brooks, "America's Coming-of-Age," in *Three Essays on America*, 39; Frank, *Our America*, 71–72.

6. Brooks, *Ordeal of Mark Twain*, 49, 61, 142.

7. Waldo Frank, "Emerging Greatness," *Seven Arts* (November 1916), 73.

8. Harold Stearns, Preface, in *Civilization in the United States*, vii.

9. Brooks, *Wine of the Puritans*, 136; Romain Rolland, "America and the Arts," Waldo Frank, trans., "An Expression of Artists for the Community," and Peter Minuit [Paul Rosenfeld], "291 Fifth Avenue," all in *Seven Arts* (November 1916), 50, 53, 64.

10. Randolph Bourne, "The Art of Theodore Dreiser," in *History of a Literary Radical*, 204; J. R. Dos Passos, Jr., "Against American Literature," *New Republic* (October 14, 1916), 270.

11. Lippmann, *Preface to Politics*, 306, 202, 307, 5, 9, 313. See also White, *Social Thought in America*. Paradoxically, for the younger generation it may have been the discovery of historicism and the sensitivity to the social context of ideas displayed by Dewey, Veblen, Beard, and others that allowed them to reject the past as an obstruction to the assertive intellect.

12. Lippmann, *Preface to Politics*, 244.

13. Randolph Bourne, "The Virtues and the Seasons of Life" and "Seeing, We See Not," in *Youth and Life*, 95–96, 217–18.

14. Brooks, "On Creating a Usable Past," 337–39. The fact that Brooks was not an academic allowed him to be open about creating rather than discovering a usable past. Peter Novick has shown how crucial the claim of objectivity was to

the development of professional history in *That Noble Dream*, esp. chap. 2. Floyd Dell took a less relativist position toward the usable past. His claim was that the "educational authorities did not want us to know the truth about this American literature. They were afraid that the real Emerson and Thoreau and Phillips and Whittier and Whitman would corrupt our young minds. So we were left to discover them for ourselves—which all too frequently we failed to do." Dell, *Intellectual Vagabondage*, 115.

15. Brooks, "On Creating a Usable Past," 340–41.

16. Macy, *The Spirit of American Literature*, 94, 14, 78, 123, 186, 155, 307. The emphasis is Macy's. Macy married Anne Sullivan, Helen Keller's teacher, in 1905. In 1912, he served with Lippmann as an aide to the Socialist mayor of Schenectady. See the "Biographical Note," in Macy, *Socialism in America*.

17. Brooks, "America's Coming-of-Age," 79–80, 88, 84–85; Paul Rosenfeld, "The American Composer," *Seven Arts* (November 1916), 91. See also Heller, "Paul Rosenfeld," 11.

18. Dos Passos, "Against American Literature," 270; Frank, *Our America*, 40, 56; Floyd Dell, "Walt Whitman and the American Temperament" (1919), in *Looking at Life*, 198.

19. Randolph Bourne, "History of a Literary Radical," in *History of a Literary Radical*, 29.

20. Brooks to J. S. Zelie, Sept. 7, 1921, Brooks Collection.

21. Lewis Mumford, Preface (1954), in *Sticks and Stones*.

22. Rosenfeld, *Port of New York*, 1.

23. Ibid., 15, 32, 57, 60.

24. Ibid., 231, 271–72.

25. Mumford, *Sticks and Stones*, 103, 115.

26. Mumford, *Golden Day*, 103–4, 118, 127, 279. The emphasis is Mumford's. H. L. Mencken, despite his iconoclasm, had never been as thoroughly dismissive of the Golden Day writers as Brooks had been. By 1924, he too was distinguishing between an adversarial and a conformist tradition: "The ancient American tradition, in so far as it was vital and productive and civilized, was obviously a tradition of individualism and revolt, not of herd-morality and conformity. If one argues otherwise, one must inevitably argue that the great men of the Golden Age were not Emerson, Hawthorne, Poe and Whitman, but Cooper, Irving, Longfellow and Whittier." H. L. Mencken, "The American Tradition," in *Prejudices: Fourth Series*, 19.

27. Mumford, *The Brown Decades*, 23, 25. In 1930, Matthew Josephson had denied the existence of what Mumford called "a continuous tradition." Although he sympathetically reevaluated the Gilded Age writers—James, Adams, Crane, Bierce, Dickinson, and Lafcadio Hearn—he concluded that they were "pitted against the steam-engine in a vain contest that could end only in retreat or flight." Thus there had been "a notable breakdown in the continuity of culture" between the New England Renaissance and the present. Josephson, *Portrait of the Artist as American*, 54, 145.

28. Edmund Wilson, "The All-Star Literary Vaudeville" (June 30, 1926), in *Shores of Light*, 245–46.

29. Edmund Wilson, "Van Wyck Brooks's Second Phase" (September 30, 1940), in *Classics and Commercials*, 10.

30. Lears, *No Place of Grace*, 257; Bender, *New York Intellect*, 239. An exception to the generally negative assessments of the *Makers and Finders* series is Thomas, "The Uses of Catastrophism."

31. Brooks to Mumford, Sept. 13, 1925, in *The Van Wyck Brooks-Lewis Mumford Letters*, 33; Brooks to Sherwood Anderson, Nov. 21, 1925, Brooks Collection. The emphasis is Brooks'.

32. Brooks, *Emerson and Others*, 39, 42, 59, 63, 5, 82, 6; Brooks to Mumford, Sept. 13, 1925, in *The Van Wyck Brooks-Lewis Mumford Letters*, 34. In his quest for an alternative tradition, Brooks was also anticipated from within the academy. As an editor at Harcourt, Brace in 1924–25, he had been responsible for bringing in Vernon Parrington's *Main Currents in American Thought*. See Hoopes, *Van Wyck Brooks*, 163.

33. Rubin, *Constance Rourke and American Culture*, 54, 57; Rourke, *American Humor*, 203.

34. Frank, *The Re-discovery of America*, 208.

35. Brooks, *The Flowering of New England*, 313, 355, 397, 154; idem, *New England: Indian Summer*, 11–13. See also Hoopes, *Van Wyck Brooks*, 210–18.

36. Brooks to Daniel G. Mason, Jan. 12, 1935, Brooks Collection; Brooks, *The Flowering of New England*, 209; Wilson, "Van Wyck Brooks's Second Phase," 15; Malcolm Cowley, "Van Wyck Brooks and the New England Legacy" (August 26, 1936), in Henry Dan Piper, ed., *Think Back on Us . . . A Contemporary Chronicle of the 1930's* (Carbondale: Southern Illinois University Press, 1967), 298.

37. Brooks, *The World of Washington Irving*, 469, 231, 165, 255.

38. Ibid., 150, 194, 470; Edmund Wilson, "A Picture to Hang in the Library: Brooks's Age of Irving," in *Classics and Commercials*, 224.

39. Edmund Wilson, "Van Wyck Brooks on the Civil War Period," in *Classics and Commercials*, 425.

40. Mumford to Brooks, July 24, 1936, in *The Van Wyck Brooks-Lewis Mumford Letters*, 137–38.

41. Stearns, *Rediscovering America*, 224, 115; idem, "The Intellectual Life," in *America Now*, 381.

42. Seldes, *Mainland*, 12–13, 48, 72, 75–76, 127, 204, 232, 240, 403, 10. Seldes at one point spoke of the "treason" of "two small but dangerously influential groups: the financiers and the intellectuals."

43. Lippmann, *The Good Society*, 379, 337, 234, 256, 330, 6, 19, 5.

44. Dos Passos, *The Ground We Stand On*, 3, 6, 18, 401.

45. "Portrait of America (1800–40)," in *Time* (Oct. 2, 1944), 96. A sketch of Brooks appeared on the cover over the caption "Van Wyck Brooks: He is rediscovering the American past."

9. Versions of Marx

1. Freeman, *American Testament*, 24. The bracketed words are Freeman's. Lyons introduced the Red Decade idea in an anti-Communist polemic. See Eugene Lyons, *The Red Decade: The Stalinist Penetration of America* (Indianapolis: Bobbs-Merrill, 1941).

2. Malcolm Cowley, "To a Revolutionary Critic" (November 8, 1933), in *Think Back On Us*, 50. *Exile's Return* was probably the text most responsible for implanting the notion of a sharp break in American intellectual history between the 1920s and 1930s. But it must be remembered that Cowley wrote not merely as a historian but as a participant in his own "narrative of ideas." Like all jeremiads, *Exile's Return* made its plea for renewed commitment by exaggerating (and perhaps even inventing) the past sins of those to whom it was addressed. Cowley's telling of Harry Crosby's story to represent the culmination of a decade's allegedly anti-social and suicidal tendencies was a clever addition to his generation's usable past—a parable of failure to encourage a redoubling of effort. For another discussion of *Exile's Return*, see Pells, *Radical Visions and American Dreams*, 157–60. While warning against categorization by decades, Pells maintains Cowley's distinctions and accepts the idea that the 1930s was characterized by a "new gospel of social commitment."

3. Frank, *Memoirs*, 196; Freeman, *American Testament*, 534, 147. The emphasis is Frank's. This yearning for community in the 1930s is discussed in Warren I. Susman, "Culture and Commitment," in *Culture as History*, 184–210.

4. Fishbein, *Rebels in Bohemia*, 39; Eastman, *Enjoyment of Living*, 354–55.

5. Reed, *Ten Days That Shook the World*, 133. The emphasis is Reed's.

6. Max Eastman, "A Letter to Romain Rolland," *Liberator* (December 1919), 24–25.

7. Max Eastman, "The Clarté Movement," *Liberator* (April 1920), 40–42. The emphasis is Eastman's.

8. Max Eastman, "Clarifying the Light," *Liberator* (June 1921), 5–7; Van Wyck Brooks, "A Reviewer's Notebook," *Freeman* (June 29, 1921), 382–83; Max Eastman, "Inspiration or Leadership," *Liberator* (August 1921), 7–9. The emphasis is Eastman's. For other discussions of the Rolland and Clarté debates, see Aaron, *Writers on the Left*, 50–55, and Gilbert, *Writers and Partisans*, 45–47.

9. Dell, *Intellectual Vagabondage*, 257, 150.

10. Max Eastman, "To Nicolai Lenin," *Liberator* (November 1918), 17.

11. Max Eastman, "Lenin—A Statesman of the New Order," *Liberator* (September 1918), 10; idem, "Lenin—A Statesman of the New Order—II," *Liberator* (October 1918), 28; idem, "About Dogmatism," *Liberator* (November 1920), 8; idem, "Hillquit Repeats His Error," *Liberator* (January 1921), 21; idem, "The Wisdom of Lenin," *Liberator* (June 1924), 8.

12. John Reed, "Soviet Russia Now" (July 1920), in *An Anthology*, 230–31; idem, handwritten note on Lenin [July 1920], published in *Anthology*, opp. page 56; idem, *Ten Days*, 125; Floyd Dell, "Lenine [*sic*] and His Time," *Liberator* (May 1919), 45; Freeman, *American Testament*, 501. Before they parted ways over Stalin,

Freeman acknowledged his intellectual debt to Eastman concerning "the torment-ing problem of how to combine a love of poetry with a passion for the revolution." See Eastman, *Love and Revolution*, 270.

13. Eastman's wife, Eliena Krylenko, appears to have envisioned a Lenin-like role for her husband. As late as 1929, she told Max of a conversation she had with Joseph Freeman in which he said that "if it was not for this 'unfortunate' situa-tion" (i.e. Eastman's anti-Stalinism), he would now be "the God Almighty" of "all the thinking radical youth" in America. In any event, she assured Max, within "another year, or perhaps less" he would "have to assume the role and the position of the intellectual and the revolutionary leader of the American move-ment." What Eastman thought of her suggestion cannot be known, although Eliena often told Max what she thought he needed to hear. The idea of Max as a revolutionary leader was probably not so far-fetched to Eliena, whose brother was one of the top Bolsheviks and who had herself traveled in the highest echelons of the Bolshevik leadership until she came to the United States with Max. Eliena Krylenko to Max Eastman, Feb. 8, 1929, Eliena Krylenko Eastman Papers.

14. Floyd Dell, "My Political Ideals," in *Looking at Life*, 149; idem, "Art under the Bolsheviks," *Liberator* (June 1919), 18. See also, for example, Michael Gold, "Two Critics in a Bar-room," *Liberator* (September 1921), 28–31.

15. Floyd Dell, "Explanations and Apologies," *Liberator* (June 1922), 25–26; Michael Gold, "Thoughts of a Great Thinker," *Liberator* (April 1922), [n.p.].

16. Eastman, *Artists in Uniform*, 216; Waldo Frank, "Values of the Revolution-ary Writer," in Hart, *American Writers' Congress*, 77. The manifesto, which the authors decided not to publish at the time, appears with a letter from Wilson to Theodore Dreiser, May 2, 1932, in Wilson, *Letters on Literature and Politics*, 222–23.

17. Gold to "the Trustees of the Garland Fund," [n.d.], Roger Baldwin to Freeman, Sept. 21, 1922, Lewis S. Gannett to Baldwin, Sept. 29, 1922, *Report of The American Fund for Public Service, Inc. for the First Six Months of Operation: July 1922–January 31, 1923*, American Fund for Public Service [AFPS] Records.

18. Mumford to Maurice Becker, Feb. 17, 1925, Dos Passos to Becker, [n.d.], List of committee members of "Dynamo," March 23, 1925, AFPS Records.

19. "Prospectus for Dynamo," [n.d.], Kirchwey to Frank, May 11, 1925, AFPS Records.

20. *New Masses* official prospectus, Dec. 1925, AFPS Records; John Dos Pas-sos, "The New Masses I'd Like," *New Masses* (June 1926), 20; Michael Gold, "Let It Be Really New!" *New Masses* (June 1926), 20–21.

21. Eastman to "The New Masses," Jan. 27, 1928, AFPS Records.

22. Egmont Arens to Baldwin, Jan. 31, 1928, AFPS Records; Michael Gold, "Trotsky's Pride" (June 1930), in Michael Folsom, ed. *Mike Gold: A Literary Anthology* (New York, 1972), 195.

23. Gold to AFPS, April 25, 1928; Earl Browder to Baldwin, Oct. 23, 1933, AFPS Records.

24. Eastman, *Marx and Lenin*, 22, 25, 37–39, 41. John P. Diggins argues that "Eastman had written the earliest and most penetrating critique of Marxist philos-

ophy in the English language, with the possible exception of Bertrand Russell's." Diggins, *Up from Communism*, 40. Eastman's debate with a younger Dewey student, Sidney Hook, is recounted in Pells, *Radical Visions and American Dreams*, 127–35.

25. Eastman, *Marx and Lenin*, 63–64, 39, 148–49, 162, 128.

26. Ibid., 203, 211.

27. Eastman to McKay, [March?] 1923 and April 12, 1923, Claude McKay Papers. These letters have been published in Wayne F. Cooper, ed., *The Passion of Claude McKay: Selected Poetry and Prose, 1912–1948* (New York: Schocken Books, 1973), 78–90.

28. Frank, *Memoirs*, 194, 185, 197; Edmund Wilson, "An Appeal to Progressives," *New Republic* (January 14, 1931), 238.

29. Wilson to Allen Tate, May 28, 1930, in Wilson, *Letters on Literature and Politics*, 196.

30. Wilson, "Appeal to Progressives," 236–38. Lewis Mumford apparently did not believe that Wilson was doing enough to take communism away from the Communists. In refusing to sign a petition circulated by Wilson and Malcolm Cowley in support of the Party's presidential candidate in 1932, Mumford wrote to Waldo Frank: "There is something unhealthy in the way in which the younger generation are *accepting* communism: they must *create* communism: it is not a patent breakfast food that was pre-digested by Marx and warmed over by Lenin." Mumford to Frank, Sept. 18, 1932, Frank Collection. The emphasis is Mumford's. Several months earlier, when Mumford, Frank, and Wilson were working together on a more general manifesto of the intellectuals, the participants agreed that they should avoid "the usual communist clichés." But they never managed to come up with language that all three writers (and John Dos Passos, whom Wilson consulted) found satisfactory. Mumford to Wilson, March 25, 1932, Wilson Papers.

31. Matthew Josephson, "The Road of Indignation," *New Republic* (February 18, 1931), 13–15.

32. Benjamin Ginzburg, "Against Messianism," *New Republic* (February 18, 1931), 16–17.

33. Frank, *Dawn in Russia*, 4, 24, 158, 252, 260, 264, 270, 246, 272; idem, *Memoirs*, 192; idem, "How I Came to Communism," *New Masses* (September 1932), 7. The emphasis is Frank's.

34. Wilson to Dos Passos, Feb. 29, 1932, Wilson to Frank, June 17, 1932, in Wilson, *Letters on Literature and Politics*, 222–23; Wilson, *Thirties*, 212–13, 208.

35. Eastman, *Artists in Uniform*, 6, vii–viii, 24–25, 29, 27; idem, "Art and the Life of Action," in *Art and the Life of Action*, 81–82, 84.

36. Joseph Freeman, "The Tradition of American Revolutionary Literature," Malcolm Cowley, "What the Revolutionary Movement Can Do for a Writer," in Hart, *American Writers' Congress*, 58, 62, 59. Earlier, Cowley had insisted that "Marxian criticism . . . does not demand a mystical immolation of one's personality or a mystical union with some collective entity, with church, nation or class; on the contrary it requires that all personal talents be developed to the highest

point they can reach." Malcolm Cowley, "A Note on Marxian Criticism" (January 30, 1935), in *Think Back On Us*, 83. In 1935, Cowley's friend Josephson remarked on the place of non-Communist intellectuals in the Popular Front: "We may work with the Marxist 'school,' and we must also look beyond it. Our usefulness would reside always in our ability to look farther ahead. If ever it becomes dishonorable to doubt, to reflect for ourselves, or use disinterested judgment, then it will be too late for everything . . ." Quoted in Josephson, *Infidel in the Temple*, 359.

37. John Dos Passos, "The Writer as Technician," Waldo Frank, "Values of the Revolutionary Writer," "Discussion and Proceeding," Kenneth Burke, "Revolutionary Symbolism in America," in Hart, *American Writers' Congress*, 80–81, 75, 72, 190, 92, 90–91, 93–94. The emphases are Frank's and Burke's. On Burke and the First Writers' Congress generally, see Aaron, *Writers on the Left*, chap. 10.

38. Brooks to Alfred Harcourt, Jan. 2, 1938, Brooks Collection; Malcolm Cowley, "Notes on a Writers' Congress" (June 21, 1939), in *Think Back On Us*, 170.

39. Wilson to Dos Passos, May 9, 1935, in Wilson, *Letters on Literature and Politics*, 263–68. On hearing that Wilson had not been invited to attend the Congress, Waldo Frank said that he was "astonished and pained." He then urged Wilson to join the League, which would "be broad enough to admit men who are less to the Left than you; and your absence would be a shame." Frank to Wilson, May 8, 1935, Wilson Papers.

40. Mumford to Daniel Aaron, Jan. 17, 1959, Mumford Collection.

41. Michael Gold, "Discussion and Proceeding," in Hart, *American Writers' Congress*, 166–67; Michael Gold, "John Reed and the Real Thing" (1927), in *Mike Gold: A Literary Anthology*, 154. Gold tried to convince Mumford that Marxism was the missing element in his writing and that its absence precluded his full effectiveness:

Lewis, you have done much brilliant work in these years and certainly fulfilled every atom of promise in that lanky, big-nosed New York goy who was such a mystery to me at the time. But you still need the iron of Marxism—with it, your work would be doubly effective and truer. You are still in the Shelley stage I believe, and today that is dangerous. We all need to be as mature as we can become, and dodge not a single factor of reality. (Gold to Mumford, Sept. 2, 1934, Mumford Collection.)

42. Joseph Freeman, Introduction, in Hicks, Gold, Schneider, North, Peters, and Calmer, *Proletarian Literature*, 12, 9, 16.

43. Gold, *The Hollow Men*, 31, 46–47, 98. Gold was particularly venomous toward Mumford, whose interventionist position at the time of German-Soviet rapprochement made him the leader of "liberal-fascism" in America. Gold consciously cast himself as the Randolph Bourne of the Second World War: the increasingly isolated hero standing against "the treason of the liberal intellectuals." See Gold, *The Hollow Men*, 118. In a review of this book, Cowley accused Gold of the greatest sin an intellectual could commit: "Mr. Gold and others like him

seem to have lost the capacity for fresh observation or independent thinking." Malcolm Cowley, "The Michael Golden Legend" (July 1941), in *Think Back On Us*, 195.

44. Wilson to Dos Passos, Jan. 31, 1935, in Wilson, *Letters on Literature and Politics*, 259. For additional discussions of *To the Finland Station*, see Paul, *Edmund Wilson*, esp. 131–39 and Castronovo, *Edmund Wilson*, chap. 4.

45. Wilson, *Travels in Two Democracies*, 252.

46. Edmund Wilson, "Marxism and Literature," in *Triple Thinkers*, 269, 266–67, 274, 276–77, 289.

47. Wilson to Eastman, Oct. 5, 1938, Eastman Papers. Wilson may have come to a critique of the dialectic on his own before encountering Eastman's book. In December 1937, he wrote that "the Marxists have been—and are still being—sadly misled through believing in the dialectic as a supernatural power which will bring them to salvation if they trust in it, without the necessity of thought or virtue on their part." Wilson to A. J. Muste, Dec. 31, 1937, in Wilson, *Letters on Literature and Politics*, 296.

48. Wilson, *To the Finland Station*, 187, 162, 189, 216, 196–97, 213.

49. Ibid., 437, 428, 197.

50. Max Eastman, Two impressions after living in Trotsky's house, July 10 and 18, 1932, Eastman Papers.

51. Eastman, *Marxism: Is It Science?*, 282, 215–16; idem, *Stalin's Russia*, 9, 45. Floyd Dell, whose career as critic and novelist had faltered in the 1930s and who was now working for the Works Progress Administration, praised Eastman for "doing simple logical justice to the subject" of Marxism and for translating into written form Dell's own "bitterness, anger, suspicion and resentment at having been swindled." Dell to Eastman, Feb. 1940, Eastman Papers.

52. Eastman, *Stalin's Russia*, 139, 136, 245, 250, 255.

53. Edmund Wilson, "Max Eastman in 1941" (February 10, 1941), in *Classics and Commercials*, 65; idem, "Marxism at the End of the Thirties" (February 22—March 1—March 8, 1941), in *Shores of Light*, 742–43.

Epilogue: Defending the Intellectual Life

1. Cowley to Wilson, Feb. 2, 1940, Wilson Papers. Part of this letter appears in Cowley, —*And I Worked at the Writer's Trade*, 155–57.

2. Brooks, *Opinions of Oliver Allston*, 131; Frank, *Chart for Rough Water*, 137.

3. Frank, *Chart for Rough Water*, 46, 95, 102.

4. Mumford, *Faith for Living*, 21–22, 42.

5. It would be a mistake, however, to claim a dramatic shift in Mumford's attitudes toward the American people. Even in the 1930s, he and many of his contemporaries remained sufficiently ambivalent about popular beliefs and values to warrant a revision of Richard Pells' observation of "a tendency among intellectuals in the 1930s to sanctify the 'people.' " While they sympathized with the victims of the Depression, critics continued to question the quality of popular culture, the susceptibility of the public to quacks and demagogues, and what they

perceived as America's banal optimism and essential conservatism. See Pells, *The Liberal Mind in a Conservative Age*, 8, and Pells, *Radical Visions and American Dreams*, throughout.

6. Mumford, *Men Must Act*, 119.

7. Mumford, *Condition of Man*, 376; Wilson, *Forties*, 44.

8. By 1950, even Gilbert Seldes had reversed his earlier stand against elitist intellectuals who failed to recognize the superiority of popular culture. In *The Great Audience*, Seldes joined with the intellectuals against the makers of "the mass man." He wrote: "The new situation, as I see it, is a persistent, unremitting, successful attack on the reasonable man of intelligence, the balanced man of thought and feeling, the individual who has so far escaped the contagion of mass thinking." Seldes, *The Great Audience*, 6, 265.

9. Eastman, *Heroes I Have Known*, xii-xiv, 326.

10. Wilson, "Max Eastman in 1941," in *Classics and Commercials*, 66. As early as the summer of 1941, Eastman was gathering information on Communist party fronts in the United States. Apparently at Eastman's request, Eugene Lyons sent him a Dies Committee chart of individuals and organizations with alleged Communist ties. See Eugene Lyons to Eastman, Aug. 22, 1941, Eastman Papers. For a discussion of Eastman's drift toward conservatism, see Diggins, *Up from Communism*, chaps. 5 and 9.

11. Frank, *Chart for Rough Water*, 46.

12. Brooks, *The Confident Years*, 607–8.

13. Leon Edel, "Edmund Wilson in Middle Age," in Wilson, *Forties*, xix; Wilson, *Forties*, 20–23. The question mark is Wilson's.

14. Rosenfeld's criticisms appeared in *Scribner's* in May 1933. For a discussion of this episode, see Aaron, *Writers on the Left*, 253–54.

15. Edmund Wilson, "Paul Rosenfeld: Three Phases," Waldo Frank, "The Listener," and Lewis Mumford, "Lyric Wisdom," in Mellquist and Wiese, *Paul Rosenfeld*, 16–17, 92, 75.

16. Jerome Mellquist, "Seraph from Mt. Morris Park," in Mellquist and Wiese, *Paul Rosenfeld*, xxxv. See also Heller, "Paul Rosenfeld," 73–80.

17. Max Eastman, "Contribution to an Apotheosis: John Reed and the Russian Revolution," in *Heroes I Have Known*, 237, 208, 212. Hicks' biography was *John Reed: The Making of a Revolutionary.*

18. Edmund Wilson, Introduction, in *Patriotic Gore*, xxxi-xxxii.

19. Mumford to Frank, July 26, 1940, Aug. 23, 1957, Aug. 29, 1959, Frank Collection; Mumford, *Condition of Man*, v, 393.

20. Mumford, unpublished ms. (1930), in *Findings and Keepings*, 208; Mumford, *Condition of Man*, 423; Mumford, *Culture of Cities*, 306. John L. Thomas discusses the passing of "the regional moment" in "Lewis Mumford: Regionalist Historian."

21. Lewis Mumford, "In the Name of Sanity" (1950), quoted in Paul Boyer, *By the Bomb's Early Light: American Thought and Culture at the Dawn of the Atomic Age* (New York: Pantheon, 1985), 351; Mumford, *Condition of Man*, 419. For an excellent discussion of Mumford's postwar years, see Miller, *Lewis Mumford.*

22. Quoted in Nelson, *Van Wyck Brooks*, 244. The whole episode of the *Partisan Review*'s confrontation with Brooks is described in Nelson, 243–47, and in Alexander, *Here the Country Lies*, 250–51.

23. Kazin, *On Native Grounds*, xi, 447–48.

24. *The Gary Schools* might be considered a book rather than an essay collection, but Bourne's best work was in the shorter form.

25. Matthews, "Social Scientists and the Culture Concept," and idem, "Paradigm Changes in Interpretations of Ethnicity, 1930–1980: From Process to Structure," in Peter Kivisto and Dag Blanck, eds., *American Immigrants and Their Generations: Studies and Commentaries on the Hansen Thesis after Fifty Years* (Urbana: University of Illinois Press, 1990), 167–188. See also Thomas, "The Uses of Catastrophism," 246–49. Matthews identifies Marxism as a structural type of thought which holds that "position in a given social structure molds what the individual human being is and can aspire to" ("Paradigm Changes," 181). But the attempts to Americanize (or pragmatize) Marxism that I described in the last chapter represent a processual orientation.

26. Pells, *The Liberal Mind*, 147, 260; Fowler, *Believing Skeptics*, chaps. 1–2 and pp. 284–86. See also Gilbert, *Writers and Partisans*, 263–82.

27. Thomas, "The Uses of Catastrophism," 247–48.

Bibliography

One of my underlying arguments is that the published writings of independent intellectuals, despite the ideal of disinterestedness and the strong element of social observation, were profoundly personal. The reflective quality of their literary output stands in dramatic contrast to the academic style they frequently disparaged. I therefore draw on published books and essays for the bulk of my evidence. Where it helps illuminate a point, I bring in private writings and archival materials as well, but my strategy of concentrating on the published sources is linked to my contention that these critics considered their personal, vocational, and creative struggles to be of public importance.

Primary Sources

I. MANUSCRIPT COLLECTIONS

American Fund for Public Service [AFPS] Records. Rare Books and Manuscripts Division, The New York Public Library, Astor, Lenox and Tilden Foundations.

Randolph Bourne Papers. Rare Book and Manuscript Library, Columbia University.

Van Wyck Brooks Collection. Special Collections, Van Pelt-Dietrich Library Center, University of Pennsylvania.

Max Eastman Papers (also Eliena Krylenko Eastman Papers, Claude McKay Papers). The Lilly Library, Indiana University.

Waldo Frank Collection. Special Collections, Van Pelt-Dietrich Library Center, University of Pennsylvania.

Benjamin W. Huebsch Papers. Manuscript Division, The Library of Congress.

Walter Lippmann Papers. Manuscripts and Archives, Yale University Library.

Lewis Mumford Collection. Special Collections, Van Pelt-Dietrich Library Center, University of Pennsylvania.

John Reed Papers. The Houghton Library, Harvard University.

Paul Rosenfeld Papers. Yale Collection of American Literature, Beinecke Rare Book and Manuscript Library, Yale University.

Margaret Sanger Papers. Manuscript Division, The Library of Congress.

Edmund Wilson Papers. Yale Collection of American Literature, Beinecke Rare Book and Manuscript Library, Yale University.

II. PUBLISHED PRIMARY WORKS

Adams, Henry. *The Education of Henry Adams.* Boston, 1918.

Addams, Jane. *Twenty Years at Hull-House.* New York, 1912 [1910].

Anderson, Sherwood. *Home Town.* New York, 1940.

————. *Puzzled America.* New York, 1935.

————. *Sherwood Anderson's Notebook.* New York, 1926.

————. *A Story Teller's Story.* New York, 1924.

Babbitt, Irving. *Literature and the American College: Essays in Defense of the Humanities.* Boston, 1908.

Beard, Charles A. and Mary R. *The Rise of American Civilization.* New York, 1930.

Bourne, Randolph S. *Education and Living.* New York, 1917.

————. *The Gary Schools.* Boston, 1916.

————. *History of a Literary Radical and Other Essays.* Van Wyck Brooks, ed. New York, 1920.

————. "John Dewey's Philosophy." *New Republic* (March 13, 1915), 154–56.

————. *The Radical Will: Selected Writings, 1911–1918.* Olaf Hansen, ed. New York, 1977.

————. *War and the Intellectuals: Collected Essays, 1915–1919.* Carl Resek, ed. New York, 1964.

————. *Youth and Life.* Boston, 1913.

Brooks, Van Wyck. *America's Coming-of-Age.* New York, 1915.

————. *An Autobiography.* New York, 1965.

————. *The Confident Years, 1885–1915.* New York, 1952.

————. *Emerson and Others.* New York, 1927.

————. *The Flowering of New England, 1815–1865.* New York, 1936.

————. "Highbrow and Lowbrow." *Forum* (April 1915), 481–92.

————. *The Life of Emerson.* New York, 1932.

————. *New England: Indian Summer, 1865–1915.* New York, 1940.

————. "On Creating a Usable Past." *Dial* (April 11, 1918), 337–41.

————. *Opinions of Oliver Allston.* New York, 1941.

————. *The Ordeal of Mark Twain.* New York, 1955 [1920].

————. *The Pilgrimage of Henry James.* New York, 1925.

————. *Three Essays on America.* New York, 1934.

————. *The Times of Melville and Whitman.* New York, 1947.

————. *The Van Wyck Brooks-Lewis Mumford Letters: The Record of a Literary Friendship, 1921–1963.* Robert E. Spiller, ed. New York, 1970.

————. *The Wine of the Puritans: A Study of Present-Day America.* New York, 1909.

———. *The World of Washington Irving.* New York, 1944.

Bryant, Louise. *Mirrors of Moscow.* New York, 1923.

———. *Six Red Months in Russia: An Observer's Account of Russia Before and During the Proletarian Dictatorship.* New York, 1918.

Burke, Kenneth. *Attitudes toward History.* 2 vols. New York, 1937.

———. *Counter-Statement.* New York, 1931.

———. *Permanence and Change: An Anatomy of Purpose.* New York, 1935.

———. *The Philosophy of Literary Form: Studies in Symbolic Action.* Baton Rouge, 1941.

Calverton, V. F. *The Bankruptcy of Marriage.* New York, 1928.

———. *Sex Expression in Literature.* New York, 1926.

Calverton, V. F., and Schmalhausen, S. D., eds. *Sex in Civilization.* Garden City, 1929.

Chase, Stuart. *The Economy of Abundance.* New York, 1934.

———. *Men and Machines.* New York, 1929.

———. *Mexico: A Study of Two Americas.* New York, 1931.

———. *The Nemesis of American Business and Other Essays.* New York, 1931.

———. *The Tragedy of Waste.* New York, 1925.

Collins, Seward. "Criticism in America." *Bookman* (June-July-October 1930), 241–56, 353–64, 400–15, 145–64, 209–28.

Colum, Mary. *The Life and the Dream.* Garden City, 1947.

Cowley, Malcolm. *—And I Worked at the Writer's Trade: Chapters of Literary History, 1918–1978.* New York, 1978.

———. *The Dream of the Golden Mountains: Remembering the 1930s.* New York, 1980.

———. *Exile's Return: A Narrative of Ideas.* New York, 1934.

———. *Think Back On Us . . . A Contemporary Chronicle of the 1930's.* Henry Dan Piper, ed. Carbondale, 1967.

Dell, Floyd. *Homecoming: An Autobiography.* New York, 1933.

———. *Intellectual Vagabondage: An Apology for the Intelligentsia.* New York, 1926.

———. *Looking at Life.* New York, 1924.

———. *Love in Greenwich Village.* New York, 1926.

———. *Love in the Machine Age: A Psychological Study of the Transition from Patriarchal Society.* New York, 1930.

———. *Moon-Calf.* New York, 1920.

———. *Were You Ever a Child?* New York, 1919.

———. *Women as World Builders: Studies in Modern Feminism.* Chicago, 1913.

Dewey, John. *The Child and the Curriculum and The School and Society.* Chicago, 1956 [1902, 1899].

———. *Democracy and Education: An Introduction to the Philosophy of Education.* New York, 1916.

———. *The Early Works of John Dewey, 1882–1898.* 5 vols. Jo Ann Boydston, ed. Carbondale, 1969.

———. *Interest and Effort in Education.* Boston, 1913.

Dewey, John and Evelyn. *Schools of Tomorrow.* New York, 1962 [1915].

Dos Passos, John. "Against American Literature." *New Republic* (October 14, 1916), 269–71.
———. *The Best Times: An Informal Memoir.* New York, 1966.
———. *The Ground We Stand On: Some Examples from the History of a Political Creed.* London, 1942.
———. *Journeys between Wars.* New York, 1938.
———. *Rosinante to the Road Again.* New York, 1922.
Eastman, Crystal. *Crystal Eastman on Women and Revolution.* Blanche Wiesen Cook, ed. New York, 1978.
Eastman, Max. *Art and the Life of Action with Other Essays.* New York, 1934.
———. *Artists in Uniform: A Study of Literature and Bureaucratism.* New York, 1972 [1934].
———. *Enjoyment of Living.* New York, 1948.
———. *Enjoyment of Poetry.* New York, 1913.
———. *Heroes I Have Known: Twelve Who Lived Great Lives.* New York, 1942.
———. *Journalism versus Art.* New York, 1916.
———. *The Literary Mind: Its Place in an Age of Science.* New York, 1931.
———. *Love and Revolution: My Journey through an Epoch.* New York, 1964.
———. *Marx and Lenin: The Science of Revolution.* New York, 1927.
———. *Marxism: Is It Science?* New York, 1940.
———. *Stalin's Russia and the Crisis in Socialism.* New York, 1940.
———. *Venture.* New York, 1927.
Foerster, Norman, ed. *Humanism and America: Essays on the Outlook of Modern Civilization.* New York, 1930.
Frank, Waldo. *America Hispana: A Portrait and a Prospect.* New York, 1931.
———. *Chart for Rough Water: Our Role in a New World.* New York, 1940.
———. *Dawn in Russia: The Record of a Journey.* New York, 1932.
———. *In the American Jungle [1925–1936].* New York, 1937.
———. *Memoirs of Waldo Frank.* Alan Trachtenberg, ed. Amherst, 1973.
———. *Our America.* New York, 1919.
———. *The Re-discovery of America: An Introduction to a Philosophy of American Life.* New York, 1929.
———. *Salvos: An Informal Book about Books and Plays.* New York, 1924.
———. *Virgin Spain: Scenes from the Spiritual Drama of a Great People.* New York, 1926.
Freeman, Joseph. *An American Testament: A Narrative of Rebels and Romantics.* New York, 1936.
Gilman, Daniel Coit. *University Problems in the United States.* New York, 1969 [1898].
Glaspell, Susan. *The Road to the Temple.* New York, 1927.
Gold, Michael [Irwin Granich]. *The Hollow Men.* New York, 1941.
———. *Jews Without Money.* New York, 1930.
———. *Mike Gold: A Literary Anthology.* Michael Folsom, ed. New York, 1972.

Grattan, C. Hartley, ed. *The Critique of Humanism: A Symposium.* New York, 1930.

Hackett, Francis. *American Rainbow: Early Reminiscences.* New York, 1971.

Hapgood, Hutchins. *A Victorian in the Modern World.* New York, 1939.

Hart, Henry, ed. *American Writers' Congress.* New York, 1935.

Hicks, Granville; Gold, Michael; Schneider, Isidor; North, Joseph; Peters, Paul; and Calmer, Alan, eds. *Proletarian Literature in the United States: An Anthology.* New York, 1935.

James, William. *Memories and Studies.* New York, 1911.

Jay, Paul, ed. *The Selected Correspondence of Kenneth Burke and Malcolm Cowley, 1915–1981.* New York, 1988.

Josephson, Matthew. *Infidel in the Temple: A Memoir of the Nineteen-Thirties.* New York, 1967.

———. *Life among the Surrealists: A Memoir.* New York, 1962.

———. *Portrait of the Artist as American.* New York, 1930.

———. *Zola and His Time.* New York, 1928.

Kirchwey, Freda, ed. *Our Changing Morality: A Symposium.* New York, 1924.

Krutch, Joseph Wood. *The Modern Temper: A Study and a Confession.* New York, 1929.

Lawrence, D. H. *The Letters of D. H. Lawrence: Volume IV, June 1921–March 1924.* Warren Roberts, James T. Boulton, and Elizabeth Mansfield, eds. Cambridge, 1987.

Lewisohn, Ludwig. *Cities and Men.* New York, 1927.

———. *The Creative Life.* New York, 1924.

———. *Expression in America.* New York, 1932.

———. *Mid-Channel: An American Chronicle.* New York, 1929.

———. *Up Stream: An American Chronicle.* New York, 1922.

Lippmann, Walter. *Drift and Mastery: An Attempt to Diagnose the Current Unrest.* Madison, 1985 [1914].

———. *The Good Society.* New York, 1937.

———. *Liberty and the News.* New York, 1920.

———. "An Open Mind: William James." *Everybody's* (December 1910), 800–801.

———. *The Phantom Public.* New York, 1925.

———. *A Preface to Morals.* New York, 1929.

———. *A Preface to Politics.* New York, 1913.

———. *Public Opinion.* New York, 1922.

Luhan, Mabel Dodge. *Edge of Taos Desert: An Escape to Reality, Volume Four of Intimate Memories.* New York, 1937.

———. *Movers and Shakers: Volume Three of Intimate Memories.* New York, 1936.

Macy, John. *Socialism in America.* Garden City, 1916.

———. *The Spirit of American Literature.* Garden City, 1913.

McKay, Claude. *A Long Way from Home.* New York, 1970 [1937].

———. *The Passion of Claude McKay: Selected Poetry and Prose, 1912–1948.* Wayne F. Cooper, ed. New York, 1973.

Mellquist, Jerome, and Wiese, Lucie, eds. *Paul Rosenfeld: Voyager in the Arts.* New York, 1948.

Mencken, H. L. *A Book of Prefaces.* New York, 1917.

———. *In Defense of Women.* Rev. ed. New York, 1922.

———. *Letters of H. L. Mencken.* Guy J. Forgue, ed. New York, 1961.

———. *The New Mencken Letters.* Carl Bode, ed. New York, 1977.

———. *Notes on Democracy.* New York, 1926.

———. *Prejudices: First Series.* New York, 1919.

———. *Prejudices: Second Series.* New York, 1920.

———. *Prejudices: Third Series.* New York, 1922.

———. *Prejudices: Fourth Series.* New York, 1924.

———. *Prejudices: Fifth Series.* New York, 1926.

———. *Prejudices: Sixth Series.* New York, 1927.

Mumford, Lewis. *The Brown Decades: A Study of the Arts in America.* New York, 1971 [1931].

———. *The Condition of Man.* New York, 1944.

———. *The Culture of Cities.* New York, 1938.

———. *Faith for Living.* New York, 1940.

———. *Findings and Keepings: Analects for an Autobiography.* New York, 1975.

———. "Fruit." *Forum* (December 1914), 889–92.

———. *The Golden Day: A Study in American Experience and Culture.* New York, 1926.

———. *Herman Melville.* New York, 1929.

———. *Men Must Act.* New York, 1939.

———. *My Works and Days: A Personal Chronicle.* New York, 1975.

———. *Sketches from Life: The Early Years.* New York, 1982.

———. *Sticks and Stones: A Study of American Architecture and Civilization.* New York, 1955 [1924].

———. *The Story of Utopias.* New York, 1922.

———. *Technics and Civilization.* New York, 1963 [1934].

Munson, Gorham B. *Destinations: A Canvass of American Literature since 1900.* New York, 1928.

———. *Robert Frost: A Study in Sensibility and Good Sense.* New York, 1973 [1927].

———. *Style and Form in American Prose.* Garden City, 1929.

———. *Waldo Frank: A Study.* New York, 1923.

Naumburg, Margaret. *The Child and the World: Dialogues in Modern Education.* New York, 1928.

Nock, Albert Jay. *Memoirs of a Superfluous Man.* New York, 1943.

Oppenheim, James. "The Story of the *Seven Arts.*" *American Mercury* (June 1930), 156–64.

Parrington, Vernon Louis. *Main Currents in American Thought.* 3 vols. New York, 1927–30.

Parsons, Elsie Clews. *Fear and Conventionality.* New York, 1914.

———. *The Old-Fashioned Woman: Primitive Fancies about the Sex.* New York, 1913.

————. *Social Freedom: A Study of the Conflicts between Social Classifications and Personality*. New York, 1915.

————. *Social Rule: A Study of the Will to Power*. New York, 1916.

Perry, Ralph Barton, ed. *The Thought and Character of William James*. 2 vols. Boston, 1935.

Pratt, Caroline, ed. *Experimental Practice in the City and Country School*. New York, 1924.

Reed, John. "Almost Thirty." *New Republic* (April 15 and 29, 1936), 267–70, 332–36.

————. *An Anthology*. Moscow, 1966.

————. *The Day in Bohemia or Life among the Artists*. Riverside, 1913.

————. *Insurgent Mexico*. New York, 1983 [1914].

————. *Ten Days That Shook the World*. New York, 1935 [1919].

————. *The War in Eastern Europe*. New York, 1916.

Rosenfeld, Paul. *The Boy in the Sun*. New York, 1928.

————. *By Way of Art: Criticisms of Music, Literature, Painting, Sculpture and the Dance*. New York, 1928.

————. *Men Seen: Twenty-Four Modern Authors*. New York, 1925.

————. *Port of New York*. Urbana, 1961 [1924].

Rourke, Constance. *American Humor: A Study of the National Character*. New York, 1931.

————. *The Roots of American Culture and Other Essays*. Van Wyck Brooks, ed. New York, 1942.

Rugg, Harold and Shumaker, Ann. *The Child-Centered School: An Appraisal of the New Education*. Yonkers, 1928.

Sanger, Margaret. *An Autobiography*. New York, 1938.

————. *The Pivot of Civilization*. New York, 1922.

————. *Woman and the New Race*. New York, 1920.

Santayana, George. *Character and Opinion in the United States*. New York, 1920.

————. *The Genteel Tradition: Nine Essays by George Santayana*. Douglas Wilson, ed. Cambridge, 1967.

Seldes, Gilbert. *The Great Audience*. Westport, 1970 [1950].

————. *Mainland*. New York, 1936.

————. *The Seven Lively Arts*. New York, 1962 [1924].

————. *The Stammering Century*. New York, 1928.

————. *The Years of the Locust (America, 1929–1932)*. Boston, 1933.

Sergeant, Elizabeth Shepley. *Fire under the Andes: A Group of North American Portraits*. New York, 1927.

————. *Shadow-Shapes: The Journal of a Wounded Woman, October 1918–May 1919*. Boston, 1920.

Sheridan, Clare. *My American Diary*. New York, 1922.

Stearns, Harold E. *America and the Young Intellectual*. Westport, 1973 [1921].

————. "Apologia of an Expatriate." *Scribner's* (March 1929), 338–41.

————. "The Confessions of a Harvard Man." *Forum* (December 1913 and January 1914), 819–26, 69–81.

Stearns, Harold E. *Liberalism in America: Its Origin, Its Temporary Collapse, Its Future*. New York, 1919.

———. *Rediscovering America*. New York, 1934.

———. *The Street I Know*. New York, 1935.

———, ed. *America Now: An Inquiry into Civilization in the United States by Thirty-Six Americans*. New York, 1938.

———, ed. *Civilization in the United States: An Inquiry by Thirty Americans*. New York, 1922.

Steffens, Lincoln. *The Autobiography of Lincoln Steffens*. New York, 1931.

———. *The Letters of Lincoln Steffens*. 2 vols. Ella Winter, ed. Westport, 1966 [1938].

Stein, Gertrude. *The Autobiography of Alice B. Toklas*. New York, 1933.

Soule, George. *The Coming American Revolution*. New York, 1934.

———. *A Planned Society*. New York, 1932.

———. *The Useful Art of Economics*. New York, 1929.

Veblen, Thorstein. *The Higher Learning in America: A Memorandum on the Conduct of Universities by Business Men*. New York, 1918.

———. *The Theory of the Leisure Class: An Economic Study of Institutions*. New York, 1927 [1899].

Vorse, Mary Heaton. *A Footnote to Folly: Reminiscences of Mary Heaton Vorse*. New York, 1935.

———. *Rebel Pen: The Writings of Mary Heaton Vorse*. Dee Garrison, ed. New York, 1985.

———. *Time and the Town: A Provincetown Chronicle*. New York, 1942.

Wilson, Edmund. *The American Jitters: A Year of the Slump*. New York, 1932.

———. *Axel's Castle: A Study in the Imaginative Literature of 1870–1930*. New York, 1931.

———. *Classics and Commercials: A Literary Chronicle of the Forties*. New York, 1950.

———. *The Cold War and the Income Tax: A Protest*. New York, 1963.

———. *Discordant Encounters: Plays and Dialogues*. New York, 1926.

———. *The Forties: From Notebooks and Diaries of the Period*. Leon Edel, ed. New York, 1983.

———. *I Thought of Daisy*. New York, 1929.

———. *Letters on Literature and Politics, 1912–1972*. Elena Wilson, ed. New York, 1977.

———. *Patriotic Gore: Studies in the Literature of the American Civil War*. New York, 1962.

———. *A Prelude: Landscapes, Characters and Conversations from the Earlier Years of My Life*. New York, 1967.

———. *The Shores of Light: A Literary Chronicle of the Twenties and Thirties*. New York, 1952.

———. *The Thirties: From Notebooks and Diaries of the Period*. Leon Edel, ed. New York, 1980.

————. *To the Finland Station: A Study in the Writing and Acting of History*. New York, 1940.

————. *Travels in Two Democracies*. New York, 1936.

————. *The Triple Thinkers: Ten Essays on Literature*. New York, 1938.

————. *The Twenties: From Notebooks and Diaries of the Period*. Leon Edel, ed. New York, 1975.

————, ed. *The Shock of Recognition: The Development of Literature in the United States Recorded by the Men Who Made It*. New York, 1955.

Secondary Sources

Aaron, Daniel. *Writers on the Left: Episodes in American Literary Communism*. New York, 1979 [1961].

Abrahams, Edward. *The Lyrical Left: Randolph Bourne, Alfred Stieglitz, and the Origins of Cultural Radicalism in America*. Charlottesville, 1986.

Alexander, Charles C. *Here the Country Lies: Nationalism and the Arts in Twentieth-Century America*. Bloomington, 1980.

Alpern, Sara. *Freda Kirchwey: A Woman of the Nation*. Cambridge, 1987.

Bender, Thomas. *Community and Social Change in America*. New Brunswick, 1978.

————. "Lionel Trilling and American Culture." *American Quarterly* 42, No. 2 (June 1990), 324–47.

————. *New York Intellect: A History of Intellectual Life in New York City, from 1750 to the Beginnings of Our Own Time*. Baltimore, 1987.

Blake, Casey Nelson. *Beloved Community: The Cultural Criticism of Randolph Bourne, Van Wyck Brooks, Waldo Frank, and Lewis Mumford*. Chapel Hill, 1990.

Blum, D. Steven. *Walter Lippmann: Cosmopolitanism in the Century of Total War*. Ithaca, 1984.

Bode, Carl. *Mencken*. Carbondale, 1969.

Bourke, Paul F. "The Social Critics and the End of American Innocence, 1907–1921." *Journal of American Studies* 3, No. 1 (July 1969), 57–72.

————. "The Status of Politics, 1909–1919: *The New Republic*, Randolph Bourne and Van Wyck Brooks." *Journal of American Studies* 8, No. 2 (August 1974), 171–202.

Bruccoli, Matthew J. *The Fortunes of Mitchell Kennerley, Bookman*. New York, 1986.

Cain, William E. *F. O. Matthiessen and the Politics of Criticism*. Madison, 1988.

Callahan, Raymond E. *Education and the Cult of Efficiency: A Study of the Social Forces That Have Shaped the Administration of the Public Schools*. Chicago, 1962.

Cantor, Milton. *Max Eastman*. New York, 1970.

Carroll, Berenice A. "The Politics of 'Originality': Women and the Class System of the Intellect." *Journal of Women's History* 2, No. 2 (Fall 1990), 136–63.

Carter, Paul J. *Waldo Frank*. New York, 1967.

Castronovo, David. *Edmund Wilson*. New York, 1984.

Clayton, Bruce. *Forgotten Prophet: The Life of Randolph Bourne*. Baton Rouge, 1984.

Cohen, Ronald D., and Mohl, Raymond A. *The Paradox of Progressive Education: The Gary Plan and Urban Schooling.* Port Washington, NY, 1979.

Cooney, Terry A. *The Rise of the New York Intellectuals: Partisan Review and Its Circle, 1934–1945.* Madison, 1986.

Coser, Lewis A. *Men of Ideas: A Sociologist's View.* New York, 1965.

Cott, Nancy F., *The Grounding of Modern Feminism.* New Haven, 1987.

Cott, Nancy F., and Pleck, Elizabeth H., eds. *A Heritage of Her Own: Toward a New Social History of American Women.* New York, 1979.

Cremin, Lawrence A. *The Transformation of the School: Progressivism in American Education, 1876–1957.* New York, 1961.

Davis, Allen F. *American Heroine: The Life and Legend of Jane Addams.* New York, 1973.

Diggins, John P. *The American Left in the Twentieth Century.* New York, 1973.

———. *The Bard of Savagery: Thorstein Veblen and Modern Social Theory.* New York, 1978.

———. *Up from Communism: Conservative Odysseys in American Intellectual History.* New York, 1975.

Dorfman, Joseph. *Thorstein Veblen and His America.* New York, 1934.

Douglas, Ann. *The Feminization of American Culture.* New York, 1977.

Douglas, George H. *Edmund Wilson's America.* Lexington, 1983.

Duffey, Bernard. *The Chicago Renaissance in American Letters, A Critical History.* Lansing, 1954.

Dykhuizen, George. *The Life and Mind of John Dewey.* Jo Ann Boydston, ed. Carbondale, 1973.

Fishbein, Leslie. *Rebels in Bohemia: The Radicals of The Masses, 1911–1917.* Chapel Hill, 1982.

Forcey, Charles. *The Crossroads of Liberalism: Croly, Weyl, Lippmann and the Progressive Era, 1900–1925.* New York, 1961.

Ford, Hugh. *Four Lives in Paris.* San Francisco, 1987.

Fowler, Robert Booth. *Believing Skeptics: American Political Intellectuals, 1945–1964.* Westport, 1978.

Gardner, Virginia. *"Friend and Lover": The Life of Louise Bryant.* New York, 1982.

Garrison, Dee. *Mary Heaton Vorse: The Life of an American Insurgent.* Philadelphia, 1989.

Geiger, Roger L. *To Advance Knowledge: The Growth of American Research Universities, 1900–1940.* New York, 1986.

Gilbert, James. *Designing the Industrial State: The Intellectual Pursuit of Collectivism in America, 1880–1940.* Chicago, 1972.

———. *Writers and Partisans: A History of Literary Radicalism in America.* New York, 1968.

Gnizi [Genizi], Haim. "Edmund Wilson and *The Modern Monthly*, 1934–5: A Phase in Wilson's Radicalism." *Journal of American Studies* 7, No. 3 (December 1973), 301–19.

———. "V. F. Calverton: Independent Radical." Ph.D. dissertation. City University of New York, 1968.

Goldman, Arnold. "The Culture of the Provincetown Players." *Journal of American Studies* 12, No. 3 (December 1978), 291–310.

Gray, Madeline. *Margaret Sanger: A Biography of the Champion of Birth Control.* New York, 1979.

Green, Martin. *New York 1913: The Armory Show and the Paterson Strike Pageant.* New York, 1988.

Groth, Janet. *Edmund Wilson: A Critic for Our Time.* Athens, Ohio, 1989.

Hahn, Emily. *Mabel: A Biography of Mabel Dodge Luhan.* Boston, 1977.

———. *Romantic Rebels: An Informal History of Bohemianism in America.* Boston, 1966.

Hare, Peter H. *A Woman's Quest for Science: Portrait of Anthropologist Elsie Clews Parsons.* Buffalo, 1985.

Hart, John E. *Floyd Dell.* New York, 1971.

Haskell, Thomas L., ed. *The Authority of Experts: Studies in History and Theory.* Bloomington, 1984.

———. *The Emergence of Professional Social Science: The American Social Science Association and the Nineteenth-Century Crisis of Authority.* Urbana, 1977.

Hawkins, Hugh. *Pioneer: A History of the Johns Hopkins University, 1874–1889.* Ithaca, 1960.

Heller, David B. "Paul Rosenfeld: Forgotten Pioneer in the Quest for an American Artistic Tradition." Honors thesis. Harvard University, 1989.

Hicks, Granville. *John Reed: The Making of a Revolutionary.* New York, 1936.

Higham, John. "Hanging Together: Divergent Unities in American History." *Journal of American History* 61, No. 1 (June 1974), 5–28.

Higham, John, and Conkin, Paul, eds. *New Directions in American Intellectual History.* Baltimore, 1979.

Hobson, Fred C., Jr. *Serpent in Eden: H. L. Mencken and the South.* Chapel Hill, 1974.

Hoeveler, J. David., Jr. *The New Humanism: A Critique of Modern America, 1900–1940.* Charlottesville, 1977.

Hoffman, Frederick J. *Freudianism and the Literary Mind.* Westport, 1977 [1957 ed.].

Hoffman, Frederick J.; Allen, Charles; and Ulrich, Carolyn F. *The Little Magazine: A History and Bibliography.* Princeton, 1947.

Hofstadter, Richard. *Anti-Intellectualism in American Life.* New York, 1963.

Hofstadter, Richard, and Smith, Wilson, eds. *American Higher Education: A Documentary History.* 2 vols. Chicago, 1961.

Hollinger, David A. *In the American Province: Studies in the History and Historiography of Ideas.* Baltimore, 1989 [1985].

Hoopes, James. *Van Wyck Brooks: In Search of American Culture.* Amherst, 1977.

Hughes, Thomas P., and Hughes, Agatha C., eds. *Lewis Mumford: Public Intellectual.* New York, 1990.

Jacoby, Russell. *The Last Intellectuals: American Culture in the Age of Academe.* New York, 1987.

Joost, Nicholas. *Scofield Thayer and The Dial: An Illustrated History*. Carbondale, 1964.

———. *Years of Transition: The Dial, 1912–1920*. Barre, Mass., 1967.

Jumonville, Neil. *Critical Crossings: The New York Intellectuals in Postwar America*. Berkeley, 1991.

Kaplan, Justin. *Lincoln Steffens: A Biography*. New York, 1974.

Kazin, Alfred. *On Native Grounds: An Interpretation of Modern American Prose Literature*. New York, 1942.

Kennedy, David M. *Birth Control in America: The Career of Margaret Sanger*. New Haven, 1970.

Kloppenberg, James T. *Uncertain Victory: Social Democracy and Progressivism in European and American Thought, 1870–1920*. New York, 1986.

Kramer, Dale. *Chicago Renaissance: The Literary Life in the Midwest, 1900–1930*. New York, 1966.

Kuklick, Bruce. *The Rise of American Philosophy: Cambridge, Massachusetts, 1860–1930*. New Haven, 1977.

Lainoff, Seymour. *Ludwig Lewisohn*. Boston, 1982.

Lasch, Christopher. *The American Liberals and the Russian Revolution*. New York, 1962.

———. *The New Radicalism in America [1889–1963]: The Intellectual as a Social Type*. New York, 1965.

———, et al. "Prophecy Reconsidered: Articles on Lewis Mumford." *Salmagundi*, No. 49 (Summer 1980).

Lawson, R. Alan. *The Failure of Independent Liberalism, 1930–1941*. New York, 1971.

Lears, T. J. Jackson. *No Place of Grace: Antimodernism and the Transformation of American Culture, 1880–1920*. New York, 1981.

Levy, David W. *Herbert Croly of The New Republic: The Life and Thought of an American Progressive*. Princeton, 1985.

Ludington, Townsend. *John Dos Passos: A Twentieth Century Odyssey*. New York, 1980.

Lynn, Kenneth S. "The Rebels of Greenwich Village." *Perspectives in American History* 8 (1974), 335–77.

Matthews, F. H. "The Americanization of Sigmund Freud: Adaptations of Psychoanalysis before 1917." *Journal of American Studies* 1, No. 1 (April 1967), 39–62.

Matthews, Fred. "Social Scientists and the Culture Concept, 1930–1950: The Conflict between Processual and Structural Approaches." *Sociological Theory* 7, No. 1 (Spring 1989), 87–101.

May, Henry F. *The End of American Innocence: A Study in the First Years of Our Own Time, 1912–1917*. New York, 1959.

Miller, Donald L. *Lewis Mumford: A Life*. New York, 1989.

Mott, Frank Luther. *A History of American Magazines: Volume V, Sketches of 21 Magazines, 1905–1930*. Cambridge, 1968.

Myers, Gerald E. *William James: His Life and Thought.* New Haven, 1986.

Nash, Roderick. *The Nervous Generation: American Thought, 1917–1930.* Chicago, 1970.

Nelson, Raymond. *Van Wyck Brooks: A Writer's Life.* New York, 1981.

Novick, Peter, *That Noble Dream: The "Objectivity Question" and the American Historical Profession.* New York, 1988.

Oleson, Alexandra, and Voss, John, eds. *The Organization of Knowledge in Modern America, 1860–1920.* Baltimore, 1979.

O'Neill, William L. *The Last Romantic: A Life of Max Eastman.* New York, 1978.

Parry, Albert. *Garrets and Pretenders: A History of Bohemianism in America.* New York, 1960 [1933].

Paul, Sherman. *Edmund Wilson: A Study of Literary Vocation in Our Time.* Urbana, 1965.

Pells, Richard H. *The Liberal Mind in a Conservative Age: American Intellectuals in the 1940s and 1950s.* New York, 1985.

———. *Radical Visions and American Dreams: Culture and Social Thought in the Depression Years.* New York, 1973.

Perry, Lewis. *Intellectual Life in America: A History.* New York, 1984.

Phillips, John Oliver Crompton. "John Dewey and the Transformation of American Intellectual Life, 1859–1904." Ph.D. dissertation. Harvard University, 1978.

Potter, Hugh. "Paul Rosenfeld: Criticism and Prophecy." *American Quarterly* 22, No. 1 (Spring 1970), 82–94.

Purcell, Edward A. *The Crisis of Democratic Theory: Scientific Naturalism and the Problem of Value.* Lexington, Ky., 1973.

Quandt, Jean B. *From the Small Town to the Great Community: The Social Thought of Progressive Intellectuals.* New Brunswick, 1970.

Reed, James. *From Private Vice to Public Virtue: The Birth Control Movement and American Society Since 1830.* New York, 1978.

Rosenberg, Rosalind. *Beyond Separate Spheres: Intellectual Roots of Modern Feminism.* New Haven, 1982.

Rosenstone, Robert A. *Romantic Revolutionary: A Biography of John Reed.* New York, 1975.

Rubin, Joan Shelley. *Constance Rourke and American Culture.* Chapel Hill, 1980.

Rudnick, Lois Palken. *Mabel Dodge Luhan: New Woman, New Worlds.* Albuquerque, 1984.

Sacks, Claire. "The *Seven Arts* Critics: A Study of Cultural Nationalism in America, 1910–1930." Ph.D. dissertation. University of Wisconsin, 1955.

Schwarz, Judith. *Radical Feminists of Heterodoxy: Greenwich Village, 1912–1940.* Lebanon, NH, 1982.

Scruggs, Charles. *The Sage in Harlem: H. L. Mencken and the Black Writers of the 1920s.* Baltimore, 1984.

Shaw, Eric W. "Harold E. Stearns: Eternal Expatriate." Honors thesis. Harvard University, 1959.

Shi, David E. *Matthew Josephson: Bourgeois Bohemian*. New Haven, 1981.

———. *The Simple Life: Plain Living and High Thinking in American Culture*. New York, 1985.

Sochen, June. *Movers and Shakers: American Women Thinkers and Activists, 1900–1970*. New York, 1973.

———. *The New Woman: Feminism in Greenwich Village, 1910–1920*. New York, 1972.

Steel, Ronald. *Walter Lippmann and the American Century*. Boston, 1980.

Storr, Richard J. *Harper's University: The Beginnings*. Chicago, 1966.

Stott, William. *Documentary Expression and Thirties America*. Chicago, 1986 [1973].

Susman, Warren I. *Culture as History: The Transformation of American Society in the Twentieth Century*. New York, 1984.

———. "Pilgrimage to Paris: The Backgrounds of American Expatriation, 1920–1934." Ph.D. dissertation. University of Wisconsin, 1958.

Tanselle, George Thomas. "Faun at the Barricades: The Life and Work of Floyd Dell." Ph.D. dissertation. Northwestern University, 1959.

Tebbel, John. *Between Covers: The Rise and Transformation of Book Publishing in America*. New York, 1987.

Thomas, John L. *Alternative America: Henry George, Edward Bellamy, Henry Demarest Lloyd and the Adversary Tradition*. Cambridge, 1983.

———. "Lewis Mumford: Regionalist Historian." *Reviews in American History* 16, No. 1 (March 1988), 158–72.

———. "The Uses of Catastrophism: Lewis Mumford, Vernon L. Parrington, Van Wyck Brooks, and the End of American Regionalism." *American Quarterly* 42, No. 2 (June 1990), 223–51.

Tompkins, Vincent Joseph, Jr. "Twilight of Idols: American Social Criticism, 1918–1930." Ph.D. dissertation. Harvard University, 1991.

Turner, Susan J. *A History of The Freeman: Literary Landmark of the Early Twenties*. New York, 1963.

Veysey, Laurence R. *The Emergence of the American University*.Chicago, 1965.

Walzer, Michael. *The Company of Critics: Social Criticism and Political Commitment in the Twentieth Century*. New York, 1988.

Wasserstrom, William. *The Time of the Dial*. Syracuse, 1963.

Wertheim, Arthur Frank. *The New York Little Renaissance: Iconoclasm, Modernism, and Nationalism in American Culture, 1908–17*. New York, 1976.

Westbrook, Robert B. *John Dewey and American Democracy*. Ithaca, 1991.

———. "Tribune of the Technostructure: The Popular Economics of Stuart Chase." *American Quarterly* 32, No. 4 (Fall 1980), 387–408.

White, Morton G. *Social Thought in America: The Revolt against Formalism*. New York, 1949.

Wiebe, Robert H. *The Search for Order, 1877–1920*. New York, 1967.

Wilcox, Leonard. "Sex Boys in a Balloon: V. F. Calverton and the Abortive Sexual Revolution." *Journal of American Studies* 23, No. 1 (April 1989), 7–26.

Wilson, R. Jackson. *In Quest of Community: Social Philosophy in the United States, 1860–1920.* New York, 1968.

Wirth, Arthur G. *John Dewey as Educator: His Design for Work in Education.* New York, 1966.

Wreszin, Michael. *The Superfluous Anarchist: Albert Jay Nock.* Providence, 1972.

Index